EEDOM OF ASSOCIATION

THE UNIVERSITY CENTER FOR
HUMAN VALUES SERIES

AMY GUTMANN, EDITOR

FREEDOM OF ASSOCIATION

Edited by Amy Gutmann

PRINCETON UNIVERSITY PRESS

PRINCETON, NEW JERSEY

Copyright © 1998 by Princeton University Press

Published by Princeton University Press, 41 William Street, Princeton, New Jersey 08540

In the United Kingdom: Princeton University Press, Chichester, West Sussex

All Rights Reserved

Library of Congress Cataloging-in-Publication Data

Freedom of association / edited by Amy Gutmann.

p.   cm. — (The University Center for Human Values series)

Includes bibliographical references and index.

ISBN 0-691-05758-3 (cloth : alk. paper). — ISBN 0-691-05759-1 (pbk. : alk. paper)

1. Freedom of association—United States.   2. Associations, institutions, etc.—United

States.   I. Gutmann, Amy.   II. Series.

KF4778.F74   1998

344.73′0414—dc21   97-48605

                                                                                                         CIP

This book has been composed in Janson

Princeton University Press books are printed on acid-free paper and meet the guidelines for permanence and durability of the Committee on Production Guidelines for Book Longevity of the Council on Library Resources

http://pup.princeton.edu

Printed in the United States of America

10 9 8 7 6 5 4 3 2 1

10 9 8 7 6 5 4 3 2 1

(Pbk.)

CONTENTS

PREFACE AND ACKNOWLEDGMENTS

THE IDEA for this book began in a two-year long seminar of the Program in Ethics and Public Affairs at Princeton University. The program brings together faculty and students to address important moral issues of public life. The value of associational life in liberal democracies is among those issues. Eminent social scientists report a decreasing proportion of Americans have been joining traditional civic and religious associations. Many people are lamenting this decline. Others are skeptical of the lament or of the reported decline. Before joining the lament or criticizing it, we would do well to inquire into the values of associational life—and of various kinds of associations—for individual citizens and for the civic life of liberal democracy. The seminar embarked on this inquiry in a collaborative way, with the aim of writing a book that examines the value of freedom of association and its limits in American democracy.

The seminar met biweekly to discuss working drafts of the essays in this volume. Over the two-year period, there were also numerous lunches, dinners, and late-night drinks, where authors, commentators, and kibitzers argued (and occasionally agreed) with one another. The value of our association extended beyond the book that was our primary collaborative purpose. We also created an example of what one contributor to this volume calls an "insignificant community," an informal association of friends and acquaintances that may not by itself have a great societal impact but is nonetheless significant in its members' lives.

This project was made possible by the support of the University Center for Human Values and the Woodrow Wilson School, which cosponsor the Program in Ethics and Public Affairs. Special thanks for their ongoing support go to Harold T. Shapiro, President of Princeton University, and Laurance S. Rockefeller, founding benefactor of the University Center for Human Values.

Amy Gutmann
Director, The Program in Ethics and Public Affairs, and
The University Center for Human Values

FREEDOM OF ASSOCIATION

Chapter One

FREEDOM OF ASSOCIATION:

AN INTRODUCTORY ESSAY

AMY GUTMANN

AMERICANS, Alexis de Tocqueville observed, are "forever form-ing associations." The associations are of many different types. They are not only commercial and industrial organizations that are necessary for a functioning economy but also "religious, moral, serious, futile, very general and very limited, immensely large and very minute." Churches, synagogues, and mosques, colleges, universities, and museums, corporations, trade unions, and lobbying groups, sports leagues, literary so-cieties, sororal and fraternal orders, environmental groups, national and in-ternational charitable organizations, and self-help groups, parent-teacher associations, residential associations, and professional associations together make a significant difference in the lives of many Americans and in the life of American democracy. "Nothing," Tocqueville concludes, "deserves more attention."[1]

Surveying the subject over a century later, we begin with the observation that the value and limits of free association in the United States have not received the attention they deserve. Freedom of speech, for example, has received vastly more attention from moral and political philosophers than has freedom of association. American culture correspondingly offers a far richer sense of the value and limits of free speech than it does of the value and limits of free association. The neglect of the values of free association even weakens our understanding of free speech because organized associa-tion is increasingly essential for the effective use of free speech in the United States. Without access to an association that is willing and able to speak up for our views and values, we have a very limited ability to be heard by many other people or to influence the political process, unless we hap-pen to be rich or famous.

Freedom of association is valuable for far more than its instrumental re-lationship to free speech. Freedom of association is necessary to create and maintain intimate relationships of love and friendship, which are valuable for their own sake, as well as for the pleasures that they offer. Freedom of association is increasingly essential as a means of engaging in charity, commerce, industry, education, health care, residential life, religious practice, professional life, music and art, and recreation and sports. Any serious consideration of the activities on this list will indicate that not all the aims of associational activities are equally valued by individuals, or equally important for the well-being of a liberal democracy. But all are valued and valuable, and associational freedom is not merely a means to other valuable ends. It is also valuable for the many qualities of human life that the diverse activities of association routinely entail. By associating with one another, we engage in camaraderie, cooperation, dialogue, deliberation, negotiation, competition, creativity, and the kinds of self-expression and self-sacrifice that are possible only in association with others. In addition, we often simply enjoy the company. The pleasures of association are typically by-products of our associating for other reasons.

To appreciate the full value of associational freedom, we need to look beyond the explicit purposes that specific associations serve. The primary and explicit aim of most religious congregations is spiritual. But many congregations in the United States also serve important civic and political purposes that do not violate the constitutional prohibition on establishment of religion. My parents never doubted that they would join a Jewish congregation when they settled in the small town of Monroe, New York. But they had to decide whether to join an established congregation outside the town (since there was no congregation in Monroe) or to create a new congregation in Monroe with the dozen or so other newly arrived Jewish families, many of them first-generation Americans. I remember having been told as a child by my parents—my father a German Jew who had recently moved to the United States after living in India for fourteen years and my mother a New Yorker—that they had decided to undertake the task of building a new congregation because, without a local place of worship, Jews would not be treated as first-class citizens in a predominantly Protestant town. Nor would my parents have felt that Monroe was their hometown had they not established a Jewish congregation there. The new Jewish settlers in Monroe were not unusual in valuing their religious association for civic and political purposes as well as spiritual and personal ones. The primary purpose of an association, as this example illustrates, does not exhaust its value either for individuals or for liberal democracies.

The essays in this book explore the many values of associational freedom in a liberal democracy, as well as the moral and constitutional limits of claims to associational freedom. One book cannot possibly give this subject the attention it deserves. But the authors who have joined together to create this volume hope to give the subject more prominence and to encourage others to pursue many of the important issues regarding the value and limits of free association in the United States. Why is freedom of association valuable for both the lives of individuals and the life of a liberal democracy? What associations have the strongest moral and constitutional claims to freedom from political interference with their policies? The weakest? Which associations have claims to positive support from government? What are the most defensible grounds for protecting free association? For limiting it?

Recently there has been a revival among scholars of concern about associational life in the United States. The political scientist Robert Putnam reports that a decreasing proportion of Americans have been joining traditional associations such as churches and synagogues, trade unions and civic groups, parent-teacher associations and even bowling leagues, while an increasing proportion have been joining self-help groups, radical religious sects, and other traditionally less mainstream associations. Social scientists are addressing the empirical questions of who is joining which secondary associations with what social and political consequences. It is equally important that moral and political philosophers address the ethical questions of the value of freedom of association, its relationship to other important values that are essential to liberal democracy—including freedom of expression, religion, and conscience, economic opportunity, nondiscrimination, and civic equality—and the limits on freedom of association that are justifiable in light of these values. Without a more extensive examination of both sets of questions, we cannot responsibly decide whether or how to pursue the increasingly popular suggestion of encouraging more associational life in this country. Are all kinds of associational life worthy of encouragement? If not, which kinds? By whom? Defensible answers to these normative questions depend in large part on our understanding the value and limits of freedom of association in our contemporary context.

Are all kinds of associational life worthy of encouragement in a liberal democracy? The land of secondary associations is sometimes called "civic space." Some of the essays in this book warn against assuming that the label "civic" necessarily has positive moral content when it is applied to particular secondary associations. Although the Ku Klux Klan is a civic association, does it serve the positive civic functions that secondary associations in general are credibly said to serve? Putnam identifies these functions as follows:

In the first place, networks of civic engagement foster sturdy norms of generalized reciprocity and encourage the emergence of social trust. . . . When economic and political negotiation is embedded in dense networks of social interaction, incentives for opportunism are reduced. . . . Finally, dense networks of interaction probably broaden the participants' sense of self, developing the "I" into the "we," or (in the language of rational–choice theories) enhancing the participants' "taste" for collective benefits.[2]

Among its members, the Ku Klux Klan may cultivate solidarity and trust, reduce incentives for opportunism, and develop some "I's" into a "we." But the solidarity and trust, the limits on opportunism, and the "we" cannot be characterized as fostering "sturdy norms of generalized reciprocity." Quite the contrary; the associational premises of these solidaristic ties are hatred, degradation, and denigration of fellow citizens and fellow human beings. By contrast to the positive contributions that many civic associations make to putting a moral principle of reciprocity into practice, the Ku Klux Klan stands for the undermining of reciprocity. It encourages social distrust, increases incentives for white citizens opportunistically to take advantage of black citizens, and endorses a racially exclusive sense of "self" among participants, thereby weakening participants' "taste" for generalized collective benefits in society. Although the Ku Klux Klan is a civic association, its pursuits undermine rather than foster reciprocity among a diverse citizenry.

May a liberal democratic government distinguish in its policies between those civic associations that do and those that do not foster reciprocity among a diverse citizenry? Reciprocity is a general value of liberal democracy that informs more specific values, such as racial nondiscrimination.[3] Liberal democratic governments should distinguish in their policies between associations that discriminate on grounds of race and others that do not. In *Bob Jones University v. United States*, the Supreme Court rightly upheld the Internal Revenue Service's denial of tax-exempt status to Bob Jones University on grounds that Bob Jones practiced racial discrimination and was therefore disqualified as a charitable institution, even though its discriminatory policy (of prohibiting interracial dating among its students) was based on a sincere religious belief that the Bible forbids miscegenation. "The state may justify a limitation on religious liberty," Chief Justice Burger argued, "by showing that it is essential to accomplish an overriding governmental interest."[4] After finding that Congress authorized the IRS policy, the Supreme Court reasonably concluded that overcoming racial discrimination in education is a compelling governmental interest, sufficient to override a religiously run university's claim to free exercise of religion. The Bob Jones decision serves as an example of one legitimate (and extremely powerful) way in which a constitutional democracy may favor associations that foster reciprocity in the form of racial nondiscrimination above those that do not. The government may deny—indeed it should deny—tax exemption to those secondary associations that discriminate on the basis of race.

Had Bob Jones been a secular university, the case would have been more one-sided in favor of denying tax exemption. A secular university would have lacked a constitutional claim as strong as the free exercise of religion to put forward against the government's interest in overcoming racial discrimination in education. Although associational freedom generally speaking is enormously valuable—indeed, it is essential for providing the opportunity to individuals to live a good life and for constituting a just society—not every example of its exercise can therefore be claimed as a moral or constitutional right. Something similar can be said about individual freedom more generally. Freedom is essential to living a good life but it would be misleading to elevate it, without any further qualification, to the level of a moral or constitutional right.

Suppose that Bob Jones had been not a university but a church, and Bob Jones Church had claimed a right to forbid miscegenation among its congregants. A primary purpose of any university, by virtue of its being a university, is that it directly serves the social function of contributing to a system of fair educational opportunity in this society in a way that a church need not, by virtue of its being a church. Colleges and universities are educational gatekeepers to the professions and to other scarce and highly valued social offices that require advanced educational credentials.[5] Churches serve largely different social purposes. The claims of a Bob Jones Church with a religiously based policy of forbidding miscegenation among its congregants would have been significantly stronger relative to the state's claims in combating racial discrimination than were the similarly based claims of Bob Jones University. Liberal democracies legitimately depend on universities for providing fair educational opportunity in a way that they do not (and should not) depend on churches, because the primary purpose of churches is spiritual, not educational or economic. The state's claim is therefore far stronger vis-à-vis a university than it is vis-à-vis a church. The claims of a Bob Jones Church to discriminate on grounds of race therefore might be overriding as the claims of Bob Jones University are not. In the case of the church, the state could not as clearly claim to have a compelling interest in regulation as a direct means of securing educational and economic opportunity that is free from racial discrimination.

Were we to suppose yet another slightly different set of facts—a Bob Jones Church that discriminates on racial grounds in hiring its office staff, which carry out the secular functions of the church (such as maintaining the building and paying bills)—then a government's grounds for regulation may once again become compelling and capable of overriding the competing claim of free association. In its role as employer of office staff, a church directly contributes to the system of economic opportunity and does so in a way that may be sufficiently disconnected from its religious missions that the state may legitimately claim a compelling interest in enforcing the principle of racial nondiscrimination.

The case becomes morally and constitutionally different yet again if the church discriminates on racial grounds only in religious offices, but not in its secular offices. After comparing the moral and constitutional claims of churches with those of secular associations, Kent Greenawalt concludes that what gives churches greater claims to associational freedom from state interference than other associations is not primarily their lesser impact on the basic opportunities of individuals. Rather, it is the churches' greater claim to freedom from state interference based on their transcendental or spiritual purposes. The closer the church's discriminatory policy is to the "core" of its internal spiritual practices, the stronger its claims to noninterference based on its distinctively religious (or at least spiritual) associational purposes. When a church engages in secular educational and economic activities, however, which can be separated from its spiritual activities, its claims to discriminate in those secular activities as its belief system dictates weakens.

What about the claims to be free from compelled association that are made by associations that are not primarily religious or spiritual, but whose purposes are nonetheless socially valuable? Many of the most morally important and intellectually challenging issues regarding the extent and limits of free association arise when a secular association with valuable social purposes has policies of restrictive membership or restrictions on membership that are objectionable from the perspective of constitutional democracy. The landmark Supreme Court case of *Roberts v. United States Jaycees*, decided in 1984, presents just such a case, and the opinions of Justices Brennan and O'Connor in *Roberts* offer an excellent starting point for analyzing the values at stake in conflicts concerning the freedom of primarily secular associations.[6]

Before *Roberts* was decided, the national Junior Chamber of Commerce, commonly known as the Jaycees, by its charter did not permit women to become full members. In the early 1980s, the Minnesota Department of

Human Rights invoked Minnesota's Human Rights Act in support of the decision by the St. Paul and Minneapolis Jaycees to admit women as full members, rather than as only associate members (as was permitted by the national Jaycees charter). The Minnesota Human Rights Act states that it is "an unfair discriminatory practice . . . [t]o deny any person the full and equal enjoyment of the goods, services, facilities, privileges, advantages, and accommodations of a place of public accommodation because of race, color, creed, religion, disability, national origin or sex."[7]

Writing for a unanimous court, Justice Brennan distinguishes between intimate and nonintimate associations, and argues that intimate associations need to be treated separately from nonintimate associations for the purposes of determining the limits of state interference. Although Justices Brennan and O'Connor differ in their analyses in some significant ways (which are explored in the contributions of Kent Greenawalt, George Kateb, and Nancy Rosenblum to this volume), they agree that the rights of intimate associations are irrelevant for the case at hand. "Whatever the precise scope of the rights recognized in such cases [of intimate relationships]," Justice O'Connor writes in her concurring opinion, "they do not encompass associational rights of a 295,000-member organization whose activities are not 'private' in any meaningful sense of that term" (631). Were the Jaycees like a reading group of friends, then its claim to limit its membership to men would have been compelling. But the Jaycees meets none of the Court's criteria of an intimate association. It is not relatively small; it does not employ "a high degree of selectivity in decision to begin and maintain the relationship"; it does not require "seclusion from others in critical aspects of the relationship"; and "congeniality" is not essential to its purpose. Quite the contrary: the Jaycees is very large and unselective in admitting young men; it carries out its operations with substantial intermingling of men and women members; and congeniality is not a primary purpose of the association. The Junior Chamber of Commerce, as its name suggests, "is, first and foremost, an organization that, at both the national and local levels, promotes and practices the art of solicitation and management" (639).

What is the constitutional basis of this distinction between intimate associations, whose constitutional claims to freedom from outside interference are second to none, and nonintimate associations? Although freedom of association is never mentioned in the United States Constitution, it is implicated in two central places. The First Amendment protects the free exercise of religion, speech, and "the right of the people peaceably to assemble, and to petition the Government for a redress of grievances." First Amendment protection does not apply in any special way to intimate associations, but rather to religious and expressive associations, those that are instrumental in enabling citizens to exercise their rights of religious freedom, free speech, freedom of assembly, and freedom to petition and criticize government. The Fourteenth Amendment has been interpreted to provide the protection of a "zone of privacy" to intimate association, by virtue of its due process clause, which prohibits depriving "any person of life, liberty, or property, without due process of law." None of these protections amounts to absolute freedom from interference by government for intimate, expressive, or religious associations. But each points to a general type of association that warrants special constitutional protection by virtue of its primary character (intimate or religious) or primary purposes (free expression) that is not available to all types of association. The challenging issues concerning associational freedom that are the focus of this volume all lie between the extremes of absolute protection from outside interference with an association's activities and no protection. In exploring the moral, political, and constitutional territory between these extremes, we need to consider the character of the association and the primary purposes that will be served and stymied by outside interference.

To identify more clearly the territory explored in this volume, we need to extend the mapping of associational life in a different direction from that offered in either Brennan's or O'Connor's opinion in *Roberts*. At the other extreme from the intimate or "primary" associations of family and friends lie "tertiary" associations that are distant from their members in their daily operations, such as centralized lobbying organizations like the American Association of Retired Persons (AARP) and the National Organization for Women (NOW) and centralized charitable organizations like Amnesty International and Oxfam. Tertiary associations carry out their purposes without involving many of their members in regular, face-to-face associational activities. Between primary and tertiary associations lie "secondary" associations like the Jaycees, whose central functions entail bringing members together in local chapters for regular meetings and cooperative activities. It is not the size or importance of the association but the centrality and extent of cooperative membership activity that distinguishes secondary associations like the Jaycees from tertiary associations like the AARP and Amnesty International.

Secondary associations like the Jaycees are conventionally called "voluntary." But we need to be careful, as Michael Walzer warns in his essay, not to misinterpret what it means to call an association voluntary. To the extent that individuals enjoy freedom of association in a liberal democracy, we are free to form secondary associations and to exit them, but not to enter just any association of our choice at will. The freedom to associate necessarily entails the freedom to exclude, and therefore limits our freedom of entry. If I can enter any association of my choice, then you have no freedom not to associate with me. A requirement of open membership would undermine the value of many secondary associations and destroy any meaningful sense of freedom of association as it applies to secondary associations. "There can be no clearer example of an intrusion into the internal structure or affairs of an association," Justice Brennan writes in *Roberts*, "than a regulation that forces the group to accept members it does not desire. . . . Freedom of association . . . plainly presupposes a freedom not to associate" (623).

Because freedom of association is neither morally nor constitutionally absolute, we cannot conclude that an intrusion into the internal structure is unjustified before we evaluate the purposes of the intrusion and compare the merits of intrusion with those of nonintrusion into an association's internal structure or affairs. We cannot claim a presumption in favor of a right to exclude or a presumption in favor of a right not to be discriminated against without begging the question: which side carries the weight of argument in cases of conflict between the values of free association and those of nondiscrimination? There is no neutral default position in cases of conflict. In his opinion in *Roberts*, Justice Brennan recognizes, in constitutional terms, first the moral burden and then the moral value of state intrusion into the internal life of a large secondary association. Brennan concludes for a unanimous Court that a compelling state interest in securing nondiscrimination for women justifies state intrusion into the structure of the national Jaycees. The essays by Kateb and Rosenblum in this volume present powerful arguments against the Court's conclusion. What more can be said on the Court's side?

Critics and defenders of the Court's decision in *Roberts* share an important point of agreement concerning associational freedom. When the primary purpose of an association is *expression* of a point of view—whether it be religious or secular—then its freedom to select members consistently with its expressive purposes is essential to its members' exercise of free speech through the association. A government that regulates the membership of a church or a political club or a social advocacy group in a way that defies its expressive purposes is also regulating its members' speech, unjustifiably and unconstitutionally so, no matter how morally misguided or factually mistaken the government may rightly believe the association's message to be. Any meaningful right to free speech must protect associations whose primary purpose is expressive from political interference in their membership policies insofar as that interference is directly related to its expressive purposes. To regulate the membership of an expressive association against those purposes is to tell that association's members to change their expression, which is tantamount to outlawing the expressive association. If anything constitutes a clear violation of the right of free speech, this kind of intrusion in an expressive association certainly does. Not to recognize this right of expressive associations to choose their members is not to recognize how essential expressive associations are to free speech. Without the right to associate in order to express our points of view, we are increasingly powerless to speak in a way that we can be heard by many others. "Protection of the association's right to define its membership," O'Connor writes in *Roberts*, "derives from the recognition that the formation of an expressive association is the creation of a voice, and the selection of members is the definition of that voice" (633). Justice Brennan agrees, as do all the contributors to this volume.

Although many secondary associations are primarily expressive, many are not. The Jaycees is among those associations that are not primarily expressive. "Both the Minnesota Supreme Court and the United States District Court," O'Connor notes, ". . . made findings of fact concerning the commercial nature of the Jaycees' activities. The Court of Appeals, which disagreed with the District Court over the legal conclusions to be drawn from the facts, did not dispute any of these findings" (639). Were the Jaycees primarily expressive, and were its expression related in some nonarbitrary way to its membership policy, then the national Jaycees would (and should) have won their challenge to the St. Paul and Minneapolis chapters' insistence on their right to admit women as full members, and to the claim by the Minnesota Department of Human Rights that the national Jaycees were legally obligated to admit women as full members in all their Minnesota chapters. But the Jaycees was and is not primarily an expressive association, even though advocacy of political and public causes is a "not insubstantial part of what it does."[8] The same may be said of most large commercial associations, such as profit-making companies, but laws protecting nondiscrimination would clearly be ineffectual were the Court to exempt any association for which advocacy of political and public causes is a "not insubstantial part" of what it does. Most corporations would thereby become exempt from nondiscrimination laws, and for some of the same reasons as the Jaycees would be on the critics' analysis. To say that an association engages in political expression as one among its many activities therefore cannot suffice to exempt it from the constraint of nondiscrimination.

Because so many associations have some expressive purposes, in order adequately to respect values such as fair opportunity that often compete with freedom of association, it is important to distinguish between those associations whose primary purpose is expressive and those whose primary purpose is not. If the presence of any expressive purposes by an association triggers the same right to freedom from outside interference that a primarily expressive association can morally and constitutionally claim, then a democratic government would be unable to secure even the imperfect degree of fair opportunity for members of historically disadvantaged groups that now exists in United States. Just as free expression is an important civic value in a liberal democracy, so is nondiscrimination on the basis of race, color, creed, religion, disability, national origin, or sex. Both values are constitutionally protected, and neither can justifiably be elevated to absolute priority over the other.

Unjustified discrimination by secondary associations warrants criticism even in situations where it does not warrant state interference. Greenawalt offers the example of a small secular country club that does not admit Jews basically because they are Jews. State intrusion into the membership policies of private associations, as Rosenblum argues, is often worse than the prejudice that it is intended to combat. It may also be counterproductive in some cases. What Rosenblum aptly calls the logic of congruence—a logic that requires government to enforce liberal democratic principles of inclusion on secondary associations with primarily private purposes—is as indefensible as what might be called the logic of incongruence: a logic that prohibits government from enforcing liberal democratic restrictions on secondary associations with primarily public purposes. The difficult issues concerning the competing values of free association and nondiscrimination lie between these two indiscriminatory positions.

An important part of the controversy concerning the *Roberts* decision centers on what kind of association should count as private or public for the purposes of state enforcement of nondiscriminatory membership. A small exclusive country club, whose activities consist of golf, tennis, swimming, and socializing, is private in a way that the Jaycees is not. But whether the Jaycees should be counted as a public association is still subject to reasonable disagreement. Its effects on economic opportunity are uncertain. But this uncertainty does not justify noninterference any more than it justifies interference since there is no neutral default position, of state interference or noninterference. Both associational freedom and nondiscrimination are significant civic values in a liberal democracy, and neither conclusion (to interfere or not to interfere) can be justified by way of a presumption (for or against interference).

Another important part of the controversy about enforcing nondiscriminatory membership policies on secondary associations focuses on claims about the spillover effects into public life of discrimination in private life. "Even if the members [of a country club that discriminates against Jews] assure us that they will extend equal respect to Jews in political and commercial life," Greenawalt writes, "we must doubt whether most people are capable of such a sharp dichotomy between semiprivate social life and public life. If it is said the state is powerless to change such attitudes, the answer is that bastions of social exclusion perpetuate attitudes within and across generations." Rosenblum writes in response to advocates of the logic of congruence that "moral psychology is more complex than this. . . . Discrimination condoned in one sphere is not necessarily condoned, or exhibited, in all or any others." Rosenblum's observation that "there are various reasons for discrimination, not just one reason that applies uniformly in all situations," suggests the need for the kind of detailed arguments that Greenawalt offers, arguments that distinguish among the purposes of different kinds of associations, and among the different grounds that associations can legitimately claim for discrimination. Under one defensible interpretation of the Fourteenth Amendment, women and other members of disadvantaged groups that have historically been subject to discrimination need not be relegated to the status of "second-class citizens" in order to claim equal protection of the laws against discrimination by associations whose primary activities promote educational, economic, or political opportunities.

Critics and defenders of the Court's decision in *Roberts* agree that a primary purpose of the Jaycees is leadership training in business and commerce. Whether these training activities of the Jaycees have actually substantially increased the economic opportunities of young men is subject to reasonable disagreement; as often is the case, the empirical evidence is uncertain. A federal system of government permits this reasonable disagreement, based partly on unavoidable empirical uncertainty and partly on unavoidable moral uncertainty, to manifest itself in various state laws and various applications of those laws, as long as those laws fall within a range of reasonable disagreement. The Minnesota Human Rights Act and its application in *Roberts* can be seen as falling within the range of reasonable disagreement that it is the virtue of a federal system to recognize.

The Human Rights Act defines as a "place of public accommodation," subject to the antidiscrimination statute, "a business, accommodation, refreshment, entertainment, recreation, or transportation facility of any kind, whether licensed or not, whose goods, services, facilities, privileges, advantages or accommodations are extended, offered, sold, or otherwise made available to the public."[9] The Minnesota Supreme Court concluded that the Jaycees qualified as a place of public accommodation under this statute. This conclusion can be seen as reasonable, even if controversial. The Jaycees are primarily engaged in selling the goods of leadership skills and in extending the privileges and advantages of business contacts and employment promotions to its members. It operates at fixed sites and therefore qualifies as a "facility" (as do privately owned restaurants and apartment houses), and it qualifies as a public association insofar as it solicits and recruits young men as members very unselectively. (A primary criterion of success for members is the successful solicitation of new young male members. "Apart from age and sex," Brennan writes for the Court, "neither the national organization nor the local chapters employ any criteria for judging applicants for membership, and new members are routinely recruited and admitted with no inquiry into their backgrounds.") (621).

Critics and defenders of the Court's decision reasonably disagree about whether the goods, privileges, and advantages available by virtue of membership in the Jaycees are or are not sufficiently connected to economic, social, and political opportunities to warrant classifying the Jaycees as a "public accommodation." The Jaycees need not be the exclusive source of economic, social, and political opportunities in a community—any more than a restaurant or apartment house need be the exclusive source of a meal or a home—to qualify as a public accommodation. Although the Jaycees did not have a monopoly on local civic associations, they were by virtue of their history and resources in many local communities the dominant, high-status civic association whose purpose was to train young men seeking to enter the economic life of the community. Women were (and are) of course free to create and join their own civic associations in which women would be eligible for regular membership. But it is highly unlikely that a new civic association for women would have social, economic, or political influence comparable to that of the well-established Jaycees.

To sustain the decisions of the Minnesota Human Rights Department and the Minnesota Supreme Court on constitutional grounds, the United States Supreme Court did not need to claim that excluding women from full membership in the Jaycees relegated them to second-class citizenship. Rosenblum rightly warns us not to confuse second-class membership in a civic association with second-class citizenship in the state. Keeping this distinction in mind, the Minnesota Department of Human Rights could still legitimately conclude that the local Jaycees chapters were acting morally and also within their constitutional rights to admit women as full members under the Minnesota Human Rights Act, which prohibits gender discrimination in public accommodation. Not to admit women as full members may reasonably be thought to deprive young women of economic and social opportunities that should be available to them, as long as they are so indiscriminately made available to young men, even if women would not be relegated to second-class *citizenship* simply by virtue of being excluded from full membership.

In determining whether the second-class membership of women in the Jaycees deprives young women of significant economic opportunities that the Jaycees makes available to young men, the Minnesota Department of Human Rights, the Minnesota Supreme Court, and the United States Supreme Court rely on the Jaycees' own public account of its associational purposes and accomplishments. "The organization," O'Connor writes:

> claims that the training it offers its members gives them an advantage in business, and business firms do indeed sometimes pay the dues of individual memberships for their employees. Jaycees members hone their solicitation and management skills, under the direction and supervision of the organization, primarily through their active recruitment of new members. . . . Recruitment and selling are commercial activities, even when conducted for training rather than for profit. (640)

"The State of Minnesota," O'Connor concludes, "has a legitimate interest in ensuring nondiscriminatory access to the commercial opportunity presented by membership in the Jaycees" (641). O'Connor then opens her argument to unnecessary misinterpretation when she adds that "[t]he Jaycees' First Amendment challenge to the application of Minnesota's public accommodations law is meritless." There are credible First Amendment claims that even commercial associations can make, but those claims are not overriding against a state's interest in keeping the channels of commerce free of gender (and other forms of) discrimination.

Even if *Roberts* was decided on defensible moral and constitutional grounds, the central argument of Rosenblum's essay still holds: a liberal democracy should not insist on congruence between its principles of nondiscrimination and the policies that govern the internal life of all secondary associations. Even if churches, fraternities, country clubs, and various other secondary associations that discriminate on grounds of race or gender are morally wrong to do so, we can consistently defend their constitutional right to discriminate if (and only if) they do not thereby interfere with anyone's basic liberties or opportunities. A small country club that excludes Jews or women would (and should) not be subject to Minnesota's Human Rights Act. Nor would a church that allows only men to hold church offices. We need not think these discriminations are morally benign to conclude that the state should not regulate the membership of these associations. Nor need we think that the state should not regulate the memberships of any secondary associations to exempt some from compelled association.

The term "freedom of association" does not appear in the United States Constitution, and the Constitution does not readily lend itself to a defense of a general right to freedom of association. Yet freedom of association, suitably qualified, is surely an essential part of individual freedom. It is, as George Kateb writes, "integral to a free human life, to being a free person. Picking one's company is part of living as one likes: living as one likes (provided one does not injure the vital claims of others) is what being free means." Freedom of association resembles freedom of speech in this sense. Speaking one's mind is part of living as one likes; living as one likes (provided one does not injure the vital claims of others) is what being free means. Freedom of association may be limited for the same kind of reason that freedom of speech may be: it can conflict with other vital claims. Associating with others for the purpose of arson is no more justifiable (or constitutionally protected) than falsely shouting "fire" in a crowded theater. Not all kinds of associations, as this example indicates, are integral to being a free person, let alone to living a good human life. As both critics and defenders of *Roberts* agree, specific rights to free association are implicated in the First and Fourteenth Amendments.

Freedom of association cannot exist without constraints on that freedom in the form of exclusions. In the context of a society where women are still systematically relegated to lower status positions in the economy than equally talented and motivated men, there is more to be said in favor of expanding the associational freedom of (some) women even at the cost of contracting that of (some) men when the association at issue is primarily commercial in its purposes, rather than expressive, religious, or private in its purposes or intimate in its character.

Far more than the associational freedom of some men would have been morally at stake, however, were the national Jaycees a religious group whose fundamental convictions would be violated by requiring regular membership for women. Greenawalt's essay carefully defends, on both constitutional and moral grounds, the proposition that freedom of religious association warrants more protection than freedom of (some) other forms of association. A church's claim to enforce a two-tiered membership policy on its Minnesota branches would be stronger than that of the national Jaycees. Why? Not because discrimination against women by churches is less likely to have a detrimental effect on the equal status or even the economic, educational, and political opportunities of women in the United States, Greenawalt argues, but rather because respecting the freedom of churches to discriminate in this way may be necessary to respect the fundamental (and often transcendental) moral convictions of its members as expressed through their church, whose primary purpose is spiritual.

The first part of this book focuses on the value of associational freedom (and the limits of its value) in the lives of individuals. But associational freedom also has civic value, which is the focus of the second part of the book. (Most of the essays address both sets of issues.) The viability and vibrancy of liberal democracy depend in many morally important ways on the associational activities of its citizens. Shorn of associational activities, the United States would not only be unlivable for most of us as individuals, it would also be unviable as a liberal democracy. The claim that associational activities of all sorts are essential to the health of liberal democracy is more controversial than the claim that associational freedom is an essential part of individual freedom. Whereas the relationship between freedom of association and individual freedom is analytical,[10] the relationship between freedom of association and various values of liberal democracy is a partly empirical, partly moral claim. Many values of liberal democracy are put in jeopardy to the extent that citizens either are not free to join secondary associations or fail to take full advantage of their freedom. Among those values that are thought to be jeopardized by a decline in associational life are economic development, the physical safety of citizens, the efficient and effective performance of government, the ability of citizens to support themselves without unnecessary public assistance, the willingness of citizens to help those who are in need or to support a government that helps those in need, and even the stability of liberal democracy itself.

What is the relationship between laws and policies that govern our use of associational freedoms and the well-being of liberal democracy? Just as our individual use of associational freedom is typically two-edged (we choose to associate with some people by excluding others), so too the role of government in fostering or regulating associational freedom is two-edged. A government that is constitutionally dedicated to liberal democratic principles has a strong interest in supporting a vast assortment of associational activities among its citizens. But it also has a strong interest in regulating associations so that they support a liberal democratic form of government and public policies that are consistent with liberal democratic principles.

Although many associational activities in America are clearly and directly supportive of liberal democracy, others are not so clearly or directly supportive, and still others are downright hostile to, and potentially destructive of, liberal democracy. Some associations, left free to determine their own affairs, will operate in ways inimical to liberal democratic values—for example, by discriminating against blacks and drilling members in the violent overthrow of lawful government. Should governments decide to regulate and support associations according to whether or not they support liberal democratic values? A policy of tax exemption for "charitable" institutions must be based on some understanding of what should count as a charitable institution. By its very nature, the politically operative understanding of *charitable* cannot be morally neutral. Granting or denying tax exemption as a charitable institution to a university that prohibits miscegenation requires a moral judgment. We cannot avoid trying to answer the moral question of which is the more defensible basis for governmental action.

Addressing the civic value of secondary associations requires a response to several substantially different questions about the relationship between associational freedom and liberal democracy. One question is whether the *stability* of liberal democratic government depends on citizens' joining secondary associations that express, teach, or internally institute liberal democratic values. To the extent that citizens choose to join internally illiberal or undemocratic associations, is liberal democratic government in jeopardy of becoming unstable? Rosenblum's essay challenges the claim that incongruity between political norms and associational norms necessarily (or even generally) has a politically destabilizing effect.

A second and distinct question asks not about the stability of liberal democratic government but about the realization of liberal democratic *principles*. To what extent do liberal democratic principles morally bind citizens in their civic associations and, more generally, in their everyday life? The civic virtue of civility, Will Kymlicka argues:

> involves a radical extension of the obligations of liberal citizenship; for the obligation to treat people as equal citizens now applies to the most common, everyday decisions of individuals. It is no longer permissible for businesses to refuse to hire black employees, or to refuse to serve black customers, or to segregate their black employees or customers. But not just that; the norms of nondiscrimination entail that it is impermissible for businesses to ignore their black customers or treat them rudely, although it is not always possible to legally enforce this. . . . Blacks must, in short, be treated with *civility*. The same applies to the way citizens treat each other in schools or recreational associations, even in private clubs.

The obligation of civility does not mean "smiling at others no matter how badly they treat you, as if oppressed groups should be nice to their oppressors. Rather, it means treating others as equals on the condition that they extend the same recognition to you." Civility, so understood, is "the logical extension of non-discrimination, since it is needed to ensure that all citizens have the same opportunity to participate within civil society." Whether the state can or should enforce these principles on secondary associations remains a separate and significant issue, addressed by other essays. But regardless of whether civility should be legally enforced, Kymlicka argues, citizens may legitimately judge others and be judged by whether they treat each other as civic equals in their everyday lives because "liberal citizenship . . . requires this sort of civility."

Some critics argue that liberal democratic citizenship wrongly requires immigrant groups to give up their distinctive heritage and assimilate to the dominant culture. Other critics argue that multicultural demands are illiberal and undemocratic, and should give way to liberal democratic norms. Against both these claims, Kymlicka argues that the vast majority of successful multicultural demands by immigrant groups are compatible with, or even required by, liberal democratic principles. These demands include making school curricula more inclusive, revising dress codes to accommodate different cultures, providing cultural diversity training for public officials, publicly funding ethnic cultural festivals, and offering children transitional bilingual education programs in schools. We can distinguish these demands from those that would allow a group to deny its own members basic civil or political rights. An affirmative answer to the second question— which argues that liberal democratic principles can and should be furthered throughout civic life—rejects demands by any group that would authorize them to deny their members basic civil or political rights.

The United States has historically exempted a few small, radically separatist groups from this requirement of adherence to liberal democratic principles; for example, the Amish have been exempted from the state requirement of high school education for their children. This exemption is the exception that "proves" the rule precisely because the Amish are so unusual, isolated, and nonparticipatory in the political life of the United States, and therefore in this sense peripheral to the life of a liberal democracy. The Supreme Court case *Wisconsin v. Yoder*, which endorses this exemption, has rarely been used as a precedent precisely because the explicit basis for the exemption is a set of highly unusual characteristics of the Amish. If the principles of liberal democracy apply to all individuals, including children who are part of separatist sects (but not therefore under their exclusive authority), even the Amish exemption is not morally required, although it may be morally permitted. No significant social group or civic activity is morally exempt from liberal democratic principles, although some groups—national minorities that constitute themselves as separate societies within a society—have legitimate claims to their own government, rather than to be ruled by the larger territorial government. A national minority like Québécois may therefore be at least partly exempt from the political authority of the larger territorial government of Canada precisely because a national minority has legitimate claims to self-government, as other groups, including most immigrant groups, do not. The right to self-government does not exempt a national minority from liberal democratic principles; it exempts the national minority from the authority of a foreign government.

An affirmative answer to the second question applies liberal democratic principles to civil society and therefore to civic associations. It does not require that all civic associations be internally liberal and internally democratic. Peter de Marneffe's essay in this volume effectively challenges any attempt to treat different associations as if their contribution to liberal democracy must be the same. De Marneffe argues for a case-by-case consideration of the burdens of state interference versus the burdens of noninterference. He finds that the burdens of state interference are far greater for some kinds of associations than for others.

The case-by-case method employed by de Marneffe is not ad hoc or arbitrary; it is a principled casuistic method of moral and constitutional decision making. By interpreting and applying the principle of basic liberty, we can distinguish between the burdens that a state-enforced policy of nondiscrimination against women would place on the exclusionary claims of a church, a country club, and a law firm. The differential burdens of interference, de Marneffe argues, require liberal democratic governments to give churches more room than country clubs to exclude women, and country clubs more room than law firms to exclude women. This analysis offers no simple formula, but it does offer principled considerations, derived from a widely shared conception of liberal democracy, that challenge the claims that *all* secondary associations or that *no* secondary associations should be prohibited from discriminating in their membership policies. The analysis invites anyone to challenge the principles of liberal democracy on which it is based, the practical implications that are drawn from the principles, or the judgment that goes into balancing the competing moral considerations.

A liberal democracy can support the civic value of associational life in some cases by insisting that a university or chamber of commerce open its doors to blacks and women, and in other cases by insisting that other more intimate, private, or expressive associations be free to discriminate in their membership and internal policies as they see fit. But the decision whether to regulate membership and other internal policies of associations is not the only way or even the most effective way in which a liberal democracy can support civic and personal values of associational life. Yael Tamir's far-ranging essay defends another, more positive and pluralistic, way. Liberal democratic governments, Tamir argues, should secure a fair distribution of the basic opportunity for citizens to join associations that enhance their lives and the life of liberal democracy. Just as de Marneffe's essay draws out the practical implications of the liberal democratic principle of basic liberty, so Tamir's essay draws out the practical implications of the principle of basic opportunity for associational life in liberal democracies.

In light of the importance of secondary associations in the lives of citizens and the life of liberal democracy, liberal democratic governments should do more to ensure that the effective opportunity to create and join associations is fairly distributed among their citizens. How can the opportunity to associate be made effective for all citizens, and not just for those who are affluent? Tax exemption for secondary associations that serve charitable purposes is not enough, since tax exemption primarily subsidizes affluent citizens, who are already most able to create and join secondary associations. Tax exemption does nothing for the poorest citizens, who for reasons of financial hardship are least likely to create or join associations. Liberal democratic governments can financially subsidize associations that serve the interests and enlist the participation of poor citizens. Quite apart from their responsibility to fairly distribute associational opportunity, liberal democratic governments are obligated to provide adequate education, housing, health care, and child care for poor citizens. Because securing adequate associational opportunities and adequate education, housing, health care, and child care is a matter of justice, such subsidies would not violate any defensible version of "liberal neutrality" among competing conceptions of the good life. Public schools can also make the freedom to associate more effective by educating all citizens in the civic skills of creating and sustaining associations.

Yet a third question relevant to the civic value of associational life asks to what extent citizens should be free to enter and exit associations that order their internal affairs in illiberal and undemocratic ways. Many secular as well as religious associations—including many expressive and educational associations—are internally illiberal or undemocratic, or both. A liberal democracy that banned all internally illiberal or undemocratic associations would fail the fundamental test of treating its citizens as free and reasonable beings who have the right and responsibility to decide what kind of associational life is most conducive to their own well-being and the well-being of their society. The freedom to choose internally illiberal or undemocratic associations has not undermined the stability of liberal democracy. It may even serve to stabilize a liberal democratic government that can demonstrate its willingness and ability to accommodate the widest range of secondary associations that citizens value and freely choose. But a critical part of the answer to the third question requires that citizens be *effectively* free, not just *formally* free, to exit associations that are internally illiberal or undemocratic. Cults that brainwash or indoctrinate their members and residential associations that require all property to become communal upon entering and deny their members any property if they decide to exit do not satisfy the standard of freedom to exit. Even if freedom of exit in these cases is a legal formality, the legal formality is not enough. To be consistent with living the life of a free person, continued membership in an association must be a sign of ongoing consent to the association's purposes, as it cannot be in the case of an association that brainwashes or indoctrinates its members or that exacts enormous sacrifices for exiting.

Liberal democrats can consistently defend the right of citizens to form secondary associations whose internal life does not directly support liberal democratic principles, as long as membership reflects the informed consent of citizens to remain within the association (i.e., citizens are effectively free to exit the association if they wish) and the association's activities do not undermine liberal democracy. Basic liberty is a fundamental principle of liberal democracy, and some basic liberties—such as freedom of expression and religious association—entail the freedom to associate in ways that are not internally liberal or democratic. There is therefore no paradox or internal inconsistency in defending the freedom of individuals to join internally illiberal or undemocratic associations on liberal democratic grounds.

An increasing number of American citizens are joining Residential Community Associations, which are relatively ethnically, racially, and economically homogeneous. Rather than being schools of civic virtue, these relatively small, solidaristic associations are likely to produce uncivic attitudes and have detrimental effects on liberal democracy, as Daniel Bell writes:

> a decreasing sense of loyalty and commitment to the national community and the local communities in which [they] are located; for nonmembers, a decreasing tax base to provide for public services; and for the nation as a whole greater alienation from the political system and an increasing gap between rich and poor.

How, if at all, should a liberal democracy respond? Residential Community Associations should be constrained not to discriminate in their commercial activities as any other commercial association should be. The more difficult problem, however, is not direct discrimination, which can be prohibited, but rather the indirect effects of association in residential communities that become—by market choice rather than discriminatory policy—racially, ethnically, and economically homogeneous. If the priority of basic liberty has any relevance to secondary associations, then such homogeneous living situations must be permitted if they are not the product of discrimination. But their indirect effects on civic and political life remain troubling.

Governments have ways of responding to this problem that do not put anyone's basic liberty at risk. Governments may legitimately support, for example through tax exemption, only those associations that are charitable as long as they do not use the distinction between charitable and non-charitable as a subterfuge for discrimination along partisan political lines. The ruling by the Internal Revenue Service against Bob Jones University, which was supported by Congress, legitimately invoked the distinction between charitable and noncharitable associations. The distinction between charitable and noncharitable associations, as this example suggests, is morally and practically useful, even if it is not always clear or without controversy. (Neither is the distinction between night and day clear or without controversy. Dusk and dawn are hard to define, and motorists may argue with the police about just when they therefore need to turn on their headlights. The existence of gray areas is not a reason to abandon otherwise useful distinctions.)

A government morally bound by liberal democratic principles has no business selectively subsidizing Residential Community Associations, as it now does. No moral perspective on politics justifies giving financial advantages to relatively affluent and racially homogeneous Residential Community Associations over low-income housing associations. Yet many governmental policies today provide far greater financial advantages for housing to relatively rich citizens than they do to relatively poor citizens. Basic opportunity, the companion principle to basic liberty, justifies just the reverse policy: subsidizing housing for citizens who could otherwise not afford it and regulating the housing market to the extent necessary to protect against direct and invidious discrimination.

Whereas many local, relatively solidaristic Residential Community Associations probably detract from civic virtue, some large, bureaucratic organizations like the National Park Service probably contribute to it. The National Park Service, as Bell points out, takes as one of its core purposes contributing "to the public's sense of a shared national identity." It does so by creating and maintaining cultural and historic sites of national significance. Although the National Park Service is best known for maintaining parks like Yellowstone and Yosemite, historical sites like the Lincoln Memorial, the Vietnam Memorial, Ellis Island, and Gettysburg make up more than half of its sites and account for more than three-quarters of the visits. A comparison of Residential Community Associations and the National Park Service does not suggest that a liberal democracy should rely on large, bureaucratic, political institutions rather than on small secondary associations for cultivating civic virtue. Rather, it warns against the generalization that smallness, internal solidarity, and independence from government are necessary or sufficient conditions for cultivating reciprocity, solidarity, and civility among citizens. We should also be skeptical of pictures of the past that associate the cultivation of reciprocity and civility among citizens with associations that excluded blacks, women, and other historically disadvantaged groups.

Civic virtues are various. Not every association can reasonably be expected to cultivate even the most basic civic virtues, which (drawing upon the account by William Galston) include the general virtues of law-abidingness, courage, and loyalty, the social virtues of independence and open-mindedness, the economic virtues of industriousness, capacity to delay self-gratification, and adaptability to change, and the political virtues of discerning and respecting the rights of others, demanding only what can be paid for, evaluating the performance of officeholders, and engaging in public discourse and deliberation.[11] A liberal democracy must depend on a wide variety of associations to cultivate the full range of civic virtues. The National Park Service, for example, tries to cultivate loyalty to country and respect for the rights of others far more than it tries to promote industriousness, public discourse, or deliberation. Smaller and more participatory associations, like parent-teacher associations and other decentralized social service organizations, probably do more to cultivate industriousness, public discourse, and deliberation. The value of cultivating many different civic virtues provides yet another reason for liberal democracies to support a wide range of secondary associations.

Various characteristics of an association are likely to be relevant to its capacity to cultivate civic virtues. The size of an association is only one of these characteristics. Other things being equal, the more economically, ethnically, and religiously heterogeneous the membership of an association is, the greater its capacity to cultivate the kind of public discourse and deliberation that is conducive to democratic citizenship. Comparisons among associations that focus on their capacity to cultivate civic virtue therefore should try to capture their comparative advantages and disadvantages across a wide spectrum of civic virtues. Associations like the Ku Klux Klan that actively cultivate civic vices are clearly problematic in a way that associations that simply fail to cultivate civic virtues are not. Were we to discover that bowling leagues and sewing circles do not cultivate civic virtue, we could still value them as recreational. A society that does not support recreation is likely to be mighty dull, even if it is not unjust.

Associational life in America today, of the sort that fascinated Tocqueville, extends well beyond even sewing circles and bowling leagues to an enormous number of informal social groups, which congregate today in almost as many places as there are safe spaces, in homes, parks and playgrounds, bars and bookstores, coffeehouses and community centers. Samuel Fleischacker's essay calls our attention to what may be the most common set of associational activities in the United States: the informal getting together of friends and acquaintances to enjoy a good meal, down a few drinks, discuss a book, watch a movie, shoot some hoops, swim a few laps, or run a couple of miles. These associational activities rarely if ever explicitly aim to cultivate reciprocity, civility, or anything as highfalutin as civic virtue. We typically get together to socialize and have a good time, and in socializing and having a good time, we also expand our understanding of other people's desires, fears, hopes, and anxieties.

The people with whom we informally eat, drink, exercise, and schmooze are probably more like one another than are the members of most larger and more formal associations. But those in loose friendship and acquaintance circles still are likely to discover and discuss substantial differences in one another's desires, fears, hopes, and anxieties. As significantly, we may learn more about each other and cultivate deeper understandings than we would as fellow members of much larger and more formal associations. Opportunities for mutual aid are also very likely to arise in such small and fluid associations. Unwelcome and unexpected circumstances that elicit mutual aid in such informal associations may do as much to teach reciprocity as the planned charitable actions of more formal organizations. (Planned charitable actions, on the other hand, do more social good for people in the greatest need. One form of association is certainly not a substitute for the other. "A thousand points of light" generated from many charitable individuals are no substitute for the knowledge that a secure source of aid will be available to you and your family in time of need as a matter of publicly recognized justice.)

Each informal and fluid association that Americans continually create and sustain is insignificant from the perspective of its explicit purposes. But insignificant communities, as Fleischacker ironically calls informal and fluid associations, turn out to be very significant not only for our individual lives but also for the life of liberal democracy. Their value is sufficiently great that it is worth imagining how a liberal democracy might create more insignificant communities. Fleischacker calls for the creation by liberal democratic governments of "Social Houses," free and relatively unstructured public spaces that are open to all comers and for almost all purposes.

Are governmental subsidies for unstructured and unpurposive public spaces a realistic means of creating more civically valuable associations of this sort? Some civic virtues may be a bit like sleep, in that they are less likely to be cultivated the more one focuses primarily on making them happen. Governments, I suspect, are less likely to be successful in this regard if they try to create the sites of insignificant communities for adults for the primary purpose of cultivating social solidarity and reciprocity than if they try to create new facilities for more specific public purposes (such as a community swimming pool, library, or retirement community) and design those facilities in a way that is conducive to a wide range of informal associational activities. The civic virtues of solidarity and reciprocity could then be cultivated as an important by-product of the pursuit of other socially valuable ends. Designing a community swimming pool so that it is conducive to informal associational activities is an intentional activity, not an accidental one. But the public purposes are unlikely to be achieved if the pool does not satisfy the personal preferences of many community members who simply like to swim.

The satisfaction of personal preferences and the pursuit of public purposes do not always coincide. Alan Ryan's essay pursues a paradigm example of the tension between the satisfaction of personal preferences and the pursuit of public purposes. Many Americans move to the suburbs because, among the options open to them as individual decision makers and consumers, their preference is to buy an affordable house in a safe neighborhood with decent schools and within commuting distance from paid work. But these same citizens may also prefer that their options be expanded to include affordable housing in a safe urban environment where they can take convenient public transportation to work and send their children to a local public school as good as those they can find in the suburbs. Our choices among existing options can be private but our preferences for additional options are public insofar as they depend (and are known to depend) for their realization on concerted public action that creates new choices that do not now exist.

In our roles as citizens we have opportunities to influence the options that will be open to us as individual actors who must choose among already established options. But taking advantage of our opportunities as citizens is often difficult and time consuming, requiring organized and purposive associational activities. Associations that are dedicated to articulating and pursuing public purposes can make a critical difference. Even if many citizens who now live in the suburbs would greatly prefer living in a safe and affordable urban environment where their children can attend a good local public school, this option will not be realized unless many associations bring citizens together in a way that overcomes the problems of collective action. It is typically easier to realize our personal preferences among existing options than our public preferences of creating new options—but not necessarily more satisfying.

The problems of collective action are probably at their peak in suburban life. Many Americans may have no better option than to live in the suburbs, drive to work, and send their children to relatively homogeneous schools. Their public preferences may be to provide more and better public transportation, to build more affordable housing in more urban areas, and to create better public schools that attract a fairly representative cross-section of citizens. To the extent that American politics is not as conducive as it might be to collective action on behalf of such civic purposes, there will continue to be many missed opportunities to satisfy public preferences. Citizens cannot be expected to make great personal sacrifices in pursuit of collective goods, but many kinds of associations can make a difference without demanding such sacrifices on the part of their members.

Because few people are powerful enough to do very much by acting alone, associations that pursue public purposes are important. Collective decision making is not intrinsically more valuable than individual decision making, but it is instrumentally essential to realizing certain collective goods. Collective decision making is typically far more difficult than individual decision making. When you buy something, you do not have to account to anyone for your taste or for your judgment that it was worth the price you paid. When you support a public policy, you not only owe your fellow citizens an account but you also are directly dependent on at least a majority (or plurality) of them for the success of your cause. To the extent that our fellow citizens neither enjoy nor value civic life, everyone is less likely to be successful in shaping our communities in satisfying ways and everyone is more likely to be resigned to choose among the existing options, even if it is within our collective power to create new options that most of us would prefer to the old.

People who have neither experienced nor enjoyed collective decision making and action are less likely to engage in even the most undemanding aspects of liberal democratic politics, such as voting, than are people who have experienced some sort of successful civic association. People do not join secondary associations in order to practice the skills and cultivate the virtues of liberal democratic politics. Having some of those skills and virtues is probably the best entry into developing them still further, succeeding in using them, and therefore enjoying their exercise. Schools are perhaps the primary place—other than the family—where citizens can learn some skills and virtues of collective decision making and action. Yet the very aim of teaching the skills and virtues of collective decision making and action in schools also depends for its realization on collective decision making and action among citizens and their representatives. It is therefore doubly difficult to overcome the neglect of these skills and virtues in school systems if schools have neglected them in the past.

Although this book focuses on secondary associations, most of which are voluntary in some meaningful sense, it is worth noting that liberal democracies are justified in compelling adults to associate in some significant ways, such as jury service. The justification for compulsion is not that juries cultivate civic virtue but rather that they carry out justice. Compelled associations among adults are easiest to defend when they serve the cause of justice. Some governmental institutions that have compelled the association of adults have been uncommonly successful in cultivating a wide range of civic virtues. Is there any large voluntary association of adults in the United States that has been as successful, relative to the rest of society, as the military was during the period from 1950 to 1970 in cultivating cooperation and respect among people from diverse backgrounds and in breaking down racial prejudice?

Legitimate forms of compelled association among adults are usually governmental, but they are not strictly limited to government. Perhaps the most significant example of a nongovernmental association that is more compelled than it is voluntary is the union shop, which legally requires employees to join (or at least to pay dues) after they are employed by the unionized company. Is this significant limitation on associational freedom justified? (Prior to legalization of the union shop by the Taft-Hartley Act, the closed shop was legalized by the Wagner Act. A closed shop had required a person to be a prior member of the union as a condition for being hired by the company. The union shop, like the closed shop before it, is outlawed by some states.) Stuart White's essay carefully considers whether democratic governments are justified in legalizing union shops and also in promoting unions rather than taking a more strictly neutral stance toward them, as governments are constitutionally bound to do toward religious and other primarily expressive associations.

How might the compelled association of a union shop be justified? First, the union shop must be a means of carrying out the aims of justice, to secure basic opportunity goods such as adequate income and decent working conditions for employees of the company. Provision for a union shop then simultaneously provides basic opportunity goods for employees and protects all employees from the free-rider problem of some employees opting out of paying dues but still benefiting from what the union gains by virtue of other employees' contributions. Second, an uncoerced majority of workers must agree to the union shop. Third, individual employees, who must pay union dues, must not be coerced into advocating any ideological cause or engaging in partisan activities of the union against their conscientious objection. Without provision for conscientious exemption from the union's expressive activities, the government through its support of union shops would be forcing some citizens to advocate ideological positions and partisan causes in which they did not believe. Under these conditions, a union shop provides a legitimate means of ensuring that the burdens of unionization are fairly distributed among those who directly benefit from its existence.

One might challenge this conclusion by claiming that union shops are not necessary for justice: a liberal democratic government could provide all the benefits of a union shop—higher wages, better working conditions, health care benefits, and other social welfare goods—without the costs of coercing workers into joining a union. If we imagine a just society, we can also imagine away union shops. Nonetheless, union shops serve an important purpose here and now. Union shops enable some workers to have enough organized power to fight for decent wages and working conditions that are essential to justice. Even after adequate wages and decent working conditions are established, they are more likely to be maintained with the ongoing pressure of powerful unions, made possible by union shops. Workers otherwise may not have sufficient power vis-à-vis either management or government to prevent the erosion of their hard-fought gains. The example of compelled association in trade unions suggests an important qualification to any generalization that government must not compel adults to associate: adults should not be compelled to associate unless the compulsion serves an important aim of justice.

Among the general conclusions that provisionally emerge from our discussions of freedom of association are the following: Many secondary associations do not serve the cause of justice, but the freedom of an association should not be contingent upon its furthering justice. The basic liberty of individuals demands a substantial degree of freedom of association that is not so contingent. Will the use of this basic liberty by individuals support civic virtues as central to liberal democracy as reciprocity and civility? Not necessarily. Secondary associations cannot be counted upon, or legally constrained, to teach reciprocity, civility, or other important civic virtues. But many still do, even though it is rarely their primary purpose. Can secondary associations at least be legally constrained to respect some fundamental principles such as nondiscrimination that help secure basic opportunity for all individuals? Associations that are primarily religious, expressive, or intimate are exempt from this legal constraint in areas that are inseparable from their religious, expressive, or intimate purposes, but many other secondary associations are not exempt. Nondiscrimination would be a hollow hope if secondary associations whose purposes are primarily commercial, for example, were exempt from this legal constraint.

Should we be worried about the decrease in associational activity in America, if it has in fact taken place? We cannot assume that the more secondary associations that exist, the better off liberal democracy will be. More of civic importance probably depends on the nature of associations in America than on their number. How can we improve the quality of the associations among which to choose, from the perspective of their contribution to the lives of individuals and the life of liberal democracy? The range and quality of our choice among associations depends on our collective action. Without many people working politically to change the existing associational landscape, our options will remain suboptimal. Freedom of association can and should be legally protected, but citizens themselves must also constructively engage with their fellow citizens if our associational life is to improve, and with it, the life of our liberal democracy.

Notes

1. *Democracy in America* (New York: Doubleday Anchor, 1969), pp. 513–17, 522.

2. Robert Putnam, "Bowling Alone: Democracy in America at the End of the Twentieth Century," *Journal of Democracy* 6, no. 1 (January 1995): 67.

3. A detailed discussion of the principle of reciprocity, and its relationship to democracy can be found in Amy Gutmann and Dennis Thompson, *Democracy and Disagreement* (Cambridge: Harvard University Press, Belknap Press, 1996).

4. *Bob Jones University v. United States*, 461 U.S. 574 (1983).

5. I discuss and defend these and other social purposes of higher education in *Democratic Education* (Princeton: Princeton University Press, 1987), pp. 172–193.

6. *Roberts, Acting Commissioner, Minnesota Department of Human Rights, et al. v. United States Jaycees*, 468 U.S. 609 (1984).

7. *Minnesota Statute* 363.03, subd. 3 (1982). The term "place of public accommodation" is defined in the act as "a business, accommodation, refreshment, entertainment, recreation, or transportation facility of any kind, whether licensed or not, whose goods, services, facilities, privileges, advantages or accommodations are extended, offered, sold, or otherwise made available to the public" (363.01, subd. 18). Quoted in *Roberts v. Jaycees* at 615.

8. *United States Jaycees v. McClure*, 709 F. 2d 1560 (8MCIR., 1983) at 1570. Quoted in *Roberts v. Jaycees* at 639.

9. Minnesota Statute 363.01, subd. 18 (1982). Quoted in Roberts v Jaycees at 615.

10. To be free to associate with others is part of what it means to be free to live one's own life. There are limits on the freedom of association that is essential to individual freedom, but those limits do not remove the analytical connection between some substantial freedom to associate and the freedom to live one's own life. If I simply cannot choose with whom to associate, I cannot be a free person.

11. William Galston, *Liberal Purposes* (Cambridge and New York: Cambridge University Press, 1991), pp. 221–224.

PART ONE

INDIVIDUAL VALUES OF ASSOCIATION

Chapter Two

THE VALUE OF ASSOCIATION

GEORGE KATEB

WRITING in 1988, Laurence Tribe maintained that it was "unclear" how far the Supreme Court would go in moving toward a view that "concerted effort *itself* is seen as entitled to independent constitutional protection."[1] His painstaking analysis of freedom of association thus yields an uncertain result. If one has not given this freedom much thought, one could find Tribe's words surprising and perhaps disconcerting. After all, do not people have the Bill of Rights on their side when they pick their own company, their associates or fellows or colleagues, for any purpose that does not injure the vital claims of others? Does not the First Amendment protect from governmental interference the right to associate? Or if the wording of the amendment seems to cover only such association (assembly) as is necessary to petition government, would not general liberty as protected by the Fifth and Fourteenth Amendments have to include the right to pick one's company? Tribe shows that such a reflexive opinion is not supported by the reasoning of courts. Rather, the tendency has been to protect freedom of association only as it serves other rights; or it is held to be a fundamental right only when it is exercised in a narrow range of activities. But when association is merely (in Tribe's words) "for the concerted pursuit of lawful but not especially 'preferred' ends,"[2] its regulation can be and has been upheld for the sake of quite a few governmental aims, many of which go well beyond protecting the vital claims of individuals. No fundamental right of association across the whole range of human activities is unambiguously protected.

I confess that I for one find this situation disconcerting. When I read some of the main cases in which the right of association is treated, for the most part, as undeserving of the level of protection that, say, speech and religion receive, my disquiet becomes stronger. And when I read those cases in which freedom of association is upheld, my disquiet is only slightly alleviated: most of the time, association is instrumentally yoked to speech and is protected only because speech is protected, or it is held worthy of full constitutional protection only in associations of personal intimacy. Only rarely does freedom of association receive a defense that honors it as integral to a free human life, to being a free person. Picking one's company is part of living as one likes; living as one likes (provided one does not injure the vital claims of others) is what being free means. Yet some main cases, decided by the Supreme Court or lower courts, show little sympathy for this abstract proposition. Why is that so?

In this paper I explore the reasoning, as it appears in some of these cases, that has either too readily abridged freedom of association or protected it in unduly limited situations. In these cases, however, we will not find an elaborate explanation for the resistance of courts to enunciating a sturdy defense of freedom of association; rather, their opinions allow us to observe their way of conceptualizing the judicially protected kinds of associational life. This way needs to be challenged.

. . . . .

Before I turn to judicial opinions, however, I would like to make a few general remarks about association itself and hence about freedom of association. There are, of course, many kinds of association. Speaking generally, we can say that there are organizations and institutions; there are enterprises; there are ties and bonds in everyday life; and there are chosen enclaves, communes, and communities. More particularly, we can list some of the principal forms of associative life:

> businesses and economic corporations, labor unions and professional guilds, and economic lobbying groups
> voluntary noneconomic associations such as political parties and various sorts of advocacy groups
> religious denominations and organizations
> institutions such as universities, museums, charities, and other nonprofit entities
> private social clubs, fraternities, sororities
> temporary and comparatively undefined and barely coordinated movements
> personal, familial, intimate relationships of love and friendship

The boundaries between these forms are sometimes ill-marked or shifting, and I do not claim that the list is complete. Still, at first sight, it would seem that the right of association would cover the forms I have just listed. In a constitutional democracy, people should have the right, recognized by government, to associate in these ways for any appropriate purpose that does not harm the vital claims of others. Government should not interfere, except with the same restraint that it is supposed to practice in regard to any other fundamental right, like expression or property or religion.

Yet, of course, association is itself conduct and creates conduct. And as we know and say, conduct cannot be as free as expression (to leave aside the rights of religion and property), even when conduct is not intentionally harmful to others. Harms may come about unintentionally; there may be some accumulation of bad effects no one foresaw. Those who harm others may not be sensitive enough to see that what they do is actually harm. This much must be granted. Perhaps, then, the right of association requires greater control than the right of expression? In the words of Justice John Marshall Harlan (in dissent): "But as we move away from speech alone and into the sphere of conduct—even conduct associated with speech or resulting from it—the area of legitimate governmental interest expands" (*NAACP v Button*, 371 U.S. 415, 454 [1963]). So, the matter is hardly simple. The fact remains that association exists for the attainment of ends that could not be attained by someone acting alone. Different kinds of association attain, or seek to attain, different ends. History and our own observation tell us that in a free society, people associate for the sake of achieving an indefinitely large range of ends. Association is essential to their lives.

Judicial reasoning dwells on the instrumental purposes of association, except when it touches on personal intimacy. There is, however, a basic truth about almost all associative life and activity, a truth not confined to love and friendship. People find in association a value in itself. The point is obvious, but it has not received enough judicial attention or protection. In pursuing their ends, and needing to associate in order to do so, people discover numerous sources of pleasure apart from the pleasure of success in their specific pursuits. They discover numerous opportunities for many diverse kinds of experience. Associations of every form provide accommodation for experience, much of it pleasurable. To characterize any association, therefore, as a mere instrument, a mere means, is to ignore some part of its role in a person's life. The means to an end can very well transform itself in a person's feelings into an end in itself. Indeed, the means may matter more than any end: the web of relations housed in an association can take on a tremendous value, greater than the goals of the association. I am referring not to intimacy (which is not judicially posited even initially as instrumental), but to relationships less intense, more limited, sometimes more casual or episodic or artificial. These relationships have their own worth. If they are not a substitute for love and friendship, love and friendship are not a substitute for them.

To be free, to live as one likes, includes associating on one's own terms,

which means engaging in voluntary relationships of all sorts, finding or trying to find pleasure in them, and also finding in them opportunities for
many kinds of experience. The freedom is in the pleasure (or the happiness); the pleasure is in the experience. If the assembly and petition clauses
of the First Amendment do not provide the explicit guarantee of this freedom of experience through association, then recourse can be had, as I have
suggested, to the general liberty of the individual that is protected by the
due process clauses of the Fifth and Fourteenth Amendments, construed by
means of the concept of substantive due process. I follow Justice John Marshall Harlan (despite the narrowness of his applications) in understanding
substantive due process as the idea that the widest possible scope of general
liberty is mandated by the Constitution, and that *certain* kinds and degrees
of governmental regulation, although imposed by an undeniably valid political procedure, have the effect of depriving innocent persons of their
rightful liberty (or property, but that is not relevant here), and hence are
somewhat analogous to "malicious" uses of due process of law against those
who are known or probably thought to be innocent, or who should be
known to be innocent. The regulation should never have been made; as
analogously, the prosecution should never have been carried out (*Poe v. Ull-
man*, 367 U.S. 497, 539–55 [1961]).[3] Incarceration is not the only way in
which government may deprive a person of rightful liberty. Therefore, the
very basis that has permitted or required courts to protect choices in close
or intimate relationships (as instances, choice of mate across racial lines and
use of contraception inside or outside marriage) should be the basis for protecting other kinds of association. It is not up to courts (or any governmental entity) to rank associations for people, or to hold that close or intimate relationships are inherently more significant than other relationships
and therefore more deserving of protection. Even if it is true that for many
people (perhaps most people) close or intimate relationships are the most
important ones, it does not follow that other relationships can be regulated
with any less judicial scrutiny and compunction. It is often more shocking
when government interferes improperly in intimate relationships than in
unintimate ones. Personal violation usually registers on us (whether victims
or observers) more vividly. But any interference that is not strictly necessary, in any sector of an individual's life, violates freedom. Government can
violate freedom unshockingly, even slightly, and still do so improperly.
Minor freedom is still freedom, and there is always a strong case against
regulating any exercise of it that does not injure the vital claims of others.

I do not intend to give a thorough inventory of all the experiences that
associations can offer. But mention can be made of such kinds as the op-

portunity for the display of energy and shrewdness presented by business life, which often marvelously combines self-denial and self-expression (or self-aggrandizement); the activism, daring, and creativity summoned by political, moral, and cultural movements; the exhilaration that arises from involvement in political life or the life of public advocacy; the camaraderie and self-confirmation that come from social clubs; the gratification of loyally helping to maintain a tradition or way of life; and so on. The process in which people strive for particular ends and have some success in attaining them provides the occasion for most of these experiences and their pleasures; the quest must be serious if the enjoyment of association itself is to have an element of discovery or surprise and hence a special keenness. Ends such as profit or reform or power or service to God or to the dead or to the future establish the need to associate. Of the associations listed above, only social clubs, fraternities, and sororities seem to make the pleasures of association the direct end, but even there, external purposes, such as voluntary social work, are contrived to disguise or palliate the pure hedonism of association.

Now, if my emphasis on having experiences for the sake of pleasure may appear insufficient to justify a plea for constitutional protection, then I am afraid that a major passion behind the struggle for constitutional protection is in the course of being forgotten: the desire to rid society of oppression so that a life of decent adventure would become more available for larger numbers of people. Experience for the sake of pleasure is one way of saying experience for the sake of experience. That should be sufficient to merit constitutional protection in a free society. Perhaps if I said, experience for the sake of finding oneself, for rounding out or re-creating one's identity, my position would attract more sympathy. I have no objection. But I would still insist that life as a decent adventure is a weighty consideration, even if one is disposed to be embarrassed by talk about identity. What living as one likes comes to, in a society supposedly dedicated to freedom, is, precisely, living for the sake of searching out experience and its pleasures, or living for the pursuit of happiness, and not being authoritatively asked to explain or give an accounting, and being regulated only with deep constitutional regret. (I would rather avoid calling such freedom by the name of autonomy: living as one likes need not mean living up to one's best potentiality or to the highest personal standards—far from it.)

To be sure, constitutional protection under the First Amendment is already accorded to one's involvement in religious life and in public advocacy. The mention of these activities in the Bill of Rights not only consecrates them but also signifies that they would not be mentioned explicitly if they were not salient in people's lives. In contrast, the Constitution does not seem to guarantee freedom of association as such. The plausible suggestion—to which I have already referred—is that many associations are so serious in their consequences that they cannot be left as free as religion or speech. This suggestion has merit. But I think that the impulse to regulate association is driven not only by a care to protect society against harm but also by the idea that living as you like, especially in the form of picking your company in matters not close or intimate, simply does not have much importance. It must in fact be conceded that a good deal of associative life is shallow or trivial. The experience it provides is sometimes not especially good experience; its pleasures can be the lower ones; its happiness vulgar. But alas, what is freedom if not the ability to do what others may think not worth doing? Just imagine what freedom of religion or speech would remain if the standard applied to them were, say, the search for truth or the tendency to prevent, abolish, or reduce injustice. Much of protected freedom is misspent or misused, is waste, from one dignified perspective or another. Government, however, is not supposed to look skeptically or censoriously at how freedom is used (except when vital claims are involved) if people are to live in a free society. One's life is one's own.

I am proposing that a somewhat different spirit pervade the constitutional jurisprudence of the right of association. Some regulation is surely necessary to prevent or remedy serious harm to the vital claims of those outside any given association, and different kinds of association will require different kinds and degrees of regulation (or limitation). Still, regulation should proceed with a sense of gravity, with reluctance, where the harm (or alleged harm) to be prevented or remedied is unintentional or unanticipated, or not judged by the associated individuals to be harm. And the harm must really be a harm, not just some vague or speculative imperfection, or an impediment to a mere policy that has no constitutional necessity, but only some desirability (often debatable).

In short, the liberty component of substantive due process must be seen as a bar to regulating association on behalf of a value that is not constitutionally equal in worth to freedom. Only a general (or abstract) formula like "regulation is allowable only when vital claims reaching to the life, liberty, or property of others are seriously harmed" can be offered as a principle to guide governmental interference in association. The same formula already applies to almost all judicially permitted restrictions of another fundamental right, freedom of expression. Perjury, copyright, libel, incitement to imminent lawless action, and so on, are all prosecutable or litigable offenses; they all pertain to the vital claims of individuals (or secondarily to the integrity of official processes). But owing to the fact that there are numerous kinds of expression, the various restrictions do not have specific common elements to go with the common one of seriously injuring the vital claims of others. Before cases arise, there can be only a general formula. If association is a fundamental right, the same abstractness inheres in the effort to state an initial principle of allowable interference with its freedom.

I now turn to judicial reasoning.

.   .   .   .   .

In a leading case on the right of association, Justice William Brennan mentions some of the principal ways in which government may interfere with freedom of association. He says:

> Among other things, government may seek to impose penalties or withhold benefits from individuals because of their membership in a disfavored group . . . ; it may attempt to require disclosure of the fact of membership in a group seeking anonymity . . . ; and it may try to interfere with the internal organization or affairs of the group. (*Roberts v United States Jaycees*, 468 U.S. 609, 622–23 [1984], hereafter cited as *Roberts*)

In this paper I will concentrate on governmental interference when it takes the particular form of affecting "the internal organization or affairs of the group," as it did in the case from which the just-quoted words come. The internal life of associations is, by itself, a vast subject. It includes such practices as discriminating in membership or services on account of race or sex in businesses, schools, and "public accommodations," as well as in social clubs. My particular concern is with social clubs. *Roberts*, perhaps the most theoretically interesting Supreme Court opinion on association, dealt with the claimed right of a social club to deny women full, voting membership. Another reason to be interested in social clubs is that we would ordinarily think of them as a typically private kind of association. If a private social club cannot be free of governmental interference, it would seem that the scope of protected privacy dwindles, while any other kind of association that is even less private or more implicated in effects on others is left more vulnerable to interference. The right of association is left in a precarious state: if social clubs can be regulated invasively, almost any kind of association can be; and the regulation can proceed with less reluctance.

Justice Brennan is clear that when a club is ordered to admit women against its will, there can be "no clearer example of an intrusion into the internal structure or affairs of an association" (*Roberts*, 623). Yet his opinion for the Court compelled the admission of women. (Seven justices took part; Brennan spoke for himself and five others; Justice Sandra O'Connor concurred in part and concurred in the judgment.) In justifying the Court's decision, Brennan explores the nature of associative life in general.

Although I have no real interest in clubs as a subject and do not see them as major forms of association, but find them, when they are exclusive, both boring and morally dubious, I think that Brennan's attitude toward them is unacceptably insouciant. I find in his opinion, and in other judicial opinions concerning the Jaycees and other clubs,[4] a seeming indifference to the value of association as such, except for close or intimate relations. The link between being free and picking one's company for the sake of pursuing any end whatever or for the sake of the company (no end at all) is scarcely acknowledged whenever the association is not close or intimate, with the result that competing values, some of them of questionable constitutional weight, are allowed to overcome the right of association far too easily. A valid restriction turns into an invalid abridgment. Even in social clubs, the idea of freedom is at stake. The Court in *Roberts* does not give freedom its due. If left free, people can find the value of association realized in any form of association. The seriousness of the association is not inevitably proportional to the value of the experience accommodated by it. The value of such experience is a matter of taste, and in a free society, taste must be left as free as possible, as a matter of right. I am not saying that the extent of freedom that is suitable for social clubs is suitable for all forms of associations. Rather, there is a clublike feature in almost all associative life, and this feature deserves both acknowledgment and considerable weight in constitutional jurisprudence. Freedom is seriously implicated in it: the freedom to lead a life of experiences in the company one chooses. Governmental interference with the membership of a private association, even a social club, raises grave questions of freedom, which inhere in even seemingly minor curtailments.

Although the core case is *Roberts*, the Supreme Court some years before handed down a decision friendlier to social clubs. Writing for a divided Court, Justice William Rehnquist allowed a private social club to deny service at its bar to a "Negro" guest (*Moose Lodge No. 107 v. Irvis*, 407 U.S. 163 [1972]). Rehnquist gives no positive constitutional reason for allowing Moose Lodge to discriminate, to pick its company. Rather, he is intent on showing that the equal protection clause of the Fourteenth Amendment does not apply to private conduct "'however discriminatory or wrongful'" (172), citing *The Civil Rights Cases*, 109 U.S. 3 (1883). State-furnished services to the club, such as electricity, water, and police and fire protection do

THE VALUE OF ASSOCIATION   43

not make the club liable to state regulation. If these services were deemed to have that effect, "such a holding would utterly emasculate the distinction between private as distinguished from state conduct set forth in *The Civil Rights Cases, supra,* and adhered to in subsequent decisions" (173). I do not mean to endorse Rehnquist's untroubled invocation of *The Civil Rights Cases.* I only mean to say that the decision in *Moose Lodge* seems right, and the reason for noninterference not given by Rehnquist is found in freedom of association as a component of liberty under substantive due process. It is unfortunate, but not especially surprising, that Rehnquist did not employ this latter concept, but certainly the distinction between private and public, howsoever based, is indispensable to a free society. Ironically, it is one of the three dissenters, Justice William O. Douglas, who endorses the proposition that freedom of association is a fundamental right. He then proceeds, however, to curtail the right on the grounds that in Pennsylvania liquor licenses are rare, and the legal permission to serve drinks therefore makes the club a sort of public resource, even an instrument of state action—in this case, action that violates the Fourteenth Amendment. Nevertheless, apart from the defense of his vote, Douglas gives the heart of the matter:

> My view of the First Amendment and the related guarantees of the Bill of Rights is that they create a zone of privacy which precludes government from interfering with private clubs or groups. The associational rights which our system honors permit all white, all black, all brown, and all yellow clubs to be formed. They also permit all Catholic, all Jewish, or all agnostic clubs to be established. Government may not tell a man or a woman who his or her associates must be. The individual can be as selective as he desires. (180–81)

He sounds a rare note, even as his vote does nothing to support his theory. The fact that liquor licenses are comparatively few cannot establish a private club's obligation to serve people whom it does not want to serve. The insult to the black guest is reprehensible, but there are supposed to be strict constitutional limits on government's policing of the manners of private individuals. Now let us see what we find when we look at *Roberts.*

The United States Jaycees (founded in 1920 as the Junior Chamber of Commerce) is a nonprofit organization that admitted to full, voting membership only young men between the ages of eighteen and thirty-five. Women were allowed as nonvoting, associate members. The organization's purpose, in its self-description, is to "foster the growth and development of young men's civic organizations in the United States"; to "inculcate . . . a spirit of genuine Americanism and civic interest"; to provide young men with "opportunity for personal development"; and "to develop true friend-ship and understanding among young men of all nations." The Jaycees or-ganization is "a supplementary education institution." As of 1981, the Jaycees had approximately 295,000 members in 7,400 local chapters affili-ated with 51 state organizations, and 11, 915 associate members. (All quo-tations and statistics are taken from *Roberts*, 612–13.)

Two local chapters in Minnesota had begun to admit women to full mem-bership, and were therefore faced with an effort by the national organiza-tion to revoke their charters. Members of both chapters filed charges of dis-crimination against the national Jaycees and did so under the Minnesota Human Rights Act, which prohibits denial to any person of

> the full and equal enjoyment of the goods, services, facilities, privileges, ad-vantages, and accommodations of a place of public accommodation because of race, color, creed, religion, disability, national origin, or sex. (*Roberts*, 615)

The Minnesota Supreme Court had accepted the determination that the Jaycees were a public accommodation, and hence came under the jurisdic-tion of the law. The spectacle of the effort made by that court's majority to show that a private club is a public accommodation is not edifying. Its con-clusion, however, was supposed to bind the federal courts. Still, whatever the Minnesota court said, the Supreme Court could have decided that a fun-damental right was involved—the right of the Jaycees to associate on their own terms. The Supreme Court decided otherwise.

In a comparatively brief space, Justice Brennan produces a general the-ory of constitutional protection for associative life. Brennan says that deci-sions of the Supreme Court have "referred to constitutionally protected 'freedom of association' in two distinct senses" (*Roberts*, 617). (The quota-tion marks around freedom of association are a bit strange, unless seen as skeptical.) First, "intimate human relationships" have received protection as "a fundamental element of personal liberty" (618). Second, the Court has held that freedom of association is guaranteed as "an indispensable means of preserving other individual liberties" (618). In this latter connection, Brennan refers to "a right to associate for the purpose of engaging in those activities protected by the First Amendment: speech, assembly, petition for the redress of grievances, and the exercise of religion" (618). Brennan uses two key summary terms: "intrinsic" to refer to intimate relationships and "instrumental" to refer to associations that somehow (often by advocacy) promote or defend First Amendment rights. (Brennan's use of the notion of instrumentality is not always clear.) Brennan seems to think that all forms of association can be regarded in the light of these two categories. His conclusion is that associating as Jaycees has little if any intrinsic value, and thus the Jaycees cannot claim constitutional protection on that score; and that the national organization's instrumental efficacy would not be impaired by the admission of women into its Minnesota chapters over its opposition. (Although the Minnesota chapters wanted women as full members, the Roberts decision could have affected local chapters elsewhere that did not want them.)

. . . . .

Brennan remarks, early in his decision, that the "intrinsic and instrumental features of a constitutionally protected association may, of course, coincide" (*Roberts*, 618). As it develops, his meaning is that any given association may lay claim (even if not always convincingly) to both intrinsic and instrumental value: that is, value that deserves full constitutional protection. For him, one question is whether the claim to intrinsic value can be sustained. If such a claim cannot be sustained, the question then becomes whether the alternative claim to instrumental value bases itself on associating for the purpose of promoting (or defending) independently guaranteed rights, like speech or religion. Either the intrinsic claim, or any kind of instrumental claim that reaches to First Amendment rights, is sufficient, by itself, to establish a strong presumption in favor of constitutional protection.

Let us follow Brennan's sequence and take up the intrinsic claim to constitutional protection first. Brennan's premise is that an associative relationship can have intrinsic value sufficient to gain constitutional protection only when it is intimate or "personal" (618). Intrinsic value thus attaches itself to face-to-face relationships in which a few people know and care for one another. These are the only relationships valuable in themselves, for their own sake. Brennan does not seem to commit himself on whether an associative relationship that is private but not intimate can have constitutional protection, but two later Court decisions in which he joined, and which are guided by *Roberts*, seem to deny that possibility, even for a group as small as twenty.[5] The protection of privacy seems to matter only when personal intimacy is at stake. Indeed, the private seems to be equated with the personal.

What, in more detail, are the characteristic features of intimate relationships, and, next, what is the nature of their intrinsic value? About the features, Brennan says the family is the model. Its internal life is "distinguished by such attributes as relative smallness, a high degree of selectivity in decisions to begin and maintain the affiliation, and seclusion from others in critical aspects of the relationship" (620). On the other hand, local chapters of the Jaycees "are neither small nor selective," and "much of the activity central to the formation and maintenance of the association involves the participation of strangers to that relationship" (621). Running through Brennan's opinion is the assumption that all nonintimate relationships are simply inferior to intimate ones. What is personal is superior to what is impersonal, what is informal is superior to what is formal, the deeply familiar is better than the less well known or the unknown. The first-named features of association deserve full constitutional protection; the latter are not deserving of any such thing, and may be regulated—whether in membership or in any other way—for any reasonable or plausible governmental purpose. In effect, only the intimate sphere (modeled on the family) has the intensity of intrinsic value to merit constitutional protection.

Brennan tries to give an account of the superiority of intimate relationships, of the reason that they possess the intrinsic value (high value, and not instrumental) that gains them "this kind of constitutional protection" of which the Jaycees are not "worthy" (620). He gives two sorts of reason, each sort complex. There is some courage in Brennan's effort to unpack the meanings of the concept of intrinsic value, to say why some relationships have it and others lack it. Brennan does not take the way out offered by just asserting that nothing can be said (intrinsic value is inexpressible), or that nothing need be said (inquiry reaches its destination when the highest end is located, and if a skeptic refuses to recognize the end, he can provide no sensible alternative). Rather, Brennan says, first, that

> certain kinds of personal bonds have played a critical role in the culture and tradition of the Nation by cultivating and transmitting shared ideals and beliefs; they thereby foster diversity and act as critical buffers between the individual and the power of the State. (618–19)

Brennan then lists seven earlier cases that sustained the value of personal bonds, and one relevant dissent in an eighth case. All but two references pertain to close or intimate relationships (but not exclusively familial). Of these two, one pertains to compulsory disclosure of membership lists (*NAACP v. Alabama ex rel. Patterson*, 357 U.S. 449 [1958]), and the other to the use of public parks by racially discriminatory private schools (*Gilmore v. City of Montgomery*, 417 U.S. 556 [1974]).

What is striking is that Brennan's first statement of the superiority of close or intimate relationships seems to instrumentalize those relationships. (Perhaps any effort, my own included, to rationalize intrinsic value must instrumentalize.) Intimacy deserves constitutional protection, Brennan seems to say, because it is *a means* to forming and maintaining certain ideals and beliefs; in turn, these ideals and beliefs, when shared, somehow manage to help insulate "the individual" from the power of political authority. Apart from his unconscious slippage in claiming intrinsic value for relationships that are then praised instrumentally, the words employed about the usefulness of these relationships could as easily be employed—perhaps could more tellingly be employed—about relationships that take the form of large, less selective, and more formally organized associations. Parties, advocacy groups, business enterprises, and private educational institutions come to mind. All these forms of associative life specialize in "cultivating and transmitting shared ideals and beliefs" and thereby fostering diversity and acting "as critical buffers between the individual and the power of the State" (619). But let me put aside the point about comparative efficacy in behalf of diversity and of power against government and stay with the concept of intrinsic value.

Now, I do not ask for any inflexible distinction between intrinsic and instrumental value, nor for a rigorous separation between means and ends. Certainly, when means are action or activity (as relationships are to an important extent), means always verge on becoming ends themselves, becoming more important ends than the ostensible ends. But if one is going to speak at all about intrinsic value as distinct from instrumental value, then it would be better not to be exclusively instrumental in one's first attempt to explain the intrinsic value of certain relationships. However, beginning with the word *moreover*, Brennan then supplies a much better account of the intrinsic value of close or intimate relationships. Why are these relationships to be valued for their own sake? Of course, they will attain ends, but the ends will be inseparable from what is needed to attain them; the ends could scarcely be attained in any other way; one is tempted to think that the ends are indistinguishable from the means to them.

> Moreover, the constitutional shelter afforded such relationships reflects the realization that individuals draw much of their emotional enrichment from close ties with others. Protecting these relationships from unwarranted state interference therefore safeguards the ability independently to define one's identity that is central to any concept of liberty. (609)

Here, then, is Brennan's most powerful statement. A relationship has intrinsic value when it is intrinsic (if you will) to a person's *identity*, that person's sense that he or she is this unique being, not to be taken for or exchanged for another; and that if certain relationships are blocked or regulated by government, one is at risk of losing oneself, of being changed for the worse against one's will. We can say that a sense of a particular identity, a sense of being oneself, is constitutionally worthy of protection, just as much as one's personhood is. Identity is selfhood, which is different from personhood. The latter is protected when one's human dignity is recognized equally with everyone else's, and one is thus guaranteed such fundamental rights against government as the preservation of one's life against arbitrary or unjust action or passive inaction, or the preservation of one's liberty against any encroachment not strictly necessary, or the preservation of one's property against arbitrary confiscation, or taking without just compensation. Personhood is, so to speak, impersonal. But if selfhood and personhood are not the same, they are both of incalculable or inestimable value. They are their own ends: to be a self-defined self is an end in itself; to be a constitutionally defined person is an end in itself. Each human being is his or her own end, at least in the eyes of the Constitution.

Inseparable and indistinguishable from being a self—having a unique identity—is having the relationships that one wants. Even a relationship that is given (say, one's parents and relatives, or one's children conceived deliberately or accidentally) must eventually be chosen if it is to be one's own. That is one reason why the right of association is a component of liberty under substantive due process. Thus, I am my relationships; and if I as a self have intrinsic value, so do all the relationships that are inextricably interwoven with my identity. (I know that the word *relationship* is ugly; perhaps that is all the better in a discussion like this one, which may verge on sentimentality.)

The question persists: do only close or intimate relationships have intrinsic value? Are they the only relationships seriously implicated in a human being's identity? I have already said that if left free, people can find the noninstrumental value of association—the pleasure of freely picking one's company, and the pleasure taken in one's company and in the experience and the adventure given oneself by one's company—in any form of association. If personhood demands as much freedom of association as constitutionally possible, does the same go for selfhood? Does identity depend on as broad a guaranteed right of association as possible? Brennan says:

> Family relationships, by their nature, involve deep attachments and commitments to the necessarily few other individuals with whom one shares not only a special community of thoughts, experiences, and beliefs but also distinctively personal aspects of one's life. (619–20)

Brennan insists that only what is small, selective, and secluded can possibly matter to one's identity—and the family is paradigmatically small, selective, and secluded. But is it true that one's idea of oneself depends only or mainly on one's family ties? Add one's serious affective ties, to fill out the scope of the intimate. Is selfhood an achievement that only intimacy favors?

The intrinsic value of association cannot be exclusively confined to close, intimate, or personal relationships, any more than pleasure or experience or adventure is found only in such relationships. If intrinsic value is present wherever a significant contribution to identity is present, then many relationships that are not close or intimate or deeply personal may have intrinsic value. Distant or formal or mediated or even abstract relationships contribute to the process of self-discovery and self-expression; so may chance or casual encounters or dealings with strangers; they can all help to shape or reshape an identity. It is an unattractive romanticism to believe that a self discloses or enhances itself only amid loving immediacy. Indeed, if Hannah Arendt is in the neighborhood of a truth, then it is not in intimacy but in undomestic situations, often involving strangers or people with whom one is accidentally thrown or mere acquaintances or formal colleagues or fellow adventurers, that one achieves a distinctive individuation.[6] Of course, one need not go the length that Arendt does in her conceptualization of the existential importance of one particular unintimate relationship: participatory political action. All that one has to say is that insofar as a relationship's intrinsic value is a matter of its connection to identity, unintimate relationships may have a great deal of intrinsic value.

Different people will, of course, vary in the proportions of intimate and unintimate relationships they want; and many choices are made without reference to a concern to achieve or maintain or reform identity. But many people find themselves by looking, at least some of the time, outside the house. They may think that by serving as a national or state officer of the Jaycees, or by being a member of a local chapter that excludes women as full members, they are engaged in a relationship of association that means a great deal to them. They may prefer to imagine that they are reduced in their identities by being told their choices are illegal, rather than constitutionally protected. We may—I do—think that it is unadult, bigoted, silly, to think as they do, and to wish to remain constitutionally free to choose to do what they want in this particular instance. I do not believe, however, that the Court should have interfered with the internal organization of an association on the grounds (partly) that such an association consisted of relationships that lacked intrinsic value, and that, therefore, "several features of the Jaycees clearly place the organization outside the category of relationships worthy of this kind of protection" (620).

To be sure, people will often get used to their compulsory associates after a while, and then enjoy their company, and eventually become unable to imagine their situation without the company of people forced on them at the beginning. But such adaptability—admirable as it can be—does not validate the original compulsoriness, even if the situation that existed at the start could not have reformed itself. The good outcome does not validate the methods that produced it; without valid methods, the good outcome is only doubtfully good, compromised at its root.

If the right of associating on one's own terms is to give way—as any fundamental right occasionally must, it seems—some competing and overriding principle must be in play. As a principle, pragmatic paternalism toward men as wayward creatures and toward women as in need of daily help would not suffice; indeed, it would erode the Constitution, as paternalism in general does. Brennan's discussion of the reason for regulating the rules of membership of the Jaycees comes out when he takes up the question as to whether the Jaycees' organization has constitutionally protected instrumental value. We now turn to that part of Brennan's analysis that deals with instrumental value as a concept.

.   .   .   .   .

I have already said that Brennan's discussion of instrumental value is not entirely clear. One formulation he produces is this:

> An individual's freedom to speak, to worship, and to petition the government for the redress of grievances could not be vigorously protected from interference by the State unless a correlative freedom to engage in group effort towards those ends were not also guaranteed. (622)

It appears from these words that the freedoms of speech, religion, and petition are ends, and freedom of association is only a means, even though an indispensable means, to those ends. Such a view would seem, at first glance, to reduce freedom of (unintimate) association to a lower level of constitutional worthiness than the freedoms of speech, religion, and petition. Perhaps Brennan is implicitly alluding to the wording and punctuation of the First Amendment, where the clauses on assembly and petition seem to make assembly (an intermittent synonym for association) solely instrumental for petition (a regular synonym for advocacy). The relevant part of the First Amendment reads: "Congress shall make no law . . . abridging . . . the right of the people peaceably to assemble, and to petition the government for a redress of grievances." A plausible interpretation would be that the First Amendment contains no general right of free association. Nevertheless, the

First Amendment cannot be used to make freedom of association solely instrumental. If the First Amendment is silent on association, then we go, as I have said, to the due process clauses of the Fifth and Fourteenth Amendments and employ the idea of substantive due process to defend freedom of association as an essential component of liberty that must not be invaded by government.

Brennan is a friend of substantive due process; this concept is not alien to him. It plays, however, no role in his opinion for the Court in *Roberts*. He does say, however, a bit more on the instrumental nature of association:

> According protection to collective effort on behalf of shared goals is especially important in preserving political and cultural diversity and in shielding dissident expression from suppression by the majority. (622)

Brennan seems to suggest that in numbers of associated people and their combined resources there is strength, specifically the strength to apply pressure in defense of difference or diversity in the face of conformist attack. Association is a way of ensuring the existence of unpopular expression, and deserves protection. Brennan then adds a more positive note:

> Consequently, we have long understood as implicit in the right to engage in activities protected by the First Amendment a corresponding right to associate with others in pursuit of a wide variety of political, social, economic, educational, religious, and cultural ends. (622)

Strength is thus needed not only to defend the very exercise of First Amendment rights but also actively to pursue or promote many ends. Brennan's words are uncharacteristically opaque. What has the exercise of First Amendment rights got to do with a wide variety of ends, not all of them manifestly within the scope of the First Amendment? In any case, Brennan acknowledges that a right is "plainly implicated in this case" (622). That is, the Jaycees case involves the associational right of a group to defend its ability to exercise the specific First Amendment right of speech or expression (not religion or petition in this case) and to advance its specific views. The case involves "the right to associate for expressive purposes" (623). The right of association is instrumental to the end, which is (shared) expression.

To gain some perspective on the different degrees of protection that Brennan affords expression and association, let us ask, Why does he seem to posit expression as an end? I say "seem" because the reader can infer that since association is instrumental to expression, then expression is an end. It is an end, even if it is not only an end. The initial reason why anyone can call speech or expression an end is that the Constitution makes it an end by prohibiting Congress from abridging it. The prohibition makes expression a fundamental right, a near absolute. An end is what is nearly absolute, protected almost absolutely against governmental interference. But there must be at least a little more to the story. Does Brennan in *Roberts* give some indication as to why expression is, and should be deemed, a nearly absolute end? He does not explain his sense on this occasion. Let me offer a view that is compatible with his overall jurisprudence.

The point has already been made that fundamental rights are indissociably joined to personhood. When government recognizes these rights, it is recognizing the equal human dignity of all persons—their status as human beings, rather than as things or materials or animals or prey or beasts of burden or children who are never able to grow up. Recognition of rights should not be theorized as conferring a contingent advantage. Government's treatment of human beings as persons is no mere advantage. Although rights are for use, not only for the establishment of the human status, when rights are not recognized, human activities are those of subjects, not persons—of human beings legally reduced below the proper human status. Such a conception of the human status in fact dominates Brennan's jurisprudence throughout his tenure on the Supreme Court. My point is that when the role played by association in acts of expression is misconceived, damage is done not only to association but also to expression, and hence to personhood.

Let me add that there is no need to say that expression, just because it is an end, must therefore have, like association, intrinsic value. I have said that the very activity of association has intrinsic value because it houses relationships and experience that are essential to identity. Expression, on the other hand, does not have be talked about in this way; to regard it as a near absolute because it is indispensable to personhood rather than selfhood pays it its due. At the same time, I am aware that no sharp line can always be drawn between personhood and selfhood. Expressing oneself freely, saying or writing what is on one's mind, and listening to and reading others as one pleases, are crucial to "the ability independently to define one's identity" (*Roberts*, 609). We can therefore speak of the intrinsic value of expression as such, while still thinking that the content of much of it is inferior, just as we may think that the content of much of associative life is inferior.

The comprehensive view that I wish to suggest is that no fundamental right, whether or not we speak of the intrinsic value (howsoever defined) of its general exercise, should be conceptualized primarily as instrumental for those who exercise it, as if a right were some optional device that could be replaced by some other practice, now or one day in the future, in order to increase the chances of success in attaining some end. Just as government's recognition of rights is no mere advantage, so rights are no mere instruments, for those who are recognized as having them. Even when we speak of using a right, we must not be misled: exercising a right is not using an instrument. For example, the First Amendment guarantees the "free exercise" of religion. This recognized right allows one to take advantage of an opportunity to engage in religious activities with impunity. Freely exercised religion is qualitatively different from religion exercised under governmental constraint or interference. Guaranteed freedom is the medium, not merely the instrument, of any kind of activity. One also exercises or uses one's rights of expression and association in this sense. And when the exercise of one right helps to sustain another, or when some other value (knowledge or beauty or virtue or progress) is furthered by the exercise of any of them, a fundamental right is still not primarily an instrument: it is inextricably joined to one's being a full person or having a true self, and personhood and selfhood are not instrumental. (This is not to say that knowledge or beauty or virtue or progress is merely instrumental, either. Each is an end, but not a constitutionally relevant one.)

Freedom of expression is not, then, properly conceptualized as a means or instrument for persons who exercise it—at least in its primary signification. Whatever goals we attain by expression are, I think, conceptually secondary. The primary notion is that a lot of the time, one is one's expression, one lives to express, one lives by expressing. One does not merely use speech; one *is* one's speech; one's life is mostly speech. (That is why I do not wish to deny that it makes sense to claim intrinsic value for expression: identity is tied to expression.) To be free, one must express oneself freely and freely receive the free expression of one's fellows. Freedom of expression is not the whole of freedom, but its soul. Just as I said that association may exist for its own sake, so I wish to say that speech or expression exists for its own sake. It is an end and hence the right to it is an end. Even in *Roberts*, Brennan himself posits freedom of expression as an end, but he does not see that, consequently, "expressive association" cannot be conceptualized as instrumental. Ordinarily, he was in agreement with the position that when any aspect of expression is seen as merely instrumental, government is on the way to encroaching on the fundamental right of expression. In general, to instrumentalize a right is to invite abridgments of it. I say this, knowing that many incidents of expression are instrumental in purpose.

Of course, association may work in the way suggested by Brennan: to defend the right to speak or to promote certain views, or "messages," as Justice Sandra O'Connor in *Roberts* and judges in other courts reductively call public expression.[7] If associations may serve this purpose, however, other considerations figure more importantly. First, and most obviously, an association is tied together by speech; its internal relations are comprised, to a great extent, of speech. To regulate the membership of an organization is often to alter its speech and hence to regulate its speakers. Does not internal speech deserve constitutional protection as a fundamental right? Yet more is at stake. I mean that Brennan's analysis carries the implication that expression, in general, is typically an utterance coming out of oneself unaided and fully formed, and that therefore the company of others is merely a way of organizing protection for one's continued ability to utter, or to promote one's views since they happen to coincide with the views of one's associates. Such an implication ignores the process by which anyone adopts or forms or discovers or revises or abandons one's views in the company of others and because of it. We are not only one another's midwives, but inseminators also. Others are not merely instrumental to mental process, nor auxiliary to it. The process is the company. Mental life, of whatever level or quality, is a continuous movement between solitude and company, as between silence and utterance. Neither pole can be forsaken, and expression survive. To put the point formally, the individual is the main (but not exclusive) beneficiary of constitutionally protected freedom of expression, but the associated individual is often the true bearer of the right (as with the free exercise of religion).

If the most important reason that an individual should wish to be protected in freedom of expression is not instrumental, then the same holds for freedom of association. At the same time, governmental respect for both selfhood and personhood is implicated equally in both rights. Both rights are fundamental. When the exercise of one is joined to the exercise of the other to create what Brennan calls "an expressive association," regulation must be reluctant and be done only in conformity with strict necessity. After conceding that regulation of membership is interference in the life of an association, Brennan goes on to insist that the admission of women as full members of the Jaycees will not, as a consequence, impose a change on the views publicly expressed by the organization on "political, economic, cultural, and social affairs" (626). He says:

> The Act requires no change in the Jaycees' creed of promoting the interests of young men, and it imposes no restriction on the organization's ability to exclude individuals with ideologies or philosophies different from those of its existing members. (627)

In effect, Brennan is claiming that if a group of people is told that they must speak to others to whom they have indicated that they have no wish to speak, in certain situations, no constitutional harm is done.

It may well be that the views finally espoused will be the same in "content or impact" (628) after as before the command; but they will more likely be different. In this particular case, where the sex of the parties is a salient element, Brennan's claim that young women may, after their compulsory admission, contribute to the allowable purpose of "promoting the interests of young men" is absurd. The plain intention behind the command to admit women to full membership is to redefine the interests of young men, to get them to start thinking that they have no interests distinct or separate from those of young women. Such a motive is creditable, but it should not be pursued at the expense of a fundamental right, which is to espouse one's or a group's views, not those of others. But even if the views were unaffected, there is still constitutional harm in compelling an individual or a group to speak to those whom they have indicated they do not wish to speak to, in a particular place, on a particular occasion. Expression itself is being compelled. The process by which views come into being and are maintained in being must be affected by such compulsoriness, irrespective of the net outcome. Under compulsion, the original process becomes another process. The same views arising from two different processes are not, in all relevant aspects, the same views.

Brennan asserts that the Court is engaged in regulation "unrelated to the suppression of ideas" (623), "unrelated to the suppression of expression" (624), and unrelated to "hampering the organization's ability to express its views" (624). That is not believable, either in regard to final views or to the process by which they come into being and are maintained in being. To hold as the Court does is to abridge the fundamental right of expression, which is joined inextricably in this case to the fundamental right of association.

Perhaps aware that he is skating on thin ice, Brennan concedes, here and there, that, after all, the Court's opinion does abridge freedom of expression. In an un-Brennan-like gesture, he avers that:

> even if enforcement of the Act causes some incidental abridgement of the Jaycees' protected speech, that effect is no greater than is necessary to accomplish the State's legitimate purpose. (628)

He repeats that the Minnesota act "abridges no more speech or associational speech than is necessary to accomplish" its purpose (629). He is here doing the kind of balancing of interests with regard to situations of expression that simply does not consist with his overall jurisprudence. Free speech is not just one more "interest" to be weighed in the balance against other interests of an indefinitely wide range.

It is a wonder to see Justice O'Connor, in her concurrence, chide Brennan for adopting an approach that:

accords insufficient protection to expressive associations and places inappropriate burdens on groups claiming the protection of the First Amendment. (632)

In an eloquent passage, she says,

> Protection of the association's right to define its membership derives from the recognition that the formation of an expressive association is the creation of a voice, and the selection of members is the definition of that voice. (633)

The trouble is that by sleight of hand, O'Connor transforms the Jaycees into a "nonexpressive" (638) association. In her hands, the Jaycees become a "commercial association" (638) interested mainly in recruiting new members, selling new memberships. This is an odd suggestion in light of the fact that the Jaycees were denying themselves income by excluding women as full members. But O'Connor is not deterred, and engages in a remarkable bit of interest balancing, even at the expense of supposedly protected speech:

> Recruitment and selling are commercial activities, even when conducted for training rather than for profit. The "not insubstantial" volume of protected Jaycees activity found by the Court of Appeals is simply not enough to preclude state regulation of the Jaycees commercial activities. (640)

If speech is entangled with economic transactions, government may abridge the freedom of speech in order to regulate those transactions. This idea hardly accords speech the protection it deserves; it is often entangled with many activities that offer tempting targets of regulation. In chiding Brennan, O'Connor offends against free speech much more than he does.

What is the Court doing in *Roberts*? What values is it granting more weight than either association as such or what it calls expressive association? Is it protecting vital claims of individuals against harms inflicted by unregulated association? Brennan provides a series of considerations. We must remember that no state action is involved; hence it would appear that Brennan is not saying that by permitting a social club to discriminate on account of sex, a state is denying women equal protection of the laws. The Court's decision permits, but does not require, state governments to compel various associations to admit women as full members. A few years after *Roberts*, however, the slight opening left for what the Court was willing to see as essentially private clubs, like the Kiwanis Club, to practice discrimination in membership was closed in *Board of Directors of Rotary International v. Rotary Club of Duarte* and *New York State Club Association, Inc. v. City of New York.*

In both these cases, the ruling in *Roberts* was relied on and pushed to the limit. The cause of private antidiscrimination had achieved a number of victories. All were made possible by the Court's acceptance of the idea that social clubs are not private, but are public accommodations or public businesses if a state says they are.

What does Brennan maintain? As we have seen, he accepts the determination that the Jaycees are a public accommodation. The Minnesota Supreme Court had already declared that the open solicitation of dues-paying members made the Jaycees a business, and one that could no longer be considered a private organization.

> This continuous concern for growth undercuts the national organization's claim to be a private organization. . . . By virtue of its unselective, vigorous sale of memberships, the national organization is a public business. (*United States Jaycees v. McClure*, 771)

By definitional fiat, a nonprofit organization becomes a business. And by an admittedly "unusually broad definition of the term 'place of public accommodation'" (766), a nonprofit organization becomes a public business. It is worth noticing that the three dissenters on the Minnesota Supreme Court say they cannot believe that "the members of the Minnesota legislature. . . thought the Junior Chamber of Commerce, a service organization, to be 'a place of public accommodation'" (773–74). Brennan, however, shows no discomfort in the face of this definitional plasticity. Once definitions are in place, the rest follows.

Thanks to an arbitrary redescription, the Jaycees organization becomes answerable to the state government; it exists by the government's sufferance and hence is bound to serve the public interest, as defined by the government. Indeed, Brennan does eventually invoke the equal protection clause and the Civil Rights Act of 1964, which was passed in order to further the clause's aims. There can be no valid "gender discrimination in the allocation of publicly available goods and services" (625). Brennan refers to "stigmatizing injury, and the denial of equal opportunities" (625) involved in gender discrimination. Of course, these are "serious social and personal harms" (625) when such discrimination results from deliberate public policy administered by state agencies. But to saddle the Jaycees or any other social club with such wrongdoing is to rob the elevated language of indignation of its proper referent. Jim Crow legislation (or something analogous) is one thing, and the Jaycees' membership policies are quite another, altogether different. Legally administered or encouraged discrimination is one thing; private discrimination, another. Constitutional governments may not do what associated private individuals may. To be sure, businesses may not discriminate, but social clubs should be allowed to do so. It would be inconsistent for me to say that the Jaycees are a trivial organization, and to defend their freedom of association on the grounds that anything they did would not matter. Whatever I or anyone else may think of them, they are not trivial to themselves; they matter, perhaps greatly, to themselves. At the same time, if a social club like the Jaycees is a public accommodation, there is no such thing as a private association.

Their organization is not a state government; it is not a state instrument. The Jaycees are not even, despite Minnesota's casuistry, a public accommodation. If they really were, freedom of association should give way. That undesirable consequences flow from their membership policies is probably true; but the exercise of fundamental rights is fertile in undesirable consequences. Undesirable consequences do not transform a private association into a public accommodation. The Constitution is not a utilitarian document; despite some overlap, the distinction between self-regarding and (undesirable) other-regarding activity is not the same as the distinction between activity that is constitutionally protected from regulation and activity that is not. The issue is whether a given activity that is alleged to be an exercise of a fundamental right injures the vital claims of others, and hence, is not in fact an exercise of a fundamental right. And if vital claims are actually involved, abridgment would not be correctly based on a mere utilitarian calculation.

As if to recover his sense of proportion, Brennan climbs down from the noble language of equal protection and the grave harms to human dignity (personhood) that result from the denial of equal protection by government. He only sketchily introduces other considerations that are more practical. But are these considerations really sufficient to abridge free speech and free association? Are vital claims being protected against injurious free activity? After crediting Minnesota with a "functional definition" (623) of public accommodations, Brennan says,

> This expansive definition reflects a recognition of the changing nature of the American economy and of the importance, both to the individual and to society, of removing the barriers to economic advancement and political and social integration that have historically plagued certain disadvantaged groups, including women. (626)

The reference to "economic advancement" strikes me as constitutionally irrelevant, mixed in as it is with other phrases that do in fact rise to constitutional stature. Since when can the economic advancement of some be used to justify an abridgment of someone else's fundamental right? We are talking of *advancement*, not of the relief of life-threatening poverty. Such relief should have constitutional standing, but contrastingly, advancement is not a vital claim and hence does not deserve protection at the cost of abridging a fundamental right. And then Brennan weakens his case more when he endorses the reasoning of the Minnesota court that upheld the state's action:

> Thus, in explaining its conclusion that the Jaycees local chapters are "place(s) of public accommodations" within the meaning of the Act, the Minnesota court noted the various commercial programs and benefits offered to members and stated that "(l)eadership skills are 'goods' (and) business contacts and employment promotions are 'privileges' and 'advantages'. . . ." . . . Assuring women equal access to such goods, privileges, and advantages clearly furthers compelling state interests. (626)

We are now in the realm of flimsy causal connections: as if full membership in the Jaycees transforms someone into a marvel of economic prowess, and denial of full membership therefore relegates the excluded to a lifetime of second-best achievement or worse. Then too, making "leadership skills" and "business contacts" and "employment promotions" more widely available—even if the *Roberts* decision would have that effect—cannot be a compelling state interest, if that phrase is to have any force. A compelling state interest is what allows the restriction of freedom. What phrase could be used when a really compelling state interest—say, preventing or deterring incitement to imminent lawless action or desegregating once legally segregated schools—is invoked in order to affirm that a given restriction is not actually an abridgment of a rightful liberty or to undo a former and indefensible abridgment? What phrase is left?

Fundamental rights endure a hard fate in *Roberts* and its successor cases. Above all, the value of association is not appreciated and hence not constitutionally respected. A right is made to give way to what is not a right, but rather a social gain (only).

. . . . .

Toward the end of his opinion for the six-member majority in *United States Jaycees v. McClure*, Justice Otis of the Minnesota Supreme Court says,

> If the national organization now before this court were conducting its business by discriminating on the basis of race, prohibited in Minnesota since 1885, we would have no difficulty holding that its activity was prohibited. (773)

This is the most powerful moment in all the sentences written against the Jaycees' membership policy in four different courts. The plain fact is that a large part of the opinions that go against the Jaycees revolves around the issue of whether the Jaycees are a public accommodation, rather than on the wrong and harm of discrimination by a social club. But these words must give pause even to those least in sympathy with the reasoning and outcome of the case. The words of Otis have a quiet power that far exceeds anything said by him or the other justices or judges who upheld the Minnesota action. Those who think that interference with the Jaycees' membership policies is constitutionally mistaken are being asked to see an analogy between excluding women as full members and excluding blacks. But despite its power, is the analogy fair?

The history of governmental policy toward American blacks—their enslavement, legal segregation, pervasive neglect, permitted suffering and humiliation on a vast scale—weighs on the conscience to an extent no other domestic policy does (with the possible exception of the treatment of native Americans). There is no parity between the suffering caused blacks by the federal and state governments and that caused women. Truth is not served, nor is justice, when the past and present authoritatively administered suffering of all disadvantaged groups in the United States is seen as equal in kind and intensity. Given the awful past, would governmental interference in the membership policies of social clubs for the purpose of compelling admission of blacks be consistent with the position on freedom of association adopted in this paper? The painful conclusion is that it would not be, any more than compelling admission of whites or men would be, mutatis mutandis. Otis's thought experiment is striking; it is certainly not sophistical; but it is finally not persuasive.

· · · · ·

The spirit of the laws of constitutional democracy contains a paradox. It protects the ideal of living as you like, even if you choose to live, or cannot help liking to live, against the spirit of the laws; but it inspires another ideal, which is to live faithfully to the meaning of constitutionalism and democracy, which can be understood as determinate guides to the manner in which one should regard oneself and treat others in all the relationships and transactions of life.[8] It will not to do to call living as you like "license," because living as you like has always meant living as you like, provided you do not harm the vital claims of others and do let them equally live as they like. But one may choose to live in a way that is exclusive or authoritarian; one may be insensitive or bigoted, or addicted to stereotypes; one's disposition may be servile or conformist; one may refuse adventure or opportunity; and so on. Yet the spirit of constitutional democracy gives shelter to all such deviations from, or inconsistencies with, itself. It knows that it contains a paradox, and in its acceptance of that paradox, it shows its true spirit. It knows that the aspiration to greater self-consistency that it harbors is subjected to tremendous resistance: the people who live in a constitutional democracy do not fully want what they nevertheless regularly sustain by their participation and compliance. And constitutional democracy suffers when people are legally compelled, when vital claims are not involved, to become ever more constitutional and democratic in their private relationships and transactions. The workings of constitutional democracy radiate a suggestive influence on the conduct of private and institutional life, but government should not try, by its policies, to force people to move in the right direction, unless vital claims are involved.

The Aristotelian precept that a polity will tend to last longer as itself if it is only impurely itself, if it allows itself to be mixed with what is not itself, is followed, wittingly or not, in every constitutional democracy. Enclaves and episodes, sectors of life and aspects of the manners of the people, all betray evidences of the near unlivability of the pure determinate content of constitutionalism and democracy. Still, the inherent inspiration, the often conscious hope, is that eventually some of the personal and social tendencies now inconsistent with the determinate content of constitutionalism and democracy will disappear. More people, more of the time, will discover that they like to live their lives constitutionally and democratically—such is the hope. At no time will all people live their lives this way; there will always be an appreciable quantity of life lived as people like, when they do not want the full determinate content of constitutionalism and democracy. But a slight increase is always a cause for celebration.

All this is a roundabout way of saying that the discriminatory national membership policies of the Jaycees were contrary to the spirit of the laws in one sense, but that the spirit of the laws, in another sense, should have been interpreted to say that the Jaycees were within their rights to associate on their own deplorable terms.

Notes

1. Laurence H. Tribe, *American Constitutional Law*, 2d ed. (Mineola, N.Y.: Foundation Press, 1988), p. 1014.

2. Ibid., pp. 1014–15. Tribe's discussion of the right of association is most valuable. See pp. 1010–22, 1400–1409.

3. Another way of thinking about substantive due process is this: The moral reasons that lie behind the procedural guarantees given to suspects, defendants, and convicted persons in the Bill of Rights should set limits as well to government's encroachments on the liberty of individuals who are not subject to criminal procedure. The moral reasons for due process of law in criminal cases stem from a refined conception of personhood: persons are prone to mistakes great and small, but the law should always treat them with respect for their dignity. Perhaps the most profound constitutionalist moral reasons are those implicated in guarantees to individuals who are subject to criminal procedure. Due process is an inspiration for substantive governmental conduct in the whole area of public policy, whether in the form of abstention or action. That is why to speak of *substantive* due process, odd as it may sound, is entirely proper.

4. I consulted the following Jaycees cases: *United States Jaycees v. McClure*, 534 F. Supp. 766 (D. Minn. 1982), in which a federal district judge ruled against the Jaycees; *United States Jaycees v. McClure*, 305 N.W. 2d 764 (1981), in which the Supreme Court of Minnesota agreed by a vote of six-to-three that the Jaycees organization was a public accommodation; and *United States Jaycees v. McClure*, 709 F. 2d 1560 (1983) in which the United State Court of Appeals (Eighth Circuit) ruled by a two-to-one vote in favor of the Jaycees. Only in the majority opinion of the Court of Appeals did I find a readiness to recognize a fundamental right of association, but even there the Court spoke at times as if association matters mainly because of its connection to the expression of attitudes; see esp. pp. 1567–68, 1570, 1574–75. But the whole opinion by Judge Arnold is unusually instructive.

5. The two later cases are: *Board of Directors of Rotary International et al. v. Rotary Club of Duarte et al.*, 481 U.S. 537 (1987); and *New York State Club Association, Inc. v. City of New York et al.*, 487 U.S. 1 (1988).

6. See Hannah Arendt, *The Human Condition* (Chicago: University of Chicago Press, 1958), especially pp. 1–38, 175–207. For a stimulating critique of the ideology of intimacy, see Richard Sennett, *The Fall of Public Man* (New York: Knopf, 1974), esp. chaps. 1–5, 11, 14.

7. The reduction of the expression of opinion on public issues to "messages" shows a lamentably narrow view of the place of speech in political life. All public speech is likened to an exchange of signals or a string of advertisements. See O'-Connor's concurrence in *Roberts*, 633. This tendency disfigures Judge Duffy's opinion requiring a private club to allow a group of gays to march as a group with its own banners in a parade on St. Patrick's day. See *New York Country Board of Ancient Order of Hibernians v. Dinkins*, (814 F. Supp. 358, S.D.N.Y. (1993), 366–69. A much more subtle conception of public speech and of expression in general permeates the unanimous opinion of the Supreme Court written by Justice David Souter in *Hurley v. Irish-American Gay, Lesbian and Bisexual Group of Boston* (1995 Lexis 4050), where a Boston club was allowed to hold its St. Patrick's day parade without being required to include a gay group (GLIB) as "its own parade unit carrying its own banner" (28). To be sure, Souter does refer to expression as message (28, 43), but the reference is incidental to his wide-ranging analysis of freedom of speech. His unequivocal meaning is that compelled inclusion alters the meaning (if not always the

content) of expression, literal or symbolic. His opinion bears an uneasy relation to *Roberts*, despite the respectful mention and use made of it.

8. I discuss the ideal of living in accordance with the meaning of constitutionalism and democracy in *The Inner Ocean: Individualism and Democratic Culture* (Ithaca: Cornell University Press, 1992), esp. chapter 1.

Chapter Three

ON INVOLUNTARY ASSOCIATION

Michael Walzer

THE PEOPLE I know are constantly forming associations, and they greatly value the freedom to associate as they please, for all sorts of purposes, with all sorts of other people. They are certainly right: freedom of association is a central value, a fundamental requirement of liberal society and democratic politics. But it is a mistake to generalize this value and call into being, in theory or in practice, a world where all associations are voluntary, a social union composed entirely of freely constituted social unions. The ideal picture of autonomous individuals choosing their connections (and disconnections) without restraints of any sort is an example of bad utopianism. It has never made sense to sociologists, and it ought to inspire skepticism among political theorists and moral philosophers too. No human society could survive without connections of a very different sort. But how can connections of any different sort be justified to men and women who claim to be free? Doesn't freedom require the breaking of all those bonds that we have not chosen or do not now choose for ourselves?

I want to argue that freedom requires nothing more than the possibility of breaking involuntary bonds and, furthermore, that the actual break is not always a good thing, and that we need not always make it easy. Many valuable memberships are not freely chosen; many binding obligations are not entirely the product of consent. We can think of our life together as a "social construction" in which we, as individuals, have had a hand; we cannot plausibly think of it as something wholly made by ourselves. We join groups, we form associations, we organize and we are organized—within a complex set of constraints. These take many different forms, some of which I shall try to describe in such a way as to suggest their legitimacy.

There are four kinds of constraints that require consideration: all of them press us toward, even force us into, associations of a certain sort, and they also limit, though in a liberal society they cannot abolish, our right to leave. Sociologists have written about the first two; political theorists and moral philosophers have had something to say about the last two. But it is useful, I think, to regard them as items on a single list.

The first constraint is familial and social in character. We are born members of a kin group, and of a nation or country, and of a social class—and these three together go a long way toward determining the people with whom we associate for the rest of our lives (even if we hate our relatives, think patriotism sentimental, never attain class consciousness). Most of us are also admitted early on to one or another sort of religious membership through infant baptism or circumcision or adolescent confirmation or bar mitzvah. These are concrete, involuntary joinings from which, so the child will certainly be told, rights and responsibilities follow. But parental instruction, the experience of class, and religious and political socialization inside and outside the home also work more indirectly, creating background conditions that support particular adult associations and not others. A great deal has been written in recent years about family failure, but in truth most parents are remarkably successful in producing children much like themselves. Sometimes, unhappily, that is the very sign of their failure—as when parents in the underclass are unable to boost their children into mainstream society. But most parents want offspring who don't land too far off, whom they can still recognize as their own—and, mostly, they produce children like that. They get a little help, of course, from their friends.

Young people can break loose, tear themselves free from family ties and social circumstance, but only at a cost that most of them don't want to bear. That is why parental connections are by far the best predictors of their own connections—as political scientists discovered long ago with regard to party allegiance and voting behavior (to take a relatively easy example).[1] Later religious choices are, I suspect, even more reliably indicated by parental choices. Indeed, in the case of religion, *choice* is probably not the operative word. Those early rituals of adherence are remarkably effective; religious membership is best described, for most people, as an inheritance. Protestant practices like adult baptism and evangelical rebirth are obviously meant to disrupt this pattern—and do so to some extent, in ways historically helpful to voluntary association.[2] But it would be interesting to know what percentage of born-again Christians are the spiritual as well as the bodily offspring of their parents: born to be born again.

People join associations that confirm rather than challenge their identities, and their identities are, mostly, the gifts of their parents and their parents' friends. Again, individuals can break away, committing themselves to the difficult process of self-formation, like the biblical Abraham who (according to postbiblical legend) broke his father's idols, or like John Bunyan's Christian pilgrim, who ran away from his wife and children (putting his fingers in his ears so that he would not hear their cries). Social change is unimaginable without people like that, but if all people were like that, society itself would be unimaginable. Nor did Abraham encourage a similar rebelliousness in his beloved son Isaac. Unlike his father, Isaac was born a member of Jehovah's party—less admirable for that, perhaps, but infinitely more reliable. And Bunyan was compelled by his readers to bring Christian's wife and children along (in a sequel to *Pilgrim's Progress*) on what was by then a stereotypical journey to join the community of saints.[3]

Associations formed or joined against a given background can still be described as voluntary, but we need to acknowledge how partial and incomplete the description is. It will look even more incomplete after we consider the next item on my list.

The second constraint is the cultural determination of available associational forms. Associates may choose one another, but they rarely have much to say about the structure and style of their association. Marriage is the obvious example here: the match may be a true meeting of minds, but the meaning of the match is not determined by the minds that meet. Marriage is a cultural practice; its meaning and the responsibilities it entails are accepted by the partners as soon as they acknowledge one another as husband and wife. Their prenuptial agreements and contracts affect only the details of the arrangement. Similarly, men and women can form a club or league or union or party, gather together freely, and write their own by-laws. But their association is likely to be remarkably similar to that of their fellow citizens down the road or across the town, and by-laws are commonly written to a standard form.[4]

Creative individuals in periods of cultural crisis and transformation do manage, obviously, to design new associational forms, often after many false starts and failed attempts. But the norm is imitation and reiteration, interrupted periodically by reforming efforts to return the various associations to their first principles. The principles themselves are objects of allegiance even before they are objects of choice.[5] Similarly, associational competence is admired and mimicked rather than freely chosen. We don't decide to learn the social and political skills that make association possible. Like the by-laws and the principles, skill too is a cultural gift—which means that it is already possessed by some subset of parents and elders who pass it on, often without any specific effort to do so. My first association was a small group of eight year olds: the Four Friends Forever, which lasted about ten months and left me better prepared for the next time. In a culture that values association and the competence that makes it possible, breakup is more often an incitement than a disillusion.

There is, then, a radical givenness to our associational life. We meet for a purpose, discover a common interest, agree more or less on a line of argument, and form an organization. Ours is very much like all the other organizations, *and that's how we know what we are doing.* That's why our accomplishment registers with the already existing groups, who quickly figure out whether we are potential competitors or allies—or neither of these, our union a matter of indifference. We arouse conventional expectations, and these are our passport to civil society. But if we meet in secret, wear masks, communicate in code, acknowledge no public purpose, and generally behave in nonstandard ways, then we arouse uneasiness and suspicion. Perhaps we are not an association at all, but rather a cabal, a conspiracy, or something worse.

Even radically new associational practices are likely to mimic old forms— the way gay marriage mimics the modern nuclear family. The established model is found to be eminently usable, so long as one of its conventional constraints can be set aside. In somewhat similar fashion, antiparliamentary social movements drift toward partylike organization; religious sects turn themselves into churches, claiming all the while that they are actually churches-with-a-difference (which they sometimes actually are).

Imagine people coming together in wholly different, infinitely odd ways, in free-form associations, with no one sending out recognizable signals: the social world would be unbearable—pure uneasiness, endless suspicion. Imagine every marriage designed in lawless freedom by the two partners, without a standard model of any sort, not for the ceremony (this much is fairly common today), not for the commitment of husband and wife, not for the proposed living arrangements, not for the obligations to in-laws, siblings, and children. The point of the practice would be entirely lost. We would have to find or devise some other practice to stabilize expectations and responsibilities. Free choice can work only within the limits of cultural provision.

The third constraint on voluntary association is political in character. Birth or residence make us members of the political community. Membership has different meanings in different times and places, and for some individuals sometimes (colonists in a new country, for example) it can be a matter of deliberate choice. But that is not what it is for most people. The standard critique of liberal consent theory builds on this simple fact about political life. The standard response is to evoke some sort of tacit consent (as I did when I wrote about citizenship and obligation twenty-eight years ago).[6] There are good reasons for this response, but it does not touch the point relevant here: that the political community is in an important sense a closed shop. If you are here, and if you stay here, you are caught up in a set of arrangements that you had no part in designing.

Real closed shops in the economic sphere work in the same way and seem to me similarly justified.[7] Self-government, political or industrial democracy, is possible only if all the residents/workers are also citizens. They can choose to vote or not, to join this or that party or movement, to form a caucus or faction, or to avoid political activity entirely. But if they are denied, or if they deny themselves, the right to do these things, then democracy is replaced by the rule of some people over others. It may be that anyway, much of the time, but the possibility of citizen activism—associational militancy, mass mobilization, radical insurgency—at least imposes some restraint upon the rulers, and that is a possibility that citizens can keep alive without ever doing anything themselves (though sometimes, surely, they ought to do something). But there is one thing they cannot do: they cannot live here or work here and refuse the rights (and the burdens too, like taxes and union dues) of citizenship.

Compulsory membership in the state or the union is often a precondition of voluntary association and activism. Of course, noncitizen militants can associate, and often have, to demand political enfranchisement or union recognition. But this is a battle that the militants don't win if they win it only for themselves. Victory pulls in the passive others, gives them new opportunities and responsibilities. For neither of these can they plausibly be called volunteers. But they can now volunteer, if they choose to do so, for activities and organizations more widely effective than anything available to them before.

The fourth constraint on association is moral in character, which some people will take to mean that it isn't constraining at all. Violators are subject only to exhortation and reproach. Unless morality is a feature of the socialization process, or written into the cultural code, or legally enforced, it has no practical effect; it is, literally, without consequence. In fact, of course, morality is implicated in each of the first three constraints, but it is also experienced as something separate from them. It is a constraint that individuals confront not only as creatures of society, culture, and politics, but also, simply, as individuals trying to do the right thing. They hear an internal or an internalized voice of constraint, telling them that they should do this or that, which they have not (so far) chosen to do and would rather not do. Most importantly for my purposes here, they are told (they tell themselves) that they ought to join this association, participate in this social or political struggle—or that they ought not to abandon this association or withdraw from this struggle.

Moral constraints are often constraints on exit and, most interestingly, on exit from involuntary associations. The classic example is Rousseau's account of the right of emigration. Citizens, he says, can leave at any time—except when the republic is in danger. In a time of trouble they are bound to stay and help their fellow citizens.[8] This bond does not derive from their previous political participation. Even if they have been unenthusiastic and negligent citizens, never flying to the public assemblies, never voting, they are still obligated. Rousseau's assertion is unqualified. It is also entirely plausible. I have perhaps benefited from the republic's better days, or from the activism of my fellows, or from the schooling the republic provides, or from the good name of citizen, or simply from having had a secure place in the world. And now I must not walk away. Indeed, I am likely to acknowledge the constraint even if I refuse to respect it—by the excuses I offer, the urgent reasons I invent as I pack my bags.

But merely to stay where I am may not be all that I am bound to do in such a case. Perhaps (there are difficult arguments here) I should enlist in the army and march off to fight the republic's external enemies. Perhaps I should join a party, movement, or campaign against the republic's internal enemies. These would be voluntary acts, strictly speaking, so long as I am free to act differently (staying on is also a voluntary act, so long as leaving is an option). And yet, when I act in these ways, I am likely to feel that I am acting under a constraint. I am doing my duty. My action does not fit Rousseau's famous description of being forced to be free. I am not even forced to be moral. There may be considerable social presssure to "do the right thing," but I imagine myself now acting conscientiously, which is a mode of action simultaneously free and unfree. For I have neither determined nor chosen the right thing that I am now bound in conscience to do. Nor was I ever informed that my tacit consent—my residence in this place, my participation in the daily round of social activities—could have this radical consequence. Living together with other people just *is* a moral engagement. It ties me up in unexpected ways.

There are times, of course, when I ought to break these ties: here involuntary association is not different from voluntary association. Sometimes I should walk away from this group that I joined, say, a few years ago, resign from the executive committee, disengage myself from my fellow members—because the group no longer serves the purposes to which I am committed or because it now serves purposes that I oppose. The case is much the same with groups I never joined, in which I simply found myself. But perhaps these two cases differ in the extent to which I am bound to hang on, protest, and resist from the inside for as long as possible. Perhaps there is a greater obligation in the involuntary case, in much the same way as I might have to argue longer with a parent, child, or sibling who is doing something terribly wrong than I would with a spouse. At some point, I can divorce the spouse; separation from the others is harder.

· · · · ·

Can we imagine individuals without any involuntary ties at all, unbound, utterly free? The thought experiment is especially useful now, when postmodern theorists are writing so excitedly about "self-fashioning," an enterprise undertaken not exactly in a social vacuum but rather—so we are told—amid the ruins of conventional social forms. I suspect that the effort to describe a *society* of self-fashioning individuals is necessarily self-defeating. But it will be interesting to see exactly where the defeats come and how definitive they are. So let us try to picture men and women like those described by Julia Kristeva, who determine their identities and memberships "through lucidity rather than fate."[9] They decide for themselves on their life plans, choose not only their associates but the very form of their association, question every standard social pattern, recognize no bonds that they have not themselves forged. They make their lives into purely personal projects; they are entrepreneurs of the self.

No doubt, this self-creation is, as George Kateb, who advocates it, admits, "uncertain, risky, and arduous."[10] But the men and women whose project it is begin it as children; they have time to get accustomed to its difficulties. Presumably their parents (self-created men and women, like born-again Christians, still have parents) help to prepare them for the choices they will have to make. Remember, we are imagining a society of such people, not a Sartrean "series." How will the young be educated in a society like that? What exactly is involved in turning vulnerable and dependent children into free individuals?

I imagine the children being taught the values of individuality: the meaning of autonomy and integrity, the joys of free choice, the excitement of risk-taking in personal relationships and political engagements. But lessons of this sort cannot be delivered only as commands: Choose freely! Do your own thing! They are probably best conveyed in narrative form, and so the children would also be told stirring stories about how a society of free individuals was created against fierce communitarian or religious opposition;

and how earlier, more primitive, organic, or tyrannical social arrangements were escaped or overthrown. We must also assume that celebratory occasions will be lifted from this narrative and marked annually with ritual enactments of the struggle against involuntary association. This is a training for the emotions, but the mind too must be readied for freedom, so students would probably also be required to study the basic texts that explain and defend free individuality and to read the classic novels and poems written by free individuals.

All this seems to me obviously necessary. One doesn't prepare children for a life that is uncertain, risky, and arduous by letting them run free, like wild horses on the range. On the other hand, the image of corralled horses suggests nothing so much as involuntary association, which is exactly what a school is, even a school devoted to freedom. But if schooling is necessary, it is by no means sure to succeed. Finding a way to express their unique individuality is likely to be a strain for most of these children, who will long for some conventional pattern into which they can fit themselves. In principle, however, they can be given nothing more than a general account of what an individual life plan should look like. How would they choose their own way? I imagine the cohort of adolescent individuals-in-the-making swept by waves of fashionable and earnest eccentricity. I imagine them rushing in and out of a great variety of associations. But would they in the end, for all the efforts of their parents and teachers, be any more differentiated, any more individualized, than the children of committed Jews or Catholics, say, or strongly identified Bulgarians or Koreans? Would they, indeed, be any more tolerant of someone in their peer group who chose not to do the done thing, not to create himself by himself, and who announced to scandalized friends, "I am just going to copy the life plan of my parents"?

The greater number of children, of course, would not rebel in this way and so would constitute in time something like (what Harold Rosenberg once called, describing the Western intelligentsia of the 1940s and 1950s) a "herd of independent minds."[11] They would be proud of whatever differences they managed to cultivate and comfortable in the society of others like themselves. They would join voluntarily in the politics of that society—though exactly how politics would work if everyone was trying to be (or even just to look like) a dissident and an outsider, I am not sure. In any case, they would surely feel bound to defend the regime that defends their dissidence against any internal or external threats—and especially against threats that came from people proclaiming their own collective commitment and common identity. Individuals would be free to leave, but not when individuality itself was under attack.

What this account suggests, I think, is that there could not be a society of free individuals without a socialization process and a culture of individuality, and without a supportive political regime whose citizens were prepared to support it in their turn. In other words, the society of free individuals would be for most of its members an involuntary association. All the social, cultural, political, and moral ties that exist in other societies would exist in this one too—and they would have the same mixed effects, producing conformists and occasional rebels. But both the existence and the legitimacy of these ties are more likely to be denied here, especially by the conformists. And denial is dangerous; it makes reflection on and understanding of involuntary association harder and rarer than they should be. We will not be able to argue about whether the ties are too tight or too loose, whether they require official sponsorship, or private support, or active opposition, or benign neglect. These ties are involuntary only at the individual level; they are still subject to political determination or, at least, to political modification. But we cannot modify them unless we acknowledge their reality. If no one is out there except autonomous individuals, political decisions about membership and obligation would have no legitimate object.

But there are, in fact, important decisions to be made about all the unchosen structures, patterns, institutions, and groupings, for the character and quality of involuntary association determine the character and quality of voluntary association. What is involuntary is historically and biographically prior—the inevitable background of any social life, free or unfree. We move toward freedom when we make escape possible: divorce, conversion, withdrawal, opposition, resignation, and so on. But mass escape is never possible. We cannot bring the unchosen background wholly into the foreground, make it a matter of individual self-determination. The point is obvious, I think, but still worth stating clearly: free choice requires involuntary association. Without it, there won't be individuals strong enough to face the uncertainties and difficulties of freedom; there won't be clear and coherent alternatives among which to choose; there won't be any political protection against the enemies of free choice; there won't be even the minimal trust that makes voluntary association possible.

But we can *work on* the background—arguing about what is necessary in different times and places—so as to encourage a lively engagement in associational activity. We can, for example, improve the public schools in this way or that, alter the curriculum, impose national standards, establish local control, raise the pay and prestige of teachers. Socialization is always coercive, but its character and conditions are open to democratic debate and reform. Similarly, we can increase the rates of social mobility or redistribute income for the sake of greater equality. We can change the marriage laws, make divorce easier or more difficult, provide family allowances, alter the legal frame within which corporate or union by-laws are written, subsidize these or those associations. We can rethink the rights and responsibilities of resident aliens. We can make military service voluntary or compulsory, exempt this or that category of men and women, and so on. This is, in large measure, what democratic politics is about. It is not possible, again, to abolish involuntary association; indeed, there are times when we will want to strengthen it—for democratic citizenship is one of the identities it can foster. Nor is there is any one correct balance of the voluntary and the involuntary; we have to negotiate the proportions to meet the needs of the hour.

In fact, the results of this negotiation are less like a simple balance than a doubled mix of the two elements. The necessary background is only partly involuntary, since exit from its various memberships is possible (though always difficult). And the foregrounded associations, all our parties, movements, and unions, are voluntary only in a qualified sense: they represent the free choices of men and women who have been taught to make, and have been enabled to make, choices of just this kind . . . freely (some of whom prove the freedom by not making them). This last is still an immensely valuable voluntarism. It seems to me that we ought to call it freedom simply, without qualification: it is the only freedom that free men and women can ever have.

Notes

1. See Angus Campbell, Philip E. Converse, Warren E. Miller, and Donald E. Stokes *The American Voter* (New York: Wiley, 1960), pp. 147–148.

2. Helpful also to democratic politics: this is the argument of A. D. Lindsay, *The Modern Democratic State* (London: Oxford University Press, 1943), chap. 3.

3. On Abraham, see Louis Ginzberg, *The Legends of the Jews*, trans. Henrietta Szold (Philadelphia: Jewish Publication Society, 1961), 1:213–214. On Bunyan's Christian, see *The Pilgrim's Progress* (New York: New American Library, 1964), p. 19 ("The Second Part," starting on p. 151, is the sequel).

4. Consider the remarkable *Robert's Rules of Order*, which is often invoked in the internal debates of the most radical associations that are pledged to newness everywhere else.

5. Also before they are objects of reflection: the Abraham story is first told long after the establishment of the covenanted people it is meant to explain and legitimate. And Bunyan writes at the end of a century of experiment with the "gathered congregation."

6. See my *Obligations: Essays on Disobedience, War, and Citizenship* (Cambridge:

Harvard University Press, 1970), esp. the fifth essay. See also A. John Simmons, *Moral Principles and Political Obligation* (Princeton: Princeton University Press, 1979).

7. At least they are justified subject to democratic conditions, like those provided in the Wagner Act: that the closure is agreed to by an uncoerced majority of the workers. See Irving Bernstein, *A History of the American Worker, 1933–1941: Turbulent Years* (Boston: Houghton Mifflin, 1970), pp. 327–328.

8. Jean-Jacques Rousseau, *The Social Contract*, Bk. 3, chap. 18.

9. Julia Kristeva, *Nations without Nationalism*, trans. Leon Roudiez (New York: Columbia University Press, 1993), p. 35.

10. George Kateb, "Notes on Pluralism," *Social Research* 61, no. 2 (summer 1994): 531.

11. The title of pt. 4 of Harold Rosenberg, *The Tradition of the New* (New York: Horizon Press, 1959).

Chapter Four

COMPELLED ASSOCIATION:

PUBLIC STANDING, SELF-RESPECT,

AND THE DYNAMIC OF EXCLUSION

Nancy L. Rosenblum

Compelled Association

INVOLUNTARY ASSOCIATION is inescapable in daily life; as Justice Douglas remarked, "one who of necessity rides busses and streetcars does not have the freedom that John Muir and Walt Whitman extolled."[1] Legally compelled association is commonplace in public institutions like schools and the army. On the other hand, for someone to be compelled to join one or any religious association or for a group to be compelled to admit unwanted members to fellowship is plainly outside government authority in a liberal democracy. When is official interference in the membership policies of secular voluntary associations justifiable? Here, I consider the principal justifications offered for compelled association in the United States. They all aim at congruence between the internal life and practices of voluntary groups and the public culture of liberal democracy. The logic of congruence dictates that associations mirror public norms, and though few advocates would legally enforce strict congruence everywhere and "all the way down," prescriptions abound for limiting voluntary associations' autonomy to govern their own affairs, including their freedom to exclude unwanted members.

What bounds on an association's freedom to elect members are defensible? In an early case involving the Benevolent and Protective Order of Elks, a district court ruled that a black applicant's "interest in joining the private club of his choice surely does not constitute a basic right of citizenship."[2] This decision frames the issue correctly; legally compelled association is justified when exclusion denotes second-class citizenship. Other familiar reasons for compelled association such as avoiding harm to personal dignity and securing self-respect are, in contrast, indefensible. When these strands of justification are unraveled, the grounds for government interference with association freedom—to ban women from all-male eating clubs, non-Jewish women from Hadassah, or men from women's business groups, and vice versa—turn out to be severely limited, even if the membership policy is pejorative, or taken as such. The reasons for freedom of association are another subject, though I propose several contrarian points briefly at the end. I suggest that affiliation with voluntary associations in which we are wanted and willing members is a key source of self-respect; that discrimination may be safely contained in these groups; and that because associations often owe their origin to a dynamic of affiliation and exclusion, resentment and self-affirmation, liberal democracy is consistent with and even requires the incongruence between voluntary groups and public norms that always accompanies freedom of association.

When we think of voluntary associations, we think first of local groups like the Jaycees—quasi-social, quasi-civic, quasi-business organizations enlisting "upstanding" local citizens and carrying on a range of activities in the community. And when jeremiahs bemoan a falling off of membership, they have groups like the Jaycees in mind. Liberal expectancy, meaning confidence in the progressive liberalization of the internal lives of groups and the beneficial impact of membership, does not attach as spontaneously or confidently to religious associations or to flourishing new phenomena such as residential homeowners' associations or fellowship and support groups as it does to these secular, quasi-civic associations. The onus for cultivating the moral dispositions of liberal democratic citizens falls heavily on voluntary groups such as the Jaycees and their myriad counterparts. So does the demand for congruence and nondiscriminatory policies of admission, with the paradoxical result that the classic voluntary association is denied the core right of freedom of association—the ability to set restrictive membership criteria and to admit only wanted members.

We regularly form, join, and disassociate ourselves from groups that are selective. We expect restrictions on who can join. In the spirit of civic inclusion, Benjamin Franklin formed a volunteer fire department, but he also founded the American Philosophical Society and the first secret club of artisans. We can imagine open organizations with which anyone can affiliate, but they have the character of public accommodations rather than voluntary associations. If associations cannot limit eligibility and control admission, their particular projects and expressive aspects will be inhibited, diluted, or subverted. Besides, we know that sometimes the whole point of association is exhibition of some exemplary difference, whether the motivation is snobbery, celebration of some social identity without any pretense of superiority, or defensive self-protection. Voluntary associations are bounded entities. The moral (and immoral) uses of pluralism require exclusion. Small wonder that the right to choose with whom one will associate necessarily implies the right to choose with whom one will not associate. "There can be no clearer example of an intrusion into the internal structure or affairs of an association than a regulation that forces the group to accept members it does not desire."[3] Justice O'Connor put it simply: "the power to change the membership of a bona fide private association is unavoidably the power to change its purpose, its programs, its ideology, and its collective voice."[4]

"Open primary" laws are a vivid example of the threat that compelled association poses to a group's ideology, practical effectiveness, and esprit. These state laws allow not just independents but voters registered with another party to participate in the opposition primary, and they mandate that election results determine the votes that state delegates must cast at the national convention. In a divided opinion in *Democratic Party v. Wisconsin*, the Supreme Court ruled that the public interest in encouraging voter participation did not outweigh political parties' freedom of association.[5] Another familiar instance of compelled association is the union shop. Unions enjoy federally sponsored power to affect nonmembers through collective bargaining, and laws compel them to represent all employees in what amounts to a fiduciary duty. At the same time, the public policy to eliminate free riders requires all employees to support the designated bargaining unit; workers cannot join rival unions, or deal directly with employers, or disassociate at will. There is no protected conscientious objection to agency shops, and no violation of First Amendment free speech rights in compelling workers to contribute financially to a union as a condition of employment.[6] This is made palatable by depreciating its significance for members personally. No worker has to espouse the cause of unionism or attend meetings, the thinking goes; the only obligation is payment of "periodic dues, initiation fees, and assessments." This is not a case of ignoring "the shibboleth that the law cannot compel the spirit of brotherhood," since the whole point is that no such spirit is necessary.[7]

The requirement that unions fairly represent all workers brings to mind other situations where membership affects the distribution of social goods and where the cost of exclusion is high. In *Roberts v. Jaycees*, women claimed that ineligibility for full membership in the Jaycees adversely affected their business and professional advancement and civic standing. Membership in such situations may be viewed as a practical necessity, alerting us to the fact that voluntary associations can be experienced as compulsory if the privi-

leges and benefits they afford seem crucial. For pragmatic or cynical joiners, affiliation is not always as nominal as dues paying, either; Jaycees must
actively participate in the association's civic work and social life to reap the
benefits of belonging. Our subject is not the calculated advantages of joining, however, but the legal compulsion to associate: the requirement that
groups open their membership to categories of people whom they wish to
exclude.

There is no question that associations can *advocate* discrimination and exclusion or any other antiliberal belief or practice. The Jaycees has a right to
say that its organization should serve only the interests of young men, but
to practice discriminatory membership is something else. The by-laws of
the Jaycees national organization allowed women to participate as "associates" but denied them full membership. Local chapters in St. Paul and Minneapolis decided to admit women as regular members, and when the national organization threatened to revoke their charters, they challenged the
legality of the organization's by-laws under Minnesota's Human Rights Act.
Roberts v. Jaycees, decided in 1984, is the Supreme Court's most extensive
discussion of the application of state antidiscrimination law to private associations.

"Few cases in this Court's history have so deeply involved the shape and
character of the private sector," and it is not hard to see why.[8] The *Roberts*
decision goes to the heart of the kind of association the Jaycees had been
and aimed to be, an association dedicated to the advancement of young
men. Minnesota challenged both this description of the Jaycees' purpose
and the prediction that the forced eligibility of women would significantly
alter it. The challenge was legally successful but the moral case for regulation is unconvincing. The Jaycees' "voice" was undeniably altered once it
was forced to admit young women as full members along with young men.[9]
Whether we give credence to its avowed purpose or see it as committed
to preserving the exclusive privileges of male middle-manager types at the
expense of women, the association did not survive nondiscrimination law
intact.

More generally, *Roberts* clearly upset settled forms of sociability and collective activity that had never been considered matters for public regulation. It upset the prevailing understanding that "while classification on the
basis of involuntary group affiliations is subject to attack in the name of
equality, voluntary associations are protected in the name of liberty."[10] It
represented an escalation of demands for congruence, and a further step in
the "constitutionalization" of social life. Evidently, "an unbounded freedom
to dis-associate would cripple the guarantees of equality contained in the

constitution and our civil rights statutes, since every ban on discrimination would be checkmated by an assertion of individual autonomy phrased as a claim of associational freedom."[11] But *Roberts* unsettled what had been a stable equilibrium between the sphere of publicly available goods and services in which antidiscrimination law operated and a sphere of private–that is, social–activity that legislatures and courts did not seek to enter. With this, the public/private divide underwent a profound reconfiguration. Like other redrawings of this perpetually shifting boundary, designating voluntary associations like the Jaycees public accommodations was spurred by benevolent intentions and invoked widely accepted principles; but it raised expectations that could not be met, and it further clouded already confused and contested notions of discrimination.

THE LEGAL BACKGROUND: STATE ACTION, NONDISCRIMINATION IN PLACES OF PUBLIC ACCOMMODATION, AND COMPELLING STATE INTERESTS

The policy of enforcing congruence between the internal lives of voluntary associations and public norms is a distinctive step in a family of legal moves prohibiting private discriminatory actions, beginning with the repeal of laws requiring racial segregation and culminating in the 1964 Civil Rights Act, which denied associational freedom to discriminate in housing, employment, education, and access to basic goods and services, facilities of commerce, and common carriers—in short, "places of public accommodation," though they are privately owned.[12] Courts have also outlawed government support for private discrimination and exclusion, such as programs providing free textbooks to students without regard to the school's racially discriminatory policy: "a state may not induce, encourage or promote private persons to accomplish what it is constitutionally forbidden to accomplish."[13] The conduct of a private association is also regulable if it constitutes "state action," though it has proved notoriously difficult to determine when a public authority has "so far insinuated itself into a position of interdependence" with a group that it is a partner or joint venturer in the discriminatory activity.

The issue was recently joined in challenges to the exclusion of gay men and lesbians from St. Patrick's Day parades.[14] Does a city permit to march constitute state action? What about a holiday for government workers on parade day? Does the fact that the parade was sponsored by Boston until 1947 make the shift to private sponsorship an evasion of the law, so that the message of exclusion can be reasonably attributed to the city? Or, as I think, is the parade the expressive activity of a voluntary association with a moral and constitutional right to select who marches? (The recourse for those excluded is to agitate, demonstrate, shame, induce officials and others not to participate, and exercise their freedom to organize their own parade.)

The tortuous path of statutory prohibition of private discriminatory action is well documented, as are the principal public interests invoked in support of legally enforced nondiscrimination. One is to fulfill liberal democracy's promise to eliminate obstacles to equal citizenship. This promise has come to mean ensuring nondiscriminatory access to education, employment, housing, and the avenues of commercial and professional advancement. Second, there is a declared public interest in eliminating the moral harms of exclusion, among them injury to personal dignity and self-respect. However, the 1964 federal Civil Rights Act did not apply to private clubs or other establishments not open to the public. Until *Roberts*, either public accommodation laws contained specific exceptions for private associations or "public accommodation" was interpreted narrowly. When the question of regulating membership of private associations was raised, these exceptions were upheld. Justice Douglas's dissent in Moose Lodge had been the rule: "The associational rights which our system honors permit all white, all black, all brown, and all yellow clubs to be formed. They also permit all Catholic, all Jewish, or all agnostic clubs to be established. Government may not tell a man or woman who his or her associates must be. The individual can be as selective as he desires."[15] Besides, states had less stringent means to counter exclusion than mandating eligibility requirements and compelling association: they could use liquor licensing authority to withhold privileges from discriminatory groups or withdraw tax concessions such as deductions for charitable contributions or nonprofit tax-exempt status. State officials could be instructed not to appear in their public capacity at any function of an offending association and not to do any business with it. It could be made unlawful for an employer to subsidize an employee's membership in a discriminatory association, and so on.

This changed when *Roberts v. Jaycees* and two subsequent cases upheld without dissent the constitutionality of employing public accommodation law to require all-male associations to admit women.[16] The Minnesota Supreme Court had held the national Jaycees organization and its local affiliates to be a business in that it sells goods and extends privileges in exchange for annual membership dues; specifically, "leadership skills are 'goods' [and] business contacts and employment promotions are 'privileges' and 'advantages.'" It is a public business in that it solicits and recruits members based on unselective criteria. And it is a facility in that it continuously recruits and conducts activities at fixed sites within a state.[17]

Justice O'Connor's concurrence adhered to this line of thought: she distinguished commercial from expressive associations, assigned commercial associations only minimal constitutional protection, and judged that despite the group's "not insubstantial" volume of protected advocacy of political causes, the Jaycees is a "relatively easy case": it promotes and practices "the art of solicitation and management." It exists to serve the general public as "customers," not a more limited group as "members." "A shopkeeper has no constitutional right to deal only with persons of one sex," she recalls, and rules as if the Jaycees were no different.[18] The Conference of Private Organizations had anticipated this argument in its amicus brief, objecting that the Jaycees does not sell seats like the Dale Carnegie organization: "if the U.S. Jaycees is merely a commercial business, it hardly would have expended hundreds of thousands of dollars in litigation fees, in courts throughout the country, defending its purpose and right not to engage in the allegedly lucrative 'sale' of memberships to women."[19]

O'Connor held the Minnesota public accommodations statute applicable to the Jaycees because it is judged commercial, rather than because, commercial or not, the state has an interest in opening its membership to guarantee women equal public standing and personal dignity. Her categorical approach contrasts with the logic of the majority opinion, which classified the Jaycees as an expressive association but allowed the state's compelling interest in antidiscrimination to override the group's First Amendment rights. That opinion was wrong. It is gravely underprotective of expressive organizations. Justice Brennan's balance is tilted against the Jaycees at the outset because he takes a crimped view of association "voice," demanding a factual nexus between the group's membership and messages before affording it constitutional protection. This leads him implausibly to conclude that since none of the Jaycee's civic activities represents interests or political positions exclusive to young men, the impact of compelled association on the exercise of the group's First Amendment rights would be trivial.[20] Every step of this reasoning is seriously flawed. But the chief weakness, from my perspective, is the misguided nature of Brennan's definition and application of the state interest in compelling association.

In judging that Minnesota has a "compelling interest" to see that women become full members of the Jaycees, Minnesota's attorney general employed the arguments used to justify public accommodation law more generally. "Clearing the channels of commerce of the irrelevancy of sex, to make sure that goods and services and advancement in the business world are available to all on an equal basis" is a public purpose of the first magnitude. And "the deprivation of personal dignity that surely accompanies denials of equal access to public establishments," which is felt as deeply by women as persons denied it on the basis of color, is a harm the state should act to prevent.[21] Are these two arguments independent rationales for compelled association? If "deprivation of personal dignity" is distinct from denying access to publicly available goods and advantages, what does it mean?

Every item in the catalog of harms of exclusion makes an appearance in the majority opinion in *Roberts*—second-class citizenship, stigma, degradation, unequal status, injury to personal dignity and self-respect. Plainly, the idea of deprivation of dignity garners power from this overlap, here and in moral and political theory more broadly. For example: "The most heartrending deprivation of all is the inequality of status that excludes people from full membership in the community, degrading them by labeling them as outsiders, denying them their very selves."[22] This representative statement conflates several independent values. "Inequality of status" indicates someone is assigned to an inferior caste; he or she is a less than a full member of political society, is a second-class citizen. "Outsider" attributes subjective feelings to all parties; it indicates that recognized signs of "belonging" are willfully withheld, and that the person marked as alien feels alienated. This criterion is problematic if we recall that casting oneself as an outsider is a familiar self-dramatizing and often self-aggrandizing mode in the United States where nothing is more common than to invoke a unified American society or culture (Christian or Judeo-Christian, male, white, secular-humanist, middle-class) to heighten a group's distinctiveness and defiant marginality. As for "denying them their very selves," the thought is indecipherable, or plainly wrong. But it is evocative of the gamut of notions associated with "identity" and the presumptively distinct, crippling injuries to identity: harm to personal dignity and self-respect, and "misrecognition." My aim is to disaggregate and assess the claims of state interest used to justify compelled association.

CLEARING THE CHANNELS OF COMMERCE: SECOND-CLASS CITIZENSHIP

Peter Berger observes that in contrast to honor, dignity relates to "intrinsic humanity" divested of social roles and "pertains to the self as such."[23] In political theory, however, and in judicial decisions such as *Roberts*, dignity is tied to civic standing in a liberal democracy. When that connection is plain, the harm of exclusion is not subjective but a violation of actual rights or public norms of civic equality (or a generally recognizable failure to apply and enforce rights and norms consistently). The injury is "logically entailed by, rather than merely contingently caused by," the conduct.[24] It is not erased by the fact that the victim may not experience injury, though normally the pain is real enough. Historically, certain exclusions have been inescapable marks of inferior public standing in the United States, which is why Charles Black was appalled by the "artificial mist of puzzlement" surrounding the question whether racial discrimination inheres in legally imposed segregation in the twentieth century. "It is true that the specifically hurtful character of segregation, as a net matter in the life of each segregated individual, may be hard to establish," he observed, but "that a practice, on massive historical evidence and in common sense, has the designed and generally apprehended effect of putting its victims at a disadvantage, is enough for law."[25]

The historical exclusions designating second-class citizenship and their contemporary residue are familiar. In a political society with a public ideology of political equality and universal suffrage, all women and slaves and later black freedmen were denied the vote on grounds of inferiority (the rationales do not bear repeating). Where no special virtue or contribution was necessary for suffrage, where "the worst white scoundrel" was declared fit to vote, to be denied the vote was to be degraded. It "is to make us an exception, to brand us with the stigma of inferiority," Frederick Douglass wrote.[26] Second-class citizenship is also sanctioned by diluting a group's vote through gerrymandering: "it is a fixed point in a democratic culture that public institutions should not establish or reinforce the perception that some people's interests deserve less respect or concern than those of others simply in virtue of their membership in one rather than another social or ascriptive group."[27] The same rationales used to deny political rights were employed to justify other civil disabilities, of course, as regards property rights and exclusion from certain occupations. "It is hardly surprising that the middle-class feminists who came to resent being excluded from the world of gainful employment should have been quite aware of the intimate bond between earning and citizenship."[28]

The message of second-class citizenship is also communicated when the exercise of a right is frustrated or conceded in a manner that is grudging, humiliating, or effectively punitive. The message is conveyed today, for example, when receipt of means-tested public benefits is made personally difficult—when welfare departments hassle recipients, or require exhaustive and time-consuming documentation or frequent trips and reapplications; when government attaches conditions to essential public benefits as private donors do to grants; by practices that assume recipients need policing—home visits characterized as "warrantless searches" by welfare workers required to be sleuths ("no such sums are spent policing the government subsidies granted to farmers, airlines, steamship companies, and junk mail dealers"); or by arrant denials of due process.[29] In *Goldberg v. Kelley*, a 1970 case requiring a pretermination hearing before Aid to Families with Dependent Children payments could be cut off, Justice Brennan's decision linked "dignity and well-being" as the twin goals of welfare.[30]

So when the *Roberts* court characterized the Jaycees' membership policy as "invidious discrimination" and the denial of full membership to women as a "stigma," it used the most forceful terms available to say that the exclusion constituted debasement of women's public standing. "Stigma" refers not just to any prejudicial mark but to a badge of civic inferiority. It is a trigger for protective treatment. Viewed in the light of the interplay in American ideology among earning, moral improvement, and public standing, women's second-class membership in the Jaycees could be taken as a mark of second-class citizenship. Women could find exclusion from full membership in the Jaycees galling, since no demonstration of excellent performance as "associate members" could improve their status. But neither observation settles the moral or constitutional question of whether the state should compel the Jaycees to admit women as full members. In the context of the desegregation decisions, Justice Black had set aside the "interesting question," "must segregation amount to discrimination?" The Jaycees' position on the social meaning of exclusion offers a blunt answer: "The fact that a few appellants do not like the . . . policy does not convert a benign exclusion into an invidious discrimination."[31] Feminist commentators concede that "not all females resent all forms of separatism and American society remains deeply divided over which forms are invidious."[32] Is the state interest in compelled association compelling here?

Public accommodation laws set out to "clear the channels of commerce," and the chief consideration is what "valuable goods and privileges" come from membership. The Jaycees protested that it would be impossible to apply the standard fairly because there is no basis for a test of their association's "influence" in the business community or helpfulness to professional advancement. Is a factual inquiry impossible? Evidence is available in the form of testimony of members regarding the personal contacts that lead to jobs, records of business deductions of membership fees, and so on. Reviewing the exemption afforded benevolent orders in *New York State Club Association*, Justice Scalia noted the absence of a showing that lodges or fraternal organizations "significantly contribute to the problem the City Council was addressing."[33] (A less restrained district court had judged the state's interest in prohibiting discrimination in the Elks far from compelling because the group was "ludicrous, harmless, innocent, anachronistic, defensive, evanescent, inconsequential."[34]) Judge Arnold, who had decided in favor of the Jaycees in the Court of Appeals, argued that Minnesota's interest was not compelling because the record failed to show that membership was the only practicable way for a woman to advance in business or professional life.[35] Even strong proponents of compelled association would agree that membership is less significant than vigorous enforcement of the Civil Rights Act, the Equal Credit Opportunity Act, or affirmative action programs, which have proved their effectiveness. The critical matter of job segregation by race and sex is affected only indirectly by this decision. Still, it is a misunderstanding of the purpose of public accommodation provisions to say that no compelling state interest exists unless the association is the sine qua non of economic advancement for women.

Is it really of compelling importance that each sex have equal access to every organization offering privileges, however? Where other avenues exist, how strict a standard of comparable value or equality of access to the market should apply? Is the supposition that other channels of commerce are open "based upon the moribund theory of 'separate but equal'"? Or does a proliferation of associations, all male, all female, and gender integrated, affect the challenge?[36] The Appeals Court thought so: "We know that membership in the Jaycees has been of some help to the complaining individuals in their corporate careers, but we do not know whether similar organizational experience in other clubs or associations, open either to both sexes or to women only, has been or could be of similar or greater help to these or other women."[37] (It is worth observing in this connection that discrimination may restrict opportunities without necessarily harming victims economically, even in areas like employment that plainly fall under public accommodation law today. Whether discrimination is costly depends on the alternatives available: "For Jews who did not want to act like WASPS or did not know how to, joining a Jewish [law] firm was an attractive option."[38] There is no evidence that they suffered measurably less success, though there is ample testimony to the pain and rage caused by discriminatory exclusion.)

From the standpoint of "clearing the channels of commerce" to avoid conferring second-class citizenship on women, the decisive question is not whether Jaycee membership is an avenue to advancement but whether parallel channels, adequately effective, are closed to women. It is worth recalling the circumstances of the case. It involved an internal dispute over eligibility. In a 1981 national referendum Jaycees voted 67 percent to 33 percent not to change the membership status of women. The St. Paul and Minneapolis chapters violated the organization's by-laws by admitting women as full members, and when the national organization threatened to revoke their charters, the Minnesota chapters brought action under the state Human Rights Act. The complaint was brought by members themselves. This is not surprising; associations engaged in a range of commercial and civic activities are highly permeable; the moral and social forces that led to legislation prohibiting gender discrimination in the mid 1970s were "out there," and local activists a decade later were not immune to them. This institutional history illustrates the observation that "nothing has been more characteristic of voluntary bodies than the proneness of dissidents to exercise what has been termed 'the God-given right of every American to resign, tell why, and raise hell.'"[39] It is unlikely that a court decision in favor of the national organization would have eliminated these integrated groups; the rebel local chapters would have separated permanently from the parent organization and gone their independent ways. Indeed, given the moral climate and organizational impetus of women's push for equality, the integrated Jaycees and parallel groups would very likely have been invigorated. ("It is almost a rule of associations," Grant McConnell advises, "that they have greater animosity for rivals than for opponents.")[40] In large cities, unreconstructed male Jaycees might have been marginalized in their own clubs.

Of course, it is also unlikely that compelled association eliminates restrictive groups; discriminatory commercial and social relations go on defiantly "underground" all the time. The only sure result of compelled association is that male Jaycees join the company of those historically discriminated against in seeing themselves as victims of powerful, hostile social forces and of a government indifferent to their freedom of association. The Rotary amicus brief expressed this plainly, invoking constitutional protection for the Jaycees as an embattled, politically unpopular group: "At the present time, male-only organizations such as the Jaycees and Rotary are encountering governmental and social hostility akin to that directed at the NAACP in the 1960s."[41] (NOW was an amicus on the winning side.) In short, the alternatives were not segregation and exclusion on the one hand and compelled association on the other. There was also voluntary association, separation and schism, and competition among groups.

Justice Brennan's decision was, I think, wrong. He was right to reason that the creation of second-class citizenship is legitimate cause for regulating associations. To the extent that he firmly tethers dignity harms to second-class citizenship, and attempts to tie both to exclusion from the specific goods meted out in places of public accommodation, his logic is sound. Minnesota's extension of public accommodation law, Brennan wrote, "reflects a recognition of the changing nature of the American economy and of the importance, both to the individual and to society, of removing the barriers to economic advancement and political and social integration that have historically plagued certain disadvantaged groups, including women."[42] If this reasoning is correct, where does the decision go wrong? Brennan was wrong to classify the Jaycees as a public accommodation. The group was not a general source of publicly available goods. Other associations were open to women; the Jaycees was not the exclusive purveyors of advantages or privileges. Indeed, legally compelled association may have slowed the multiplication of groups capable of providing more people with a wider range of opportunities for commercial and professional advancement. These are arguable matters of judgment, however. There is no bright line to indicate when exclusion from the option of participating in the advantages of association membership makes equal public standing so difficult that association should be legally compelled.

The critical problem with Brennan's decision is that he does not scrupulously preserve the tie between second-class citizenship and access to publicly available goods and services. Perhaps because the association's importance as an avenue to salient public goods is doubtful, this justification for interfering with association freedom seemed to need reinforcement. The public accommodation rationale is merged with another, broader argument for compelled association; in fact, it is swallowed up by the claim that second-class membership in this sort of voluntary association implies second-class citizenship tout court. The judgment that subordination in the Jaycees is a substantial barrier to economic advancement recedes; in its place Brennan invokes an unsupported structural parallel (political theorists propose a causal connection as well) between subordination of women in the Jaycees on the one hand and in society at large and as citizens on the other. Second-class membership is simply identified with second-class citizenship.

Once the justification for compelled association is loosed from its tether to public accommodation law and the aim of "clearing the channels of commerce," there is nothing to stop the argument from expanding to cover every arbitrary and unjustified subordination and exclusion. A brake is needed, for the perfectly good reason that commitment to equal citizenship is "not identical to the general right of all citizens not to be arbitrarily discriminated against."[43] And because, as I will show, the conflation of second-class membership with debased public standing is strangely seductive, it amounts to an invitation to set aside sociological and psychological realism.

SECOND-CLASS MEMBERSHIP = SECOND-CLASS CITIZENSHIP?

The national Jaycees' organization admitted women as "associate members" but they could not hold office, vote for officers or for organization policy, or receive achievement awards (though they participated in the programs upon which awards were based). The state's "overpowering interest," Justice Brennan explained, stems from the fact that "discrimination based on archaic and overbroad assumptions about the relative needs and capacities of the sexes forces individuals to labor under stereotypical notions that often bear no relationship to their actual abilities."[44] With this, the stigma of subordinate status within the association becomes key.

Full association membership and public standing are seen as interdependent in the present on the assumption that social habits and moral dispositions cultivated and expressed in voluntary associations are carried over willy-nilly to public life. Congruence is necessary because moral dispositions are of a piece in their origins and effects, and spill over from sphere to sphere. Second-class membership, the argument goes, is inseparable from debased public standing because their sources are the same. (So are their consequences for victims: affront, outrage, "misrecognition," and self-loathing.) This position has the appeal of simplicity and holism: "Men who are uncomfortable associating with women in such social settings are unlikely to become less so if discomfort remains a valid justification for exclusivity. And such discomfort is not readily confined. Those who have trouble treating women as equals at clubhouse lunches will not readily escape such difficulties in corporate suites or smoke-filled rooms."[45]

Perhaps. But moral psychology is more complex than this, casting doubt on this assumption as a justification for legally compelled association. Discrimination condoned in one sphere is not necessarily condoned, or exhibited, in all or any others. For one thing, there are various reasons for discrimination, not just one reason that applies uniformly in all situations. "Myopic" prejudice may be amenable to correction by experience, and if irrational prejudice were at work, compelled association might encourage male Jaycees to acknowledge women's contributions to their association, spilling over into appreciation of equality generally. The Court assumed myopic prejudice, and in a related case involving Rotary clubs took an overtly paternalistic line, announcing that the exclusion of women was not in the association's interest. The club's mission—providing humanitarian service, encouraging high ethical standards in all vocations, and helping build world peace—would be improved by opening membership to women, Justice Powell prescribed, and would permit the Rotary to "obtain a more representative cross-section of community leaders with a broadened capacity for service."[46] Paternalism was misplaced. It is doubtful that male Rotarians or Jaycees were myopic, or that their membership practices were based on a stereotypical belief that women could not recruit new members or organize charity drives. After all, as "associates" women contributed to the group's effectiveness.

Their point in challenging the applicability of Minnesota's law was not to defend a generalization about whether or not women could perform adequately as members, but to preserve the group as an association of young men. The subordination of women illustrates "principled discrimination," which is cold-eyed and persists even where measurable costs are known: in this case it trumps economic self-interest (insofar as Justice O'Connor is right in characterizing them as a commercial enterprise) and maximum recruitment. Moreover, principled discrimination is normally not a permanent disposition, unconsciously carried over from one sphere to another.[47] Here, hierarchical membership is a defining element in the Jaycees' pursuit of its avowed goal: the self-development and advancement of male management-types under the age of thirty-five (which is why they humorlessly object to the expression "old boys' network.") Compelled association is not a correction of irrational prejudice but an interference with the association's deliberate, self-chosen purpose.

Those who see a seamless web of public and private life and a unity of moral disposition deny that people have the capacity or inclination to discriminate discriminatingly. Beyond that, they argue that when government fails to interfere with membership restrictions and to protect against "second-class membership," it "morally legitimizes and potentially encourages a practice both courts and legislatures have decried as one of the most significant evils in modern society."[48] On this view, government has an obligation to mandate moral education, affirming the equal worth of excluded individuals, redressing dignity harms broadly understood, and enforcing acceptable democratic behavior in almost every arena except for the most intimate (small businesses are exempt from antidiscrimination law on the presumption that they are family affairs.)[49] Government has many avenues for public communication and the promotion of approved conduct and messages, of course, not only in its authoritative capacity as educator but also in its activities as employer, owner, grantor, and patron. But this extravagant case for the obligation to educate demands more than seizing official occasions for proclamations and exhibitions of liberal democratic practices, and more than prohibiting "state action" in which government is insinuated into private conduct. Advocates of congruence are stern didacts, and would use the law to compel voluntary associations to promote approved messages and to prohibit disfavored ones. They are willing to "press club members into service to send society a message of inclusion and equality." They reject the liberal fundamental "that private individuals may not be used as the involuntary instruments of a state lesson."[50]

Plaintiffs in the Tiger Inn case, for example, acknowledged that the purpose of requiring Princeton University's all-male eating clubs to admit women was to send a message of equality to club members and society at large. "College years are very formative years, and students should not be taught the lesson that discrimination is acceptable and legitimate."[51] The same didactic intent informs arguments for the mandatory gender integration of Greek letter societies: "Integration may help teach young men and women to view one another as complete human beings rather than merely as potential sexual partners. Living together on a daily basis should encourage members of both genders to accept one another as social and intellectual equals."[52] This argument proves too much; it would make coed dormitories obligatory, for example. It is insensitive to the range of personal needs, and sexual and moral maturity, of students. And it does not tell us when the "formative" years are over. In any case, the justification for compelled association has shifted from avoiding presumptive harm to the public standing of those excluded to the moral education of discriminating members.

As a general matter we expect "circular reinforcement of politics, private attitudes and behavior, and constitutional law."[53] But as a general matter, government is not said to "morally legitimize and potentially encourage" a group's practices when it leaves the control of membership to members. Freedom of association is no stamp of public approval of the internal life of an association in a liberal democracy. If it were, the fundamental principle of toleration would be meaningless. All associations would be vulnerable to the logic of congruence—indeed, to the social preferences of the party in power.

PUBLIC STANDING AND SELF-RESPECT

Those who think that discrimination is one thing, that it cannot be contained, and will spill over from sphere to sphere, see victimization as uniform across spheres as well. Stigmatizing reduces the victim "from a whole and usual person to a tainted discounted one," Erving Goffman wrote, and described stigma as "spoiled identity."[54] The idea is that those discriminated against and excluded internalize images of inferiority and incapacity. This psychological logic was used effectively by Kenneth Clark and the NAACP in their argument in *Brown* opposing government-mandated racial discrimination in public schools. The Court found officially inflicted harm to students, which Chief Justice Warren described as "a feeling of inferiority as to their status in the community that may affect their hearts and minds in a way unlikely ever to be undone." The psychology is widely invoked, but there is little reason to think that what holds for black children's motivation to learn in officially segregated schools (and in an overtly racist public environment) is generalizable.

The assumption that second-class citizenship inexorably injures self-respect—a commonplace in discussions of democratic equality—is even more troubling than the conflation of second-class membership with second-class citizenship. It is not just that self-respect is too vague and subjective a state of mind to be the ground for public policy ("the consequences of discrimination both real and imagined, depend on an individual's temperament and past experience"—or the thickness of our skin).[55] Beyond that, the two are independent. This may seem to claim too much. I could say, more modestly, that public standing is a necessary but not sufficient condition for dignity and self-respect, but I want to make the stronger claim.

Why? For one thing, the admonition that second-class citizenship is intolerable is not enhanced by heaping on the presumption of injury to self-worth. Its "elemental wrongness" is unchanged, whether or not victims suffer. The obligation of democratic government (and of citizens personally and individually) to ensure equal public standing and refrain from public shows of disrespect is not diminished by my declaration of their independence. More important here, the assumption that self-respect is mediated by public standing is an unproved overstatement with serious consequences. It would be foolish to deny that second-class citizenship, accompanied as it normally is by public expressions of denigration and hate, can cause self-loathing. It would be just as silly to insist on stoic detachment, which has it that debasement and humiliation disrupt the equilibrium of only those willing to be harmed. Simply, there are good reasons not to overstate the capacity of law and public institutions to instill or to secure self-respect, and even better reasons to acknowledge that exclusion and "invidious discrimination" are not inherently harmful to it.

Self-respect is rightly characterized as a "primary good," vital to well-being. It is a condition for any purposive action beyond the most narrowly instrumental: "The importance of self-respect is that it provides a secure sense of our own value, a firm conviction that our determinate conception of the good is worth carrying out. Without self-respect nothing may seem worth doing, and if some things have value for us, we lack the will to pursue them."[56] We know little about the conditions that instill self-respect, though, apart from the necessity of attachment and basic trust in early childhood (a deficit at this stage is said to be irreparable). We know even less about how self-respect is damaged or reversed—in particular, what conditions exacerbate or mitigate the effects of the public stigma of second-class citizenship. But because liberal theorists fear that self-respect is vulnerable to unequal public standing, and because ardent civic-minded theorists positively insist it *should* be so, there is a strong impetus to accept as a democratic tenet that self-respect is inexorably tied to first-class citizenship. With it comes the impetus to urge a uniform spirit of civic equality throughout public and private life; congruence requires that not only political institutions and public accommodations but also voluntary social groups function as mini–liberal democracies, with a view to cultivating and sustaining self-respect. (And it is a short step to the "politics of recognition," whereby groups cannot be civic or social equals unless their "specific experience, culture, and social contributions are publicly affirmed.")[57] In short, the consequence of insisting that public standing is a necessary condition of self-respect is to assume a positive public obligation to ensure self-respect, which is neither possible nor desirable.

Moreover, the claim that we cannot have one without the other is careless and unintentionally cruel insofar as it imposes heroic obligations on victims. By tying self-respect to public standing, defending oneself against discrimination becomes a moral imperative, and by implication those who do not resist unjust treatment are lacking in moral backbone or psychological core. Hannah Arendt warned that the school desegregation decisions required heroism of children, and she feared for black children forced into social stituations where they were not wanted. She was contradicted by Ralph Ellison, who explained that these children are required to master the inner tensions created by their racial situation, and must be inured to struggle.[58] The exchange reminds us that antidiscrimination law is not self-enforcing. Enforcement is dispersed, and in this respect the *Roberts* case, which was an intraorganizational dispute brought by local chapters against the national organization, is misleading, since it entailed few personal risks or costs to complaining members. In most cases, effecting rights to equal treatment in housing, employment, education, and so on requires the personally consuming commitment of individual victims to righting the wrong through formal institutional proceedings or in court. It means overcoming concrete obstacles: the costs of counsel, technicalities of evidence and burdens of proof, lack of legal knowledge of what sorts of complaints are cognizable and what are not (after all, many forms of prejudicial treatment are permissible). Complainants must be prepared to verify their subjective experience of wrong in the form of records and evidence. Moreover, discrimination occurs unostentatiously in the course of ordinary interpersonal relations, and self-assertion in accord with public procedures threatens to disrupt day-to-day life. We tend to forget or depreciate the need to make the mundane calculation that one's situation will actually be improved.

Second-class citizens must call publicly for legal protection, and dedicate themselves to showing they deserve it.[59] To insist that self-respect requires this of them is more onus than inspiration. Of course, there are sound political reasons for activists to organize and motivate people to defend their rights or to *want people* to mobilize themselves, reinforced by the thought that activism itself is vitalizing and contributes to self-respect. But this is entirely different from the implication that asserting one's public standing is imperative, and from the suggestion that passivity (or alternative strategies of self-defense) indicates that second-class citizens are not self-respecting. In a well-meaning effort to enhance the importance of equal citizenship by saying it is a necessary condition of self-respect, and in what appears superficially to be a demonstration of empathy with victims, advocates come perilously close to confirming that people treated as second-class citizens are degraded.

Like all subjective harms, the effects of second-class citizenship will vary among individuals, who must make the personal decision whether or not to defend their rights in legally specified ways. Understandably, if victims fear that formal complaint and legal intervention will worsen their condition, they will devise alternative strategies. These responses include angry confrontation, stoic endurance, and exit—taking another job or moving to other housing. Christopher Jencks describes gender differences in the strategies African American men and women have developed for dealing with discrimination:

> When a black man thinks someone has shown him disrespect or treated him unfairly, he is likely to show his anger, perhaps because this is the only way he can maintain his self-respect. Women are less likely to feel that their self-respect requires them to challenge their boss. . . . They tell one another sto-

ries about how unfair their boss's behavior is, or why they deserved the promotion someone else got.[60]

One strategy is more constructive than the other from the point of view of
keeping one's job, but the point is not that women are more disciplined
calculators. Both not complaining and lashing out may be expressions of
dignity. People maintain a sense of pride "by withstanding pain, avoiding
confrontations, or completing humble work."[61] Self-respect may lie in re-
signing oneself to mistreatment for the sake of fulfilling other obligations
such as supporting a family. My point here is that tension between other
roles and responsibilities and defense of public standing is aggravated by a
public ideology that identifies self-respect with public standing and describes affirming one's public standing as its premier expression.

Expecting prejudice, seeing it rooted in individual personality (the of-
fender is "immature" or "just plain ignorant"), viewing stoicism as strength
of character may be unhelpful from the point of view of public education and
political progress; we know that confrontations in the aggregate and over
time can stem exhibitions of prejudice. But they are perfectly consistent with
a keen perception of stereotypes others have of one's group. And from the
point of view of self-respect, little good can come from denying that victims
have or demonstrate it unless they take up what is not just self-defense, after
all, but a public cause. Otherwise, they are assigned the obligation to morally
educate violators. And they must publicly demonstrate that they are not lacking in self-respect—that they do not see themselves as "spoiled."

The same caution holds for the identification of employment with self-
respect; it can boomerang on the intended beneficiaries. If paid work is represented as a condition not only of public standing but also of self-respect,
then reasons multiply for why the unemployed must take work, why public policy should make them work, and why government must guarantee
work (or job training), and we are liable to lose sight of the fact that it is not
necessarily a source of personal dignity. In fact, when it comes to work, public standing and self-respect may conflict. It seems that any work that earns
a living suffices for public standing; it signifies that able-bodied adults have
to take on the common obligations of citizenship, or at least prove that they
are not idlers, burdens on taxpayers. But self-respect may require useful or
"decent" work, or work that calls upon specific capacities and talents. Work
may diminish self-respect if the job itself or treatment there are considered
demeaning, or if it is manifestly make-work. Michael Sandel argues the republican case that by itself labor for a wage does not necessarily cultivate

the qualities of character necessary for self-government, which should be the aim of political economy, and he quotes Robert Kennedy's prescription: "dignified employment at decent pay, the kind of employment that lets a man say to his community, to his family, to his country, and most important, to himself, 'I helped to build this country. I am a participant in its great public ventures.'"[62] This is to say that not just any job will do for anyone, that contingencies of age and environment complicate whether or not particular work or conditions of employment, including wages, are considered self-respecting. Some jobless will take any job they can get, some do not want a job at all, and some want only a "good job," as Christopher Jencks explains: "Minimum-wage jobs are acceptable to many teenagers, who have no family to support and just want pocket money. But no native-born American male can imagine supporting a family on $3.35 [at the time of this writing $4.25] an hour. If that is the only 'respectable' alternative, he will usually conclude that respectability is beyond his reach."[63]

By definition, the marks of first-class citizenship are the chief public exhibitions of respect. It is a failure of moral imagination to think that public standing is the sole, chief, guaranteed, or necessary condition of self-respect, however, or that public shows of disrespect normally cause self-loathing, for the dynamic also works in reverse. Self-respect bolsters us against slights and prejudice, social exclusion and second-class membership, and even second-class citizenship. These goods are not as unambiguously related as political theory would have it.

So it should not be surprising that my advisory against identifying self-respect with public standing holds with greater force for exclusion from voluntary associations or subordination within them. What is wrong with assuming that personal dignity is mediated by "recognition" of the sort that comes from admission to membership? For one thing, it assumes that the intention to stigmatize and harm by exclusion is successful. It aggrandizes discriminators, and it diminishes their targets by assuming they have no resources to resist being "spoiled." It is also too stringent: under the guise of protecting people against injury to self-respect, it may simply protect them from "the raw insult of being kept out." The fine line between disrespect and insensitivity is added reason to restrict official policy to exclusions that are inescapably intended and regarded as marks of second-class citizenship, and to concede that self-worth falls outside the public, legal purview. Those who unjustifiably exclude others from consideration as candidates for membership may be guilty of a moral wrong or, more likely, of the "ordinary vice" of snobbery, but lack of consideration as a result of prejudice and ill will is not a public harm, and is not officially corrigible. What is taken as an expression of superiority may be unintended.

> As we join a multiplicity of groups that include some people, we also exclude most others. These little societies are by no means equal in social standing and neither are their individual members. Inevitably some outsiders will be rebuffed and hurt, and this would be the case even if there were no groups that make social exclusion their chief business. Given any degree of inequality and any kind of choice of intimacies and interests, there is bound to be snobbery in effect.[64]

This is not to deny the painfulness of "the raw insult of being left out." "Psychologically," Arendt observed, "the situation of being unwanted (a typically social predicament) is more difficult to bear than outright persecution (a political predicament)."[65]

Besides, there is no reason to ennoble would-be joiners by assuming that their motives for wanting to belong to a restricted membership group are laudable. The grim self-righteousness of opponents of Princeton's eating clubs is unmistakable. Those storming the gates of elitism may be frankly disposed to shut the door behind them. We have all witnessed the depressing spectacle of people desperately trying to appear at home in some milieu they imagine is better than others—it can operate, for example, as forcefully among women in traditionally male bastions as across cultural groups and social classes. Characters without personal pride, who abandon one group and push their way into another, have been unwholesome staples of the novel from its inception. Self-righteousness, hypocrisy, social climbing, and envy do not undermine the principled justifications (and good motives) for compelled association—but they help explain the moral ambivalence we may feel about crusading crashers. They also provide insight into the passionate resistance of groups that want to preserve their exclusive characters; sheer illiberal prejudice is not the only force at work.

It can seem harsh to recommend those excluded from voluntary associations to exhibit once-aristocratic-now-democratic pride, though it is less rare than political and legal theorists think (regrettably, empathy is typically restricted to weakness). It deserves moral approval. There is nothing inherently lamentable about individuals thrown back on themselves to "dredge up the meaning and stability" they require, rather than to find it in membership in an association.[66] That is what we all must do, in practice. No matter how emotionally identified we are (or imagine we could be) with a particular group, voluntary associations do not "constitute" us. (Nor for that matter does public standing as a citizen, no matter how fulsome official rituals of recognition.) Personal resources and moral courage are not all we have to draw on in response to exclusion, in any case. Social attachments and membership in voluntary associations where they are welcome members buffer individuals from public shows of disrespect, and theorists of civil society rightly describe these as the chief settings for cultivating a sense of self-worth. (We can think of other conditions that favor self-respect: the belief that one is smiled upon is common among natural athletes, for example.) Because social resources are supplied and inner resources reinforced by voluntary association, the excluded disagree about whether the best response is compelled association or self-affirmation through their own restrictive voluntary groups. Organized "support" is a major industry today; innumerable self-help groups, fellowship groups, and self-styled "identity groups" form around personal disabilities and social disadvantages, stigmas, real or imagined victimization, disappointment and rejection of all kinds. Long lists of meetings fill local newspapers and bulletin boards. COYOTE (Call Off Your Old Tired Ethics), to take one example, has as its primary goal providing an educational and support network "to raise the overall self-esteem of women and men in the sex industry" and end the stigma surrounding "sexwork."[67] For those who are not heroic individualists, associations of one's own are the democratic response to exclusion and rebuff.

THE PERMANENT DYNAMIC OF ASSOCIATION AND EXCLUSION: THE DEMOCRATIC USES OF "COMPARING GROUPS"

John Rawls is surely right that to be self-respecting more is needed than public recognition as demonstrated in the distribution of fundamental rights and liberties. Individuals need some place where their values and opinions are affirmed, their contributions acknowledged, where the likelihood of failure is reduced and they find support against lurking self-doubt. Voluntary associations provide these contexts even if they are not congruent with liberal democratic norms and institutions.[68] Rawls also proposes that membership in associations protects against harms to self-respect by mitigating the effects of inequalities of income and wealth, a necessary function even if inequalities are just, as they are in his ideal scheme. A plurality of associations "tends to reduce the visibility, or at least the painful visibility, of variations in men's prospects." Associations "tend to divide it [society] into noncomparing groups" and to act as a brake on competition, rivalry, and hostile outbreaks of social envy.[69] Freedom of association operates as the antidote to its own vices if everyone has occasions for inclusion and exclusion, opportunities for self-protection and for experiencing a sense of self-worth.

A sociological precursor to Rawls's account is the 1892 essay "The Great American Safety-Valve," which characterized voluntary associations as relatively harmless outlets for "these ambitions for precedence which our national life generates, fosters, and stimulates, without adequate provision for their gratification."[70] This suggests that even if voluntary associations temper economic comparisons, as Rawls proposes, they are fertile ground for exhibitions of earned or unmerited superiority, organized elitism, separatism, snobbery, and genuinely hateful, prejudicial exclusion—to say nothing of the pleasures of sheer contrast. Associations are formed to demonstrate some exemplary difference from "mainstream" society as a whole. (Thus, the life history of the odyssey of first-generation American to assimilated citizen and member—Jaycee!—has its counterpart in the life history of the shallow assimilationist discovering his or her roots, as did Malcom X, and claiming superiority over "plain" Americans.) Or associations are formed to reaffirm commitment to the public values of democratic society, exhibiting members' exemplary civic-mindedness and civility. "The Americans' unsystematic desire to identify with intermediary groups . . . may be based on real or imagined descent, on old or newly adopted religions, on geographic area of origin, socialization or residence, on external categorization, on voluntary association, or on defiance. In all of these cases," Werner Sollors explains, "symbolic boundaries are constructed in a perplexing variety of continuously shifting forms."[71]

Anyone observing children's cliques gets a taste of the sheer arbitrariness of selective association in action, its irrepressibility and manifest cruelty. I do not want to suggest an essentialist psychology or appear to concede that "tribalism" is primordial. On the contrary, the dynamic I describe is distinctively democratic, and habits are learned early. Regardless of an association's purpose or members' intentions, selective groups will be seen as advancing some claim to preference, privilege, or desert, and they will provoke accusations that they violate the public ethos of democratic equality. As *Roberts* demonstrates, egalitarian opposition to restrictive secular associations is endemic in the United States.

The history of voluntary associations here reflects the permanent dynamic of snobbery and exclusion, and opposition in the name of democratic equality. The first collective enterprises apart from churches in the colonial era were nonsectarian benevolent societies such as the American Bible Society, which charged churches with elitism.[72] Preoccupation with a "regal fungus," with "entails, nobility, hierarchy, and monopolies," emerged full force in the Jacksonian era.[73] Social critics added professionals to the seemingly endless list of "social classifications" and "combinations" that smacked of pride and privilege. Every one of these groups would, "if our Government were converted into an aristocracy, become our dukes, lords, marquises, and baronets."[74] The "voluntary principle" was the proposed democratic antidote, meaning free competition and voluntary association. Even among Jacksonians, however, a few observers like Nathaniel Hawthorne were wary of the enthusiasm for meritocratic striving (nothing was more foolish "than the eagerness with which gaunt and gosling-like youths strive to break through the barriers")[75]; Hawthorne predicted that the purported cure for hereditary social hierarchy and traditional exclusion—competing voluntary associations—would be an enormous generator of restrictiveness and resentment in turn. Hawthorne was right. Despite recurrent populist charges of elitism and subversion, Americans are not opposed to exclusive and even secret organizations for themselves: "The plain citizen sometimes wearied of his plainness," and wanted rites as well as rights, ceremonials, grandiloquent titles, exotic regalia, and comradeship.[76] According to David Brion Davis, "the subversive group was essentially an inverted image of Jacksonian democracy and the cult of the common man."[77]

There are always fresh waves of exclusiveness. As some forms of descent are thrown off as undemocratic fetters, others are invented, and groups based on ancestry are an American commonplace: pedigreed associations of the Sons and Daughters of the American Revolution, the Society of Mayflower Descendants, and the like; commemorative associations of survivors of the Civil War and heritage organizations such as the Sons of Confederate Veterans, which inspired the formation of groups of Jewish War Veterans, among others. Nativist anti-Catholic societies like the Order of United Americans and Brotherhood of the Union arose in response to the Ancient Order of the Hibernians, imported by Irish Catholics in 1836, and the dozens of Jewish fraternal orders, including B'nai Brith in 1843. The premier example of the dynamic is the American penchant for secret societies and the groups formed in reaction, to combat their "conspiracies"—the Masonic fraternity, for example, and the rabid associations, also secretive, organized to counter Masonic power. Exclusive associations generate resentment, reverse snobbery, and self-defensive affiliation in turn; every restrictive association spawns not only accusations that it is subversively antidemocratic but also the formation of counterpart groups, mirror images of exclusiveness.

I belabor this point because it is rarely noted. Except for in the political science literature on political interest groups and grass-roots community organizing, group formation is a relatively neglected aspect of pluralism, and in these writings the dynamic of self-respect and self-protection, snobbery and exclusion, has no place. The standard thesis on voluntary association in America sees the process as determinedly practical, stressing cooperation in socially useful tasks. In contrast to aristocratic orders, Tocqueville explained, the "independent and feeble" citizens of a democratic nation must "learn voluntarily to help one another." Collective action is a practical imperative, and he remarked on "the extreme skill with which the inhabitants . . . succeed in proposing a common object to the exertions of a great many men, and in getting them voluntarily to pursue it."[78] The heyday of association in America was the rush into clubs in the mid-nineteenth century: "The churches, clubs, lodges, temperance and reading societies of natives and immigrants encouraged social ties that made the formation of death benefit, accident, and unemployment pools possible."[79] This is the "civic culture" social scientists look to for the social capital that overcomes free riding and the tragedy of the commons. It is similar to pragmatists' enthusiasm for "communities of inquiry and practice" that generate their own internal discipline and organization to encourage the perfection of a craft, skill, or science, product, technique, or performance.[80] The Jaycees put themselves in this company when they warn that compelled association would have a "chilling effect" on their charitable works and civic activities.

This standard, sanguine view of association suffers from a naive liberal expectancy. It has always had its acid detractors. Washington's Farewell Address condemned "all combinations and associations, under whatever plausible character, with the real design to direct, control, counteract, or awe the regular deliberation and action of the constituted authorities," and accusations of faction, real or imagined, are leveled at every imaginable group.[81] Civic republicans follow Rousseau in devising schemes to eliminate "Hobbesian" self-preferring groups and the social hierarchies that get their foothold in private circles; clubs, lodges, parishes, and gangs "were not media which could nourish effective and inclusive community growth. [A] city of such private associations was a city of closed social cells."[82] There are innumerable "lapsarian theories of groups" as combinations of individuals corrupted by self-love. And romantic individualists see all joining as a pitiful lack of self-reliance. The usefulness of groups escaped Thoreau entirely; the best neighborliness is "minding your own business," he thought, and the true reformer is "one perfect institution in himself."[83] "At the name of a society all my repulsions play," Emerson confessed. "Men club together on the principle: "I have failed, and you have failed, but perhaps together we shall not fail.'"[84] In liberal democracy, romantic aloofness is as insufferable as exclusive groups; it too is perceived as aristocratic self-distancing, and generally despised. Nonetheless, romantic individualism points up the dark underside of gregariousness: dependence, craving for the good opinion of others, hypocrisy, and the desire of those excluded to join together and inflict the same on others. These are not just incidental accompaniments of voluntary association; they are among its sources.

The permanent dynamic of affiliation and exclusion is linked not only to the social and cultural pluralism of an open liberal democracy but also to the fact that our conceptions of social status are unstable. It is reported that "private social clubs with discriminatory membership policies are fast becoming extinct" (the average age of membership is sixty-two). The reasons doubtless have less to do with legal challenges than with changing ideas about social precedence. Freemasons, Shriners, Elk, and Moose are endangered species when groups of middle-aged white men are eyed with suspicion, and when prospective members find secret handshakes and the Moose's cape and tah (hat spelled backwards) laughable. The St. Andrews Society recently contemplated admitting women to their 237-year-old club dedicated to upholding Scottish traditions and Scottish charity. They debated whether the association could survive without women members or whether St. Andrews did enough for women already by allowing them to attend the annual banquet (seated at segregated tables in the balcony) and the Tartan Ball (where they could sit at tables with men). It is fair to suppose that potential younger members were not so much outraged by the group's discriminatory practices as put off by the fact that St. Andrews could not possibly satisfy contemporary desires for social status, and its affairs did not appear to be fun.

The contemporary "politics of recognition" bears a family resemblance to the dynamics of affiliation and exclusion, particularly insofar as theorists emphasize the variability of cultural group membership, symbolic boundaries, and "ethnic options." But at least among academic theorists and as regards cultural (not racial) groups, the terms of discussion are often idealized. "Identity," "recognition," the emergence of self-understanding from "dialogue" with "significant others" are maddeningly benign. We have lost Hawthorne's cold eye on the snobbery and malice of associations, whether they have power and privileges or not. Association and exclusion, the creation of boundaries that others regard as discriminatory and antidemocratic go on everywhere, except perhaps at the very bottom. Yet it is considered disrespectful to say that people who have been subject to discrimination want the solace and revenge of compensatory, exclusive, and sometimes hostile associations of their own. The dynamic of exclusion is a virtual taboo, or is attributed entirely to vulnerability and the contingent need for self-protection. The motivational root of members' expressions of affiliation with cultural groups is supposed to be the "epistemological comforts of home," not access to jobs and positions, social status, or sheer resentment.[85] Only rarely do we observe that language emphasizing identity and values "has often provided the excuse—as well as the emotional fuel" for action aimed at getting a share, fair or not, of social and economic goods, and not only at the top.[86] Sociologists may be wrong in describing the revival of ethnic groups in the United States as a self-conscious racist response to the civil rights movement and to celebrations of racial and ethnic identity by nonwhite groups, but they are right to be skeptical that these associations advance mutual understanding.[87]

To the extent that the public culture and institutions of liberal democracy are strong, and sentiments of exclusiveness cannot result in withholding legal rights and publicly available goods, the dynamic of exclusion will take the form of avid voluntary association. The dynamic is eminently democratic. Indeed, as gains in first-class citizenship by previously marginal groups and real security for public standing increase, we can expect to see the number and intensity of these associations grow too. The genuinely antiliberal, antidemocratic claim that "we" are the "real citizens" and others permanently second class because their inferiority is a matter of inherited or unalterable attributes will never disappear, but voluntary associations can contain even this discrimination, as the "safety-valve" thesis suggests.[88] What Rawls's picture of "noncomparing groups" gets wrong, then, is that the morally useful world of multiple associations and multiple hierarchies is one of comparing groups. Without this dynamic, which operates more freely in a liberal democracy than anywhere else, there would be many fewer sources of the "primary good" of self-respect—and less containment of irrepressible exclusiveness.

Coda: Democracy and Disassociation

The moral imperative of compelled association misses the mark. The critical dilemma for liberal democracy in the United States today is not exclusion from restricted membership groups but isolation. Genuine anomie is evidenced less by declining membership in traditional associations (others are burgeoning) than by the way ghettoization, chronic unemployment ("unemployment means having nothing to do—which means having nothing to do with the rest of us"),[89] and characterological impediments to sociability (among them aggressiveness and depression) put the whole range of associational life beyond reach. In the case of anomic individuals condemned to a "culture of segregation," both public standing and self-respect may well depend almost entirely on being drawn into voluntary associations. But these are the very people who lack resources for organizing groups and occasions for being recruited into existing ones. A newspaper report on the decline of the Loyal Order of Moose Lodge in Roxbury, Massachusetts, described the lodge's plan to give up its capes and to attract young men by launching a drum and bugle corps. The difficulty seemed immense even to the hopeful Moose: "If they're already into drugs, it'll be hard to get them into the drum and bugle corps."[90] We know very little about how to get socially isolated individuals to become joiners, still less about how to keep them. Accounts of recruitment by gangs and hate groups indicate that young men are not attracted to them because these groups reflect their own racist ideas and ambitions but simply because they are solicited. They have nothing better to do and nowhere else to go. Given this scenario, it is no surprise that the life span of membership in racist groups is short and that members cycle away, often into persistent disassociation and personal chaos.[91]

Recruiting the disassociated or supporting the creation of associations of their own requires intensive effort "on the ground." It is unlikely that the energy and flux of voluntary association can be directed from above; associations implanted from outside have a high failure rate.[92] Recognizing that indigenous local efforts are the most successful, government programs have sought to fill the associational void by exploiting every potential group as a basis for positive social organizing. One proposal cast street gangs as sources of social capital, if only they could be diverted from apprenticeship for crime and self-destruction. We can sympathize with Nathan Glazer, sceptical but stumped: "In the absence of the natural forms of informal social organization, what alternatives do we have"?[93] The terrible, palpable self-exclusion of anomie may be intractable. But if it is not, the process of association that is capable of generating stable membership and self-respect in anomic outsiders will replicate the dynamic not only of affiliation but also of exclusion, of "comparing groups." It is another reason—not sanguine to be sure, but familiarly democratic—to minimize legally compelled association and the logic of congruence on which it rests.

Notes

1. *International Association of Machinists v. Street*, 367 U.S. 740 (1961) at 775.

2. *Cornelius v. The Benevolent Protective Order of the Elks*, 382 Fed. Suppl. 1182 (1974) at 1199.

3. *U.S. Jaycees v. McClure*, 709 F.2d 1560 (8th Cir 1983) at 1576.

4. *Roberts v. Jaycees*, 468 U.S. 609 (1984) at 633.

5. *Democratic Party of the U.S. et al v. Wisconsin Ex Rel. La Follette*, 450 U.S. 107 (1980) at 130.

6. On freedom of expression and membership see *Abood v. Detroit Board of Education*, 431 U.S. 209 (1976).

7. Harry H. Wellington, "The Constitution, the Labor Union, and 'Governmental Action,'" *Yale Law Journal* 70 (1961): 345.

8. Cited in Douglas O. Linder, "Freedom of Association after *Roberts v. United States Jaycees*," *Michigan Law Review* 82 (August 1984): 1881.

9. See Nancy L. Rosenblum, "Membership and Voice," in *Membership and Morals: The Personal Uses of Pluralism in America* (Princeton: Princeton University Press, 1998).

10. Kathleen Sullivan, "Rainbow Republicanism," *Yale Law Journal* 93, (July, 1988): 1714–15.

11. Brief Amicus Curiae for the American Civil Liberties Union in *Roberts v. Jaycees*, cited in Linder, "Freedom of Association," p. 1880.

12. I will not take up the question whether gender distinctions are as invidious as racial distinctions and should be treated as presumptively unconstitutional. Federal and state governments have progressively broadened both the number of facilities and the groups covered; New York City's Human Rights Law covers the physically or mentally handicapped and individuals discriminated against because of actual or perceived sexual orientation.

13. *Norwood v. Harrison*, 413 U.S. 455 at 465–66.

14. *Hurley and South Boston Allied War Veterans Council v. Irish-American Gay, Lesbian and Bisexual Group of Boston*, 115 S. Ct. 2388 (1995).

15. *Moose Lodge No. 107 v. Irvis*, 407 U.S. 163 (1972) at 180.

16. *Board of Directors of Rotary International v. Rotary Club*, 481 U.S. 537 (1987); and *New York State Club Association v. City of N.Y.*, 487 U.S. 1 (1988).

17. The District Court found in favor of the state. The Eighth Circuit Court of Appeals overturned, finding in favor of the Jaycees, though it split sharply. The Supreme Court decision was unanimous, though Chief Justice Burger and Justice Blackmun, past members of the St. Paul and Minneapolis Jaycees respectively, took no part in the decision.

18. *Roberts* at 636, 638, 633. O'Connor's typology is amenable to different interpretations. On the first, constitutional protection is determined by whether an association's particular purposes or activities are predominantly expressive or commercial. O'Connor also suggests that even an expressive association forfeits protection by engaging in commerce, though it is unclear how much commercial activity gives the state warrant to intervene.

19. Brief of Amicus Curiae, 83–724.

20. I take up the other issues in *Membership and Morals.*

21. Appellants brief appeal from the U.S. Court of Appeals for the Eighth Circuit, 83–724.

22. Kenneth Karst, *Belonging to America: Equal Citizenship and the Constitution* (New Haven: Yale University Press, 1989), p. 4.

23. Peter Berger, "On the Obsolescence of the Concept of Honor," in Michael Sandel, ed., *Liberalism and Its Critics* (New York: New York University Press, 1984), pp. 149–158, 153.

24. For a discussion in the context of tort law see Robert C. Post, *Constitutional Domains* (Cambridge: Harvard University Press, 1995), p. 56.

25. Charles L. Black, Jr., "The Lawfulness of the Desegregation Decision," *Yale Law Journal* 69:427.

26. Cited in Judith Shklar, *American Citizenship: The Quest for Inclusion* (Cambridge: Harvard University Press, 1991), p. 56.

27. Charles Beitz, *Political Equality* (Princeton: Princeton University Press, 1989), p. 110.

28. Shklar, *American Citizenship*, p. 84.

29. Cited in *Wyman v. James*, 400 U.S. 309 (1970) at 332.

30. *Goldberg v. Kelley*, 397 U.S. 254 (1970) at 265; Sylvia Law, "Some Reflections on *Goldberg v. Kelley* at Twenty Years," *Brooklyn Law Review* 56 (1990).

31. Appellee brief, the United States Jaycees, in *Roberts v. Jaycees*, 83–724. The Jaycees argued that the crux is whether "private" association is a sham for excluding no one except a minority group. The class here is young men with like interests and backgrounds between the ages of eighteen and thirty-five. Jaycee membership is not a cross-section of young men, either: 30 percent are upper management and another 20 percent middle management, though far less than half the population from which Minneapolis members are drawn is either; in the St. Paul chapter no more than five of four hundred work in government, though of all cities in Minnesota it is the most heavily populated by government employees. The group does not exclude young black men (and does not argue that the right of association would allow it to if it would).

32. Deborah L. Rhode, "Association and Assimilation," *Northwestern University Law Review* 81 (1986): 106. Deborah Rhode argues that the Jaycees "perpetuate male hierarchies, not male sanctuaries" and favors a rule that would integrate all-male associations while leaving all-female associations alone. Legal differentiation is defensible because "separatism imposed by empowered groups carries different symbolic and practical significance than separatism chosen by subordinate groups."

33. Cited in *New York Club*, 487 U.S. 1 at 5–6, 16–17, 20, 21.

34. *Cornelius v. Elks* at 1203.

35. *U.S. Jaycees v. McClure* at 1572.

36. Linder, "Freedom of Association," p. 1890.

37. *U.S. Jaycees v. McClure* at 1572.

38. Christopher Jencks, *Rethinking Social Policy: Race, Poverty, and the Underclass* (Cambridge: Harvard University Press, 1992), p. 48.

39. Arthur M. Schlesinger, "Biography of a Nation of Joiners," *American Historical Review* 50, no. 1 (October 1944): 1–25, 23.

40. Grant McConnell, "The Public Values of Private Associations," *Voluntary As-*

sociations, Nomos XI, ed. J. Roland Pennock and John W. Chapman (New York: Atherton Press, 1969), p. 158.

41. Brief amicus curiae, Rotary International.

42. *Roberts* at 608.

43. Arthur Kinoy, cited in Karst, *Belonging to America,* p. 60.

44. *Roberts* at 624.

45. Rhode, "Association and Assimilation," p. 123.

46. *Rotary* at 538.

47. Jencks, *Rethinking Social Policy,* p. 40.

48. William P. Marshall, "Discrimination and the Right of Association" *Northwestern University Law Review* 81 (1986): 70.

49. The partial exceptions are religious associations and certain political groups protected by the First Amendment.

50. "Note: State Power and Discrimination by Private Clubs: First Amendment Protection for Non-expressive Associations," *Harvard Law Review* 104:1849.

51. Ibid., 1854, 1849, 1853.

52. Daniel Schwartz, "Discrimination on Campus: A Critical Examination of Single-Sex College Social Organizations" *California Law Review* 75:2123.

53. Karst, *Belonging to America,* p. 79.

54. Erving Goffman, *Stigma: Notes on the Management of Spoiled Identity* (Englewood Cliffs, N.J., Prentice-Hall, 1963), pp. 105–6.

55. Jencks, *Rethinking Social Policy,* p. 48.

56. John Rawls, *Political Liberalism* (New York: Columbia University Press, 1993), p. 316.

57. Iris Marion Young, *Justice and the Politics of Difference* (Princeton: Princeton University Press, 1990), p. 174.

58. Hannah Arendt, "Reflections on Little Rock," *Dissent* 6, (winter 1959): 45–56. For a discussion of the alternatives between shielding a minority or disabled child from dislike as a way of developing self-esteem and alerting and preparing her see Martha Minow, *Making All the Difference* (Ithaca: Cornell University Press, 1990), pp. 39–40.

59. Kristin Bumiller, *The Civil Rights Society: The Social Construction of Victims* (Baltimore: Johns Hopkins University Press, 1988), p. 109; this paragraph is indebted to her argument.

60. Jencks, *Rethinking Social Policy* pp. 48–49.

61. Bumiller, *Civil Rights Society,* p. 70.

62. Michael Sandel, *Democracy's Discontent: America in Search of a Public Philosophy* (Cambridge: Harvard University Press, 1996), p. 303.

63. Jencks, *Rethinking Social Policy,* pp. 127, 158: "No one has yet undertaken the kind of research that would be necessary to determine what sorts of jobs the long-term jobless are really willing to take".

64. Judith Shklar, *Ordinary Vices* (Cambridge: Harvard University Press, 1984), p. 88.

65. Arendt, "A Reply to Critics," *Dissent:* 179.

66. Erving Goffman, "The Nature of Deference and Demeanor," *American Anthropologist* 58, no. 3 (1956): 473–502, 479.

67. Cited in *Extremism in America*, ed. Lyman Tower Sargent (New York: New York University Press, 1995), pp. 271–72.

68. Rosenblum, *Membership and Morals*.

69. John Rawls, *A Theory of Justice* (Cambridge: Harvard University Press, 1971), pp. 441, 544, 545.

70. Cited in Schlesinger, "Biography of a Nation of Joiners," p. 24.

71. Werner Sollors, *Beyond Ethnicity* (Oxford: Oxford University Press, 1986), pp. 29, 175–76.

72. Schlesinger, "Biography of a Nation of Joiners," p. 7.

73. Steven Simpson, "Political Economy and the Workers," in *Social Theories of Jacksonian Democracy*, ed. Joseph Blau (New York: Bobbs-Merrill, 1954), pp. 145, 156.

74. William Leggett, "Rich and Poor," in Blau, *Social Theories*, p. 67.

75. "Hints to Young Ambition," in *The Complete Writings of Nathaniel Hawthorne* (Boston: Houghton Mifflin, 1990), 17: 241.

76. Schlesinger, "Biography of a Nation of Joiners," p. 15.

77. David Brion Davis, "Some Themes of Countersubversion: An Annal of Anti-Masonic, Anti-Catholic, and Anti-Mormon Literature" in *Conspiracy: The Fear of Subversion in American History*, ed. Richard Curry and Thomas Brown (New York: Holt, Rinehart, Winston, 1972), p. 64.

78. Alexis de Tocqueville *Democracy in America*, ed. J. P. Mayer (New York: Harper and Row, 1969), p. 604.

79. Sam Bass Warner, *The Private City* (Philadelphia: University of Pennsylvania Press, 1968), p. 72.

80. Charles Anderson, *Pragmatic Liberalism* (University of Chicago Press, 1990), p. 19, 23, 89.

81. Schlesinger, "Biography of a Nation of Joiners," p. 8.

82. Warner, *Private City*, p. 62.

83. Cited in Leo Stoller, *After Walden* (Stanford, Calif.: Stanford University Press, 1967), p. 17; in "Economy," Nancy L. Rosenblum, ed., *Thoreau: Political Writings* (Cambridge: Cambridge University Press, 1996) p. 34.

84. Schlesinger, "Biography of a Nation of Joiners," p. 20.

85. Russell Hardin, *One for All* (Princeton: Princeton University Press, 1995), p. 217.

86. Karst, *Belonging to America*, p. 89.

87. Mary C. Waters, *Ethnic Options* (Berkeley: University of California Press, 1990), p. 157.

88. Hannah Arendt made a similar argument in "Reflections on Little Rock," though she drew the boundary line in the wrong place, exempting schools and places of public accommodation. If discrimination is permitted in the social sphere and confined there, it is less likely to erupt and to color politics (she condones civil rights activity on behalf of voting rights) or personal life (the "most outrageous" violation of human rights is antimiscegenation laws criminalizing mixed marriage). "Discrimination is as indispensable a social right as equality is a political right." "Reflections on Little Rock," pp. 60–1, 66, 45–56.

89. Robert Kennedy, cited in Sandel, *Democracy's Discontent*, p. 302.

90. *Boston Globe*, May 31, 1993, p. 1.

91. See Rosenblum, *Membership and Morals*, for an extended discussion of secret societies and hate groups.

92. See for example, Daniel J. Monti, "People in Control: A Comparison of Residents in Two U.S. Housing Developments," in *Ownership, Control, and the Future of Housing Policy*, ed. R. Allen Hays (Westport, Conn.: Greenwood Press, 1993), p. 188.

93. Nathan Glazer, "The Street Gangs and Ethnic Enterprise," *Public Interest* 28 (summer 1972): 89.

Chapter Five

FREEDOM OF ASSOCIATION
AND RELIGIOUS ASSOCIATION

KENT GREENAWALT

THIS ESSAY about freedom of association and religious association concentrates on the constitutional law of the United States, but makes broader normative claims about associations within liberal democracies. I focus on freedoms that associations do or should have, paying special attention to whether religious associations are special. I also ask how associational ties affect certain claims of individuals to be exempt from ordinary legal requirements.

Although the reader should glean a sense of established standards and possibilities in American constitutional law, my main objective is *not* to provide a summary account of that law. Rather, nuanced differences in constitutional principles show how grand abstractions about associational freedom may be "cashed out."

Two initial distinctions clarify the questions I address. To say that an association should be free means that the state should not circumscribe its choices in certain respects. Someone who says that associations *are free* to choose members might mean that the law leaves them free or that a written constitution guarantees that freedom. Similarly, a comment that associations *should be free* might refer to an absence of regulation or to constitutional protection. This paper is mainly about protected constitutional rights, but other meanings of freedom dominate in countries that lack written constitutions.[1]

A second distinction is between rights as ideally formulated and rights as they should be formulated, given legally authoritative norms, cultural characteristics, and difficulties of finding facts and drawing lines. Someone might say: "Treating religious associations differently from other associations is not justified. *Some* nonreligious associations exhibit many characteristics that matter most for freedom and are common among religious groups. That is true, for example, of centrality in the life of members. Some members hold their nonreligious associations as dear as most members hold their churches, synagogues, and the like. Freedom related to associational life should not depend directly on whether a group is religious."

A person focusing on rights in the United States might respond: "Religious associations enjoy a special place because the First Amendment gives them one. Further, the United States Bill of Rights reflects historical truths that apply to many countries. Not including the family, religious associations have been by far the most important associations in their members' lives. They have also been the associations most frequently making claims that members owe a higher allegiance to them than to the state. This renders relations between them and governments particularly sensitive and makes them a crucial counterbalance to tendencies of governments to abuse power. Drawing a line between religious and nonreligious is complicated, but it is more feasible than determining which individual associations *really matter* to their members or which constitute a significant obstacle to political abuse. In light of such factors, some legal distinctions between religious groups and nonreligious associations make sense." Thus, while conceding that in some ideal sense religious associations might not warrant special treatment, someone might assert forcefully that that treatment is desirable in an actual constitutional regime.

In this essay the value of nongovernmental associations is, for the most part, supposed rather than explicitly defended. I assume that associations do not possess value that is independent of individuals. Some associational ties may be constitutive of the lives of members, but associations are valuable because they represent human choices about how to live and because of their influence on people's lives. Many purposes that people have can be carried out only in association with others. Associations are a crucial context in which individuals develop a capacity for choice and learn to deal fairly with their fellows. Political virtues of respect, equality, deliberation, discussion, compromise, and self-sacrifice grow out of associational life. Associations help prevent a tyranny of the majority and forestall absolutist pretensions of government officials.

A mention of these virtues of association reminds us that associations do not exemplify them equally. Indeed, some groups may have a powerful negative influence on the development of democratic political virtues; the Ku Klux Klan, the Nazi Party, and the Michigan Militia are not breeding grounds for liberal democrats. If associations contribute differentially to the life of liberal democracies, how should the law take account of this?

We can imagine three strategies. One is to make individualized, contextualized judgments about the value of associational life, giving benefits or exemptions to associations that contribute most to liberal democracy (and *perhaps* to independent values, such as human autonomy). This strategy promises a close link of social value and associational benefit, but it presents an obvious disadvantage. A government making such decisions about social contribution is likely to favor associations that support it. Given the conflicts and prejudices that often accompany governments' picking and choosing *among* religions, this strategy for religious groups is fraught with danger.

A second strategy is to distinguish among broad kinds of associations— religious groups, universities, opera companies, fraternal orders, and softball leagues. Some officials would make broad judgments about the places of kinds of association, but would eschew judgments among the same kind of association. This approach allows less refined judgments about the quality of particular associations, but avoids the difficulties that such individualized judgments carry.

A third approach is to identify valuable *activities* and to assist groups that engage in them. Thus, the government may help finance private hospitals, nursing homes, adoption agencies, and soup kitchens. No one assesses the *overall* quality of sponsors. Rather, officials decide how well a hospital is operated, and so forth. These judgments are less freighted and subject to bias than are general judgments about the virtues of an association.

I turn now to an account of constitutional principles in the United States. The general themes will reemerge as I analyze the central cases and constitutional possibilities.

My "methodology" in this essay may roughly be characterized as intuitive. I offer various judgments about what American courts would and should decide. Many of these judgments are controversial. Present uncertainties about religion-clause interpretation yield insecure foundations for estimates of likely decisions;[2] intense dispute about how cases should be resolved precludes agreement about normative judgments.

This essay is not the occasion to explore in depth the significance of my conclusions. For most of them, I provide arguments, but often without trying to explain why those arguments seem stronger than counterarguments. Sometimes, but not always, I could provide a fuller argument. When I indicate what a court would do, I draw on *one* specialist's sense of the development of First Amendment law. My normative conclusions rest partly on some notions of "fit" with settled law, but they also reflect my appraisal of how the law should develop. I invite readers to measure their appraisals against mine. Even readers not familiar with First Amendment interpretation can ask themselves which approaches fit their reflective ideas about associations in liberal democracies.

NONRELIGIOUS ASSOCIATIONS AND THE UNITED STATES CONSTITUTION: ROBERTS V. UNITED STATES JAYCEES

The United States Supreme Court's protection of the rights of nonreligious associations has two strands. Both are discussed in *Roberts* v. *United States Jaycees*.[3]

The Jaycees is a nonprofit corporation founded as the Junior Chamber of Commerce. Prior to *Roberts*, full membership was limited to young men, although young women could be associate members and participate in most activities. When the Minneapolis and St. Paul chapters began accepting women as regular members, the national organization threatened to revoke their charters. Members of the local chapters brought proceedings in the state, charging that the national by-laws were illegal in Minnesota. Minnesota, like many states and the federal government, has a law that forbids discrimination by race, religion, and sex (among other categories) in places of public accommodation. The Minnesota Supreme Court had determined that the Jaycees organization is a "place of public accommodation" within the meaning of the state's act.[4] The Supreme Court had to decide whether Minnesota's forbidding discrimination against women in membership violated a federal constitutional right of the Jaycees to select members as it chose.

Within the Supreme Court, Justice Brennan wrote the Court's opinion for five justices. Justice O'Connor agreed with only part of Brennan's opinion.[5]

Justice Brennan begins his analysis by distinguishing two senses in which the Supreme Court has referred to freedom of association. He writes, "In one line of decisions, the Court has concluded that choices to enter into and maintain certain intimate human relationships must be secured against undue intrusion by the State because of the role of such relationships in safeguarding the individual freedom that is central to our constitutional scheme."[6] The other line of decisions has recognized a right to associate to engage in activities protected by the First Amendment, including speech, assembly, and the exercise of religion. An example of the first kind of decision is *Griswold v. Connecticut*,[7] protecting the right of a married couple to use contraceptives. An example of the second kind is *NAACP v. Button*,[8] which held that the NAACP did not have to comply with certain state restrictions when it provided legal services to advance social objectives. In a somewhat confusing formulation, Justice Brennan also speaks of the intrinsic (intimate human relationship) and instrumental (free speech, etc.) aspects of protected association.

The Court's opinion first treats the principle that "certain kinds of highly personal relationships [must be afforded] a substantial measure of sanctuary from unjustified interference from the State."[9] It indicates that "certain kinds of personal bonds have played a critical role in the culture and traditions of the Nation by cultivating and transmitting shared ideals and beliefs; they thereby foster diversity and act as critical buffers between the individual and the power of the State" (618–19). Further, since "individuals draw much of their emotional enrichment from close ties with others . . . [p]rotecting these relationships . . . safeguards the ability independently to define one's identity that is central to any concept of liberty" (619). Given this language, one might suppose that many religious groups strongly partake of the elements of intrinsic association: they cultivate and transmit shared ideals and beliefs; they foster diversity and act as critical buffers between the individual and the power of the state; they provide emotional enrichment and contribute to the self-definition of members.

Justice Brennan, however, proceeds to suggest that "the personal affiliations that exemplify these considerations . . . are those that attend the creation and sustenance of family" (619). Families "are distinguished by such attributes as relative smallness, a high degree of selectivity . . . and seclusion from others. . . . As a general matter, only [such] relationships . . . are likely to reflect the considerations that have led to an understanding of freedom of association as an intrinsic element of personal liberty" (620). When one thinks about intense but not particularly selective religious groups, one doubts whether smallness, high selectivity, and seclusion are so tightly connected to the considerations the opinion has discussed. Subsequently, the Court notes, "Determining the limits of state authority over an individual's freedom to enter into a particular association . . . entails a careful assessment of where that relationship's objective characteristics locate it on a spectrum from the most intimate to the most attenuated of personal attachments" (620).

The Court's comments about the "intrinsic" features of association attempt to develop a general rationale for decisions protecting matters related to family. The rationale extends to other associations, including many religious groups, but the Court doubts that it will extend the same protections to those other groups. Since the Jaycees does not qualify, the Court equivocates about any extension, settling for a theory of the family cases that is vague and not satisfactorily concentrated on the family.

Justice Brennan next addresses First Amendment freedom of association: About this, he says, "According protection to collective effort on behalf of shared goals is especially important in preserving political and cultural diversity and in shielding dissident expression from suppression by the majority" (622). Interferences with the right to associate for expressive purposes may be justified by "regulations adopted to serve compelling state interests . . . that cannot be achieved through means significantly less restrictive" (623).

The Jaycees had taken public positions on diverse issues; a "not insubstantial part" of its activities constituted protected expression. Nonetheless, its constitutional claim fails. The state has a compelling interest in prohibiting gender discrimination in places of public accommodation. According to Justice Brennan, "the Jaycees has failed to demonstrate that the Act imposes any serious burdens on the male members' freedom of expressive association" (626). But even if there were an incidental abridgment of the Jaycees protected speech, it would be acceptable (628).

Justice Brennan links religious activities with other expressive activities. Someone who looked at the *Roberts* opinion alone might conclude that the constitutional status of discrimination by churches and other religious groups would have the same status as discrimination by the Jaycees, but that conclusion is highly doubtful.

Can the government conceivably regulate how churches choose their members and officers? Suppose a church openly discriminates on grounds of race, ethnic origin, or gender. One argument for absolute liberty is that the government's interest in ending such discrimination is not strong, that religious association is in a private sphere, more removed from public affairs than the activities of the Jaycees, and that discrimination by religious groups little affects ordinary political and social opportunities. But, given the central place of churches in many communities, I find that argument unconvincing. If religious bodies should have more latitude to discriminate than the Jaycees does, the crucial difference lies in their claim to freedom, not in the weight of the public interest in ending discrimination. Were the government to enforce standards of choosing members and officers on churches and like organizations, that would involve an unacceptable encroachment of the government in religious affairs.

Justice O'Connor challenges much of the Court's opinion. She claims that the Court's approach both overprotects and underprotects associational claims. She regards the Jaycees as essentially a commercial association. She notes that shopkeepers and labor unions can be forbidden to discriminate on grounds of gender, and that the state need only establish a rational basis (a much weaker hurdle than compelling interest) for that leg-islation. She argues that an association should be treated similarly unless its activities—in contrast to those of the Jaycees—are "predominantly of the type protected by the First Amendment" (635). Justice O'Connor also ob-jects that the Court's mechanical application of a compelling interest test would afford an association "engaged exclusively in protected expression" too little protection. She writes, "Protection of the association's right to de-fine its membership derives from the recognition that the formation of an expressive association is the creation of a voice, and the selection of mem-bers is the definition of that voice" (633). She implies that the choice of members should be absolutely protected for an association that exclusively or predominantly engages in protected expression.[10]

Justice O'Connor's approach would give political organizations the same protection in choosing members that I have suggested religious organiza-tions have. Hers is only one voice against five,[11] but *Roberts* is not a reliable indication of what a majority would decide about restrictions on member-ship choices of a genuinely expressive association, an association, for ex-ample, that limits its members to African Americans or women and whose overriding purpose is to promote the rights and interests of those respec-tive groups. Insofar as what divides the majority from Justice O'Connor is *how* absolute is the privilege of membership selection of dominantly ex-pressive associations, *that issue* is not yet settled.

Some Variations on Associational Claims to Discriminate

To test how extensive a right to choose members and officers should be and whether the religious character of an association should matter, it helps to explore some nuances in discrimination by associations. After briefly treat-ing discrimination that bears a close relation to an association's expressive aims or religious understanding, I discuss, in turn, discrimination that does not appear relevant to expressive or religious activities, discrimination that the organization itself forbids, and discrimination in relation to marginal activities.

Discrimination with a Close Relation to Purposes

What the opinions in *Roberts* mainly consider is discrimination that is the announced policy of an association and has some relation to its aims. The clearest right to "discriminate" involves ideological screening. A politically active group may restrict members or officers to people who subscribe to its purposes.[12] A religious body may accept only those who accept the tenets or practices of the religion. American law often forbids discrimination on the basis of religion, but makes an exception for religious organizations. Since statutes do not forbid ideological discrimination based on political or social views, no exception is needed for organizations pursuing political or social agendas. Should a legislature ever attempt to forbid a church from using religious criteria for membership or to forbid a political organization from using political criteria, such a law would strike at the very core of associational identity; courts would declare it invalid.

Resolution is not *so* simple if members or officers must be part of the group on whose behalf an organization is formed. Suppose organizations dedicated to the political advancement of women, men, blacks, or native Americans choose to restrict membership or official positions to just those persons. Since a man may care about the advancement of women, a white about the advancement of blacks, and so on, such restrictions are not exactly ideological. Nevertheless, most of those within an association may believe that only members of the groups they benefit can be trusted, or that one critical avenue of advancement is holding positions of power, for the purpose of formulating and executing policies uninfluenced by outsiders. For such discrimination by predominantly expressive groups, Justice O'Connor proposes more absolute protection than the *Roberts* majority.[13] Associations created for political and social advocacy need to compose themselves as they deem best.[14] Absolute protection of such choices is appropriate.

Religious organizations whose doctrines give special status to women or men, blacks or whites, should have similar liberty. The government cannot tell the Nation of Islam ("Black Muslims") to admit whites; it cannot tell a white supremacist church to admit blacks.

Discrimination with a Remote Relation to Purposes

When associations self-consciously engage in forms of discrimination, but outsiders can identify no important relation between the discrimination and the organization's underlying purposes, a right to discriminate becomes more debatable. *Roberts* indicates that when fulfillment of an organization's purposes will not be frustrated by ending discrimination, the state may require that.[15] Associations of particular kinds may put forward "privacy" or "expressive" claims against the application of such laws.

Since association itself is a valued activity, perhaps government intervention should occur only when membership significantly affects public and commercial opportunities. This was the basis on which New York City successfully restricted large private clubs.[16] What of a golf club of three thousand members that does not allow Jews to join and is near other golf clubs that do admit Jewish members? The club's position is that its members prefer to associate with non-Jews. The idea that people should be able to associate on whatever bases they choose, if they do not affect public life, certainly has considerable force. Still, this discrimination is troubling. If the club admits atheists, and indeed makes no inquiry about religious beliefs, the club's rationale cannot be that members want to associate with persons who share their religious perspectives. And, if the club screens for "congeniality," any assertion that "our members feel they would get along less well with Jews" can hardly reflect some valid generalization about personal characteristics. The assertion can reflect only a prejudice against Jews. The sentiment is a preference to avoid social contacts with Jews because they are Jews. Whether public and commercial opportunities are directly affected, such attitudes are not healthy in a liberal democracy. *Even if* the members assure us that they will extend equal respect to Jews in political and commercial life, we must doubt whether most people are capable of such a sharp dichotomy between semiprivate social life and public life. If it is said the state is powerless to change such attitudes, the answer is that bastions of social exclusion perpetuate attitudes within and across generations.

The state may argue that discrimination in such sizable social associations implements and reinforces attitudes that are undesirable within liberal democracies. It may also argue that large clubs do affect political and business opportunities, because business is transacted there and because membership in a "leading" club confers status.[17] The members' interest in associating with whom they please is supportive of a right to discriminate; but this interest is weaker than in small, close-knit associations like reading groups of friends that meet in living rooms. Whether a state should prohibit such discrimination is a difficult question. If a state adopts a ban, the members' constitutional right to associate should not protect their discrimination. The Supreme Court has sustained such restrictions against large New York clubs,[18] and one would expect the same outcome even if a law's application was tied less directly to trade and business than was the city's Human Rights Law.[19]

What of a claim to discriminate by a dominantly expressive or religious group self-consciously engaging in discrimination that bears no discernible relation to its purposes? To take the first possibility, imagine that an environmental group refuses to admit any African Americans, or bars them from official positions. Although Justice O'Connor's absolute liberty makes sense when an organization produces a plausible, substantial reason why its limits on members or officers relate to its objectives, other discrimination should not be regarded as carrying an absolute constitutional privilege.[20]

If the reason a religious group discriminates relates substantially to its basic tenets, its privilege to choose members and officers should be absolute, as courts would certainly say. Suppose the connection of discrimination and belief or practice is not apparent. Even for secular officials to judge whether purported religious reasons suffice to sustain practices of discrimination presents a real danger to religious liberty and separation of church and state. Choices of members and officers lie too close to the core of internal practice of churches to permit intervention. In other words, religious groups[21] should have an absolute right to discriminate even when others deem their grounds for doing so to be flimsy. This is probably what courts *would* say were the issue sharply presented.

Discrimination the Association Forbids

Can an association have any basic right to discriminate if it has announced that it does not discriminate on certain grounds, and an individual claims that she has nevertheless suffered such discrimination? Without showing any failure of the association to comply with its own *procedures*, a woman asserts that the group denied her membership or an office because of her gender. If *all* the state does is to enforce a policy of nondiscrimination in which the organization concurs, perhaps no serious interference occurs.

For religious groups, matters certainly are not so simple. The difficulty is clearest for officials, especially ministers and rabbis. The state should not dictate who leads organizations whose purposes are substantially transcendent. To identify discrimination, officials must undertake inquiries and make factual findings; they must decide that someone would have been hired if standard criteria for the job had been used. How can officials be confident that a woman was not hired as a minister because she was a woman rather than because of a subtle sense of spiritual qualities? No administrative official or court is fit to decide who should be a spiritual leader.

How to resolve some variations on this illustration is less clear. First, a local group announces that it has refused to hire a woman in contravention of the stated, and controlling, policy of its denomination.[22] Courts still should not order that any applicant be hired as minister, but monetary damages would be an acceptable remedy for discrimination that unambiguously violates the law and church policy.

Second, suppose a local church engages in a continuing pattern of passing over highly qualified women. Since people long habituated to male clergy might unconsciously suppose that women typically lack some central element for spiritual leadership or are unlikely to be forceful preachers,[23] then it may still be difficult to conclude that *self-conscious discrimination* has taken place. Because of the desirable autonomy of religious organizations, probably only self-conscious discrimination should give rise to recovery; if that is established, damages for the probable victims are the remedy.[24]

For most religious groups, accepting members is significantly different from choosing officers. Most groups are comparatively unselective about membership. Prospective members may have to undertake study, engage in practices, affirm beliefs. But no one makes a searching inquiry of their honesty or spiritual qualities. Those who have completed the study, accepted the practices, affirmed the beliefs, are received as members.[25] If African Americans who apply for membership are rebuffed, no one can doubt that racial discrimination has transpired. At present, membership in a church organization is not an interest the law protects. If the state forced a church with a policy against discrimination to take members, that would not be as troublesome as forcing it to take clergy, but the interference with church autonomy should still be regarded as too great.[26]

The state's latitude to restrict other expressive groups should be somewhat greater than what I have sketched for religious bodies. Suppose an applicant asserts that a local branch of a national expressive organization denied her membership on grounds of race or gender, contrary to national organization policy.[27] If the organization lacks transcendental or spiritual aspirations, public enforcement of nondiscrimination in membership is appropriate. Government should not require expressive organizations to place people in high positions, but damages for discrimination in choosing officers are all right.

Discrimination in Marginal Activities

Religious and expressive associations often engage in activities that are not obviously religious or expressive. The status of employment decisions that relate to such activities was raised when a building engineer in a gymnasium run by organizations of the Church of Jesus Christ of Latter Day Saints was fired because he failed to qualify for a temple recommendation certifying his good standing in the Mormon Church.[28] Federal civil rights law forbids religious discrimination, but makes an exception for religious organizations. Prior to 1972, the exemption covered only religious activities of those organizations; it was then extended to cover all activities. The Supreme Court decided that exempting secular nonprofit activities of religious organizations was not an impermissible establishment of religion. The majority offered the controversial ground that the law was all right because discrimination was by the religious group, not the state. All the justices united behind the rationale that it would be an interference with the autonomy of religious organizations for the government to decide which non-profit activities are religious and which are not.[29] Avoidance of that delicate inquiry was a sufficient reason to justify Congress's broad exemption for nonprofit activities.[30]

What about nonreligious expressive groups? Neither federal nor state law now forbids ideological discrimination in general,[31] but it could be altered to cover that. Expressive associations would undoubtedly retain a First Amendment right to use ideological standards to choose leading personnel for their expressive activities. The National Rifle Association could refuse high positions to persons who favor strict gun control. Such associations should not be able to employ ideological criteria for positions unrelated to their expressive activities. If the NRA had a gymnasium open to a wide public, it should use nonideological standards for building engineers. If Congress adopted a law forbidding discrimination based on political opinion and extended an exemption for all nonprofit activities of expressive organizations, such a broad exemption probably should not succeed.[32] The NRA could assert that the government should not decide which activities relate to expressive purposes; but the argument would be much weaker than it was for religious organizations. Most expressive associations are less all-embracing in their purposes than religious groups are, and the domain of their objectives is more comfortably assessed by public officers.

Present laws provide no exemption for discrimination based on gender or race. An ordinary expressive association lacks a plausible argument that it should be allowed to engage in such discrimination for activities that bear slight relation to its expressive purposes. The argument for autonomy of choice for marginal activities is somewhat stronger for religious groups, but the state's interest in achieving equality is ample to overcome it.[33]

Avoidance of Doctrinal Judgments

One interesting comparison between religious and nonreligious associations concerns a segment of law that is now well established for religious groups. In many states, when courts used to be faced with competing factions laying claim to church property, they would ask whether the faction that would otherwise prevail had departed from the basic doctrines of the church. This inquiry required courts to identify earlier doctrines and to assess their centrality. The Supreme Court, with the support of a much earlier precedent under federal common law,[34] has said over the last twenty-five years that such examinations are barred by the religion clauses.[35] Courts can say neither what doctrines are true nor which doctrines validly carry forward a religious tradition. When courts now decide whether a national or local church should control property, or which of two local factions genuinely represents the church, they must *either* defer to governmental structures within the religious organization *or* they must apply neutral principles of law, interpreting deeds, and so forth, without resolving disputed matters of doctrine. Although determining what are the authoritative bodies within a church may implicate doctrine to some extent,[36] courts are usually able to resolve legal disputes between religious groups without entering into debatable religious questions.

No similar principles apply to the resolution of disputes between factions of other associations. Given what the Supreme Court says in *Roberts* about the diversity generated by intimate associations, we could *imagine* a legal regime in which courts would not pass on whether parties are faithful to the purposes of an intimate association. Indeed, the movement in the law is toward *fewer* judgments about appropriate family life, as evidenced by no-fault divorces and recognition in certain respects of nontraditional families. But the state still largely defines the obligations of marriage and parenthood; and it identifies failures to comply in many instances.

Is the analogy between religious associations and expressive associations more promising? Suppose that an environmental organization has been given a generous grant to pursue the objective of preserving the environment. Somehow, the officers, backed by a majority of members, turn to support mining development and logging. A minority claims that they are entitled to carry on with the money because the majority has departed from the donor's objectives. The majority may counter that courts should not be deciding what *really* counts as environmental protection. There is some risk if courts decide which members of an association are faithful to a public policy objective, but the prospect is far less disturbing than are similar inquiries about religion. The inquiries are more manageable, and the intertwining of the state with a private organization less disquieting.

General Reasons for Differentiation

I have made a number of judgments thus far about appropriate treatment of religious organizations and other expressive associations without defending many of the differences I suggest. The crucial factors boil down to these: (1) religions make claims on the whole lives of their members; (2) typically they are grounded in beliefs about transcendent or immanent reality far removed from everyday human experience and ordinary political affairs; (3) forms of religious "reason" and justification differ in substantial degree from those used in ordinary affairs; (4) historically, ties between church and state have been divisive and have threatened both church and state; and (5) legal support for special treatment in the United States is provided in the religion clauses. It is, of course, possible to imagine nonreligious expressive associations that exhibit some of these features, but many do not. There is good reason, as Justice O'Connor explains, for the government to keep its hands off the membership choices of genuine expressive associations; but certain government restrictions on nonreligious expressive associations are acceptable, even though similar restrictions on religious associations are not acceptable.

Without undertaking a full examination, I need to explain briefly how I understand the fifth factor, constitutional law, as relating to the other four. On my own understanding, both constitutional cases and the conceptions of people at the time the Bill of Rights and Fourteenth Amendment were adopted point toward some differences in the treatment of religious organizations. Were I persuaded that approach is seriously unjust or unwise from the standpoint of political theory, as some commentators believe, I would, however, favor development of constitutional law toward elimination of difference. Thus, I do not claim the religion clauses somehow *require* differential treatment regardless of the strength of the other factors. For American society, I believe the other four factors (as well as constitutional law) incline toward difference in treatment.

Can one believe that religious groups should receive different treatment without supposing that religion is "intrinsically good"? In the history of this country, most people have supposed that religion in some form (if not religion in general) is intrinsically good for human beings. Someone who holds that belief, or who acknowledges that the belief is embedded in our culture (though not personally holding the belief) has some reason to support special treatment for religious groups;[37] but I contend that the factors I have mentioned have independent force, apart from that belief. They should be persuasive to someone who thinks religion is a matter of indifference and who places no weight on a contrary cultural view.[38]

Religious Groups Receiving Less Favorable Treatment

My discussion so far has focused on situations in which religious groups may have greater rights than do other associations. But in some respects religious groups do, and should, receive less favored treatment. Although the Supreme Court has recently held that state universities must finance student expressions of religious opinions if they finance expressions of other opinions,[39] most of the justices continue to assume that outright public funding of churches from tax money is impermissible, even if churches fall into some broader class of organizations that receive funding.[40] Further, government may not publicly endorse the aims of religious groups, as it may publicly endorse the aims of the Red Cross or the Sierra Club. The same factors that point toward more favorable treatment of religious groups for some matters also suggest a distance between government and religion that produces less favorable treatment in other regards.

One crucial lesson of a careful treatment of associational rights is the need for nuanced evaluation. Easy generalizations about how religious bodies compare with expressive associations are bound to be too simple. In some respects their basic rights are the same; in other respects differences are justified.

Associations and "Ordinary" Illegal Activities of Individuals

People who perform illegal acts sometimes make claims based on associational membership. Prosecuted for a crime or sued, individuals may assert a privilege to act as they did because of their religious beliefs and associations. For any such claim of a privilege, we can ask how claims in three other situations would be treated: (1) when an individual has a religious belief but no associational relationship; (2) when an individual is connected to a nonreligious association; (3) when an individual lacks either a religious belief or an associational connection. My analysis, again, mostly occupies the terrain of American constitutional law, but has broader implications for how governments should approach types of associations.

I first address possible exemptions from criminal statutes. The most important Supreme Court case is *Wisconsin v. Yoder*, decided in 1972.[41] The Court overturned convictions of Amish parents who had declined to send their children to school past the eighth grade, in violation of the state's compulsory school-attendance law. The Amish parents claimed that sending their children to school beyond eighth grade was contrary to their religion and way of life and would endanger the salvation of the children and themselves.

The Court recounted in some detail the separateness of Amish communities, their belief in making a living by farming and closely related activities, their strength as a community and their mutual support, their refusal to rely on public welfare, their effective informal vocational education which well prepares even those young people who subsequently decide to leave the Amish community, their objection to the worldly influence of education past the eighth grade.

The Court said it "must be careful to determine whether the Amish religious faith and their mode of life are, as they claim, inseparable and interdependent. A way of life, however virtuous and admirable, may not be interposed as a barrier to reasonable state regulation of education if it is based on purely secular considerations. . . . If the Amish had rejected contemporary secular values in the manner of Thoreau at Walden Pond, their choice would be philosophical and personal rather than religious and would not "rise to the demands of the Religion Clauses" (216). But "the traditional way of life of the Amish is not a matter of personal preference, but one of deep religious conviction, shared by an organized group and intimately related to daily living" (216).

When it turned to evaluate the state's interest in compulsory education, the Court accepted the state's claim that education is needed "to prepare citizens to participate effectively and intelligently in our open political system" and to be "self-reliant and self-sufficient participants in society" (221). It considered the Amish to be productive and law-abiding, and conveniently neglected the objective of educating citizens for political participation, which the Amish do not do. The Court also omitted to mention the obvious reality that someone who leaves school at the end of eighth grade will be at a distinct disadvantage in pursing a career (such as medicine) that requires extensive education, if that is what she wants to do when she chooses to leave the Amish community. The Court determined that the state's interest in compulsory education for the Amish children past the eighth grade was not great enough to override the parents' claim of free exercise.

Yoder was decided more than two decades ago. What is the present significance of the case, and how would one expect analogous claims that do not involve organized religious groups to fare? The *Yoder* Court indicates it would reject claims of individual parents detached from religious affiliation. It explicitly says that parents who adopted Henry Thoreau's philosophical rejection of materialist society would not succeed under the religion clauses, and it assumes the absence of any alternative constitutional basis to sustain the parents' claims. The Court prefaces its reference to Thoreau by saying "the very concept of ordered liberty precludes allowing every person to make his own standards on matters of conduct in which society as a whole has important interests" (15–16). This language, as well as the Court's strong emphasis on the nature of the Amish community, shows that the Court would not sustain a claim by individual parents, even one sincerely religious, if the claim is unconnected to membership in a religious group.[42]

Three strong reasons support making an exemption depend on group membership. Without a group, one could have little confidence that children withdrawn from school after the eighth grade would do well. One could also have little confidence that as they grew older, they would continue to endorse their parents' choice.[43] Sincerity is another problem. Some parents have an economic interest in children working at home after eighth grade. If these parents say that they have a religious objection to advanced schooling developed from their private study of Scripture, officials will have trouble knowing whether they are telling the truth. Very few people join Amish communities for economic gain. Membership assures sincerity.

What of the person who belongs to a nonreligious association devoted to a rejection of modern complex life? Suppose two hundred "Thoreaus," less individualistic and obstinate than the historical person, establish an agricultural community. Most members are atheists or agnostics, but all agree that modern life is too hurried, stressful, and competitive. They live a simpler life and teach that to their children. If they make a claim like that of the Amish, will it be successful? According to *Yoder*, they cannot make a religious claim; the Court implies that no other claim will succeed.

How would one appraise the present prospects of cases involving religious and nonreligious associations? *Yoder* held that when someone presents a substantial religious ground for not complying with a general law, the law can be enforced against that person only if enforcement against people like him is necessary to serve a compelling state interest.[44] In a 1990 case, *Employment Division v. Smith*,[45] a bare majority of the Court said that this was not the law, that if a statute neither is directed at religion nor discriminates among religions, the government can apply it against religious claimants without making any special showing. In the *Smith* case itself, the Court held that a general law against use of peyote could be applied to participants in religious services of the Native American Church, for whom use of peyote was the center of their religion. The Court stated that legislatures might grant exemptions for such use in worship, but that they need not do so.

Smith generated an uproar among religious groups and scholars. The upshot was the Religious Freedom Restoration Act, adopted by overwhelming majorities in both houses of Congress, which purported to reinstate the compelling interest test for review of religious claims for exemptions from federal and state laws.[46] In June of 1997, the Supreme Court declared that

Congress lacked power under the Fourteenth Amendment to adopt such a law.[47] The theory of the decision covers only the law's state and local applications. Some of the Court's language reads as if the law is invalid in all applications; but the decision definitely does not preclude similar statutes by state legislatures or a new federal law limited to federal applications.

Of special interest for our purposes is how the *Smith* Court treated *Yoder*. It did not conclude that *Yoder* was incorrectly decided. It said that *Yoder* was one of a number of cases in which religious claims had been linked to other constitutional claims; in *Yoder*, the linkage was to "family" claims of parents to control the education of their children.[48] Many readers, including myself, have assumed that this approach was disingenuous (creating a novel account of previous religion cases) and indefensible (if religious claims in combination with other claims can sometimes win, how can religious claims standing alone always fail?). But the account of *Yoder* might conceivably have relevance for nonreligious claims like *Yoder*'s.

Members of a nonreligious agricultural community opposed to education past the eighth grade might draw from what *Roberts* calls rights of intimate association. Perhaps the association of a family by itself might give rise to a substantial claim for parental control of education. Lawyers could trot out language of opinions to argue that the state requires a compelling interest to override parental convictions about schooling, but an unembellished claim of parents to preclude ordinary education of their children would not succeed.

A claim of instrumental or First Amendment association looks more promising. In our hypothesized community, keeping children out of school is closely tied to beliefs about the good life. The community's practices may be understood as a form of advocacy, protected under *Roberts* unless the state demonstrates a compelling interest. Alternatively, parental rights might combine with broad First Amendment rights in a manner similar to the combination of religious and parental claims Justice Scalia says determined *Yoder*.

Although one can build an argument along these lines, one would not expect success. Even if a court employed the compelling interest test, it would not afford the secular group a right to keep its children out of school. No such secular group in the United States could demonstrate anything like the continuity of the Amish. Nor could it present a dilemma over two years of schooling that would seem as poignant as that of the Amish.

I conclude that the particular right given in *Yoder* continues to depend crucially on religious association. Individual parental claimants would lose, and parents attached to otherwise similar secular associations would also lose.

Is such favored constitutional treatment for religious groups defensible? I think so. The free exercise clause supports it. If one accepts, as I do, the theme of other Supreme Court decisions that the government cannot formally promote religion over irreligion, favoritism for religious claimants cannot be justified on the ground that their views are right. But one can recognize that the transcendent beliefs of most religious groups create dilemmas more acute than those secular groups are likely to face. The two extra years of schooling will seem to make more practical difference, and the perceived danger to salvation of allowing the schooling will generate a more serious sacrifice. A proponent of equal treatment for religious and nonreligious associations might respond that constitutional principles should be neutral; nonreligious groups might lose but only because they fail to demonstrate painful enough dilemmas. However, courts cannot easily assess the precise pain of a dilemma on a case-by-case basis. Making religious association a necessary condition to avoid compulsory education is one sensible approach. Other liberal democratic societies might treat these problems somewhat differently; the approach of American law, as I have discerned it, represents one appropriate resolution.

Shunning, Boycotts, and Invasion of Privacy

Both church discipline and the aims of expressive associations can lead people to commit what would otherwise be civil wrongs. Does association make a difference, and does it matter if the association is religious?

Shunning

Some Mennonite and other churches practice a form of separation for excommunicated members. All members of the church shun the former members in business and social matters, and spouses avoid physical and social contacts with them. In many states, organizing a boycott of someone's business and encouraging wives or husbands to refrain from contact with their spouses are civil wrongs. For churches that practice it, shunning is an aspect of church discipline, enjoined by Scripture and needed to keep the church pure[49]. Members typically are aware of the practice of shunning when they join these groups.

Three broad avenues are open to courts. They might treat religious motivation as irrelevant, the approach of *Employment Division v. Smith;* they might make religious association a virtually absolute defense; they might engage in some serious weighing process of religious practice against general public need. The import of *Smith* for shunning is uncertain.[50] Although the Supreme Court has held the Religious Freedom Restoration Act invalid as applied to states, states may adopt the compelling interest test by statutes or by interpretations of their own constitutions. Common law doctrines that forbid shunning constitute a significant burden on the free exercise of religion; they should be applied against religious groups only upon a showing that they are necessary to serve a compelling interest. (This assessment is based partly on my opinion that *Smith* was wrongly decided.)

In the 1975 case of *Bear v. Reformed Mennonite Church*,[51] the Supreme Court of Pennsylvania adopted an intermediate approach favorable to the shunned former member. Robert Bear claimed that he had been excommunicated from the Reformed Mennonite Church for criticizing its teaching and practices and that church officials had ordered all church members, including his own family, to shun him. Church officials argued that even if all Bear's claims that he was shunned were true, the free exercise clause provided a complete defense. The court responded that "the shunning practice of [the] church and the conduct of individuals may be an excessive interference within areas of 'paramount' state concern, i.e., the maintenance of marriage and family relationship, alienation of affection, and the tortious interference with a business relationship" (341 A.2d 106). The court did not quite *decide* that the state's interests were strong enough for Bear to succeed, but a trial would establish little more on *that* subject. Thus, the court's decision that Bear's action should not have been dismissed prior to a trial suggests its view that the state's interests against shunning were strong enough for him to recover.

The Court of Appeals for the Ninth Circuit, in 1987, took an approach that was substantively different, although formally similar, in *Paul v. Watchtower Bible and Tract Society of New York*.[52] Paul, who had been "disfellowshipped" from the Jehovah's Witnesses, claimed that the group had caused emotional disturbances, alienation of affections, and harm to his reputation. The Ninth Circuit said, "We find the practice of shunning not to constitute a sufficient threat to the peace, safety, or morality of the community as to warrant state intervention."[53] It continued, "Intangible or emotional harms cannot ordinarily serve as a basis for maintaining a tort cause of action against a church for its practices— or against its members."[54]

The courts in the two cases disagree over a fundamental issue: Does the state have a compelling interest in the quality of life of individual adult members of society if so few people are involved that any influence on the larger culture will be slight? Without doubt, protecting a few individuals *can* constitute a compelling interest, in American judicial understanding.

When the lives of children are at stake, courts require medical procedures the parents do not want. And *Yoder* assumes that educational impoverishment of even a few children is something the state can avoid, sustaining the claim of the Amish parents only upon determining that children withdrawn after eighth grade will not be seriously disadvantaged in life. But what about *adults* who suffer harms that are less than death and that may seem less the state's direct concern than adequate education for children? The effects of shunning can be devastating in the lives of some few individuals. But shunning involves encouraging people to behave in a way that is legally permitted for each individual. It, thus, differs from physical assault, slander, and many other torts that are wrong even if committed by an isolated individual.[55] When adults have voluntarily undertaken membership in a religious group that they know practices shunning, the state lacks a compelling state interest in protecting them from the financial and emotional consequences of that practice. It is not that their joining the religious group legally binds them to accept any penalties the group may inflict or eliminates the state's interest in their welfare vis-à-vis the group; rather, their voluntary acceptance of membership reduces the urgency of the state's interest. The fundamental freedom to exercise religion should override the effects of shunning on former members who joined a religious group and were aware of that practice.

Disclosure of Embarrassing Facts

In the highly publicized case of *Guinn v. Church of Christ*,[56] in which the elders of a Church of Christ had informed the congregation and four surrounding churches that Guinn had been engaging in fornication, the Oklahoma Supreme Court adopted an approach different from those of the shunning cases. Guinn claimed an invasion of privacy and the intentional infliction of emotional distress. The Elders explained that "this process serves a dual purpose; it causes the transgressor to feel lonely and thus to desire repentance and a return to fellowship with the other members, and secondly, it ensures that the church and its remaining members continue to be pure and free from sin" (768).

The court distinguished between members and nonmembers. Guinn had resigned shortly before the church branded her publicly. The court determined that the church elders had no right to commit torts against nonmembers. The court emphasized that if a church treats harshly those who have fallen away, the religious exercise of individuals no longer convinced by a church's values will be inhibited. As the court put it, "No real freedom to choose religion would exist in this land if under the shield of the First Amendment religious institutions could impose their will on the unwilling and claim immunity from secular judicature for their tortious acts" (779).[57] For the court, the "victim's" religious liberty becomes an important interest that the state might advance to justify its restriction on the church.

Nevertheless, the court's disposition slights the church's concern directly for people who have been very recent members and its concern for continuing members of the church who may have further relations with the former member. Churches typically do not conceive of relations with members as just like those of any voluntary club; they have a special concern with those who have belonged and fallen away that does not apply to all nonmembers.[58] Those who do not approve of this view of religious association and believe that a more voluntaristic model fits liberal democracy better may argue that *courts should employ* the voluntaristic model, as preferable from a civil point of view. This is a difficult point; but, on balance, the secular state should not prefer one understanding of a religious community to another. Thus, courts considering how churches relate to former members should not simply presume a wholly voluntaristic model.

Apart from their concern for former members, churches may conceive a responsibility to inform present members that a person who has recently been a close associate does not have the character one would expect from the fact of shared membership. If members of the Church of Christ regard avoidance of nonmarital sexual relations as very important, they will care whether a former member has found some other church to be more attractive or has continued to commit a serious sin even after being privately chastised by the elders. In this day and age, most of us blanch at the prospect of church officials disclosing the sexual behavior of nonmembers to their congregations and other churches. However, this disclosure comports with the religious understanding of the affected church, and its concern for present members should carry weight.

The free-exercise concerns of the former member are diminished if she knew what kind of church she was joining. She may have chosen at Time 1 to become a member of church that puts strong pressure on those who fall away. If she becomes subject to such pressure at Time 2, her exercise of religion is interfered with only to an extent she understood was possible, and perhaps implicitly agreed to, at Time 1. Of course, people often make choices without full understanding, and they always make choices without knowing the future. A legal rule of "no divorce" restrains liberty even if it applies only to people who have married with full awareness of the rule. A former member's prior awareness of practices like disclosure does not eliminate concern with her religious freedom, but it does diminish the force of the concern. In the *Guinn* case itself, it was far from clear that when she joined, Guinn either was aware of how the church might treat members who resigned or should have been aware of that. Reasonable ignorance makes a big difference. This is yet another nuance in the delicate calculation of what should count as sufficiently strong state interests to override religious practices.

In broad summary of these shunning and privacy cases, we may say that the church's claim of religious liberty is important, that something like the compelling interest test is the measure a court should use to assess whether ordinary civil remedies will be available. My own view is that the state lacks a compelling interest when a church engages in practices of exclusion and disclosure against former members who were aware of those practices when they joined. Thus, religious bodies should usually be able to engage in these practices against those former members.

Nonreligious Associations

Should similar freedom attach when members of nonreligious associations engage in similar activities? The bonds of intimate association would be relevant within the family setting. One member of a family can advise a second member to withdraw contact from a third. But connections of intimate association would not justify someone's organizing a large boycott of a business or announcing a person's sexual behavior to a broader public.

The more significant inquiry concerns claims of expressive association. In *NAACP v. Claiborne Hardware Co.*,[59] the Supreme Court indicated that the ordinary law regarding boycotts of business could not be applied when boycotters were engaged in a political protest. Although sympathy with the civil rights advocates who organized the boycott may have influenced the Court, the logic of its opinion protects boycotters with other legal political objectives.[60]

Claiborne Hardware raises the question of what purposes are sufficient to make objectives political. Suppose that some people object to a local retailer's committing of adultery or they object to his taking a position in favor of busing at a public school board meeting. They organize a boycott of his store. Here, no political objection exists to how he is running the store. The only "political" message is that the retailer is not living by the right moral standards or has adopted a political stance unrelated to how he runs the store. Probably neither of these aims counts as political expression in a sense envisioned in *Claiborne Hardware*. Not every harm to someone's business because one does not like his lifestyle or politics qualifies as political expression in the sense that warrants exemption from ordinary tort liabilities.

We cannot yet conclude that the freedom of churches to shun is greater than that of political groups, because the Claiborne Hardware boycott was against an outsider, whereas the religious cases involved members or former members. For the storeowner boycott, religious expression would itself be treated as favorably as political expression. If a store owner ran his business in a manner that offended a groups's religious principles, it could publicize its religious objection by a boycott. If religious objections were to the personal life of a store owner who had never had any connection with a church and whose operation of a store did not offend the church, courts would not accept the church's organizing a general boycott that would otherwise be illegal. Perhaps it should matter *who* is encouraged not to patronize the store. If the church limits encouragement to its own members, urging them not to associate with a serious sinner, its claim of religious freedom would be stronger than if it tried to draw the general public into the boycott.

The more interesting comparison involves an expressive group boycotting a former member who joined aware of their practice. Should the nonreligious group have the same privilege as a church? Probably it will have more difficulty showing that the boycott is related in some crucial way to its associational identity and purposes; if it can show this, it should have the same privilege. One argument is that internal discipline within an expressive association should count as an expressive activity, or be regarded as closely enough connected to expressive activity to receive constitutional protection. The message that religions project to nonmembers is affected both by the quality of their members and the nature of their disciplinary practices, and the same may be true about organizations for racial justice or environmental quality. Discipline might plausibly be seen as an aspect of expression; but forms of discipline, especially those involving what amount to civil wrongs, are much less central than choice of membership to expressive associations, and typically should not generate a privilege to commit acts that would otherwise be wrong.

CUSTODY OF CHILDREN

Custody disputes raise yet different problems. One common setting is that divorcing parents make competing claims to custody of children.[77] Under the religion clauses, what relevance, if any, should courts give to the parent's religious beliefs and associations? If the basic principle is that the state should be neutral among competing religious views and groups, what implications does that principle have if the religious views of one parent require an upbringing at odds with what would be regarded as healthy under broad cultural standards? A comparative question can be asked about non-religious beliefs and associations.

The 1967 dispute of *Quiner v. Quiner* starkly posed the issues about religion.[62] I will disregard some features of the actual case presented to California's intermediate appellate court, which took as the fundamental issue whether a wife's religious beliefs and practices could in any way count as negative in the battle for custody. This problem is simplest to consider if we assume that a court is making an initial decision about custody, that factors other than those related to religious belief and practice tip slightly in favor of the mother, and that the overall standard for evaluation is the "best interests of the child."[63]

When the Quiners married, both were members of a group called the Plymouth Brethren. Disagreement arose and the group split, with Mr. Quiner joining a faction that did not accept the majority's move toward exclusivity and separation. Mrs. Quiner remained with the more exclusive group, of which her father was a leader. Mrs. Quiner believed she had to be "separate" from her husband, who "had chosen to be out of the fellowship." She could not eat meals or have sexual intercourse with him. She acknowledged that she would instruct her son, John Edward, in her religious faith and that if he accepted the faith, he would "separate" from the "spiritually unclean" father. Nevertheless, Mrs. Quiner said she would teach her son to love his father as a father and to respect and obey him.

The Exclusive Brethren of which Mrs. Quiner was a member, counseled children not to eat in the school cafeteria but to eat a box lunch alone, separate from their schoolmates; the children could not affiliate with any outside organization and could not participate in any extracurricular activity; they could not visit and play with other children; they could not have toys or pets; they could not watch television or listen to the radio; and they were discouraged from reading anything except schoolwork and the Bible. Adult members did not vote or participate in civic or government activities; they did not have television or radio in their homes. Mrs. Quiner attended religious meetings six nights per week and three times on Sunday, and she took her child to many of these. According to an encyclopedia on religion and ethics to which the court referred, women are not allowed to speak when members are assembled for such meetings. The boy might be converted to a full member as early as the age of six. According to the trial court, "such a schedule leaves practically no time for defendant to spend in the normal activities of mother and child in training, recreation and otherwise attending to her child's needs." Mr. Quiner also had Protestant Fundamentalist beliefs, but he did not live "separate" with all the limitations that concept entailed.

The court announces that the basic standard for judgment is "the best interests of the child," but it accepts Mrs. Quiner's claim that an award of custody to her husband "penalized her for her religious beliefs."[64] The court construes the federal and state constitutions as forbidding any legal penalty "imposed upon a person because of any religious beliefs which are not immoral, illegal or against public policy" (510–11). The court says it cannot conclude that John Edward will not grow up to be a constructive, happy, law-abiding citizen. It emphasizes that had the Quiners stayed together, they would certainly have been free to raise their son as Mrs. Quiner plans to raise him. The court would be opening a "Pandora's box" if it could "weigh the religious beliefs" of each parent to decide which is in the best interests of the child (517). It comments, "Precisely because a court cannot *know* one way or another, with any degree of certainty, the proper or sure road to personal security and happiness or to religious salvation, which latter to untold millions is their primary and ultimate best interest, evaluation of religious teaching and training and its projected as distinguished from immediate effect (psychologists and psychiatrists to the contrary notwithstanding) upon the physical, mental and emotional well-being of a child, must be forcibly kept from judicial determinations" (516). If John Edward is taught not to love and respect his father, or there is actual evidence that his "emotional and mental well-being has been affected and jeopardized," the court will be able to intervene. The dissenting judge objected to a result that will "with practical certainty . . . produce tragically harmful effects inimical to the welfare of the . . . boy" (518).[65] He points out that once psychological damage is actually done, a lifetime of remedial care may not undo it. He argues that custody should be awarded on the basis of "reasonable probabilities."

The issue posed by *Quiner* is not easy. Custody disputes differ from most other cases we have considered in that the state does not have the option of "staying out."[66] It must make a decision one way or the other.

We can identify four conceivable bases, all connected to religion, on which a court might rely to award Mr. Quiner custody. It might decide (1) that Mrs. Quiner's separatist beliefs are bizarre and unsound; (2) that internal aspects of the practice of that religion (for example, that only males speak at assembly meetings) teach implicit lessons contrary to the ideals of democratic citizenship; (3) that separation is so severe, a child will be ill prepared for ordinary life in this country; (4) that there are severe risks of the son's wanting to avoid contact with his father, or being harmed emotionally by the pull of the mother's beliefs against the pull of the father's love. We can quickly dispose of the first and second possible grounds. Secular courts may not decide that some religious beliefs are intrinsically sounder than others or base decisions on judgments about how well worship services and organizational principles comport with democratic ideals.

The third and fourth potential grounds are harder. Mrs. Quiner has indicated that she will raise John Edward to have much less contact with other students and with the external, general culture than he would have were his father to have custody. John Edward is too young to make any decision about what he wishes, and each parent wants a different upbringing. One might reasonably conclude that a child not allowed to participate in any extracurricular activities, not exposed to any television or radio, not encouraged to read anything other than school assignments and the Bible, will be less well prepared for ordinary life in our broad society. Of course, he may be prepared for life within the Exclusive Brethren, but suppose he leaves?[67] One might understand a court's judgment on these factors as being based on Mrs. Quiner's proposed social life for her son, not on any religious considerations. One might take the same view of Mrs. Quiner's encouraging separation from the father.

A comparison with similar nonreligious claims is helpful. Imagine a mother who said, without any religious basis or associational tie, that she would teach her child to withdraw from social contacts, not to read books, and so forth, and to separate from his father. Courts would certainly take this as counting against custody for the mother. If Mrs. Quiner belonged to a similar nonreligious expressive association, she might argue that the state should not penalize ideological beliefs and practice; but one would not expect that a court to regard itself as disqualified from assessing likely effects on the child.

We have to understand *Quiner* as effectively qualifying the usual best-interests-of-the-child approach. Its unexpressed rule of law is, "We will award custody according to what will probably be in the best interests of the child, except that we will not make judgments about projected plans for a child when those plans relate to a parent's religious beliefs and practices, even when the difficulty with the plans (social withdrawal and possible separation from the father) can be identified without any reference to the religious beliefs themselves and can be assessed according to a nonreligious cultural understanding about a healthy upbringing."

So perceived, the principle of the case is certainly debatable. The court's approach is not to take these factors into account absent clear evidence of actual harm to the child. A different approach would be to give such factors their ordinary force. Each of these contrasting approaches might be defended as "not taking religion into account." A third, intermediate, approach would be to consider such factors, but to resolve a case based on them *only* when they point strongly against custody for the parent with the unusual religious beliefs and practices. In a case that called the approach of *Quiner* "improvident," a court held "that the requirement of a reasonable and substantial likelihood of immediate or future impairment [of the child's physical or mental well-being] best accommodates the general welfare of the child and the free exercise of religion of the parents."[68] This kind of intermediate approach seems to me most appropriate. It avoids the nearly absolutist approach of the *Quiner* court, but ordinarily treats religious practices as something more than factors to be thrown into the mix with everything else that is relevant.[69] This approach is an analogue, or even an application, of the compelling interest test.[70]

Does it matter whether a religious parent is connected to a religious group? Perhaps not for the threshold determination of how to treat factors connected to religious practice. However, in the final evaluation of those factors, religious association will loom large. John Edward will at least grow up with the support of a like-thinking group. Imagine how difficult it would be for a child who is required to separate in almost every aspect of life and has no close association with anyone other than a single parent who is doing the same. In addition to the predictable emotional strain, the child's chances of eventually rejecting that way of life seem much greater without a supportive group.[71] As with some other areas we have discussed, the person who is connected to a religious group will fare better than individuals who lack associational ties or are connected to nonreligious associations.

CONCLUSION

I have examined constitutional claims that associations, or individuals connected to associations, might make. Even when individuals might make a claim on their own, without any associational relation, membership in an association may matter, and claims deriving from religious association will often have more force than those deriving from other associations. Among other associations, predominantly expressive associations have some special privileges under the First Amendment, but their privileges will not track exactly those of religious groups.

Lest my essay give the impression that association always matters and that *religious* belief is always crucial, I may mention that as far as claims of conscientious objector status to avoid military service are concerned, the present doctrine (built on a misreading of a statute) is that neither associational membership nor religious belief (in any traditional sense) is necessary. I believe this is a correct result on constitutional grounds.[72]

Valid generalization is difficult. For some areas of individual claims of free speech and free exercise, association will not be critical, or nonreligious sources will be treated like religious sources, or both. I have discussed contexts where these things now, appropriately, make a difference in American law, and I have concentrated on those areas in which rights connected to association are greater for religious groups than for others.

Part of the broad and familiar lesson of this essay is that the law often needs to draw lines that imperfectly capture all relevant considerations. I have suggested that a crucial line is between religious and nonreligious, and I have defended this line partly on the basis that religious claims are often perceived as transcendent. Not all religions make transcendent claims.[73] Nevertheless, in most instances the critical line is between religious and nonreligious; otherwise, courts would favor transcendent religions over others. Perhaps some room for direct consideration of the transcendent nature of obligations exists when a court assesses the perceived religious harm of complying with a secular law, as in the *Yoder* case, but in most instances religious groups should be treated similarly, whether or not they assert a transcendent reality.

Much of the essay has moved between the descriptive and normative and between the American constitutional order and liberal democracies more generally. I have not attempted to demarcate every comment into one of four boxes: (1) American constitutional order-descriptive;[74] (2) American constitutional order-prescriptive; (3) liberal democracy-descriptive; (4) liberal democracy-prescriptive.

Some final comments may clarify what has gone before. When I believe that what judicial opinions say or imply is misguided, I have said so. When I have suggested "courts will probably decide," without further remark, I believe that resolution is appropriate. I at no point have attempted a descriptive account for liberal democracies in general.

I claim that conclusions about the American constitutional order have wider normative significance, but it is usually of a particular kind. On the broad problem of treating religious associations differently from other associations in particular respects, my claim is that such treatment is reasonably defensible. I do not argue that in each and every liberal democracy that approach will be preferable to one that fails to make this differentiation.

NOTES

I have benefited tremendously from discussions of this paper at the University Center for Human Values at Princeton University, Marshall-Wythe School of Law at William and Mary, Tulane Law School, and the Harvard Center for Ethics and the Professions, and in a seminar on Church and State and before the faculty at Columbia Law School. Among individuals who have provided very valuable comments are Laura Brill, Amy Gutmann, Alan Hyde, Jill Fisch, Jim Liebman, Henry Monaghan, Gerald Neuman, Carol Sanger, Jeremy Waldron, and Ken Ward (who also provided helpful research assistance). Mark Hulbert also gave me most effective research help. I am grateful to the Center for Human Values for a very pleasant leave, which allowed time for work on this essay.

1. Yet further complexities are that "freedom" may be understood in relation to nonlegal social conventions and in relation to what international documents of various sorts may guarantee.
2. I analyze these, as of the summer of 1995, in "Quo Vadis: The Status and Prospects of Religion Clause Tests," *1995 Supreme Court Review* 323.
3. 468 U.S. 609 (1984).
4. In the American federal system, federal courts, including the Supreme Court, accept the interpretations of state statutes made by state supreme courts. Narrowing the state court's rather expansive rendering of "place of public accommodation" was, thus, not an option for the Supreme Court.
5. Chief Justice Burger and Justice Blackmun (both from Minnesota) did not participate; Justice Rehnquist concurred in the judgment.
6. 468 U.S. at 617–18.
7. 381 U.S. 479 (1965).
8. 371 U.S. 415 (1963).
9. 468 U.S. at 618.
10. Justice O'Connor says that the standard for whether an association receives significant First Amendment protection is whether it is "predominantly" engaged in protected activities; she seems to assume that an association predominantly engaged in First Amendment activities (such as the National Rifle Association) should receive the same protection as one exclusively engaged in such activities.
11. For someone evaluating the two opinions, the numbers are a bit misleading. Presumably Justice Brennan assigned himself the majority opinion after a vote in conference. (Since the chief justice did not participate, Brennan, as the senior justice voting with the majority, assigned the opinion). The Jaycees was going to lose in any event; perhaps the justices did not worry too much about formulating a constitutional test that made the Jaycees' case appear stronger than it might otherwise

have seemed. Justices joining the majority opinion may not have resolved all the disagreements among themselves and they may not have been overly concerned about nuances of language that troubled Justice O'Connor but had no effect on the outcome. Further, Justice O'Connor remains on the Court and Justice Brennan (and some other members of the majority) do not.

12. Many well-known expressive associations are ones in which policy is determined and implemented by a small core of officials. Ordinary membership amounts to the privilege of donating money and confers no genuine participation. These groups typically accept the money from wherever it comes, making no inquiry about whether those making donations understand and share its purposes.

13. In *New York State Clubs Association v. New York City*, 487 U.S. 1, 19 (1988), Justice O'Connor, concurring, commented "[T]here may well be organizations whose expressive purposes would be substantially undermined if they were unable to confine their membership to those of the same sex, race, religion, or ethnic background."

For discrimination that is on the basis of the message itself, *Hurley v. Irish American Gay, Lesbian, and Bisexual Group of Boston*, 115 S.Ct. 2338 (1995), establishes that a group ordinarily has absolute control over what message it will convey. On a debatable reading of the record, the Court concluded that GLIB had been denied a place in Boston's St. Patrick's Day–Evacuation Day Parade not because of the sexual orientation of its members (they could have marched with other units), but because of its message that people of gay, lesbian, and bisexual orientation should receive unqualified social acceptance. Thus, the state's application of its public accommodations statute to require a place in the parade for GLIB violated the First Amendment rights of the parade organizers.

14. When organizations representing dominant social groups exclude those who are already disadvantaged, that can be seriously harmful; but this is a cost worth bearing to ensure freedom for associations involved in political life.

15. The Court says in *Roberts* "that the Jaycees' right of association depends on the organization's making a 'substantial' showing that the admission of unwelcome members will change the message communicated by the group's speech." But it was ready to sustain application of Minnesota's antidiscrimination law even if the group's message *would be affected*: "In any event, even if enforcement of the Act causes some incidental abridgment of the Jaycees' protected speech, that effect is no greater than is necessary to accomplish the State's legitimate purposes." 468 U.S. at 632.

16. *New York State Club Association v. New York City*, 487 U.S. 1 (1988).

17. Asking courts to make individualized contextual judgments about the disadvantages of individual exclusion from particular clubs is unwieldy, so a law may properly bar discrimination in all large clubs of this sort.

18. It *is doubtful* whether the federal government would have authority to forbid such discrimination, since there are limits to what it can do under the commerce clause and the Fourteenth Amendment.

19. See also *Board of Directors of Rotary International v. Rotary Club of Duarte*, 481 U.S. 537 (1987).

20. This approach differs from what the Court in *Roberts* suggests in the following way. The Court assumes that a compelling interest for the government is sufficient to end discrimination in expressive organizations even if the organization has

some substantial reason to discriminate. Under my suggestion a compelling interest would be sufficient *only* if the reason to discriminate is not substantially related to the purposes of the organization.

It might be objected that this proposal would encourage organizations to adopt explicit discriminatory objectives. One answer is that many organizations would hesitate to do so. People might feel more comfortable excluding blacks than announcing that their aim was to protect the environment for whites. A second answer requires closer scrutiny of what counts as crucial objectives. An "objective" that is just a cover for discrimination should not be sufficient. More importantly, an "objective" that concerns comfort in association rather than expressive purpose should confer no greater constitutional privilege than a similar "objective" in the golf club example.

21. I do not mean to cover here central religious organizations, like the National Council of Churches, who represent many religious faiths. Perhaps they should have no more right to discriminate than do nonreligious expressive organizations.

22. I specify "controlling" because an organization might involve substantial local autonomy; the central denomination might recommend policies that would not bind local churches.

23. The academic analogue is worry that a woman may not be an effective teacher of large classes.

24. I say "probable victims" because even when a pattern is clear, a court may be uncertain whether discrimination mattered in any particular instance.

25. In *this sense* of unselectivity, groups that discourage converts, as do many Jewish groups, may not differ from those that reach out to acquire new members, as do most Christian churches.

26. Since membership, by itself, carries no economic reward, it is hard to conceive what would be appropriate monetary damages.

27. As for the religious organization, see n. 22 above. I am assuming that the structure of the expressive group makes national policy mandatory for local branches.

28. *Corporation of the Presiding Bishop of the Church of Jesus Christ of Latter-Day Saints v. Amos*, 483 U.S. 327 (1987).

29. Concurring opinions by Justices Brennan and O'Connor noted that the effect of the exemption was to interfere to some degree with the freedom to choose religious practices of employees who might lose their jobs because of religious discrimination.

30. The justices by no means decided that the earlier distinction between religious and nonreligious activities was itself unconstitutional.

31. Firing or refusing to hire someone because of positions about labor relations could violate laws dealing with that subject. In some states, firing people because of political opinions might amount to a form of unlawful discharge.

32. This is a very difficult question of constitutional law. Such an exemption could be defended on the grounds that the organization, not the state, discriminates and that the free speech clause lacks the "no establishment" content that would preclude discrimination. My position in the text requires rejecting the first basis for the majority's decision in *Amos* and discerning an antidiscrimination principle in the free speech and equal protection clauses.

33. I have dealt with direct restrictions on discrimination. A related question is when the government may, and should, remove otherwise available tax exemptions because of discrimination that offends public policy. The *Bob Jones* case (accepting a somewhat artificial reading of what the statutory word *charitable* entails) establishes that a religious university that engages in racial discrimination may be ineligible for an exemption. *Bob Jones University v. United States*, 461 U.S. 574 (1983). The government's interest in ending racial discrimination overrides any free exercise claim of the university to carry out its religious understanding of appropriate relations between the races. The Court's resolution seems appropriate in respect to independent activities carried on by religious groups; but tax exemptions given to churches *as churches* should not depend on whether such discrimination exists. See also *Gay Rights Coalition of Georgetown University Law Center v. Georgetown University* 536 A. 2d 1 (D.C. App. 1987), holding that a Catholic university need not grant official recognition to gay rights groups but cannot, under the city's Human Rights Law, deny tangible benefits based on the sexual orientation of a group's members.

34. *Watson v. Jones*, U.S. (13 Wall.) 679 (1872). At the time of *Watson v. Jones*, federal courts were not required to follow state common law; they could decide nonstatutory cases on the basis of judicial principles they deemed most appropriate. Under modern law, matters of ordinary common law are viewed by the federal constitution as within the province of states. Federal courts, including the Supreme Court, must follow state doctrines unless they violate the federal Constitution or federal statutes.

35. See *Presbyterian Church in the United States v. Mary Elizabeth Blue Hull Memorial Presbyterian Church*, 393 U.S. 440 (1969); *Jones v. Wolf*, 443 U.S. 595 (1979).

36. I was once involved in a case where the minority members of a local congregation of Plymouth Brethren urged that the religion was essentially hierarchical against a competing claim that it was congregational.

37. There is a complicating wrinkle. If one believes that the right religion is intrinsically good but others are intrinsically bad, and one acknowledges that the government may not favor one religion over other religions, one might conclude that religious groups in general should not receive special treatment.

38. Someone who thinks religion is positively evil might well resist any favored treatment.

39. *Rosenberger v. Rector and Visitors of the University of Virigina*, 115 S. Ct. 2510 (1995).

40. I discuss these matters in Quo Vadis, n. 2 above.

41. 406 U.S. 205.

42. However, in *People v. DeJonge*, 442 Mich. 266, 601 N.W. 127 (1993), the Supreme Court of Michigan sustained a free exercise claim that parents should be free to educate children at home without meeting teaching certification requirements. The Court assumed no sacrifice in educational quality was involved and noted that the vast majority of states no longer had such requirements for home teaching. The state requirements *were upheld* against a nonreligious parental claim. *People v. Bennett*, 442 Mich. 316, 501 N.W. 2d 106 (1993).

43. Justice Douglas was bothered in *Yoder* by the possibility that the children involved might have beliefs different from those of their parents, but the rest of the Court assumed a congruence of outlook.

44. However, the compelling interest standard was applied with much less stringency in religious liberty cases than in free speech and equal protection cases.

45. 110 S. Ct. 1595 (1990).

46. Religious Freedom Restoration Act of 1993, Pub. L. No. 103– 141, sec. 2, 107 (Stat. 1488, codified at 42 U.S.C.A. sec. 2000bb-2000bb-4 (Law. Co-op. Supp. 1994).

47. *City of Boerne v. Flores*, 117 S. Ct. 2157.

48. That parents have some such rights was supported by two cases from the early 1920s holding that states cannot deny parents the opportunity to have their children educated in private schools and instructed in the German language. Thus, state statutes requiring all children to be educated in public school and forbidding instruction in the German language were unconstitutional. Justice Scalia's opinion in *Smith* raises the possibility that these decisions may stand on some general (substantive due process) principle of parental rights. However, the point of the opinion is that religious exercise claims will succeed only when combined with other constitutional grounds, not to suggest that the other grounds will usually be sufficient by themselves. The decisions were rendered before the Court had applied most of the Bill of Rights against the states and were based on a general doctrine of substantive due process under which courts reviewed a wide range of interferences with liberty. In the 1930s, this substantive due process review shriveled to insignificance, and most people have thought since that the results of the earlier decisions could be defended only on the basis of religious exercise and broader freedom of thought and speech.

49. Even among churches that separate themslves from the rest of the society, former members are then excluded more rigorously than people who have never been members. For example, members typically engage in some business relations with nonmembers, and wives and husbands whose spouses have never been members will be able to continue marital relations with them.

50. It might be argued that shunning has to do with the organization of membership, an internal church affair; but it is hard to see why a church should have more latitude in dealing with excommunicated members than in determining its basic worship service, the issue in *Smith*. Another possible argument for avoiding *Smith* is that shunning involves religious exercise *and* expression, making the claim on its behalf a combination claim somewhat like that involved in *Yoder*.

51. 462 Pa. 330, 341 A.2d 105 (1975).

52. 819 F. 2d 875 (9th Cir. 1987).

53. The court drew from language of *Sherbert v. Verner*, 374 U.S. 398 (1963), a case holding that unemployment compensation could not be denied for an unwillingness to work on Saturday if the unwillingness was based on religious convictions.

54. 819 F. 2d at 883.

55. That the wrongs committed by the shunning of former members do not impinge on vital state interests is shown by the infrequency of recovery for group boycotts that are not motivated by economic gain and by the abolition of recovery for alienation of affections in many states.

56. 775 P.2d 766 (1989).

57. Ibid. at 779. Judge Wilson, in a separate opinion, also emphasized the claimant's religious freedom and suggested that if she were not protected, the court would be aiding the church in violation of the establishment clause (at 790).

58. This differentiation is acute in at least some understandings of Islam, which acknowledge much greater religious freedom in those who have never been Muslims than in those who have once adhered to the faith.

59. 458 U.S. 886 (1982).

60. In *Federal Trade Commission v. Superior Court Trial Lawyers Association*, 483 U.S. 411 (1990), the Supreme Court declined to protect boycotters whose immediate objective was their own economic advantage.

61. Another issue about religion is whether one parent may take a child to religious services if the child is being raised in the religion of the other parent. See, e.g., *Pater v. Pater*, 63 Ohio St. 3d 393, 588 N.E.2d 794 (1992); and *Zummo v. Zummo*, 574 A.2d 1130 (Pa. Super. 1990). Still a different kind of custody question is whether adherence to the religion of natural parents or others previously having custody should count in favor of a claim to custody. That issue is most troublesome when the child is too young to have yet had any religious upbringing.

62. 59 Cal. Rptr. 503.

63. In the actual case, John Edward, the child, had spent the years from two and a half to five with his father, in accord with the trial court's award of custody. The appellate court treated the then existing law as requiring a grant of custody of a child of tender years to a fit mother, barring truly extraordinary circumstances. That approach is now regarded as violative of the equal protection clause, under which women and men must be treated equally in respect to custody. Mothers continue to receive custody of small children in the vast majority of circumstances, but courts do not invoke any nearly automatic principle. Finally, appellate courts generally defer to the discretion of trial courts that have decided on custody. An appellate court may accept a custody determination different from the one it would have made itself.

64. 59 Cal. Rptr. at 510.

65. Dissenting opinion of J. Herndon.

66. This also is true of property disputes between factions of churches.

67. For this aspect of the inquiry, the track record of the Exclusive Brethen might be relevant. If *most children* reared in this and similar groups remain within the fold, the risk of poor preparation may be tolerable. If most children eventually leave such groups, the chances are high that John Edward's rearing will leave him less well prepared for the life he will eventually choose.

68. In re *Marriage of Hadeen*, 619 P.2d 374, 382 (Ct. App. Wash., Div. 1 1980). See In re *Marriage of Short*, 698 P.2d 1310, 1313 (Colo. Sup. Ct. 1985); *Morris v. Morris*, 271 Pa. Super. 19, 412 A.3d 139, 144 (1979).

69. A case that approximates this position is *Petersen v. Rogers*, 433 S.E.2d 770 (N.C. App. 1970). See also *Pater v. Pater*, 63 Ohio St. 3d 393, 588 N.E.2d 794 (1992).

70. One might conclude that the state has a compelling interest in seeing that individual children, in those rare cases in which factors related to religion strongly tip the balance, have custody determined in accord with their best interests.

71. Another consideration, although not one a court is likely explicitly to rely upon, is that an individual who arrives at such beliefs on her own is much more likely to be viewed as emotionally unstable than someone who has participated in group life. (In Mrs. Quiner's case, the leadership of her father provided a quite natural explanation of why she was attached to the group she was.)

72. See Kent Greenawalt, *Conflicts of Law and Morality*, (New York: Oxford Uni-

versity Press 1987), pp. 322–28. A relatively recent case has held that an exemption from required membership in labor unions was invalid because the law was limited to members of religious groups that had been historically conscientiously opposed to membership. *Wilson v. NLRB*, 920 F.2d 1282 (6th Cir.), cert. den., 112 S.Ct. 3025 (1992).

73. On the complex question of what count as religions for American constitutional purposes, see K. Greenawalt, "Religion as a Concept in Constitutional Law," *California Law Review* 72 (1984).

74. By "descriptive," I mean here to include not only an account of what courts have said, but also predictions of what they will say and do.

Chapter Six

RIGHTS, REASONS, AND FREEDOM
OF ASSOCIATION

PETER DE MARNEFFE

IN *On Liberty*, Mill identifies "liberty of combination" as one of the liberties essential to a free society—along with liberty of thought and discussion and liberty of tastes and pursuits—and he argues that as such it is wrong for the government to limit this liberty to prevent adults from harming themselves.[1] Rawls too identifies freedom of association as a basic liberty[2]—along with freedom of thought, liberty of conscience, freedom of the person, and political liberty—and he argues that as such it is wrong for the government to limit this liberty either to promote human excellence or the welfare of society as a whole.[3] To identify freedom of association as a fundamental liberty within the liberal tradition is thus to claim that it is wrong for the government to interfere with this liberty for certain reasons.

Do these constraints on reasons apply equally to *all* forms of association, though, or only to some of them? Suppose we think that the freedom of two single adults to enter into a monogamous marriage with each other is a fundamental liberty, and that it is therefore wrong for the government to prohibit them from doing so either for their own good or for the good of society. Must we also agree that it is wrong for the government to prohibit polygamy either for the good of women who might enter into polygynous marriages or for the welfare of society as a whole?[4] It seems that the constraints on reasons identified by Mill and Rawls might apply only to some forms of association and not to others, which raises the question, to which forms of association do they apply and why?

Freedom of association is not the only fundamental liberty about which we could ask this question. We could ask about liberty of thought and discussion; does it include the freedom to post obscene images on the Internet as well as the freedom to read and discuss the *Communist Manifesto*? We could ask about freedom of conscience; does it include the freedom to take cocaine for recreation as well as the freedom to take communion? We could ask about freedom of the person; does it include the freedom to sell sexual favors as well as the freedom from involuntary servitude? There is nothing especially problematic about freedom of association, then. Still, it is worth examining freedom of association as a particular case of fundamental liberty, both to see what we learn about freedom of association itself and the nature of fundamental liberty in general.

RIGHTS

To identify a general category of liberty as fundamental is to claim that there are moral rights against government interference with certain specific liberties that are naturally thought to fall within this general category; and to claim that there is a *moral right* against government interference with a specific liberty is to claim it is morally wrong for the government to interfere with this liberty *for certain reasons*. For instance, to claim that freedom of expression is a fundamental liberty is to claim, among other things, that there are moral rights against government interference with freedom of political speech, where this is to claim that it is morally wrong for the government to limit the expression of beliefs about the wisdom of government policy for certain reasons—that their content offends or upsets people, for example.

Some may think of rights as "absolute," believing that to say that there is a *right* to some liberty is to say that the government may not interfere with this liberty for *any* reason. But if this is how rights are understood, there are virtually no rights to liberty—because for virtually every liberty there will be *some* morally sufficient reason for the government to interfere with it. Consider freedom of political speech. If there are any rights to liberty, there is a right to this one, and yet it seems morally permissible for the government to limit even this liberty for *some* reasons—to prevent the communication of information on how to build weapons of mass destruction, for example. To say that there is a moral right against government interference with a liberty is not to say that it is wrong for the government to interfere with this liberty for *every* reason, then; it is only to say that it is wrong for the government to interfere with this liberty for *some* reasons.[5]

Now, there are two different ways in which it might be wrong for the government to interfere with a liberty for a certain reason. First, the reason to interfere might be a bad reason in itself. That is, the proposition that purportedly supports the judgment that the government ought to interfere is false or inadequately supported,[6] or, while true and adequately supported, it fails to provide any support to the judgment that the government ought to interfere. Consider the reason to prohibit the public expression of certain political beliefs that their expression will result in revolution. If this proposition is false or inadequately supported, then it is a bad reason in itself for government interference. Or consider the reason to prohibit the public expression of certain political beliefs that they contradict some ancient religious text. Even if true and adequately supported, this proposition alone provides no support at all to the judgment that the government ought to interfere with their expression. These are bad reasons in themselves for government interference, then, and it is therefore morally wrong for the government to interfere for these reasons.

The second way in which it might be wrong for the government to interfere with a liberty for a certain reason is that while it is a good reason in itself for interference—it is adequately supported and supports the judgment that the government ought to interfere—there is a reason against interference that has *moral priority* over this reason to interfere. A reason against interference with a liberty has *moral priority* over a reason to interfere, on my view, if it identifies a burden that interference would impose on someone that is substantially worse than any burden imposed on someone by noninterference that is identified by the reason to interfere. Consider, for example, the reason against prohibiting the public expression of beliefs about the wisdom of government policy that it will make it difficult for those who hold these beliefs to influence the political process in ways favorable to their legitimate interests. This reason identifies a burden that is substantially worse than the burden of being upset by hearing these beliefs expressed. So there is a reason against interference with the freedom to publicly express beliefs about the wisdom of government policy that has moral priority over the reason to interfere that the expression of these beliefs upsets people, and it is therefore morally wrong for the government to interfere with this freedom for this reason.

When the government interferes with a liberty for a reason that is a bad reason in itself, it violates a general moral right, which I will call the *right against arbitrary government interference*. When, on the other hand, the government interferes with a liberty for a reason that is a good reason in itself, but there is a reason against interference with this liberty that has moral priority over this reason to interfere, then there is a *specific moral right* against government interference with this liberty. To claim that a general category of liberty, such as freedom of association, is fundamental is to say that there are specific moral rights of this kind against interference with specific forms of association. The question raised at the outset, then, is which specific moral rights of this kind are there and why?

Fundamental liberties, it might be said, are those whose recognition and protection is essential to democracy. This suggests that in order to determine what specific rights to association there are we need only consider what specific freedoms of association are essential to democracy. Broadly understood, however, "democracy" is just a political regime in which individuals' moral rights are recognized and protected. So to know what freedoms of association are "essential to democracy" in this broad sense we must already know what specific moral rights to association there are. We might interpret "democracy" more narrowly to mean only a political regime in which the political process is open, free, and fair. But then the criterion of being "essential to democracy" would fail to identify the moral rights there are to freedom of religious or intimate association. This is because only freedom of political association is essential to democracy in this narrow sense. The notion of being essential to democracy does not help much, then, in answering the question of what specific associational rights there are.

Liberal theories of rights to liberty suggest a different approach. They suggest that to determine what specific rights there are to freedom of association we should reason from general principles that prohibit the government from limiting any form of freedom of association for certain kinds of reason. Thus Mill suggests it is always wrong for the government to limit a person's freedom of voluntary association for his or her own good; and Rawls suggests that it is always wrong for the government to limit a person's freedom of voluntary association to promote human excellence or the general welfare. In this essay, I will consider two general principles of this kind. The first is that it is wrong for the government to interfere with voluntary associations for reasons of equality. The second is that it is wrong for the government to interfere with voluntary associations for paternalistic reasons. I will argue that neither of these general principles is correct. While it is morally wrong for the government to interfere with some forms of association for these reasons, it is not wrong for it to interfere with every form.

If this is correct, we must wonder whether there is any correct general account of associational rights. I will argue that there is not. That is, I will argue there is no smallish set of general principles that correctly tells us what specific moral rights there are against government interference with freedom of association. To determine what specific moral rights there are, we must consider the good reasons that exist to interfere with each specific form of freedom of association and then consider whether or not there is some reason against interference that has moral priority over these reasons to interfere. If so, then there is a specific moral right against this form of interference; if not, there is no such right.

FREEDOM AND EQUALITY

One of the practical tasks for political philosophy in modern democracies, it is sometimes said, is to reconcile the conflicting claims of freedom and equality.[7] This conflict arises because there are good reasons of equality for the government to interfere with individual liberty. There is a good reason of equality for the government to require the Roman Catholic Church to ordain women as priests, for example, because the church's policy of ordaining only men deprives women of important opportunities. Interference with this liberty would interfere with the freedom of conscience of members of the Catholic Church, however. How, then, are conflicts of this kind between freedom of association and equality of opportunity to be resolved—in favor of freedom or equality?

Rawls endorses a general principle that he calls "the priority of liberty," according to which the government should not limit a basic liberty except better to protect a basic liberty or to make the system of basic liberty as a whole more secure,[8] and he identifies freedom of association as a basic liberty.[9] The priority of liberty thus implies that the government should never limit freedom of association to promote social and economic equality.[10] But this seems implausible without a qualification. Consider the freedom of restaurant owners not to serve members of racial minorities in their restaurants. It seems permissible for the government to interfere with *this* form of freedom of association, not only better to protect basic liberties, but also to promote social and economic equality. The priority of liberty does not seem valid, then, as a completely general principle ordering freedom of association and equality of opportunity in every case of conflict.

Here it is natural to respond that the *basic liberty* of freedom of association is properly understood to include only the freedoms of political, religious, and intimate association, and not the freedoms of commercial association. Rawls's priority of liberty would then imply that while it is wrong for the government to interfere with the freedom of the Roman Catholic Church not to ordain women as priests, it is not wrong for the government to interfere with the freedom of restaurant owners not to serve members of racial minorities, which seems right. Can we address conflicts between freedom of association and equality of opportunity by appeal to Rawls's priority of liberty, then, once the basic liberty of freedom of association is interpreted in this way?

There are at least three difficulties with leaving the matter here. First, it is doubtful that it *is* always wrong for the government to interfere with religious associations to promote equality of opportunity. Consider laws that prohibit religious colleges from refusing to admit members of racial minorities, or effectively do so by removing funding or tax exemptions from colleges that have discriminatory admissions policies. It is doubtful that this form of interference with freedom of association is wrong even though the association in question is in some sense religious. Second, it is questionable whether it is always permissible for the government to interfere with commercial associations to promote equality. Consider the casting of actors in movies. Even though the association between actor and producer is a form of commercial association and the hiring patterns of production companies may not provide as many good acting opportunities for women as for men, there may be good reasons of artistic integrity against forcing production companies to hire as many women actors as men actors that have moral priority over the reasons of equality to interfere. We cannot assume, then, that just because a form of association is commercial that it is permissible for the government to interfere with it to promote equality. Finally, once the basic liberty of freedom of association is interpreted to include freedom of political, religious, and intimate association, but not commercial association, the priority of liberty leaves some conflicts that arise between freedom of association and equality of opportunity unresolved. Consider laws that would require private social clubs to admit women as members to promote equality of business opportunity. Social clubs are not forms of political, religious, or intimate association, but they are not forms of commercial association either. So the priority of liberty does not resolve this conflict between freedom and equality once interpreted in this way.

These difficulties with addressing conflicts between freedom of association and equality of opportunity by reference to a general principle like Rawls's priority of liberty suggest that we should approach conflicts between freedom of association and equality of opportunity case by case. What I will do in the rest of this section is to consider three specific freedoms of association and consider whether it is permissible for the government to interfere with these specific freedoms of association for reasons of equality. They are the freedom of law firms not to hire women as lawyers; the freedom of private social clubs not to admit women as members; and the freedom of the Roman Catholic Church not to ordain women as priests.

It is natural to make a distinction between public and private associations and argue that while it is permissible for the government to interfere to promote equality with associations, such as the military, which it creates and maintains, it is not permissible for the government to interfere to promote equality with associations, such as private law firms, which it does not create or maintain. If my account of moral rights to liberty is correct, however, there is nothing wrong with government interference with private associations to promote equality unless it imposes a burden on someone that is substantially worse than the burdens of noninterference identified by the reasons of equality to interfere. And this is presumably not always the case.

Once we allow that the government may interfere with private as well as public associations, however, it may seem that the three cases I have just mentioned stand or fall together. It may seem that if it is permissible for the government to interfere with the freedom of law firms to hire only men to promote the equality of women, it must also be permissible for the government to interfere with the freedom of private social clubs to admit only men as members, and with the freedom of the Roman Catholic Church to ordain only men as priests. The only way around this, it might be thought, is to hold that these cases are different because of the different general categories of association within which they fall. But, I have just argued, the fact that a form of association falls within a general category—commercial, social, religious—is insufficient to settle whether it may or may not be limited for a certain kind of reason. What I want to argue, then, is that there are nonetheless important moral differences between these three forms of association that support different conclusions about the permissibility of government interference with them.

The hiring of lawyers by law firms is a form of a commercial association, but this fact alone is not sufficient, I have suggested, to show that it is permissible for the government to interfere with this freedom of association for reasons of equality. What may give the impression that it is always permissible for the government to interfere with freedom of commercial association to promote equality is that reasons of profitability against interference do not generally have moral priority over reasons of equality to interfere. In some cases reasons of profitability might have moral priority over reasons of equality to interfere, however—when, for example, interference would have such a destructive effect on profitability that it would destroy the very opportunities that are to be distributed equally.[11] And in other cases there may be reasons other than profitability against interference that have moral priority over the reasons of equality to interfere—such as reasons of artistic integrity—even though the primary purpose of the association is commercial. To determine whether it is permissible for the government to interfere with any specific form of freedom of commercial association, we must therefore consider the specific case to see whether there are specific reasons against interference that have moral priority over the reasons of equality to interfere.

If there is any reason against government interference with the freedom of law firms to hire only men as lawyers, it is either that law firms will be less profitable if they hire women—because women make less productive lawyers because of their maternal obligations, say, or their presence distracts the male lawyers from their work—or that women lawyers will make the work atmosphere less comforting or congenial for partners and their clients. Not only is it doubtful that these things are true, but, even if they were, they would not identify burdens on partners or their clients that are substantially worse than the burdens on women of noninterference. The opportunity to work as a lawyer in a law firm is valuable in our society, not only for the financial rewards, the power and the prestige, and the intrinsic satisfactions of lawyering, but also because it is strategically valuable as an entryway to many other valuable opportunities in business, politics, and social life. If law firms were not to hire women as lawyers, women would thus have fewer opportunities for many important social goods, which is a substantial burden, and one that is worse than whatever loss of profitability or comfort partners and their clients might suffer as a result. So there is no moral right against government interference with this form of freedom of association. This is not because the freedom of law firms not to hire women is a form of commercial association, but because the moral weight of the specific reasons against interference in this case is not great enough to outweigh the reasons of equality to interfere.

Does it follow from this argument that it is permissible for the government to interfere with the freedom of private social clubs to promote the equality of women? Consider the policy of some elite social clubs to admit only men as members. In the large metropolitan areas in which these clubs operate, these policies presumably have only a very small negative impact, if they have any, on the business and social opportunities of women. This is because there are so many business opportunities in large metropolitan areas, and very few are tied to membership in these clubs. Furthermore, membership in comparable women's clubs is available. If the government prohibits social clubs from admitting only men as members—or effectively does so by refusing to grant liquor licenses to clubs that have these membership policies—it will put an end to a social environment that some male members have reason to value for the feelings of comfort, familiarity, and comradeship that it makes possible outside the home. And given how minimal the burdens on women of noninterference appear to be, this burden is arguably substantially worse than the burdens of women of failing to interfere. If so, then this form of government interference would violate the moral rights of the male club members to freedom of association. The fact that it is permissible for the government to interfere with the freedom of law firms not to hire women as lawyers does not imply, then, that it is also permissible for the government to interfere with the freedom of private social clubs not to admit women as members.

This argument also does not imply however, that it is *always* wrong for the government to prohibit social clubs from admitting only men as members. Imagine that most of the business in a small town is conducted at the town's single country club, that women are not admitted to this club, and that as a result they cannot participate fully and effectively in the business life of the community. Business is a central path to making money and achieving social status, and the male club members have many other opportunities to enjoy each other's company without the company of women—by hunting or golfing together, for example. Under these conditions the burdens imposed by the membership policies of this club on those individual women who wish to participate fully and effectively in the business life of the community seem worse than the loss to the members of the special social environment provided by the club. It is therefore permissible for the government to interfere with the membership policies of this club to promote equality of opportunity for women.

But if it is permissible for the government to require law firms to hire women as lawyers, and it is sometimes permissible for the government to require social clubs to admit women as members, then it might be thought to follow that it is also permissible for the government to require the Roman Catholic Church to ordain women as priests. This form of association is religious, to be sure. But what moral difference does this make, since employment and social opportunities of women are at stake in this case as they are in the first two? Interference with this freedom of association may interfere with freedom of conscience. But how can we consistently hold that the first two kinds of interference are permissible while also holding that the third kind is not? It may seem that we must either judge that interference with this form of freedom of conscience is permissible, or conclude that it is wrong for the government to interfere in the other two cases as well.

Those in the Catholic hierarchy who are charged with ordaining priests endorse a religious doctrine according to which they are morally obligated to obey canon law. According to canon law, only men may be ordained as priests. Whatever a bishop might like to do, then, he may not ordain women as priests because he is prohibited from doing so by the religious doctrine he accepts. If the government were to require bishops to ordain women as priests, or if it were to punish their church in some other way for not doing so—say, by removing its tax exemption—it would thereby prohibit people from acting in accordance with their sense of duty or would penalize them for doing so. Law partners, by contrast, do not endorse any religious or moral doctrine according to which they have a duty not to hire women as lawyers; nor do the members of social clubs endorse a religious doctrine according to which they have a duty not to admit women as members. So there is a good reason of conscience against government interference with the freedom of the Roman Catholic Church not to ordain women as priests, and no such reason against government interference with the freedom of law firms not to hire women as lawyers,[12] or with the freedom of social clubs not to admit women as members.

To appreciate the moral significance of this difference, consider the difference in our attitudes toward the pacifist who seeks to avoid military service because he believes that he has a moral duty not to kill other human beings and toward the businessman who seeks to avoid military service because he believes that he can make a more profitable use of his time if he does not go to war. The fact that the pacifist believes it is his duty not to kill is a reason against drafting him that has substantially greater moral weight than the businessman's belief that he can make a more profitable use of his time—and it has substantially greater moral weight even if the pacifist's belief is actually false and the businessman's belief is actually true. Some people may, of course, have unreasonable beliefs about their duty—that they have a duty to kill people who work at abortion clinics, for example—and if a person's judgment of duty is unreasonable, the fact that she holds it is not a reason of much weight against government interference with her freedom to perform it, even if she is sincere.[13] But if a person's judgment of duty is reasonable in the sense that it is warranted by a moral or religious doctrine that can be affirmed through intelligent and informed reflection, as is the case with the pacifist's belief, then this judgment is a reason of substantial moral weight against government interference. And those in the Catholic hierarchy who are charged with ordaining priests believe they have a duty to ordain only men in light of a religious doctrine that can be affirmed as the result of intelligent and informed reflection. There is an important moral difference, then, between the freedom of the Roman Catholic Church not to ordain women as priests and those in the freedom of law firms not to hire women as lawyers and the freedom of social clubs not to admit women as members.

The fact that there is a good reason of conscience against government interference with the freedom of the Catholic Church to ordain only men as priests does not alone show that it is wrong, however. Whether it is wrong depends upon whether the burdens that would be imposed by interference are substantially worse than the burdens on women of non-interference identified by the reasons of equality to interfere. So, before we conclude that this form of government interference would violate someone's moral rights, we must consider what the burdens of noninterference on women actually are.

The Roman Catholic Church does not impose a duty on women to be priests, so no woman who fully endorses Roman Catholic doctrine can coherently believe that she has this duty. She may believe that she has a calling to serve God and man as a cleric, but she may pursue this calling by leaving the church. This might be a considerable loss for her, but if she regards it as her *duty* to remain within the church, then it is doubtful that she can coherently believe that she has a duty to serve as a priest within the church. And if she does not regard staying within the church as her duty, then it is doubtful that she can coherently regard serving as a priest within the church as a duty. The burdens of noninterference on women are different in kind, then, from the burden that would be imposed on those in the Catholic hierarchy if they were forced by the government to ordain women as priests.

Still, these burdens are substantial. If the government does not require the Catholic Church to ordain women, then Catholic women will be unable to achieve a kind of special status within their religious community or to have a certain kind of job that they might enjoy within that community. What we must consider, then, is whether or not being prohibited from acting in accordance with one's reasonable sense of duty is substantially worse than the loss of these valuable opportunities.

Given the choice between securing the freedom to perform what one reasonably regards as one's duty and securing the opportunity to occupy a certain position of status within one's religious community or to have a job one enjoys in that community, it seems that a conscientious person would choose to secure the former over the latter. This is because performing what we reasonably regard as our duty is more central to our integrity as moral persons than enjoying these other opportunities. This suggests that the burden of interference on those in the Catholic hierarchy is substantially worse than the burden of noninterference imposed on Catholic women, and that the reason of conscience against interference has moral priority over the reasons of equality to interfere. Interference with this form of freedom of association for these reasons of equality would therefore violate the moral rights of those in the Catholic hierarchy who are charged with ordaining priests.

Note that it does not follow from this argument that it is *always* wrong for the government to interfere with freedom of religious association to promote equality. Imagine that the decisions of American bishops not to ordain women as priests were based not on canon law, but merely on uncodified local tradition. Then there would be no good reason of *conscience* against government interference, and the burdens on women of noninterference would seem to be worse than the burdens of interference on those in the Catholic hierarchy. Rawls maintains that "the freedom and integrity of the internal life of religious associations" is an essential aspect of the basic liberty of freedom of conscience to which the priority of liberty applies.[14] And in the case of the freedom of the Roman Catholic Church to ordain only men as priests, this seems correct. In other cases of religious association, however, there may be no good reasons of conscience against interference. The fact that a form of freedom of association is religious is not sufficient to show, then, that it is an essential aspect of freedom of conscience to which the priority of liberty applies.

There are a number of general principles on the basis of which one might seek to resolve conflicts between freedom of association and equality of opportunity: that freedom of association as a basic liberty always takes priority over equality of opportunity; that the freedoms of political, religious, and intimate association always take priority as basic liberties over equality of opportunity; that freedom of private association always takes priority over equality of opportunity. All these general principles are implausible, I believe. This is because whether it is permissible or impermissible for the government to interfere with a liberty for reasons of equality depends not upon the category of liberty it falls within, but upon the relative weight of this reason of equality and the reasons against interference. We should resolve conflicts between freedom of association and equality of opportunity not by considering general principles, then, but by considering the details of each case.

PATERNALISM

One understanding of the claim that freedom of association is a fundamental liberty is that no form of freedom of association may be limited for reasons of equality. This claim is implausible, I have argued, but a similar claim might still hold for other kinds of reason for interference. It might hold for paternalistic reasons, for example. Indeed, this is just what Mill seems to have meant in identifying "liberty of combination" as one of the liberties essential to a free society[15]—that it is wrong for the government to interfere with freedom of association to promote the physical or psychological health, well-being, or development of the adults who wish to associate voluntarily.

If my account of fundamental liberty is correct, however, it is puzzling why this should be so. To say that freedom of association is a fundamental liberty on this view is to say that there are specific moral rights against interference with some forms of association, and to say that there is a specific moral right against interference with a certain form of association is to say that a reason against interference has moral priority over some good reason to interfere. Government interference with freedom of association for paternalistic reasons is always wrong, then, only if there is always a reason against interference with freedom of association that has moral priority over the good paternalistic reasons there are to interfere. This is hard to believe.

"The strongest of all arguments against the interference of the public with purely personal conduct," Mill writes, "is that, when it does interfere, the odds are that it interferes wrongly and in the wrong place."[16] This statement about "odds" implies that the public might interfere with purely personal conduct "rightly and in the right place," which happens, one assumes, when it prohibits individuals from doing something that there is actually sufficient reason for them *not* to do even in the absence of a law that prohibits them from doing it. The public interferes "wrongly and in the wrong place," then, just when it prohibits individuals from doing something that there *is* sufficient reason for them to do in the absence of such a law. Mill's main argument against paternalism, then, is that if the government is permitted to prohibit people from doing things for their own good, it is likely to prohibit some individuals from doing what there is actually sufficient reason for them to do.[17]

A natural response is that while the government may be likely to interfere "wrongly and in the wrong place" in *some* areas of purely personal conduct, it is not likely to interfere "wrongly and in the wrong place" in *other* areas. So let us suppose that the government is likely to interfere wrongly if it interferes for paternalistic reasons with the freedom of adults to engage in private, noncommercial, consensual sexual relations. We might still suppose that it is unlikely to interfere wrongly if it interferes for paternalistic reasons with the freedom to drive motorized vehicles without using certain safety devices such as seat belts or helmets. And if this is correct, then, while it might show it is wrong for the government to interfere for paternalistic reasons in the area of private, noncommercial, consensual sexual conduct, Mill's argument would not show that it is wrong for the government to interfere for paternalistic reasons in the area of driver safety.

This response may not get to the heart of Mill's objection to paternalism, for it still seems that any kind of paternalistic interference is likely to prohibit *some* individuals from doing what there is sufficient reason for them to do—even in the area of traffic safety. To illustrate the problem, suppose the government passes a law requiring motorcyclists to wear helmets for the reason that wearing a helmet reduces the risk of death and permanent brain damage to those who ride motorcycles. Let us assume that most people who wish to ride a motorcycle without a helmet are young men who have poor judgment about their own personal safety, and that while they believe they ought to ride a motorcycle without a helmet, they are in fact mistaken. Despite what they believe, there is sufficient reason for them not to ride a motorcycle without a helmet, even in the absence of a law prohibiting them from doing so, and paternalistic interference with their freedom to do so is therefore "right and in the right place." The problem is that this form of interference is likely to prohibit others from riding a motorcycle without a helmet who do have sufficient reason to do so. So imagine a mature man of good judgment who has a terminal illness and who enjoys the experience of riding his motorcycle without a helmet because it reminds him of the freedom of his youth. There is sufficient reason for this person to ride a motorcycle without a helmet, let us suppose. So if there is a general law against riding a motorcycle without a helmet, someone will be prohibited from doing what he has sufficient reason to do, and the government will therefore interfere "wrongly and in the wrong place."

This argument against paternalism indicates a morally relevant distinction between paternalistic legislation and egalitarian legislation. When the government is justified in interfering with someone's freedom for an egalitarian reason, we might say, it is always and only because there is sufficient reason for those whose liberty is limited to act differently from how they believe they ought to act. Thus if laws that prohibit racial discrimination in places of public accommodation are justified, it is because, regardless of what they happen to believe, those who discriminate in these places actually ought not to do so. But, it might be said, this is not the case with paternalism. Paternalistic legislation will typically prohibit not only conduct that people have sufficient reason *not* to engage in, but also conduct that they *do* have sufficient reason to engage in. And this is why paternalistic legislation is wrong.

The fact that someone has sufficient reason to do something is not generally a reason against government interference with his liberty to do it, however, that has moral priority over the good reasons to interfere. Thus, in the absence of a law imposing a sixty-five mile-per-hour speed limit, a good driver might have sufficient reason to drive eighty miles per hour on the highway, but this reason against imposing a sixty-five mile-per-hour speed limit does not have moral priority over the reason to impose this limit that doing so will make driving on the highway safer for others. Why, then, should the fact that someone has sufficient reason to ride his motorcycle without a helmet be a reason against motorcycle helmet laws that has moral priority over the paternalistic reasons of safety for them?

In the case of speed limits, one might argue, the liberty of those who have sufficient reason to do something is limited for the safety of *others*; but this is also true of motorcycle helmet laws: the liberty of those who have sufficient reason to ride without a helmet is limited for the safety of others who have sufficient reason to wear one. One might argue that the two cases are importantly different because those who are in greater danger as a result of not wearing a helmet can reduce this risk to themselves without government interference—simply by wearing a helmet. But those who are in greater danger as a result of others driving fast on the highway can also reduce the risk to themselves—by not driving on the highway. Forcing people to choose between being less safe and not driving on the highway imposes a burden on them, to be sure. But then the absence of motorcycle helmet laws is a burden too, because an incentive is not provided that is necessary to motivate those who have sufficient reason to do so to protect their heads properly when they ride motorcycles. And this burden seems roughly as heavy as the burden of having to choose between being less safe on the highway and not driving on the highway at all. So it is hard to see why the mere fact that motorcycle helmet laws are likely to prohibit someone from doing what there is sufficient reason for him to do is a reason against them that has moral priority over the good paternalistic reasons for them. And for this reason Mill's "strongest argument" against paternalism does not seem very strong.

The point here is not that paternalism is never wrong. Surely it sometimes is. The point is rather that when paternalism is wrong, it is not wrong simply because it prohibits someone from doing what there is sufficient reason for him to do; it is wrong because it imposes a more specific burden on those who are interfered with, and one that is substantially worse than any burden imposed on someone by noninterference identified by the paternalistic reason to interfere. When we consider the issue of paternalistic interference with freedom of association, we cannot therefore dismiss all such interference as unjustified on the grounds that any such interference is likely to prohibit some people from doing what there is sufficient reason for them to do. Rather, in each case where there is a good paternalistic reason to interfere, we must consider whether interference would impose a more specific burden on someone that is substantially worse than any burden imposed by noninterference identified by the paternalistic reason to interfere. If so, then such interference is morally wrong; if not, it is not.

To illustrate this approach, consider the paternalistic reason to prohibit homosexual relationships that this will motivate some people who would otherwise not be so motivated to seek heterosexual relationships, which can produce the biological children of both partners. Let us suppose that laws that prohibit homosexuality actually do have this effect, and that relationships that produce biological children have a meaning, purpose, and psychological completeness that relationships that cannot produce biological children lack. There is a good paternalistic reason, then, for the government to prohibit homosexuality. If the government prohibits homosexual relationships, though, it will prohibit some adults from having the sorts of consensual intimate relationships that feel the most natural to them and are the most emotionally satisfying, and this burden on them is substantially worse than the burden that would be imposed on them or others if the government were not to deter them from having relationships that cannot produce children. After all, having children is not the only thing that makes intimate relationships valuable, and lives without children can be satisfying. Furthermore, those to whom having biological children with their partner is very important will presumably be adequately motivated to seek heterosexual relationships even if homosexual relationships are not illegal. So there is a reason against government prohibition of homosexual relationships that has moral priority over this paternalistic reason to interfere, and interference with this form of freedom of association for this paternalistic reason therefore violates individuals' moral rights.

Contrast this case with paternalistic laws that prohibit brothels. Let us suppose that an individual's work as a prostitute in a brothel is typically degrading in that (*a*) it inflicts a certain kind of psychological injury that can be detected by psychologically astute persons and that is not adequately compensated for by the money the prostitute receives in return; (*b*) it inhibits emotional development; and (*c*) it is experienced as demeaning by the

RIGHTS AND REASONS   161

prostitute in a way that makes her hate herself. And let us suppose that work as a prostitute in a brothel is typically exploitive in that women who do this work typically do so only because their capacity for self-protection and for insisting that others treat them with respect is substantially diminished. The fact that work as a prostitute in a brothel is typically degrading and exploitive in these ways, if it is a fact, seems to be a good paternalistic reason in itself for prohibiting these establishments. So if this form of paternalism is wrong, it is only because there is a reason against this kind of interference that has moral priority over this paternalistic reason to interfere.

Let us assume that some women have sufficient reason to work as prostitutes in brothels even though this work is typically degrading and exploitive in the way just described. Because they possess an unusual psychology, let us suppose, they are not actually degraded and exploited by it, and they can make more money by doing this work than they otherwise could. The mere fact that someone has sufficient reason to do something is not a reason against government interference with her freedom to do it that has moral priority over the good paternalistic reasons there are to interfere. Or so I have just argued. So if there is reason against prohibiting brothels that has moral priority over the paternalistic reason for prohibiting them, it is that this form of interference imposes a more specific burden on someone. What burden might this be?

The main burden that a government prohibition of brothels would impose on individual women is that it would close a way for them to make more money than they otherwise could. There are normally other ways of making enough money to live on, though—by waitressing, for example. So the burdens imposed on individual women under normal economic conditions by prohibiting brothels are not great. The burdens of government toleration or legalization of brothels are considerable, however. This is because a policy of tolerance would make it significantly more likely that women who have an unusually low capacity to protect themselves and to insist on respect from others will engage in an activity that injures them psychologically in substantial ways. The reason against government interference that it will prohibit a means of making money does not seem to have moral priority, then, over the paternalistic reason to interfere that the work is typically degrading and exploitive, and interference for this reason does not therefore violate anyone's moral rights.[18]

Some have argued that the government violates a person's "right to moral independence" if it interferes with personal conduct for the reason that it is degrading,[19] and one might attempt to summarize the argument for this position as follows.[20] Each citizen has a general right that his or her government treat him or her with equal respect. On the liberal interpretation of equal respect, the government treats its citizens with equal respect only if it shows equal respect for each citizen's conception of the good. Equal respect for each citizen's conception of the good is inconsistent with the government's limiting a person's liberty for the reason that his or her conception of the good is unworthy of respect or less worthy of respect than others.[21] And if the government limits individual liberty for the reason that a form of conduct is degrading, then it limits the liberty of those whose conceptions of the good counsel this conduct for the reason that their conceptions of the good are unworthy of respect. The government thus violates a person's moral rights—the right to moral independence—if it limits a person's liberty for the reason that the conduct counseled by their conception of the good is degrading.[22] Why, though, if a conception of the good counsels conduct that is degrading, is it entitled to equal respect from the government? Perhaps this is what liberalism entails, but then why accept liberalism?

The idea that it is wrong for the government to interfere with associational conduct for the reason that it is degrading gains most of its credibility, I believe, from the fact that the government may sometimes interfere with associational conduct for this reason when the conduct in question is not actually degrading, or when the proposition that it is, is not adequately supported. So suppose the government prohibits homosexuality for the reason that it is degrading. If it is false that homosexuality is degrading or if the proposition that it is, is not adequately supported, then this is a bad reason in itself for the government to interfere with this conduct, and interference for this reason violates the general moral right against arbitrary interference. The fact that it is wrong for the government to interfere with conduct for the reason that it is degrading when it is *not* degrading should not mislead us into thinking, though, that it is wrong for the government to interfere with conduct for the reason that is degrading when it actually *is*. After all, it is also wrong for the government to interfere with conduct for the reason that it threatens others' health and safety when it does not. It is wrong for the government to prohibit marijuana use for the reason that it threatens others' health and safety, for example, if it does not. But this does not mean that it is wrong for the government to interfere with conduct for the reason that it threatens others' health and safety when it actually does.

Some may conclude from the two cases I have just discussed that while it is permissible for the government to interfere with commercial forms of intimate association for paternalistic reasons, it is impermissible for the government to interfere with noncommercial forms of intimate association for paternalistic reasons, but this conclusion is not warranted. Consider laws that would prohibit movie actors from playing love scenes together for the paternalistic reason that playing such scenes sometimes has a destructive impact on their marriages. Such laws would interfere with a commercial form of intimate association, but they might still be impermissible. And consider laws that prohibit sexual relations between family members for the reason that such relationships are generally psychologically destructive. Such laws may be permissible even though the form of intimate association they interfere with is noncommercial. Whether it is permissible or impermissible for the government to interfere with a freedom of association for paternalistic reasons depends, then, not upon the category of association within which this freedom falls, but solely upon the relative weight of the specific reasons for and against interference in that particular case. Paternalistic interference with freedom of association is thus to be evaluated in the same way as egalitarian interference: case by case.

Systematicity

There is no general right against interference with freedom of association for reasons of equality, I have now argued, and no general right against interference with freedom of association for paternalistic reasons—not even paternalistic reasons that might be regarded as "moralistic." To determine whether a form of government interference with a form of association is wrong, we must consider whether there is a good reason for this form of interference, and, if so, whether there is nonetheless a reason against it that has moral priority over this reason to interfere. If so, there is a right against this form of interference; if not, there is no such right.

I have now considered several forms of freedom of association, and offered my opinion on whether or not it is wrong for the government to interfere with them for certain reasons. Some readers will no doubt disagree with these opinions, and may wonder what demonstrates they are correct. These judgments are correct, I answer, if they assign the relevant burdens their proper relative weight. There is ultimately only one test of whether or not they do, which is whether or not the judgment that they do withstands the critical scrutiny of informed and reflective persons over time.[23] The reader must judge for herself or himself whether or not this is the case.

This conclusion may seem inadequate. It may seem that a philosophical discussion of freedom of association must aim to identify general principles of freedom of association on the basis of which more specific judgments about associational rights can be explained and defended. So in this section I will explain why I do not think that any general theory of associational rights can be both correct and complete.

A general theory of moral rights to freedom of association is correct and complete, I will suppose, if and only if it identifies a general reason—or smallish set of general reasons—to value freedom of association that leads us, either directly or through a natural course of reflection, to all and only those more specific reasons against interference with specific freedoms of association that have moral priority over the good reasons there are to interfere. To illustrate the apparent difficulty with finding such a theory, consider a theory that identifies as the general reason to value a form of freedom of association that the government must recognize and protect this freedom if each person is to have a fair chance to advance his or her legitimate interests through the political process. This account would explain why there are moral rights to freedom of *political* association—because the freedom to join with others to advance common political aims seems necessary for each person to have a fair chance to advance his or her legitimate interests through the political process—but it would not explain why there are moral rights to the freedoms of religious and intimate association, at least not directly or through a natural course of reflection. This is because as long as each person has the right to vote and to run for office, and to advocate his or her views through the media, as well has as adequate material means to communicate these views, then even if some are prohibited by law from associating with each other for purely religious purposes or from having certain kinds of intimate relationship with each other, each person will still have a fair chance to advance his or her legitimate interests through the political process.[24] This general account is incomplete, then, because it fails to identify all the moral rights there actually are to freedom of association.

It is natural to respond here that this account fails to account for moral rights to freedom of religious association and freedom of intimate association because it does not identify the value of individual autonomy as the basis for regarding liberties as fundamental. If we start from the value of autonomy, it might be said, we can arrive at a general theory of freedom of association that is both correct and complete. "Individual autonomy" picks out a number of different values, though, so it cannot be the basis of a determinate theory of associational rights until we are precise about which specific value we mean. And once we are precise, it is hard to formulate a theory of associational rights in terms of this value that identifies all and only those freedoms of association to which there are moral rights.

Suppose we say that autonomy is having the ability to act, and generally acting, after critical reflection on all the feasible alternatives. Or suppose we say that autonomy is being able and willing to decide in general what one should believe and how one should act without checking with someone else whom one regards as having general authority over these decisions. These are both sensible notions of individual autonomy, but they do little to explain the distinctions we make between those freedoms of association to which we have moral rights and those to which we do not. They do little to explain the distinction we make, for example, between freedom of religious association, on one hand, and the freedom to discriminate against members of racial minorities in places of public accommodation, on the other. This is because people might exercise their autonomy equally, in both senses, in deciding to worship with others and to discriminate against them.

Suppose we say, then, that people are autonomous if they enjoy the prerogative to make certain decisions about, and are thereby free to exercise active control over, certain important areas of their lives. Or suppose we say that people are autonomous if they actually exercise active control over certain important areas of their lives by making all the important decisions they have the prerogative to make in these areas. These too are sensible notions of individual autonomy, but they provide no general theory of associational rights until they are accompanied by a general theory of what areas of life, or what decisions in these areas, are "important." So, we may ask, is the prerogative to decide who may eat in one's restaurant necessary for one to exercise active control over an important area of one's life? If not, why not?

Suppose we say, then, that there is a moral right to some form of freedom of association if people need to exercise this liberty in order to act autonomously in the narrow sense of doing what one believes one ought to do. This identifies too many associational rights. Thus, people who discriminate against others in places of public accommodation presumably believe that this is what they ought to do, but there is no moral right to discriminate in this way. We might address this particular objection by saying that there is a right to a liberty if people need to exercise this liberty in order to act autonomously in the ideal sense of doing what one *really* ought to do for the reason that one really ought to do it. But even this identifies too many associational rights. Thus, in the absence of a law limiting bakers' hours to sixty hours a week, some bakers might have sufficient reason to work for eighty hours, but this does not show there is a moral right to this form of freedom of association, which would be violated, say, if it were limited by the government to protect the health of other bakers.

Consider, then, the general theory of freedom of association suggested by Rawls's discussion of basic liberty: there is a moral right against government interference with a form of association if the social conditions necessary for the full development and exercise of our capacities for practical reason will not be secure unless the government recognizes and protects this form of association.[25] This theory is informative and it is not obviously incorrect. So, to illustrate, let us assume that in order to develop and exercise their capacities for practical reasoning fully, persons must be able to act in accordance with those duties that are imposed by the reasonable religious or moral doctrine that they endorse. And let us assume that no reasonable moral or religious doctrine requires people to discriminate against racial minorities in places of public accommodation. Then, unlike some of the other suggestions we have just considered, this theory of associational rights can explain the distinction we make between the freedom of the Roman Catholic Church not to ordain women as priests, on the one hand, and the freedom of restaurant owners to refuse to serve members of racial minorities on the other.

To be *complete*, however, a theory of associational rights must identify a general reason to value liberty that leads us, either directly or through a natural course of reflection, to all and only those more specific reasons against interference with liberty that have moral priority over the reasons there are to interfere. And here it is doubtful that this theory succeeds. So let us suppose that there is a moral right against the government prohibiting two single adults from entering into an interracial marriage for the reason that the children of such unions have a more difficult time forming a racial identity, which, let us suppose, creates a mild form of psychological stress. If this account of associational rights is complete, then it must be the case that the government's recognition and protection of the freedom to enter into interracial marriages is necessary to secure the social conditions necessary for the full development and exercise of the capacities for practical reason. But is it? The freedom of people to marry whom they wish is not necessary for people to *deliberate* about what is right and good, nor is it generally necessary for people to act in accordance with the duties imposed by the reasonable religious or moral doctrine they endorse.[26] And while it may be necessary for people to act on their considered judgment about what is good, many other liberties to which there are no moral rights may be necessary in this way too, such as the liberty to drive fast or to discriminate against others. So it seems that this theory of associational rights is either incomplete or incorrect: either it fails to identify the freedom to marry as one to which there are moral rights or it identifies too many other moral rights as well.

There are many freedoms of association to which we might think there are moral rights: the freedom to form and conduct friendships as we think best, consistent with our obligations to others; the freedom not to associate socially with anyone with whom we do not want to associate; the freedom to marry whom we wish to marry and, at least under some circumstances, to divorce; the freedom to worship with others according to shared religious beliefs; the freedom not to worship with anyone; the freedom to live with others in religious or other kinds of social community; the freedom to form political parties and political interest groups; and many others. To determine what moral rights exist against interference with these forms of association, however, we must consider the specific reasons against interference with them that have moral priority over the reasons there are to interfere with them. It would be interesting to have a general theory of freedom of association that would identify all and only those specific reasons against interference that have this kind of moral priority. The activities that people pursue in exercising these liberties are so varied, however, and the distinctions we make between different forms of these liberties are so fine, that the prospects for such a theory seem dim. The reasons against interference that have moral priority over the reasons there are to interfere are simply too diverse. There is nothing that all the good reasons against government interference with freedom of association have in common, no master value that generates or collects them all. It does not follow, though, that we cannot say anything interesting or informative about associational rights. We can—by identifying the good reasons there are against interference in each case and considering carefully whether these reasons have moral priority over the good reasons there are to interfere. This is what I have attempted to do here.

Constitutional Rights

I have now outlined a view of what makes freedom of association fundamental as a general category of liberty—there are specific moral rights against government interference with certain forms of association—and I have expressed my opinion about whether there are indeed specific moral rights against government interference with certain identified forms of association for egalitarian and paternalistic reasons. Given the place the notion of fundamental liberty has in our constitutional law, it is natural to wonder about the relation between the claims made here and constitutional interpretation, so I will briefly say something about this in conclusion.

According to the substantive interpretation of the due process clause of the Fourteenth Amendment, the Fourteenth Amendment licenses the Supreme Court to evaluate the constitutionality of state legislation that limits freedom of association according to the following scheme: if the freedom of association is "fundamental," then the legislation is constitutional only if it is necessary to promote a "compelling state interest"; but if the freedom of association in question is not "fundamental," then the legislation is constitutional if and only if it advances (or is reasonably believed to advance) a "legitimate state aim." To identify a form of freedom of association as fundamental in constitutional law is thus to say that it may not be limited by the government for reasons that would otherwise be sufficient, which is also to say that there is a specific moral right against government interference with a form of freedom of association, in my view. This structural similarity may lead one to think that the claims made here about moral rights to freedom of association are implicitly claims about what constitutional rights there are, but this is incorrect.

To say that someone has a *moral right* to some liberty is to say it is *morally wrong* for the government to limit this liberty for a certain reason. To say that someone has a *constitutional right* to some liberty, by contrast, is to say that the courts *ought* (all things considered) to make the judgment that it is *illegal* for the government to limit this liberty for a certain reason (when it is not to say that they *have made* this judgment already). One very important reason for the courts to judge that it is illegal for the government to limit a freedom of association is that there is a moral right against this kind of interference. But this moral reason is not necessarily decisive. Suppose, for example, that laws that prohibit interracial marriage violate people's moral rights. At an earlier time, a judgment by the Supreme Court that such laws are illegal might have (wrongly) struck so many citizens as unjustified that this judgment would have had the political effect of weakening the obedience of the other branches of government to the Court's decisions, and this reason against making this judgment might have been sufficiently weighty to be decisive even though these laws violated citizens' moral rights. The fact that a form of government interference violates a person's moral rights is thus not always a decisive reason for the courts to judge that it is illegal, and so not always sufficient to show that it is unconstitutional.

The fact that a form of government interference violates a person's moral rights often does warrant the conclusion that it is unconstitutional, however. So consider the issue taken up in *Bowers v. Hardwick*:[27] the constitutionality of laws that prohibit sodomy. These laws impose a substantial burden on homosexuals because they prohibit the only kind of consensual sex that adults who are homosexual can have with each other. Unless there is a reason for these laws that identifies a burden that noninterference would impose on someone that is comparable to these burdens, these laws violate people's moral rights to freedom of intimate association. Let us suppose, then, that noninterference does not impose any such burden on anyone, and that these laws do therefore violate people's rights. There does not now seem to be any morally weighty political or pragmatic reason against judging these laws illegal. So the fact that these laws violate individuals' moral rights would seem to warrant the judgment that they are unconstitutional.[28]

The fact that a form of government interference *does not* violate a person's moral rights may also warrant the judgment that it is constitutional. Consider *Roberts v. United States Jaycees*.[29] In that case, the Supreme Court considered whether the state of Minnesota violated the Jaycees' constitutional right to freedom of association by requiring it to admit women as full voting members. The Court argued that since this form of interference does not impose any serious burdens on the male membership—either with respect to their ability to express their political beliefs or with respect to their ability to control the nature of their personal relationships—this form of interference is permissible to promote equality of opportunity for women. The Court thus argued, in effect, that since there is no moral right against this form of interference—no reason against this form of interference that has moral priority over the reason of equality to interfere—there is no constitutional right against it, and this seems correct.

The fact that there is no moral right against interference with a form of freedom of association does not necessarily imply that there is no constitutional right to it, however. It might happen, for example, that settled constitutional doctrine clearly supports the conclusion that a form of government interference with freedom of association is illegal even though there is no moral right against it. There is no identity of constitutional and moral rights, then, even though there is an important connection between them.

The judgment that a form of government interference violates a person's rights is always an important moral argument to make against it, though, even if this does not warrant the judgment that it is unconstitutional. If government interference with a form of freedom of association violates a person's moral rights, then it is wrong in principle for any private citizen to advocate or vote for legislation that limits this freedom for this reason, and it is wrong in principle for any government official to do so too. Private citizens and public officials may, of course, have the right to do what is wrong. Thus, even if a person advocates limiting a person's liberty for a bad reason, he may have a right not to be silenced for this reason. This is because there may be reasons against this kind of interference that have moral priority over this reason to interfere—that political decisions will become less responsive to citizens' legitimate interests over time if the government does not observe a general rule that prohibits it from silencing people for the reason that what they advocate is wrong, for example. To say that someone has a duty not to advocate limiting another person's liberty for a bad reason is not to say, then, that he has no right against government interference with his freedom to do so.[30] Still, it is an important moral criticism of a person's support for a policy that it violates others' moral rights, and a criticism well worth making when true. My aim here has been to understand the abstract content of this criticism, and to consider a few cases in which it might be true of freedom of association.

Notes

I thank the participants in the Program in Ethics and Public Affairs seminar at Princeton University, where a draft of this essay was first discussed; their questions and comments led to extensive revisions. I am also indebted to Katrin Borland, Arthur Kuflik, Jeffrie Murphy, and Thomas Scanlon for their comments on later drafts.

1. J. S. Mill, *On Liberty*, ed. Elizabeth Rapaport (Indianapolis: Hackett Publishing Co., 1978), 1.12.12 (references are to chapter, paragraph, and page).
2. John Rawls, "The Basic Liberties and Their Priority," in *Political Liberalism* (New York: Columbia University Press, 1993), pp. 291, 309, 313, 332, 335, 337, 341.
3. Rawls, "The Basic Liberties and Their Priority," p. 294.
4. Mill himself discusses the issue of polygamy in *On Liberty*, 4.20.89–90.
5. It follows from my view that rights to liberty cannot conflict with each other or with other rights. The thought that rights conflict arises, I believe, partly from a failure to notice the important distinction between saying that it is wrong for the government to interfere with a liberty for a *certain* reason and saying that it is wrong for the government to interfere with a liberty for *any* reason. It also arises from conflating the notion of a right and the notion of a legitimate interest. Legitimate interests may conflict with respect to liberty because there may be good reason for one person to want to exercise a liberty while there is good reason for another person to want him not to exercise it. A right to liberty cannot conflict with any other right, however, because to say that a person has a right to a specific liberty is just to say that there is a reason against interference with this liberty that has moral priority over some reason to interfere, and if this claim is correct, then no other valid claim of the same kind can conflict with it.
6. A belief is adequately supported, I assume, if and only if the available evidence

gives more support to the judgment that it is true than to the judgment that it is false.

7. See, for example, Rawls, "Justice as Fairness: Political Not Metaphysical," *Philosophy & Public Affairs* 14 (summer 1985): 223–51. See, too, Ronald Dworkin, "What Rights Do We Have?" in *Taking Rights Seriously* (Cambridge: Harvard University Press, 1978).

8. This formulation is found in Rawls, "The Basic Liberties and Their Priority," p. 295. See, too, Rawls, *A Theory of Justice* (Cambridge: Harvard University Press, 1971), p. 244.

9. See Rawls, "The Basic Liberties and Their Priority," pp. 291, 309, 313, 332, 335, 337, 341.

10. See Rawls, *A Theory of Justice*, p. 244; and Rawls, *Political Liberalism*, pp. 6, 291.

11. In cases of this sort one might deny that there are any *good* reasons of equality to interfere and might argue that in cases of this sort the reasons of equality to interfere are only apparent. If this is the correct description, then it might be true that reasons of profitability never have moral priority over *good* reasons of equality.

12. *Conscience*, strictly speaking, is the capacity for judgments of *duty*; it is not the more general capacity for judgments about what to do.

13. Of course, even if it were reasonable for people to believe that they have a duty to kill people who work at abortion clinics, it would not follow that the government must tolerate this kind of behavior, for this reason of conscience not to interfere would certainly not have moral priority over the obvious reasons there are to interfere.

14. See Rawls, "The Basic Liberties and Their Priority," p. 341.

15. Mill, *On Liberty*, 1.12.12.

16. Ibid., 4.12.81.

17. Mill also argues earlier that paternalistic interference with individual liberty is not "authorized" by "the permanent interests of man as a progressive being." See Mill, *On Liberty*, 1.11.10. But these interests do seem to warrant some forms of paternalism. Thus, if we understand the permanent interests of man as a progressive being to include staying alive and having a functioning brain, these interests seem to warrant motorcycle helmet laws. Mill seems to believe that the permanent interests of man as a progressive being will be effectively advanced over time only if people are always free to do what they actually have sufficient reason to do. I find this claim implausible.

18. This is not to say that the prohibition of brothels is *good policy* or the best thing to do, all things considered. The distinction between the claim that a form of government interference violates a person's moral rights and the claim that it is bad policy is an important one that needs explication, but I cannot offer that here.

19. See, for example, Dworkin, "Do We Have a Right to Pornography?" *A Matter of Principle* (Cambridge: Harvard University Press, 1985), pp. 353–54.

20. The argument that follows is a brief reconstruction of the arguments given by Dworkin in "Do We Have a Right to Pornography?" pp. 353–54, and "Liberalism," pp. 190–92, in *A Matter of Principle* (Cambridge: Harvard University Press, 1985).

21. This claim is related to Dworkin's principle that the government should be "neutral" among conceptions of the good. Properly understood, the principle of neutrality forbids the government from depriving any citizen of opportunities and resources *for the reason that* their conception of the good is unworthy of respect or less worthy of respect than those of other citizens. See Dworkin, "Liberalism," p. 191. For a similar understanding of neutrality, see Bruce Ackerman, *Social Justice and the Liberal State* (New Haven: Yale University Press, 1980). While the idea of neutrality has recently come under fierce attack, it is not clear how many critics actually reject it. So Joseph Raz, who criticizes the idea of neutrality, also accepts the harm principle in some form, and this would seem to commit him to roughly the same kind of neutrality that Dworkin and Ackerman have in mind. See Joseph Raz, *The Morality of Freedom* (New York: Oxford University Press, 1986), chap. 5 and 6, for discussion of neutrality, and chap. 15, for endorsement of the harm principle.

22. It is open to question, of course, whether anyone's *conception of the good* counsels them to work at a brothel. If not, then I suppose that, strictly speaking, laws against brothels would be compatible with this version of liberalism.

23. I do not claim here that the statement that these judgments are correct *means* that they pass this test; I claim only that this test is ultimately the only *method* we have for assessing the correctness of these judgments.

24. I assume here that the idea of a fair chance to advance one's legitimate interests through the political process is not defined in terms of any particular outcome. If this is not the case, then perhaps this idea does identify moral rights to the freedoms of religious and intimate association. But then to provide a *theory* of associational rights one would need to provide a theory of what outcomes for liberty define a fair process and why, and no such theory is clearly implicit in the idea of a fair political process alone.

25. See Rawls, "The Basic Liberties and Their Priority," pp. 331–40.

26. Might not one have a duty to marry for love? One might *feel* that one has a duty to marry for love, to be sure, but one might also *feel* that one has a duty not to serve members of racial minorities in one's restaurant—a duty of solidarity to one's own race, for example. If the sense of duty is to mark a genuine distinction between the freedom of the Roman Catholic Church to ordain only men as priests and the freedom of restaurant owners to serve only whites, it must therefore be interpreted strictly to require acting only in accordance with those duties that are actually imposed by a reasonable religious or moral doctrine. Is there a doctrine of this sort that imposes a *duty* on people to marry for love? If so, I am unaware of it.

27. 476 U.S. 186 (1986).

28. This is not what the Court actually decided in *Bowers v. Hardwick*, and against my conclusion it might be argued that the judgment that sodomy laws are illegal is not licensed by the "text" of the Constitution. It is arguable that a liberty is "fundamental" in the sense relevant to applying the substantive interpretation of the due process clause, though, when its limitation imposes a burden on someone of substantial moral weight, and that the state has a "compelling interest" in limiting a liberty that is fundamental in this sense only when not limiting it would impose a burden on someone of comparable moral weight. So if the substantive interpretation of the due process clause of the Fourteenth Amendment is correct, then the conclusion that sodomy laws are illegal *is* arguably warranted by the "text" of the Con-

stitution, and in *Bowers* four out of nine justices seem to have reached the same conclusion.

29. 468 U. S. 609 (1984).

30. Rawls makes a closely related point in "The Idea of Public Reason" when he says that the idea of public reason "is not a matter of law" (pp. 213, 253); and in "The Idea of Public Reason Revisited" when he says that the duty of civility "is not a legal duty, for in that case it would incompatible with freedom of speech," *University of Chicago Law Review* 64, no. 3 (summer 1997): 769.

PART TWO

CIVIC VALUES OF ASSOCIATION

Chapter Seven

ETHNIC ASSOCIATIONS AND
DEMOCRATIC CITIZENSHIP

WILL KYMLICKA

ENTHUSIASM for associational life is running high among both political scientists and normative political theorists. Participation in the many groups and associations that compose civil society is said to help foster collective trust and solidarity. Membership in these groups, and the civic engagement it leads to, often cuts across major social cleavages, and thereby promotes a sense of "horizontal connectedness" among citizens. Associational life becomes a breeding ground for civic virtues and a crucial support for a viable democratic order. Indeed, the importance of associational life is so great, it is argued, that consideration should be given to providing state recognition and support to these groups.[1]

But many people's enthusiasm for associational life diminishes when the relevant groups are defined on an ethnic basis. There is a widespread backlash today against "multiculturalism," in whose name ethnic associations have demanded, and sometimes received, public funding and recognition. Whereas associational life in general is commended as helping to produce solidarity and trust, multiculturalist support for ethnic groups is increasingly decried as helping to produce balkanization, tribalization, and the "disuniting of America."

So we find ourselves in the paradoxical situation in which associational life is widely applauded and encouraged, but in which one of the few serious attempts at promoting associational life—namely, multiculturalism—is increasingly denounced. This is perhaps less of a paradox than it might seem. After all, ethnicity is precisely one of the great social cleavages that associational life is supposed to overcome. And recent events around the world have, if anything, confirmed the threat that ethnocultural divisions can pose to the sort of solidarity and trust needed for the proper functioning of democracy. To endorse and support associations that are defined on ethnic grounds seems, to many critics, the wrong way to enhance the sense of horizontal connectedness amongst citizens.

In this paper, I want to examine the relationship between ethnic associations and democratic citizenship, and the impact of "multiculturalism" on that relationship. I will argue that assessing this impact is much more complicated than critics often assume. I hope to highlight two common mistakes that plague many discussions of multiculturalism. On the one hand, accounts of multiculturalism are often guilty of overgeneralizations and of ignoring important differences between various ethnic groups. Commentators talk about "ethnic politics" in general (or, even more generally, of "identity politics"), as if all groups had the same aspirations and faced the same obstacles. To properly evaluate the role of ethnic associations, I will argue, we need to look carefully at the particular demands of particular groups, in the light of their historical treatment, present circumstances, and goals for the future. But on the other hand, accounts of multiculturalism are also guilty of focusing too much on the details of particular debates or controversies and of ignoring the larger context. They often miss the forest for the trees, because they examine multiculturalism in isolation from the larger array of governmental and institutional policies that affect the horizontal connectedness of citizens. This, indeed, is the main point of my paper. My aim is to situate multiculturalism within the broader range of government policies that affect the social, cultural, and political integration of ethnic groups.

I will begin the paper, therefore, by examining the role of the state in shaping the ethnocultural identities of its citizens. It is often assumed that liberal democracies are, or can be, neutral regarding the ethnocultural identities of their citizens. I will argue, however, that liberal states have engaged in systematic efforts at "nation-building" that involve promoting and diffusing a common national culture, and which aim at the sociocultural integration of minority groups.

I discuss in the second section how different ethnocultural groups respond to this nation-building project. I argue that ethnocultural groups have three basic options—marginalization, integration, or nationalist separatism—each of which has been adopted by a specific type of ethnocultural group. Generally speaking, the marginalization option has been accepted by a few religious sects, for whom participation in the modern world is seen as corrupting; the integration option has been adopted by most immigrant groups; and the nationalist option has been adopted by many nonimmigrant national minorities. We can also identify three distinctive forms of multiculturalism that correspond to these options. The forms sought by religious sects, immigrant groups, and national minorities have, I will argue in the remainder of the chapter, very different implications for democratic citizenship.

NATION-BUILDING IN LIBERAL DEMOCRACIES

In order to understand the impact of multiculturalism on democratic citizenship, we need first to understand the larger context of the relationship between ethnic groups and the state. Some theorists argue that liberal-democratic states should treat culture generally in the same way as religion—that is, as something that people should be free to pursue in their private life, but that is not the concern of the state. Just as liberalism precludes the establishment of an official religion, so too there cannot be official cultures that have preferred status over other possible cultural allegiances. Multiculturalism policies, for these theorists, involve a new and dangerous attempt by liberal states to influence the ethnocultural identities of their citizens.

Indeed, some theorists argue that what distinguishes liberal "civic nations" from illiberal "ethnic nations" is precisely their refusal to support any particular societal culture or ethnonational identity. Ethnic nations take the reproduction of a particular ethnonational culture and identity as one of their most important goals. Civic nations, by contrast, are 'neutral' with respect to the ethnocultural identities of their citizens, and define national membership purely in terms of adherence to certain principles of democracy and justice.

For example, Michael Walzer argues that liberalism involves a "sharp divorce of state and ethnicity." The liberal state stands above all the various ethnic and national groups in the country, "refusing to endorse or support their ways of life or to take an active interest in their social reproduction." Instead, the state is "neutral with reference to [the] language, history, literature, calendar" of these groups. He says the clearest example of such a civic nation is the United States, whose ethnocultural neutrality is reflected in the fact that it has no constitutionally recognized official language.[2] For immigrants to become American, therefore, is simply a matter of affirming their allegiance to the principles of democracy and individual freedom defined in the U.S. Constitution.

But this is inaccurate, both as a historical account of American policy and as a conceptual account of the relationship between states and cultures within liberal democracies. The fact is that the U.S. government very actively promotes not only a particular set of political principles, but also a particular kind of sociocultural integration. Immigrants are required to swear allegiance to the Constitution, but they must swear allegiance *in English*. It is in fact a legal requirement for immigrants (under the age of fifty) to learn the English language and American history to acquire American citizenship. It is also a legal requirement for children to learn the English language and American history in schools; it is a de facto requirement for employment in government that the applicant speak English; court proceedings and other government activities are typically conducted only in English; and the resulting legislation and bureaucratic forms are typically provided only in English. All levels of American government—federal, state, and municipal—have insisted that there is a legitimate governmental interest in promoting a common language, and the Supreme Court has repeatedly affirmed that claim in upholding laws that mandate the teaching and use of English in schools and government functions. Indeed, as Gerald Johnson put it, "It is one of history's little ironies that no polyglot empire of the old world has dared to be so ruthless in imposing a single language upon its whole population as was the liberal republic 'dedicated to the proposition that all men are created equal.'"[3]

In short, the United States has deliberately promoted integration into what I call a "societal culture" that is based on the English language. I call it a *societal* culture to emphasize that it involves a common language and social institutions, rather than common religious beliefs, family customs, or personal lifestyles. Societal cultures within a modern liberal democracy are inevitably pluralistic, containing Christians as well as Muslims, Jews, and atheists; heterosexuals as well as gays; urban professionals as well as rural farmers; conservatives as well as socialists. Such diversity is the inevitable result of the rights and freedoms guaranteed to liberal citizens—including freedom of conscience, association, speech, political dissent, and rights to privacy—particularly when combined with an ethnically diverse population.

So a societal culture is a territorially concentrated culture, centered on a shared language that is used in a wide range of societal institutions, in both public and private life, such as schools, media, law, economy, government, and so forth. Participation in such societal cultures provides access to meaningful ways of life across the full range of human activities, including social, educational, recreational, and economic life, encompassing both public and private spheres.

The American government has deliberately promoted integration into such a societal culture—that is, it has encouraged citizens to view their life chances as tied up with participation in common societal institutions that operate in the English language. Nor is the United States at all unique in this respect. Promoting integration into a societal culture is part of a nation-building project that all liberal democracies have engaged in. When I speak of the "integration" of ethnic groups, therefore, I am speaking of integration in this very specific sociocultural sense—that is, the extent to which the members of ethnic groups integrate into an existing societal culture and come to view their life chances as tied up with participation in the range of societal institutions based on a common language that define that societal culture.

Obviously, the sense in which English-speaking Americans share a common "culture" is a very thin one, since it does not preclude differences in religion, personal values, family relationships, or lifestyle choices. But while this sort of common culture is thin, it is far from trivial. On the contrary, as I discuss below, attempts to integrate people into such a common societal culture have often been met with serious resistance. Although integration in this sense leaves a great deal of room for both the public and private expression of individual and collective differences, some groups have nonetheless vehemently rejected the idea that they should view their life chances as tied up with the societal institutions conducted in the majority's language.

It is important to note that governments need not promote only one societal culture. It is possible for government policies to encourage the sustaining of two or more societal cultures within a single country—indeed, as I discuss below, this is precisely what characterizes "multination" states. However, historically, virtually every liberal democracy has, at one point or another, attempted to diffuse a single societal culture throughout all of its territory. Nor should these efforts at assimilation be seen purely as a matter of cultural imperialism or ethnocentric prejudice. This sort of nation-building serves a number of important and legitimate goals. For example, a modern economy requires a mobile, educated, and literate workforce. Standardized public education in a common language has often been seen as essential if all citizens are to have equal opportunity to work in this modern economy. Also, participation in a common societal culture has often been seen as essential for generating solidarity within modern democratic states. The sort of solidarity required by a welfare state requires that citizens have a strong sense of common identity and common membership, so that they will make sacrifices for each other, and this common identity is assumed to require (or at least be facilitated by) a common language and history. Promoting integration into a common societal culture has been seen as essential to social equality and political cohesion in modern states.

So all states have engaged in this process of nation-building—that is, a process of promoting a common language, a sense of common membership in, and equal access to the social institutions based on that language.[4] Far from being neutral with respect to citizens' ethnocultural identities, state decisions regarding official languages, core curriculum in education, and the requirements for acquiring citizenship all were made with the express intention of diffusing a particular culture throughout society and of promoting a particular national identity based on participation in that societal culture.

Because these nation-building projects can be seen not merely as ethnocentric prejudice, but rather as an extension of freedom and equality to all citizens, they have not always been resisted by minority groups. Some ethnocultural groups have accepted the call to integrate. And in some countries, the result of these nation-building programs has been to extend a common societal culture throughout the entire territory of the state. These are the paradigmatic nation-states—for example, England, France, Germany. But in other countries, territorially concentrated minorities have resisted integration into the dominant societal culture. In such multination states—like Canada, Switzerland, Belgium, and Spain—one or more national minorities, each with its own distinct languages and separate institutions, exist alongside the dominant societal culture.

THE CHOICE OF MARGINALIZATION, INTEGRATION, OR SELF-GOVERNMENT

So the state, far from being neutral with respect to ethnocultural identity, has engaged in systematic efforts at diffusing a common societal culture. As a result, the members of ethnocultural minorities are faced with a basic question about how they wish to relate to this state-supported societal culture.

As Charles Taylor notes, the process of nation-building inescapably privileges members of the majority culture:

> If a modern society has an "official" language, in the fullest sense of the term, that is, a state-sponsored , -inculcated, and -defined language and culture, in which both economy and state function, then it is obviously an immense advantage to people if this language and culture are theirs. Speakers of other languages are at a distinct disadvantage.[5]

This means that the members of minority cultures face a choice. If all public institutions are being run in another language, minorities face the danger of being marginalized from the major economic, academic, and political institutions of the society. To avoid perpetual marginalization, minorities must either integrate into the majority culture or seek the sorts of rights and powers of self-government needed to maintain their own societal culture—that is, to create their own economic, political and educational institutions in their own language.

Not all groups wish to avoid marginalization. This would seem to be true, for example, of certain immigrant ethnoreligious sects, like the Amish in the United States or the Hutterites in Canada. But the option of accepting marginalization is likely to be attractive only to ethnoreligious sects whose theology requires them to avoid all contact with the modern world. The Hutterites and Amish are unconcerned about their marginalization from universities or legislatures, since they view such "worldly" institutions as corrupt. They have demanded and received special exemptions that reduce their exposure to the larger world in general and to state institutions in particular—for example, exemption from military service and the right to withdraw their children from schools before the legal age of sixteen.

The rationale for this voluntary marginalization was religious, not linguistic. These groups objected to integrating into the mainstream anglophone society not because they wished to preserve their ancestral Germanic language, but because they wanted to create a "sacred space" free from corrupting influences. Since they did not desire integration, they had less motivation to learn English than most immigrants, and the extent of their isolation meant that they faced less pressure to learn English than did most immigrants. As a result, these groups maintained their ancestral language for a longer period than other immigrant groups did. But language maintenance was never the main reason for their isolation, and over time English has gradually supplemented German as the language of community life (except for church services).

We can say that the special status of such ethnoreligious sects constitutes a kind of multiculturalism—one that protects their ability to maintain themselves as a closed and permanently marginalized community within the larger society. It is anachronistic to use this term, since the exemptions accorded these groups date back to the turn of the century, long before the adoption of any principle of multiculturalism. Moreover, these exemptions were accorded on an ad hoc basis for very small groups, rather than as a precedent or model for immigrants or religious communities generally. But these groups do exhibit a specific type of ethnocultural accommodation, which I will call "isolationist multiculturalism." I will evaluate its impact on democratic citizenship in the section on ethnoreligious sects and isolationist multiculturalism.

However, isolationist multiculturalism is a peripheral phenomenon, restricted to religious sects whose theology prohibits contact with the modern world. Virtually all other ethnocultural minorities seek to participate in the modern world, and to do so, they must either integrate or seek the self-government needed to create and sustain their own modern institutions. Faced with this choice, ethnocultural groups have responded in different ways. Some have accepted integration. This is particularly true, historically, of immigrant groups. Why have immigrants historically accepted integration? One reason is that most immigrants have voluntarily left their own culture with the expectation of integrating into another national society. That is just what it means to become an immigrant. If they found the idea of integrating into another culture repugnant, they would not have chosen to become immigrants. (Obviously this does not apply to refugees.) Moreover, since they typically emigrate as individuals or families, rather than as entire communities, immigrants lack the territorial concentration or corporate institutions needed to form a linguistically distinct society alongside the mainstream society. To try to re-create such a distinct parallel society would require tremendous support from the host society—support that host governments are reluctant to offer.

Some commentators think that the sort of multiculturalism policies demanded by immigrants today are precisely an attempt to gain this sort of support. I believe that this perception reflects a misunderstanding of what is in fact required for an ethnocultural group to create and sustain a separate national culture. It would require changes in virtually all areas of public policy and all political institutions—demands that no immigrant group has made and that no host government would even consider accepting. I hope to show that the nationalist option is neither desirable nor feasible for immigrants. And indeed there are very few (if any) examples in the Western democracies of immigrant groups forming nationalist movements for self-government or secession. If we look carefully at the actual substance of immigrants' multiculturalism demands, we will see that they involve simply renegotiating the terms of integration so as to enable immigrant groups to express their particularity within mainstream institutions. Immigrants still accept the expectation that they will integrate into common institutions operating in the English language, but insist that these institutions be adapted to accommodate their identities and practices. I will call this "pluralist multiculturalism," and discuss its impact on democratic citizenship in the sections on immigrant groups and pluralist multiculturalism.

By contrast, nonimmigrant national minorities have strongly resisted integration, and instead have fought for self-government. By "national minorities" I mean historically settled, territorially concentrated, and previously self-governing cultures whose territory has become incorporated into a larger state. The incorporation of such groups has typically been involuntary, due to colonization, conquest, or the transfer of territory between imperial powers, but in some cases reflects a voluntary federation. Such groups include the Québécois and Puerto Ricans in North America, and the Flemish, Catalans, and Basques in Europe.

Immigrants rarely object to the imposition of a common language, since they have already chosen to leave their old culture behind and since the option of re-creating a culturally distinct society alongside the existing national culture is not feasible. For national minorities, however, the imposition of the majority language threatens their existing culturally distinct society. Their language and historical narratives are already embodied in a full set of social practices and institutions, encompassing all aspects of social life, which then become threatened by the majority's efforts to diffuse a common societal culture. Such groups almost inevitably resist integration, and seek official recognition of their language and culture. Indeed, Walker Connor goes so far as to suggest that few if any examples exist of recognized national groups in this century having voluntarily assimilated to another culture, even though many have faced significant economic incentives and political pressures to do so.[6]

This demand for official recognition need not take the form of a secessionist movement for a separate state. It could instead take the form of demanding some form of local autonomy, perhaps through a system of federalism, that would give local control over education, language, and perhaps even immigration. But whatever the exact form, it typically involves the demand for the sorts of legal rights and legislative powers necessary to ensure the survival of a distinct societal culture alongside the majority society.

National minorities have rarely advanced their claims for self-government under the rubric of multiculturalism. They have rather appealed to the older and more well-established norms and vocabularies of nationalism and of "the self-determination of peoples," which long predated the current discourse of multiculturalism. However, for the purposes of this paper, we can consider this as a distinctive form of multiculturalism—what I will call "nationalist multiculturalism"—and I will evaluate its impact on democratic citizenship below.

To sum up, then, faced with the nation-building project of the state, ethnocultural groups must choose between marginalization, integration, or separatist nationalism. Given these options, a few ethnoreligious sects have chosen marginalization; immigrant groups are likely to choose integration;

while national minorities are likely to choose the nationalist strategy. This is certainly the historical pattern in the United States and Canada.

Of course, this is just a general trend, not a universal law. In some countries, immigrant groups have not been allowed or encouraged to integrate (e.g., Turks in Germany). Even in the United States, the usual tendencies toward immigrant integration have sometimes been deflected, particularly if the newcomers were expected to return quickly to their country of origin (as with the original Cuban exiles in Miami); or if the immigrants were illegal, and so had no right to employment or citizenship (as with illegal Mexican migrants in California). These groups were exempted or precluded from the usual state-imposed pressure to integrate.

The extent to which national minorities have been able to maintain a separate societal culture also varies considerably. In some countries, national minorities have been almost completely integrated (e.g., Bretons in France). Even in the United States, the extent (and success) of nationalist mobilization varies. For example, compare the Chicanos in the Southwest with the Puerto Ricans. The Chicanos were unable to preserve their own Spanish-speaking judicial, educational, or political institutions after being involuntarily incorporated into the United States in 1848, and they have not mobilized along nationalist lines to try to re-create these institutions. By contrast, Puerto Ricans mobilized very successfully to defend their Spanish-language institutions and self-government rights when they were involuntarily incorporated into the United States in 1898, and continue to exhibit a strong nationalist consciousness. The extent of nationalist mobilization also differs among the various native Indian tribes in America. Moreover there are some groups that do not fit any of these categories—most obviously African Americans—whose unique history has led to a very distinctive, and somewhat ambivalent, form of multiculturalism.[7]

There are many such complicated cases that do not fit neatly into the "ethnoreligious sect," "immigrant," or "national minority" patterns. I will return to some of these "in-between" cases later on. But we can best understand the complexities and ambiguities of these cases if we first have a clear picture of the more standard cases, since the demands of in-between groups are often a complex hybrid of different (and sometimes contradictory) elements drawn from the more familiar models of ethnoreligious marginalization, immigrant integration, and separatist nationalism.

Corresponding to each of these three main options (marginalization, integration, separation) is a specific form of multiculturalism—which I have called, respectively, isolationist, pluralist, and nationalist. In the rest of the paper, I would like to examine these forms more carefully, to consider what sort of associational life they imply for ethnic groups and what sort of impact they have on democratic citizenship. To evaluate them, however, we need an account of what democratic citizenship involves.

The Virtues of Liberal Democratic Citizenship

I began the paper by noting the fear that participation in ethnic associations does not promote the sort of habits and virtues needed for a healthy liberal democratic society. But what are these virtues? William Galston divides the virtues required for responsible citizenship into four groups: (1) *general* virtues: courage, law-abidingness, loyalty; (2) *social* virtues: independence, open-mindedness; (3) *economic* virtues: work ethic, capacity to delay self-gratification, adaptability to economic and technological change; and (4) *political* virtues: capacity to discern and respect the rights of others, willingness to demand only what can be paid for, ability to evaluate the performance of those in office, willingness to engage in public discourse.[8]

It is the last two virtues—the ability to question authority and the willingness to engage in public discourse—that are the most distinctive components of liberal democratic citizenship. The need to question authority arises in part from the fact that citizens in a representative democracy elect representatives who govern in their name. Hence, an important responsibility of citizens is to monitor those officials and judge their conduct. The need to engage in public discourse arises from the fact that the decisions of government in a democracy should be made publicly, through free and open discussion. But as Galston notes, the virtue of public discourse is not just the willingness to participate in politics or to make one's views known. Rather, it "includes the willingness to listen seriously to a range of views which, given the diversity of liberal societies, will include ideas the listener is bound to find strange and even obnoxious. The virtue of political discourse also includes the willingness to set forth one's own views intelligibly and candidly as the basis for a politics of persuasion rather than manipulation or coercion."[9]

This is sometimes called the virtue of "public reasonableness." Liberal citizens must give reasons for their political demands, not just state preferences or make threats. Moreover, these reasons must be "public" reasons, in the sense that they are capable of persuading people of different faiths and nationalities. Hence, it is not enough to invoke Scripture or tradition. Liberal citizens must justify their political demands in terms that fellow citizens can understand and accept as consistent with their status as free and equal citizens. It requires a conscientious effort to distinguish those beliefs that are matters of private faith from those that are capable of public defense, and to see how issues look from the point of view of those with differing religious commitments and cultural backgrounds.

The importance of public reasonableness depends, in part, on how politically active people are. For those who are politically apathetic, learning the virtue of public reasonableness is less important. But even for such politically passive citizens, the requirements of liberal citizenship are by no means trivial. The obligations of liberal citizenship are often described in purely negative terms—that is, the obligation not to break the law and not to harm others or restrict their rights and liberties. But that ignores one of the most basic requirements of liberal citizenship, albeit one that is often neglected in theoretical discussions. This is the virtue of "civility" or "decency," and it is a virtue that even the most passive citizen must learn, since it applies not only to political activity, but also—indeed, primarily—to our actions in everyday life, on the street, in neighborhood shops, and in the diverse institutions and forums of civil society.

Civility refers to the way we treat nonintimates with whom we come into face-to-face contact. To understand civility, it is helpful to compare it with the related requirement of nondiscrimination. The legal prohibition on discrimination initially applied only to government actions. Government laws and policies that discriminated against people on the basis of race or gender have gradually been struck down in Western democracies, since they violate the basic liberal commitment to equality of opportunity. But it has become clear that whether individuals have genuinely equal opportunity depends not only government actions, but also on the actions of institutions within civil society—corporations, schools, stores, landlords, and so forth. If people are discriminated against by prejudiced shop owners or real estate agents, they will be denied equal citizenship, even if the state itself does not discriminate. Hence, legal requirements of nondiscrimination have increasingly been applied to "private" firms and associations.

This extension of nondiscrimination from government to civil society is not just a shift in the scale of liberal norms; it also involves a radical extension in the obligations of liberal citizenship, for the obligation to treat people as equal citizens now applies to the most common, everyday decisions of individuals. It is no longer permissible for businesses to refuse to hire black employees, or to refuse to serve black customers, or to segregate their black employees or customers. But not just that; the norms of nondiscrimination entail that it is impermissible for businesses to ignore their black customers or treat them rudely, although it is not always possible to legally enforce this. Businesses must in effect make blacks feel welcome, just as if they were whites. Blacks must, in short, be treated with *civility*. The same applies to the way citizens treat each other in schools or recreational associations, even in private clubs.

This sort of civility is the logical extension of nondiscrimination, since it is needed to ensure that all citizens have the same opportunities to participate within civil society. Now it extends into the very hearts and minds of citizens. Liberal citizens must learn to interact in everyday settings on an equal basis with people for whom they might harbor prejudice. The extent to which this requirement of civility can (or should) be legally enforced is limited. It is easier to compel businesses to be nondiscriminatory in hiring than to compel them to treat black customers with civility. But the recent spread of laws and regulations against sexual and racial harassment, both in society generally and within schools and businesses, can be seen as an attempt to ensure a level of civility, since they include forms of offensive speech as well as physical intimidation. And while it is obviously impossible to compel civility between citizens in less formal settings—for example, whether whites smile or scowl at an Asian family in the neighborhood park—liberal citizenship nonetheless requires this sort of civility.

It is easy to trivialize this requirement of civility as being simply good manners. Philip Rieff, for example, dismisses the insistence on civility as a superficial facade that simply hides a deeper indifference to the needs of others. As he puts it, "We have long known what 'equality' means in American culture: it means . . . a smile fixed to the face, demanding you return a smile."[10] It is true that liberal societies have reinforced, and thereby partially conflated, the moral obligation of civility with an aesthetic conception of "good manners." For example, the expectation of civility is sometimes used to discourage the sort of forceful protest that may be needed for an oppressed group to be heard. For a disadvantaged group to make a scene is often seen as in bad taste. This exaggerated emphasis on good manners can be used to compel passivity. True civility does not mean smiling at others no matter how badly they treat you, as if oppressed groups should be nice to their oppressors. Rather, it means treating others as equals on the condition that they extend the same recognition to you. While there is some overlap between civility and a more general politeness, they are nonetheless distinct—civility involves upholding norms of equality within the public life of a society, including civil society, and thereby upholding essential liberal values.[11]

These three virtues are arguably the bedrock of liberal democratic citizenship—civility, public reasonableness, and the commitment to hold public officials accountable. Without a significant measure of these virtues among citizens, it is difficult to see how democratic cooperation is possible. It is important, therefore, to determine the impact of the various types of multiculturalism on these virtues. I will start with the case of isolationist multiculturalism before turning to nationalist and pluralist multiculturalism.

ETHNORELIGIOUS SECTS AND ISOLATIONIST MULTICULTURALISM

What is the impact of isolationist multiculturalism on democratic citizenship? Allowing groups to, in effect, opt out of the public life of the country clearly impedes, rather than promotes, the sort of habits and virtues needed for good democratic citizenship. To be sure, by protecting the associational life of the Amish, isolationist multiculturalism promotes many nonpolitical virtues. For example, the Amish are widely admired for their work ethic, law-abidingness, family loyalty, and religious devotion. But the Amish show no interest in the political virtues of citizenship. They do not learn the ability to evaluate the performance of those in elected office—indeed, they take no interest in elections, and neither vote nor run for elected office. Nor do they learn to engage in public discourse or to interact civilly with others in the institutions of civil society—indeed, the very idea of interacting extensively with non-Amish is strongly discouraged. (When this sort of interaction is unavoidable, it is done through paid intermediaries.) And this sort of multiculturalism does not promote horizontal connectedness among citizens or a shared sense of solidarity or loyalty. Isolationist multiculturalism, in effect, absolves the Amish from their responsibilities as citizens to deal with the country's problems. It absolves them from any responsibility to think about the problem of inner-city neighborhoods, or how to pay off the national debt, or of how to respond to injustices overseas.

But while this sort of multiculturalism does not promote democratic citizenship, neither is it very harmful to the overall functioning of liberal democracies, precisely because the Amish are so politically passive and socially isolated. It is not that the Amish participate in politics in an irresponsible or selfish manner; it is simply that they do not participate at all. Similarly, it is not that the Amish discriminate against others in civil society; it is rather that they do not enter the larger society. They are, to use Jeff Spinner's term, "partial citizens."[12] They have, in effect, waived both the rights and responsibilities of democratic citizenship. They do not accept their civic responsibilities, but neither do they exercise their political rights or seek political office.

Spinner argues that such groups should be tolerated and their special exemptions granted, so long as they remain socially withdrawn and politically passive, and so long as members are free to leave. My own view is that we should continue to respect the special exemptions that were historically promised to certain groups (particularly when it was the promise of such exemptions that led these groups to settle where they are now). However, I do not believe that liberal democratic states have any obligation to make it possible for new groups to acquire this status (e.g., Christian fundamentalist survivalist groups).[13]

In any event, isolationist multiculturalism is peripheral to modern democracies. The more pressing issue concerns the multiculturalism claims of immigrants and national minorities, to which I now turn.

National Minorities and Nationalist Multiculturalism

I noted earlier that historically, immigrants and national minorities have responded differently to the state's efforts at nation-building: the former accepting integration, the latter pursuing self-government. Many people worry, however, that immigrant demand for multiculturalism reflects a rejection of the historical tendency toward integration and the quest for something closer to the rights and powers of national minorities.

I think this is seriously mistaken. Below, I will examine several immigrant multiculturalism policies and show that they are not opposed to integration, but rather assist it. However, to see this, we need first to consider what would be required for an ethnocultural minority to consolidate its own societal culture within a larger state. In this section, therefore, I want to look at nationalist multiculturalism of the sort pursued by national minorities. The thought that multiculturalism could enable immigrant groups to form and sustain their own societal cultures rests, I believe, on a failure to recognize what is actually involved in such a project. The fact is that to maintain a separate societal culture in a modern state is an immensely ambitious and arduous project.

We can get a sense of what this involves by thinking about what the Québécois have had to do to maintain their societal culture within Canada. Obviously, the first demand was that their children be able to attend French-language schools. This is a pivotal step in reproducing a societal culture, since it guarantees passing on to the next generation the language and its associated traditions and conventions. But this by itself did nothing to create or sustain French-language public institutions. It ensured that children learned the language, but it did not ensure that they had opportunity to speak it in public life. It is very difficult for languages to survive in modern industrialized societies unless they are used in public life—for example, in political, economic, and academic institutions. Given the high demands for literacy in work and the widespread interaction citizens have with government agencies, any language that is not a public language becomes so marginalized that it is likely to survive only among a small elite, in isolated rural communities, or in a ritualized form, not as a living and developing language underlying a flourishing culture.

The Québécois also, therefore, fought for various substantial positive rights to use their language when interacting with government institutions—that is, in courts, legislatures, welfare agencies, health services, and the like. But this is not sufficient either, since people interact with the state only on an episodic basis. The real key to the reproduction of a societal culture is the ability to use one's language in one's day-to-day employment.

Hence, the Québécois sought the right to use their language within government employment. It is important to remember that the government is a very large employer. In modern states, public expenditures often account for 50 percent of the economy. To survive, therefore, minority groups must have a fair share of government employment and government contracts. For example, consider the army. In many countries, the army is a major employer, and of course military service is often compulsory. If all units in the army operate in the majority language, military service becomes a crucial tool for integrating minorities. This is true, for example, in Israel, where military service has been the single most important institution for integrating immigrants into a Hebrew-speaking society. It was also a pivotal institution for integration in France. A classic study has shown that the spread of the French language—which was largely restricted to Paris at the time of the French Revolution—was primarily the result of the fact that conscripts had to learn French. The army was key in "turning peasants into Frenchmen."[14]

A minority that is content to accept marginalization can avoid integration by simply seeking exemption from military service. This is true of the Amish and Hutterites. But if a minority seeks to maintain a modern national society, then they will instead demand that some army units operate in their own language. Hence, the Québécois have fought for the right to French-language military training and French-language military units.

The same applies to other areas of government employment—from food inspectors to tax accountants. In all of these cases, some part of the public service must be conducted in the minority's language. It is not enough that one can interact with the state in one's language—given the role of the state as the single largest employer, minorities must also be able to work within the state in their own language. But the state is not the only large employer, and so considerable efforts have been made to ensure that French is the language of the workplace even in private firms. This is an important—and largely successful—feature of Quebec's language laws. And in order to train the doctors, scientists, and skilled workers who will staff these public institutions and private workplaces, the minority must create its own higher education system—not simply at the elementary and secondary school levels, but up to university and professional schools. Hence the insistence on forming several French-language universities and colleges.

The requirements for sustaining a national culture go even further. For example, decisions regarding immigration and naturalization also affect the viability of societal cultures. Immigration can strengthen a culture, so long as the numbers are regulated and immigrants are encouraged (or required) to learn the nation's language and history. But if immigrants into Canada integrate into the majority anglophone culture, then the Québécois will be increasingly outnumbered and, so, increasingly powerless in political life, both federally and within Quebec. A minority that seeks to sustain a distinct societal culture must, therefore, have some control over immigration policies. And control over immigration has been one of the key features of modern Quebec nationalism—including the right of the Québécois to define their own immigration criteria (which favor French speakers), to set their own target levels (based on their calculations regarding the absorption capacity of their society), and, indeed, to send their own immigration officers overseas.

So the historical experience of the Québécois suggests that a minority can sustain its societal culture only if it has substantial powers regarding language, education, government employment, and immigration. If the minority can be outvoted on any of these issues, their hope of sustaining their societal culture will be seriously jeopardized. But they can exercise these powers only if they have some forum of collective decision making. That is, there must be some political body or political unit that they substantially control. This is reflected in the Québécois commitment to federalism—that is, to a system that decentralizes power to federal subunits and whose boundaries are drawn so that the Québécois form a majority within one of these subunits. And to ensure that they are not deprived of their self-government, the Québécois have insisted that the boundaries of their province and the powers it exercises themselves be constitutionally guaranteed, so that the majority cannot unilaterally reduce their self-governing powers.

This is just a brief sketch of the measures that the Québécois have found necessary to sustain their societal culture in the face of the anglophone majority in Canada. One could list many other factors, from bilingual product labels to bilingual currency. But most commentators would agree that *la survivance* in Quebec has depended on a number of these very basic conditions: French-language education, not only in childhood, but through to higher education; the right to use one's language, not only when interacting with government, but also in one's day-to-day job, whether in public service or private employment; the right not only to exempt francophone immigrants from the requirement to learn English to gain citizenship, but also the right to select, integrate, and naturalize immigrants; the right not only to a fair share of political power at the federal level, but also the right to self-government, as embodied in a constitutionally defined federal subunit that has the power to make decisions with respect to education, employment, and immigration.

A similar story could be told about the conditions that have proven necessary to sustain a distinct societal culture in Puerto Rico, or in Flanders, or in Catalonia. For example, Puerto Rico has not only demanded Spanish-language schools, up to and including at the university level, but also that Spanish be the language of government employment and that immigrants be able to naturalize in Spanish rather than English. (Puerto Rico is the only place within the United States where immigrants are exempt from the requirement to know English to gain citizenship.)

It is important to reflect on how onerous these efforts at cultural reproduction have been. Sustaining a societal culture in the modern world is not a matter of yearly ethnic festivals or a few classes taught to children in their mother tongue. It is a matter of creating and sustaining a set of public institutions that enables a minority group to participate in the modern world through the use of its own language.

To put it another way, it is not enough for a minority simply to resist the majority's efforts at diffusing a single common language. The minority must also engage in its own competing form of modern, state-sponsored nation-building. Nationalists in Quebec or Puerto Rico realize that to sustain their national culture, they too must seek to diffuse a common culture and language throughout their society so as to promote equality of opportunity and political solidarity. And they must use the same tools that the majority nation uses in its program of nation-building—that is, standardized public education, official languages, including language requirements for citizenship and government employment, and so forth. As I noted earlier, the historical evidence is that the capacity and motivation to undertake such an ambitious nation-building project is found only in national minorities, rather than in immigrant groups. And as I discuss in the next section, there is no basis for thinking that this is changing.

What is the impact of this nationalist form of multiculturalism on democratic citizenship? Obviously, the project of maintaining a separate and self-governing society, with its own complete set of institutions operating in its own distinct language, does not promote horizontal connectedness among citizens. On the contrary, the almost inevitable result is to make democratic cooperation across national boundaries more difficult. The problem here, unlike the case of the Amish, is not that national minorities lack the virtues of public reasonableness or civic engagement. The problem, rather, is that they see themselves as belonging to a separate political community and as having only a secondary, and often ambivalent, bond to the larger state. After all, most national minorities have been involuntarily incorporated into the larger state, and even those that do not actively seek secession nonetheless insist that the authority of the larger state over them is limited.

One could say, therefore, that this form of multiculturalism is balkanizing. But this is to beg the question, for the whole point of nationalist multiculturalism is to insist that national minorities form separate political communities, with the right to govern themselves. Their concern is with the democratic functioning of their own political community, and nationalist multiculturalism is intended precisely to promote trust and solidarity within their own national society. They care about democratic virtues, but their concern is, in the first instance, with promoting these virtues within their own polity, and they see nationalist multiculturalism as building the common institutions and public spaces within which civic engagement can take place and within which democratic virtues can be developed.

This raises an important point. The claim that associational life promotes democratic virtues may be true, but as with most claims about democracy, it tells us nothing about where the relevant boundaries of the democratic unit should be. Democracy is the rule of "the people," and the evidence suggests that democracy functions best when "the people" are engaged in civil society. But what if there are two or more peoples in the state, each with the right to rule themselves and each with its own civil society? In such multi-nation states, the impact of nationalist multiculturalism on democratic citizenship is to be evaluated not just by its effect on democracy at the federal level, but also by its effect on democracy at the level of the self-governing national community.

Put this way, it seems likely that nationalist multiculturalism promotes democracy at the level of the self-governing nation, but renders democratic cooperation more difficult at the federal level. Québécois nationalism has led to a flourishing francophone civil society within Quebec, but has not promoted the participation of Québécois in the pan-Canadian anglophone civil society. To reject nationalist multiculturalism on the grounds that it impedes democratic cooperation at the federal level, therefore, is to assume precisely what national minorities dispute—namely, that for the purposes of evaluating democratic functioning, the country as a whole forms a single "people," rather than two or more peoples each with the right to govern itself. Of course, one might respond that national minorities are wrong to think that they have a right to govern themselves. I cannot address that objection, except to say that in situations where national minorities have been involuntarily incorporated into a larger state through conquest or colonization or the imperial cession of territory, I think that they do have a very powerful right to self-government. Indeed, to oppose nationalist multiculturalism under such circumstances on the grounds that it interferes with democratic cooperation at the federal level is not a defense of democracy but of colonialism.[15]

IS IMMIGRANT MULTICULTURALISM SEPARATIST?

Isolationist multiculturalism and nationalist multiculturalism are longstanding phenomena that in fact predate the rise of "multiculturalism" as a concept in public debate. By contrast, the sort of pluralist multiculturalism sought by immigrant groups really is a new phenomenon. Prior to the 1960s, immigrants to the United States, as to Australia and Canada, were expected to shed their distinctive heritage and assimilate to existing cultural norms. This is known as the "Anglo-conformity" model of immigration. Indeed, some groups were denied entry if they were seen as unassimilable (e.g., restrictions on Chinese immigration in Canada and the United States, the "whites-only" immigration policy in Australia). Assimilation was seen as essential for political stability, and was further rationalized through ethnocentric denigration of other cultures. However, beginning in the 1970s, under pressure from immigrant groups, all three countries rejected the assimilationist model and adopted more tolerant and pluralistic policies that allow and indeed encourage immigrants to maintain various aspects of their ethnic heritage. It is now accepted that immigrants should be free to maintain some of their old customs regarding food, dress, religion, and recreation and to associate with each other to maintain these practices. This is no longer seen as unpatriotic or un-American. The demand for multiculturalism policies is a natural extension of this change. If it is acceptable for immigrants to maintain pride in their ethnic identity, then is it not right that these identities be recognized and accommodated by the state?

Perhaps because it is so new, many people are fearful of immigrant multiculturalism. Critics worry that it involves repudiating not just Anglo-conformity but the entire idea of integration and treats immigrant groups as if they were national minorities. Like nationalist multiculturalism, it is seen as promoting balkanization or separatism and encouraging the "fragmentation of the national community into a quarrelsome spatter of enclaves, ghettoes, tribes . . . encouraging and exalting cultural and linguistic apartheid."[16]

I think this is quite mistaken. I will consider the impact of specific multiculturalism policies on democratic citizenship in the next section. Before we can look objectively at the impact of these policies, however, we need to confront the fear of balkanization and apartheid that has distorted most discussions of multiculturalism.

Consider any of the sorts of policies commonly associated with immigrant multiculturalism, whether it is curriculum reform in schools (e.g., revising the history and literature curriculum within public schools to give greater recognition to the historical and cultural contributions of ethnocultural minorities; creating bilingual education programs at the primary school level for the children of immigrants), or institutional adaptation (e.g., revising work schedules or dress codes to accommodate the religious holidays and practices of immigrant groups; adopting workplace or school harassment codes prohibiting racist comments; adding federal regulatory guidelines about ethnic stereotypes in the media), or public education programs (e.g., antiracism educational campaigns; cultural diversity training for the police, social workers, or health-care professionals), or cultural development programs (e.g., funding of ethnic festivals and ethnic studies programs; providing mother-tongue literacy courses for adult immigrants), or affirmative action (e.g., preferential treatment of visible minorities in access to education, training, or employment).

Each of these policies raises its own unique issues, and so it is misleading to talk about "the impact of multiculturalism" in general, as if all of these policies have the same motivations and consequences. Having said that, however, it is important to note that *none* of them—either by themselves or taken together—involves anything close to a program of nation-building. For example, none of these policies involves creating Spanish-language army units or Vietnamese-language universities. And none of them involves creating new political units that would enable Ukrainians or Somalis to exercise self-governing powers over government employment or immigration. Nor have any of these types of measures been demanded by these immigrant groups.

One might think that existing multiculturalism policies are first steps down the road toward a protonationalist project of maintaining a separate societal culture and away from integration. As I argue below, I think that is an implausible interpretation of these demands. On the contrary, most of them actually promote and consolidate the societal integration of immigrants. However, let us imagine, for the sake of argument, that an immigrant group within the United States or Canada—say, the Chinese—really did want to form and maintain their own societal culture. It is worth emphasizing how much farther such a group would need to go, in terms of its institutional capacities and political powers.

It is certainly possible *in theory* for Chinese to become a national minority, if they settle together and acquire self-governing powers. After all, this is what happened with English colonists throughout the British Empire, to Spanish colonists in Puerto Rico, and to French colonists in Quebec. These colonists did not see themselves as "immigrants," since they had no expectation of integrating into another culture, but rather aimed to reproduce their original society in a new land. It is a defining feature of colonization, as distinct from individual immigration, that it aims to create an institutionally complete society rather than integrating into an existing one. It would, in principle, be possible to encourage Chinese immigrants today to view themselves as colonists.

Think about what this would require. As we have seen, reproducing a societal culture requires not only that children be taught Chinese in public schools, but also that there be Chinese-language universities; it requires not only that there be Chinese-language ballots or welfare forms, but also that Chinese be the working language of the government workplace, including Chinese-language army units or hospitals; it requires not only that Chinese not be underrepresented in parliament, but also that there be a political body within which Chinese form a majority; it requires not only that Chinese need not learn English to acquire citizenship, but also that the Chinese community can maintain itself over time by selecting and naturalizing future immigrants on the basis of their integration into the Chinese-speaking community.

The simple fact is that existing multiculturalism policies have not created *any* of the public institutions needed to create and sustain a separate societal culture for Chinese or any other immigrant group. None of the academic, political, or economic institutions that would enable an immigrant group to participate in modern life through their mother tongue have been created. If Chinese Americans want to access the opportunities made available by modern society, then they must do so within the economic, academic, and political institutions of the anglophone societal culture.

This should not be surprising, because multiculturalism has not replaced any of the broader panoply of government policies and structures that sponsor societal integration. For example, it is still the case that immigrants must learn to speak English to gain citizenship, or to graduate from high school, or to get government employment, or to gain professional accreditation. As I discussed earlier, these are the basic pillars of government-supported integration within liberal democracies, and none of them has in any way been eroded by multiculturalism policies. Nor was multiculturalism intended to erode these.

This leaves open the possibility that some leaders of ethnic groups hope that multiculturalism policies will provide a springboard to a more comprehensively separatist policy. If so, it is a vain hope that massively underestimates the sort of support needed to create and sustain a separate societal culture. It makes more sense, I believe, to simply accept the obvious: there is no rational basis for the fear that multiculturalism policies will be used to enable immigrant groups to sustain their own societal cultures. It is a red herring, without any basis in reality. There is simply no evidence from any of the major Western immigration countries that immigrants are seeking to form themselves into national minorities or to adopt a nationalist political agenda.

Once we let go of this red herring, we can look more objectively at the actual intentions and implications of immigrant multiculturalism policies. As I noted earlier, if a nationalist movement for self-government is either undesired or unfeasible, then minorities have two choices. They can either integrate into one of the existing societal cultures or accept permanent marginalization—that is, become isolated enclaves that do not participate in the larger society and that lack the public institutions needed to form their own societal cultures.

The fundamental question regarding immigrant multiculturalism policies, I believe, is whether we view them as integrative or marginalizing. There are some examples of groups accepting permanent marginalization—for example, the Amish. But as I noted earlier, these groups are unique in wishing to avoid the modern world. They do not want to become police officers, or doctors or engineers or legislators. Therefore, they have no interest in controlling their own political units or universities. These groups are the exception that proves the rule that participating in modernity requires integration into a societal culture.

Do multiculturalism policies encourage immigrants today to become marginalized like the Amish? Or are they instead simply revising the terms of integration, encouraging immigrants to integrate into the anglophone societal culture while still maintaining pride in their ethnic and religious identities, and thereby enriching and pluralizing the larger societal culture? Do these policies promote what Spinner calls "partial citizenship":—that is, passive isolationism and withdrawal from mainstream society and political life? Or do they promote active participation and responsible citizenship among immigrants?

Immigrant Groups and Pluralist Multiculturalism

To help focus the question, here is a list of twelve policies that are often discussed under the rubric of multiculturalism:

1. Affirmative action programs that seek to increase the representation of immigrant groups (or women and the disabled) in major educational and economic institutions

2. A certain number of seats in the legislature or in government advisory bodies reserved for immigrant groups (or women and the disabled)

3. History and literature curriculum revision within public schools to give greater recognition to the historical and cultural contributions of immigrant groups

4. Revised work schedules that accommodate the religious holidays of immigrant groups (e.g., scheduling professional development days on major Jewish or Muslim holidays; exempting Jewish and Muslim businesses from Sunday closing laws)

5. Dress code revisions that accommodate the religious beliefs of immigrant groups (e.g., an army dress code that allows Orthodox Jews to wear their skullcaps; an exemption for Sikhs from mandatory motorcycle helmet laws or construction site hard hat laws)

6. Antiracism educational programs

7. Workplace or school harassment codes that seek to prevent colleagues/students from making racial (or sexist or homophobic) statements

8. Cultural diversity training for the police or health care professionals that trains them to recognize individual needs and conflicts within immigrant families

9. Government regulatory guidelines about ethnic stereotypes in the media

10. Government funding of ethnic cultural festivals and ethnic studies programs

11. Services to adult immigrants in their mother tongue rather than requiring that they learn English as a precondition for accessing public services

12. Bilingual education programs for the children of immigrants, in their earliest years of education as a transitional phase to secondary and postsecondary education in English

This list is not comprehensive, of course, but it gives a fairly accurate reflection, I think, of the sorts of issues that are raised in the public debate over immigrant multiculturalism and that have been adopted or at least seriously proposed by Western governments. I have also chosen these policies because they seem particularly relevant for assessing the question of balkanization versus horizontal connectedness.

Needless to say, this is not the only important question raised by immigrant multiculturalism. For example, some proposals raise the question of the relationship between multiculturalism and individual rights. This is the primary concern regarding the practice of female clitoridectomy, for example, or proposals for the legal recognition of compulsorily arranged marriages and *talaq* divorces, or the legal enforcement of traditional Muslim family law, or with proposals to allow husbands to cite "culture" as a defense when charged with beating their wives. Although these practices are sometimes debated under the label of multiculturalism, they have not been adopted by any Western government. They have been rejected not because they would directly affect the societal integration of immigrant groups in terms of their participation in mainstream economic, academic, and political institutions, but rather because they involve a denial of individual liberties and equality rights.

This raises an entirely separate set of issues from the ones I have been discussing in this chapter. I have tried to discuss these issues at length elsewhere. Let me just say here that in my view, a liberal state must reject any proposals that would allow a group to oppress its own members by limiting their basic civil and political rights.[17] So I think it is right and proper that immigrant multiculturalism policies have not extended to the accommodation of such practices.

My concern in this paper, however, is with the sorts of policies that have been adopted by governments, and with their impact on civic engagement and democratic citizenship, so I will focus on the twelve issues listed above. I will start with the first ten policies, since they are examples of diversity accommodated within common institutions, and then examine the final two policies, which are more complicated, since they involve a degree of institutional separateness.

I do not have the space to discuss all of these policies in detail. But to briefly go through the list, affirmative action policies and guarantees of group representation in the political process are clearly integrationist in their aim. They are intended precisely to increase the numbers of immigrants who participate within mainstream institutions, by guaranteeing them a certain share of the positions in various academic, economic, or political institutions. They bring members of different groups together, require them to cooperate in common tasks and common decision making, and then require them to abide by these common decisions. They are, therefore, the very opposite of policies designed to promote ethnic separatism. (Whether they are *fair* ways to promote the integration of immigrants is a separate question).

Affirmative action and group representation, then, are intended to help immigrants enter mainstream societal institutions. The next seven multiculturalism policies are intended to make immigrant groups feel more comfortable within these institutions once they are there. This is true, for example, of demands that the curriculum in public schools be revised so as to provide greater recognition for the historical contributions of immigrant groups; or of demands that public institutions recognize the religious holidays of immigrant groups (e.g., recognizing Muslim and Jewish as well as Christian holidays); or of demands that official dress codes for schools, workplaces, and police forces be amended so that Sikh men can wear turbans, or Jewish men can wear skullcaps, or Muslim women can wear the *hijab*; or of demands that schools and workplaces provide a welcoming environment for people of all races and religions by prohibiting hate speech; or of demands that the media avoid ethnic stereotyping and give visible representation to society's diversity in their programming; or of demands that professionals in the police force, social work, and health care be familiar with the distinctive cultural needs and practices of the people in their care.

None of these policies involves encouraging immigrant groups to view themselves as separate and self-governing nations with their own public institutions. On the contrary, they are intended precisely to make it easier for the members of immigrant groups to participate within the mainstream institutions of the existing society. Immigrant groups are demanding increased recognition and visibility within the mainstream society. In short, these multiculturalism policies involve a revision in the terms of integration, not a rejection of integration per se. They are rejecting Anglo-conformity but not integration.

Critics of these policies typically focus entirely on the fact that they involve public affirmation and recognition of immigrants' ethnic identity—a process that is said to be inherently separatist. But they ignore the fact that this affirmation and recognition occurs *within common institutions*. There is no sense in which any of these policies encourages either an Amish-like withdrawal from the institutions of mainstream society or a Québécois-like nationalist struggle to create and maintain separate public institutions. On the contrary, these policies are flatly in contradiction with both ethnic marginalization and ethnonationalism, since they encourage integration into mainstream institutions. They encourage more immigrants to participate within existing academic, economic, and political institutions, and modify these institutions to make immigrants more welcome within them.

Of course, these policies may cause a backlash among nonimmigrant groups. For example, the demand by Sikh men to be exempted from the requirement to wear the ceremonial headgear of the national police force was seen by many Canadians as a sign of disrespect for one of Canada's "national symbols." But from the immigrants' point of view, such accommodations are integrative. The fact that Sikh men wanted to be part of Canada's national police force is ample evidence of their desire to participate in and contribute to the larger society, and the exemption they were requesting should be seen as promoting, not discouraging, their integration.

Indeed, it is the failure to adopt such policies that creates the serious risk of marginalization. For example, without the accommodation of their religious beliefs in school holidays and dress codes, immigrant groups might feel compelled to leave the public school system and set up separate schools. And without affirmative action, fewer immigrants would feel that they have a realistic chance at succeeding within mainstream institutions. These policies can only realistically be seen as helping to fight the potential sources of marginalization.

The situation gets more complicated when some form of institutional separateness is involved. Consider, for example, the issue of mother tongue education for adult newcomers, such as recent programs to teach illiterate newcomers how to read and write in their mother-tongue. Such experimental programs reflect a significant departure from the traditional assumption that adult immigrants must learn English first as a precondition for accessing any further education or government services.

The idea of separate classes for people of a particular ethnic group is very worrisome to some people, as is the idea that immigrants should be encouraged to use and develop their mother tongue. Are these policies the first steps toward either marginalization or nationalism, rather than integration? It should be obvious by now, I hope, that these policies are not guided by any ideal of nation-building. The assumption that immigrants who want to learn basic literacy in their mother tongue will subsequently demand mother-tongue universities or army units is deeply implausible. But are these policies marginalizing? That depends, I believe, on their long-term consequences. Critics assume mother-tongue programs prevent or discourage immigrants from learning English. This is a serious concern, because the evidence is clear that fluency in English is pivotal to the economic prospects of most immigrants and, indeed, to their more general ability to participate in social and political life.

But does teaching literacy in the immigrant's mother tongue in fact diminish the likelihood that he or she will successfully learn English? There is little evidence for this assumption. On the contrary, the evidence suggests that many people have great difficulty learning literacy in English until they acquire literacy in their mother tongue.[18] Under existing policies, they are effectively permanently marginalized from the larger society. Providing literacy classes in a newcomer's mother tongue, therefore, may be the first step toward enabling literacy in English.

In other cases, people may be psychologically unprepared for learning a new language upon arrival in their new country. This is particularly true if they are refugees fleeing violence and family tragedy. But it may also be true of other immigrants who have to cope with the trauma of struggling to survive and to make a home for oneself and one's family in a strange new country without any of the social supports that one is accustomed to.

For newcomers who are likely to take many years to acquire English, the goal of integration might best be served if they have access to various services or classes in their mother tongue in the early years after their arrival. For example, they could learn more about their new country, such as the nature of the legal system and job market, through mother-tongue classes. Or they could upgrade some of their job skills by taking classes in their mother tongue.

The issue is not whether immigrants should be encouraged to learn English. As I noted earlier, failure to acquire literacy in English is likely to lead to serious marginalization. Moreover, this disadvantage often gets passed to the next generation if neither parent is able to communicate with his or her children in English. The issue is much more practical—what sort of policy actually works best to enable various types of immigrants to learn

English? The current expectation that all immigrants should try to learn English as soon as they arrive is simply not working for certain groups of immigrants. It condemns to perpetual marginalization anyone who cannot learn English quickly when they arrive.[19]

It may seem logical to say that people will integrate best if they are encouraged to participate in fully integrated institutions as quickly as possible. But how immigrants learn English best is not a question of logic. It is a complicated empirical question of pedagogy and socio-linguistics. The same holds true for the related case of bilingual education for immigrant children. To try to decide these questions without reference to the facts is unhelpful, and potentially counter productive.

In short, none of these multiculturalism policies for immigrant groups necessarily promotes either ethnonationalism or marginalization. The first ten policies are, I believe, clearly integrationist, and while the latter two involve short-term forms of institutional separateness, they can be seen as promoting long-term institutional integration. If we examine genuine cases of marginalization—such as the educational and military exemptions accorded ethnoreligious sects that enable them to live apart from the mainstream society—we find that they predate the multiculturalism policy. Many of the criticisms that are wrongly leveled at multiculturalism policies are much more plausibly leveled at the policies adopted early in this century toward the Amish and Hutterites. Indeed, one could argue that there is an element of racism in the way that many Americans and Canadians accept the historical accommodations made for these white Christian sects—accommodations that are genuinely separatist and marginalizing—while bitterly opposing the accommodations made for more recent nonwhite, non-Christian immigrant groups, even though these accommodations are integrationist.

What is the impact of these policies of democratic citizenship? It should be clear, I hope, that they promote horizontal connectedness at least at an institutional level. But the fact that immigrants have accepted this sort of *institutional* integration does not necessarily mean that they have "integrated" in a more purely psychological sense. That is, immigrants who accept the need to participate in English-language institutions in the United States may have little sense of being "American." They may show little interest in learning about the rest of the country, and may wish to focus as much as possible on the glories of the Old World, rather than on embracing the opportunities available in the New World.

The idea that multiculturalism is promoting an apartheid-like system of institutional separatism is, I think, wholly misplaced. But is it promoting a kind of *mental* separatism, encouraging immigrants to dwell on the life they left behind, rather than on the opportunities available in their new country? This is a more plausible worry. However, if the theory of associational life is correct, then this worry is overstated; it is one of the key claims of theorists of associational life that institutional integration is likely to generate over time a sense of psychological identification. The fact that common institutions bring together the members of different ethnic groups has important ramifications both personally and politically. At the personal level, it means that people meet (and indeed often fall in love with) members of other ethnic groups, which promotes interethnic friendships and marriages. These relationships are intimately tied up with one's new life here, not with the Old World. Politically, it means that people must learn how to negotiate with the members of other ethnic groups. An immigrant group might want to incorporate material about their homeland into the school curriculum, but since these are common institutions, they will have to persuade the members of other groups about the value of this material. The inevitable result is that groups must focus on how to contribute to the new life here, rather than simply dwelling on the society left behind. In short, institutional integration makes possible the kind of civic engagement that supports democratic citizenship. It promotes participation in a larger civil society, and encourages the development of civility and public reasonableness.[20]

This form of multiculturalism is "pluralist" in two distinct senses. Unlike isolationist or nationalist multiculturalism, its aim is not to separate the minority group from the larger society, but rather to encourage it to participate in the larger society, and thereby pluralize it. But pluralist multiculturalism also promotes pluralism within immigrant groups themselves. When liberal societies promote public reasonableness and civility in civil society, they not only protect immigrant groups; they also limit their ability to maintain their cultural distinctiveness. Civility and public reasonableness in civil society means that cultural boundaries tend to break down. Members of one ethnic group will meet and befriend members of other groups, and adopt new identities and practices. Conversely, practices associated with one group will become adopted by members of the larger society. Over time, liberal citizenship results in "pluralistic integration."[21] This does not involve the preservation of distinct cultures (since ethnic identities weaken and incorporate aspects of the larger culture), nor is it assimilation (since ethnic groups change the larger society as they integrate).

Of course, even if pluralist multiculturalism policies are integrationist from the point of view of immigrants, they may create ethnic tensions, and so inhibit integration if they lead to a backlash on the part of native-born citizens. I cannot deal with this issue at length, except to note that this problem is not new. Much of the fear that native-born citizens express today regarding the integration of Muslims, for example, is virtually identical to the rhetoric expressed one hundred years ago regarding the integration of Catholics. Catholics were perceived as undemocratic and unpatriotic, since their allegiance was to the pope, and as separatist, since they demanded their own schools. Every new wave of immigration brings its own stresses, conflicts, and misunderstandings, which take time to overcome. In any event, if the real problem is not with the willingness of immigrants to integrate, but rather with the backlash against immigrant multiculturalism among native-born citizens, then the problem we need to address is the lack of civility and public reasonableness among the majority, not the impact of multiculturalism on the civic virtue of the immigrants themselves.

The picture I have presented so far of immigrant multiculturalism is very different from the picture painted by its critics. Whereas critics see it as promoting balkanization and separatism, I have argued that its goal is to promote better and fairer terms of integration. But how is it working in practice? Since this sort of pluralist multiculturalism is relatively new, it may be too early to assess the actual implications of these policies. However, evidence is gradually accumulating. The first country to adopt an official multiculturalism policy was Canada in 1971, followed shortly thereafter by Australia, so we now have twenty-five years of experience to assess. And the evidence, so far, is very positive. For example, on every major indicator of integration, immigrants integrate more quickly in Canada today than they did before the adoption of the multiculturalism policy in 1971. Moreover, immigrants integrate more quickly in those countries that have official multiculturalism policies (like Canada and Australia) than in countries which do not (like the United States and France). And these immigrants are not only institutionally integrated, but also active participants in the political process, strongly committed to protecting the stability of mainstream institutions and to upholding liberal-democratic values.[22]

In short, there is no evidence at all that immigrant multiculturalism is promoting balkanization or cultural and linguistic apartheid or partial citizenship. On the contrary, the evidence—while still preliminary—shows that multiculturalism is doing what it set out to do: namely, to promote better and fairer terms of integration for immigrant groups.

If I am right about the consistency of multiculturalism and immigrant integration, why have so many people assumed that these policies are balkanizing? There are several reasons, but the main problem, I think, is that people ignore the big picture. They look at multiculturalism in isolation from other government policies, and so assume that multiculturalism is the only policy that bears on the decision of immigrants to integrate. But in fact multiculturalism is a relatively minor policy in the overall scheme of things. The primary pillars of government-sponsored integration are the policies on naturalization, education, and employment—and all of these pillars of integration remain fully in place.

Relatedly, people underestimate how difficult it would be for a minority to actually establish and reproduce a distinct societal culture. It requires a vast panoply of public institutions and political powers, none of which has been granted under the multiculturalism rubric, and which could be achieved only by changes in virtually all areas of public policy and in all political structures. The idea that an immigrant group might use multiculturalism policies to form and maintain a separate society seems feasible only because people ignore the big picture.

But this just pushes back the problem a level. Why do people ignore the big picture? After all, there is nothing mysterious about the way governments promote sociocultural integration. The evidence is there in plain view, available to anyone who takes even a cursory glance at naturalization laws or education policies. The answer, I think, is that many commentators have been seduced by the myth of "civic nationalism," which I discussed in the first section, according to which membership in the nation is just a matter of subscribing to certain political principles, and not a matter of integration into a societal culture. Since this model provides no justification for encouraging immigrants to integrate into an anglophone societal culture, commentators conveniently overlook all of the government policies that do precisely this. And having ignored all the government policies that promote integration, they then adopt an exaggerated, almost hysterical view of the disintegrating effects of multiculturalism policies.[23] To get a balanced view of the impact of multiculturalism policies for immigrants, we need a more honest view of the role of states in promoting and diffusing national cultures.

The Mixed Case of Hispanics

So far, I have focused on three sharply distinguished cases of multiculturalism—the isolationist marginalization of ethnoreligious sects; the nationalist multiculturalism of national minorities; and the pluralist multiculturalism of immigrant groups. But as I noted earlier, there are many in-between cases of ethnocultural groups that do not fit neatly into one category or another, and that often combine different forms of multiculturalism. Moreover, attempts are sometimes made to encourage different kinds of ethnocultural groups to amalgamate and to view themselves as sharing a common identity and political program.

A very interesting and important example of this concerns the Hispanics in the United States. The American government has decided to treat Hispanics or Latinos as a single ethnocultural category (e.g., in the census), when they are in fact a heterogenous collection of different kinds of ethnocultural groups. Hispanics in America include national minorities (the Puerto Ricans), legal immigrants (from Central America), exiles (Cubans in Miami), and illegal immigrants (from Mexico). In the past, each of these types of groups had its own needs and aspirations, and hence its own conception of multiculturalism. For example, Puerto Ricans exemplify the standard pattern of a nationalist national minority, whereas legal immigrants from Guatemala or Honduras exemplify the standard pattern of an immigrant group that integrates into the anglophone society (indeed, among Latino immigrants "assimilation to the English group occurs more rapidly now than it did one hundred years ago").[24]

The situation of Cuban exiles and illegal immigrants is more complicated. These groups do not fit the standard pattern of immigrant integration, precisely because they were never subjected to the usual state policies promoting integration. As the experience of other countries shows, a real danger of marginalization arises when newcomers are exempted or excluded from the normal policies promoting integration. But we should not conflate the experience of these two groups with that of other Hispanic groups.

The divergent experiences of Hispanic groups helps to explain why there has been considerable difficulty in getting Hispanics to mobilize as a single group with a single political program. However, efforts are sometimes made to describe a singular form of "Hispanic" multiculturalism. And given that the American government is implicitly promoting the view that Hispanics form a single group, a new sense of a unified Hispanic identity may yet emerge. But what sort of an identity will it be? Will Hispanics come to view themselves as a national minority, with rights to self-government and to public institutions in their own language not just in Puerto Rico, but throughout the United States? Some commentators oppose offering statehood to Puerto Rico on precisely the grounds that it will promote such an attitude among Hispanics and encourage the idea that the United States should be officially bilingual.[25] Or will Hispanics come to view themselves as a broad coalition of immigrant groups, like the Asians, who are seeking fairer terms of integration into the anglophone mainstream of America? This is what some Hispanic leaders have promoted.[26]

Neither of these seem like plausible scenarios, at least for the foreseeable future. The histories and aspirations of Hispanic groups are simply too divergent to create a single form of multiculturalism appropriate for all Hispanic groups. Indeed, the net result of treating Hispanics as a single group may simply be to obscure the real needs of the various Hispanic groups. In particular, Hispanic immigrants, who should be treated like other immigrant groups under the umbrella of pluralist multiculturalism, may instead be exempted from some of the expectations to integrate. This could easily to lead to marginalization, since outside of Puerto Rico (and perhaps Miami) they are unlikely to possess the economic and political resources or legal rights necessary to create or sustain a flourishing Spanish-language societal culture. They may then end up with the worst of both worlds—marginalized from the mainstream anglophone society but unable to sustain a viable Hispanic society. All too often, this is the fate of ethnocultural groups that fall in between the standard categories of immigrants and national minorities.[27]

CONCLUSION

I began by noting the paradox that many people applaud associational life in general but denounce one of the few attempts to actually promote associational life, namely, multiculturalism. The explanation for this apparent paradox is that civic engagement is applauded precisely because it often cuts across ethnic lines, and thereby promotes democratic virtues of solidarity, trust, civility, and public reasonableness. Many commentators conclude that it is therefore unhelpful, indeed counterproductive, to support associations defined on ethnic lines. Supporting ethnic associations is assumed to promote insularity and balkanization, not a wider horizontal connectedness among citizens. I hope to have shown that we need a more nuanced approach to the impact of multiculturalism on democratic citizenship. I have tried to show that multiculturalism can, and often does, promote the sort of civic engagement that helps develop important democratic virtues.

I have discussed three forms of multiculturalism: (a) the isolationist multiculturalism of certain religious sects, which hinders the development of democratic citizenship but which is of peripheral importance to the larger society; (b) the nationalist multiculturalism of national minorities, which promotes democratic citizenship at the level of the self-governing nation but makes democratic cooperation more difficult at the level of the state as a whole; (c) the pluralist multiculturalism of immigrant groups, which promotes participation within a larger civil society, and so encourages the sort of civic engagement that supports democratic citizenship. These are just trends, of course, and one could cite many examples of groups that do not fit neatly into these characterizations. But it should be clear, I hope, that it is misleading to claim that multiculturalism in general supports or hinders democratic citizenship.

Notes

1. For two representative examples, see Michael Walzer, "The Civil Society Argument," in Chantal Mouffe, ed., *Dimensions of Radical Democracy: Pluralism, Citizenship, and Community* (London: Routledge, 1992); and Mary Ann Glendon, *Rights Talk: The Impoverishment of Political Discourse* (New York: Free Press, 1991).

2. Michael Walzer, "Comment," in Amy Gutmann, ed., *Multiculturalism and the "Politics of Recognition"* (Princeton: Princeton University Press, 1992), pp. 100–101. See also Walzer, *What It Means to Be an American* (New York: Marsilio, 1992), p. 9.

3. Gerald Johnson, *Our English Heritage* (Westport, Conn: Greenwood Press, 1973), p. 119.

4. For the ubiquity of this process around the world, see Ernest Gellner, *Nations and Nationalism* (Oxford: Basil Blackwell, 1983); Benedict Anderson, *Imagined Communities: Reflections on the Origin and Spread of Nationalism* (London: New Left Books, 1983).

5. Charles Taylor, "Nationalism and Modernity," in J. McMahan and R. McKim, eds., *The Morality of Nationalism* (New York: Oxford University Press, 1997), p. 34.

6. Walker Connor, "Nation-Building or Nation-Destroying," *World Politics* 24 (1972): 350–51; "The Politics of Ethnonationalism," *Journal of International Affairs* 27, no. 1 (1973): 20. For a more recent survey of ethnonational conflicts around the world, which shows clearly the important differences between immigrant groups and incorporated national groups, see Ted Gurr, *Minorities at Risk: A Global View of Ethnopolitical Conflict* (Washington, D.C.: Institute of Peace Press, 1993).

7. I have discussed the multiculturalist demands of African Americans—and the tension between integration and nationalism that they exhibit—in *Finding Our Way: Rethinking Ethnocultural Relations in Canada* (Toronto: Oxford University Press, forthcoming), chap. 5.

8. William Galston, *Liberal Purposes* (Cambridge: Cambridge University Press, 1991), pp. 221–24.

9. Ibid., p. 227.

10. Rieff quoted in John Murray Cuddihy, *No Offense: Civil Religion and Protestant Taste* (New York: Seabury Press, 1978), p. 6.

11. My discussion here draws extensively on Jeff Spinner's account of civility in

The Boundaries of Citizenship: Race, Ethnicity, and Nationality in the Liberal State (Baltimore: Johns Hopkins University Press, 1994), chap. 3.

12. Ibid., p. 98.

13. See my *Multicultural Citizenship: A Liberal Theory of Minority Rights* (Oxford: Oxford University Press, 1995), pp. 116–20.

14. E. Weber, *Peasants into Frenchmen: The Modernization of Rural France 1870–1914* (London: Chatto and Windus, 1976).

15. I discuss the self-government rights of national minorities at length in *Multicultural Citizenship*, particularly chaps. 2, 6, and 8.

16. Arthur Schlesinger, *The Disuniting of America* (New York: Norton, 1992), pp. 137–38. For similar claims about multiculturalism in Canada, see Neil Bissoondath, *Selling Illusions: The Cult of Multiculturalism in Canada* (Toronto: Penguin, 1994); Richard Gwyn *Nationalism without Walls: The Unbearable Lightness of Being Canadian* (Toronto: McClelland and Stewart, 1995).

17. Insofar as multiculturalism involves certain "group rights," it is important to distinguish two kinds of group rights. A liberal state can accept the idea that a group might have certain rights against the larger society, rights that make it easier for members of the group to affirm and express their identity. But it cannot accept the idea that a group has rights against its own members, rights that limit the freedom of individual members in the name of "tradition" or "cultural purity." See *Multicultural Citizenship*, chaps. 2 and 8.

18. See Barbara Burnaby, "Official Language Training for Adult Immigrants in Canada: Features and Issues," in B. Burnaby and A. Cumming, eds., *Socio-Political Aspects of ESL* (Toronto: OISE, 1992).

19. For an in-depth discussion, see Susan Donaldson, *Un-LINC-ing Language and Integration* (master's thesis, Department of Linguistics and Applied Language Studies, Carleton University, 1995).

20. There is no reason to leave this sort of psychological integration completely to chance, and it is worth examining specific policies to see if they can be improved on this score. In assessing policies regarding the funding of ethnic studies programs or ethnic presses, for example, I think it is right and proper that the government be encouraging immigrant groups to focus primarily (though not necessarily exclusively) on their contribution to their new country, not on the accomplishments of the society they have left behind. Similarly, government-funded bilingual education programs for children or mother-tongue literacy programs for adults should be used primarily as a vehicle for teaching immigrants about their new country, not about the history of the Old World.

21. See Spinner, *Boundaries of Citizenship*, p. 73 for a useful discussion of what he calls "pluralistic integration."

22. For the statistical evidence, see my *Finding Our Way*, chap. 1.

23. This is my best explanation for the otherwise incomprehensibly paranoid misinterpretations of immigrant multiculturalism in the works of Schlesinger, Lind, Hughes, et al.

24. R. de la Garza and A. Trujillo, "Latinos and the Official English Debate in the United States," in D. Schneiderman, ed., *Language and the State: The Law and Politics of Identity* (Cowansville, Quebec: Les Editions Yvon Blais, 1991), p. 215.

25. Alvin Rubinstein, "Is Statehood for Puerto Rico in the National Interest?"

In Depth: A Journal for Values and Public Policy (spring 1993): 87–99; Nathan Glazer, *Ethnic Dilemmas, 1964–1982* (Cambridge: Harvard University Press, 1983), p. 280.

26. Linda Chavez, *Out of the Barrio: Toward a New Politics of Hispanic Assimilation* (New York: Basic Books, 1991).

27. For a more detailed discussion of this point, see my "Do We Need a Liberal Theory of Minority Rights?" *Constellations* 4, no. 1, (1997): 72–87.

Chapter Eight

REVISITING THE CIVIC SPHERE

YAEL TAMIR

> Among laws controlling human societies there is one more
> precise and clear, it seems to me, than all others. If men
> are to remain civilized or to become civilized, the art of
> association must develop and improve among them
> at the same speed as equality of conditions spreads.
> *(Tocqueville, Democracy in America)*

THIS PAPER is, first and foremost, an attempt to sound a note of caution against the wave of renewed enthusiasm for civic associations that seems to have swept political theory. In the recent literature, the revival of *civic associations* and the *civic sphere* is offered as a panacea for all the main illnesses of modern society—alienation, isolation, excessive anarchic and individualistic capitalism, social disintegration, and political indifference.[1]

As one reviewer has recently written: "In the world of ideas, civil society is hot. It is almost impossible to read an article on foreign or domestic politics without coming across some mention of the concept. And 'civil society' has bipartisan appeal; from Hillary Rodham Clinton to Pat Buchanan, politicians of all stripes routinely sing its praises."[2]

This excited response is not restricted to politicians. According to Robert Putnam, the new guru of civic society, trust, toleration, civic virtue, and even personal satisfaction with one's life are closely linked to the flourishing of associational life. Happiness, he concludes "is living within a civic community."[3]

What can account for the growing interest in the civic sphere and the overwhelming support of efforts to revive civic associations? The answers lies in a rare overlap between arguments drawn from three schools of thought. Each produces a cluster of justifications that highlights different aspects of associational life.[4] Taken together, the three clusters capture the rich gamut of virtues and values associated with the civic sphere. Justifications that form the core of the first, democratic cluster emphasize the instrumental role associations play in fostering democratic attitudes such as trust, respect, reciprocity, tolerance, responsibility, cooperation, public deliberation, and participation. Justifications that constitute the second, liberal cluster are predicated on the close relationship between personal autonomy, freedom of association, and freedom of expression. The third cluster encompasses communitarian justifications praising intimacy, privacy, solidarity, and mutual support, as well as the proliferation of cultural pluralism and group identity.

One feels embarrassed to break this happy and unusual union and mention that not all the personal and communal goods and liberties embodied in the different clusters coincide. Nevertheless, it is the purpose of this paper to highlight such tensions, and especially to remind those who support civic associations and the civic society because they want to promote what the Romans called *civitas*, "that is, public-spiritedness, sacrifice for the community, citizenship, even nobility,"[5] that not all civil society is civic-minded. Some associations have the contradictory effect; they threaten social cohesion, erode the social capital, frustrate social equality and equal opportunity, and violate individual rights.

What are we to do about these associations? If we value associational life *only* because we see civic associations in an instrumental light, as a seedbed of democracy, we will permit the state to intervene in the civic sphere, encourage the formation of associations that foster democratic skills and dispositions, and marginalize the role played by associations that undermine democratic virtues, social responsibility, and civic-spiritedness. If we care less about social cohesion and popular sovereignty and endorse a liberal position that emphasizes freedom of association and freedom of expression or a communitarian perspective that stresses the importance of intimacy and communal life, we will advocate a policy of nonintervention and claim that the state should treat all associations equally.

Which of these two alternatives is preferable? What role should the civic sphere play in a liberal democratic state? In this paper I advocate a policy of nonintervention in the civic sphere for both practical and ideological reasons. In the first sections I question the efficiency of such intervention and point to its limitations. I then adopt the liberal view that argues that the autonomy of the civic sphere should be retained since it advances the ability of individuals to exercise their freedom of association and expression, and the communitarian claim that the autonomy of this sphere is imperative since in it communal, religious, and cultural lives are shared and enjoyed.

My preference for the liberal and the communitarian perspectives should not be seen as grounded in indifference for the fate of democracy or in a belief that democratic virtues and skills would necessarily emerge out of a free market of ideas. Rather, it expresses a firm belief in the responsibility of democratic states to nurture, in state-governed institutions, democratic competence and attitudes.

The approach presented in this chapter defends the autonomy of the civic sphere, and yet it insists that this freedom should be exercised within the framework of a powerful, liberal democratic welfare state. Such a state ought to be committed to balancing the harmful effects of associational activities. Namely, it ought to protect human rights, promote social equality and equality of opportunities, and provide a safety net ensuring individuals that they will not be left unprotected even if they exercise their right to exit the associations with which they are affiliated. Only then will the freedom of the civic sphere promote the rights of individuals and allow them to give public expression to their identity without sacrificing either democracy, social justice, or human rights.

A MATTER OF DEFINITION

A methodological clarification is in order before we reach the core of the discussion. The term *civic association* is very loosely defined. It covers any kind of formalized, non-governmental, human interaction, from cooperation among the tenants of one house to the international network of non-governmental organizations (NGOs); from loose organizations such as Oxfam, whose members do not interact with each other and have no more than occasional mail contact with the association's officers; to churches and neighborhood associations, whose members are engaged in daily, face-to-face interactions. Consequently, when the praises of associational life are sung, it is hard to know what exactly is being acclaimed.[6]

I will not attempt to offer here a systematic categorization of all the different kinds of associations, though some classification will emerge in the course of the discussion. One basic observation must, however, be made at the start—not all associations allow their members to enjoy the intimacy or communal support associational life is thought to provide. Many large associations—Amnesty International, Save the Children Fund, Friends of the Metropolitan Museum—are far too loose to provide such benefits. In turn, many small and intimate associations that do dispense such advantages— for instance, ethnic and religious communities—are nonvoluntary or semivoluntary and have very restrictive membership rules regulating the rights of entry and exit. Hence, though they contribute to their members' ability to enjoy the benefits of associational life, they do not allow them to practice freedom of association. Consequently, we can conceive of a society where associational life thrives, but in which individuals have little opportunity to exercise their freedom to join the associations of their choice or exit the ones they are members of, or of a society in which individuals enjoy the freedom to join and exit the associations of their choice but in which stable, active, and rich associational life is lacking.

According to Walzer the latter option is typical of the United States. The decaying state of communal engagements, he argues, could be explained by reference to the freedom of exit and entry. There are no borders around our cultural groups, and, of course, no border police:

> Men and women are free to participate or not as they please, to come and go, withdraw entirely, or simply fade away into the peripheral distances. This freedom, again, is one of the advantages of an individualistic society; at the same time, however, it doesn't make for strong and cohesive associations.[7]

The American experience that forces members of different ethnic communities and social groups to function "as if they were voluntary associations,"[8] blurs the distinction between social groups, which are nonformal collectives of individuals whose unity is grounded in shared cultural forms, practices, or way of life, and associations, which are formal organizations whose unity is fictional and legal. As Young recognizes, in the United States, "civic groups more often than not are organized along the lines of gender, race, religion, ethnicity or sexual orientation, even when they have not explicitly aimed to do so."[9] And most of these groups are neither purely voluntary nor purely ascriptive; many of them have a loose formal structure but also a set of unwritten norms and practices. No wonder then, that the discussion in the literature swings back and forth between groups, communities, and civic associations. I make no attempt to remove this ambiguity, and in what follows I will use the term *civic associations* in the broad and equivocal way in which it is used in the literature.

SEEDBED OF DEMOCRACY

The perception of civic associations in political philosophy has been heavily influenced by their impassioned description in Tocqueville's *Democracy in America*. The most democratic country in the world at that time, he argued, "was that in which men have in our time carried to the highest perfection the art of pursuing in common objects of common desires and have applied this new technique to the greatest number of purposes."[10] Rather than as an incidental feature, then, Tocqueville viewed voluntary associations as a necessary building block of liberal democracy. For him and his followers, membership in secondary associations is essential for cultivating democratic dispositions ranging from "modest law-abidingness, willingness to work, and the self-control necessary to refrain from violence and public shows of disrespect (hence, the 'civil' in civil society) to more demanding dispositions such as tolerance, habits of cooperation, and if not full blown civic virtue, at least a minuscule of concern for the common good."[11] Associations are thus praised as a "seedbed of civic virtue," as "schools of democracy," participation in which helps citizens develop competence, self-confidence, and a broader set of interests.

The idea that associational life offers experiences that have edifying qualities is adopted and developed by Rawls, who takes the "morality of association" to be a necessary stage of moral development. In this stage, individuals acquire cooperative virtues: "those of justice and fairness, fidelity and trust, integrity and impartiality,"[12] broaden their moral horizons, and learn to consider the needs and interests of others: "In due course the *reciprocal effects* of everyone doing his share strengthen one another until a kind of equilibrium is reached."[13]

While Rawls is describing an ideal society governed by the principles of justice, in the real world it is unrealistic to expect that in a voluntary process, free from state intervention, associational life will foster tolerance, modesty, trust, and reciprocity; strengthen liberal democratic beliefs and tendencies; restrain the rule of the majority; balance the activities of the state; give individuals a public voice, and stabilize democracy. A few associations may indeed fulfill all (or most) of these functions effectively, but many will fail to do so. Some ethnic associations may limit majority rule but will, at the same time, have destabilizing effects on the political system as a whole. Religious groups may educate individuals to submit to religious authority at the same time they cast doubt on the authority of the state; other associations may foster feelings of trust and reciprocity among members but only at the expense of nurturing animosity and mistrust toward outsiders.

Tocqueville himself noticed that the values fostered by some associations may be in sharp contradiction to liberal democratic ones. For example, he acknowledged that the nature of religious associations may vary quite considerably, and that Islam and Judaism, which are practice-oriented religions, may have difficulties adapting to a liberal political system.[14] Muhammad, Tocqueville argues, brought down from heaven and put into the Koran

> not religious doctrines only, but political maxims, criminal and civil laws, and scientific theories. The gospels, on the other hand, deal only with the general relations between man and God and between man and man. Beyond that, they teach nothing and do not oblige people to believe anything. That alone, among a thousand reasons, is enough to show that Islam will not be able to hold its power long in ages of enlightenment and democracy while Christianity is designed to reign in such ages, as in all others.[15]

This prediction has proven incorrect. More and more illiberal associations, religious and others, are emerging in liberal democratic societies. This proliferation of illiberal associations suggests that the harmonious picture drawn by Tocqueville and reiterated by so many other social thinkers is inaccurate. Liberal democratic values and politics may indeed have gained considerable popular support in the last several decades, but their success has by no means been conclusive. When allowed to associate, individuals quite often opt for illiberal, authoritarian, nondemocratic options. As Nancy Rosenblum rightly remarks, as long as freedom of association is respected, civic society will be home to every imaginable type of association—authoritarian, elitist, bureaucratic, hierarchic, sexist, racist, and blindly traditionalist. Such associations may foster nondemocratic tendencies, sharpen social cleavages, foster mutual distrust, and advocate disobedience of the law.[16]

Putnam recognizes this danger, though only in a footnote. Not all associations of the like-minded are committed to democratic goals nor organized in an egalitarian fashion, he argues; "consider, for example, the Ku Klux Klan or the Nazi party."[17] It is perfectly possible "for intermediate associations to be as undemocratic as primary groups, or even more so." Life upon the secondary levels, Eckstein reminds us, "was very vigorous in the Weimar period—and very incongruent with democracy."[18] But one need not evoke the Weimar Republic, the KKK, or the Nazi Party in order to support the claim that not all associations are democratic. Many current religious and ethnic associations are hierarchical and antidemocratic by nature. Even soccer associations, which Putnam claims are a major vehicle for democracy in Italy, can induce violent, racist, and uncontrolled behavior, as English soccer hooliganism proves. We should then be careful *not* to presuppose that the very existence of civic associations will necessarily support democracy and foster civic virtues and respect for the principles of justice.

There is no reason to believe that, left on their own, associations will serve as a seedbed of democracy. We must then ask: Should democratic states see the civic sphere through the prism of its benefits and costs to the state and consequently intervene in it when needed? Or should they see it through the prism of associational rights and liberties and therefore treat equally all the various kinds of associations individuals form, regardless of their social and political impact?

INVITING THE STATE TO RESHAPE THE CIVIC SOCIETY

Two interesting models that adopt the instrumental-democratic viewpoint have been offered recently. Both assume that democratic states cannot be indifferent to the spread of civic virtues; since these virtues do not emerge "naturally" or through the action of some "invisible hand," democratic states must cultivate them using not only formal state institutions, but also civic associations. We would, Macedo argues, think "more constructively about moral and political education if we think less about the simple and direct means of pedagogy, such as school curricula. The very structure of our social lives educates us indirectly, and exerts influences over our lives. The heavy hand of direct public control may be far from the best way of promoting the character traits and virtues on which our polity depends."[19]

Membership in overlapping associations—or more precisely, overlapping associations that are of a particular kind—is thus seen by Macedo as an important social tool that should be used to foster liberal democratic virtues. To achieve this end, group life should be *constituted and shaped* so as to be of use to our political order." Liberal democratic states must therefore *plan* for citizens' virtue by promoting "the *right* patterns of community life. . . . While heavy-handed interventions in religious life or other 'private' matters may be neither necessary nor permissible, liberals should not shy away from the important work of *shaping* community life for civic virtue."[20]

By emphasizing the contribution of the civic sphere to indirect civic education, Macedo's science of group life redefines the social role of this sphere. Deviating from the traditional liberal emphasis on the contribution of an independent civic sphere to the ability of individuals to achieve their ends, express their opinions, pursue their life plans and restrict the powers of the state, Macedo emphasizes the contribution of this sphere to the ability of the governing bodies to stabilize the political system, thus shifting the delicate balance between the individual and the state in favor of the latter. This imbalance is intensified by the endorsement of private charities and by assigning to these charities edifying roles, a move that further weakens individuals and curtails their autonomy. Let me clarify this claim: Citing Beito's work, Macedo praises self-help and mutual aid associations, arguing that "the moral resources and moral education furnished by such societies stand in sharp contrast with those provided by the welfare state, in which benefits are provided without any behavioral demands (or in which, if behavioral demands are made, they will be ineffective because imposed from the outside)."[21] This claim may indeed be true; the moral rules of mutual aid associations may be both more acceptable to their members and more effectively enforced on deviators, and yet one may wonder whether the redistribution of goods and services should be made dependent on moral performance. The basic idea of the modern welfare state is quite the opposite—welfare is a service that individuals deserve, not one earned through performance.

In fact, many social democrats suggest that the state should assure its citizens certain welfare rights and services precisely because it ought to allow individuals to free themselves from their communal bonds if they find them too oppressive or moralizing. In discussing the Alamo Case,[22] Rosenblum rightly argues that

> the court's decision to extend fair labor protection to members contributed to voluntarism and to the possibility of actually experiencing pluralism. Like all rights and benefits, its impact is edifying as well as practical. FLSA [Fair Labor Standards Act] protection is an affirmation of the dominance and inescapability of liberal democratic civil culture. To members of a self-styled totalistic religious community it is both a public declaration and a material demonstration of the associates' standing as citizens. And it helps make exit conceivable. It removes at least an impediment to the ongoing moral uses of pluralism.[23]

The state, according to the court's view, is expected to balance the power of associations rather than contribute to it. Indeed, this may weaken the influence of these associations on their members and hinder attempts to use their power for the purpose of indirect education. And yet such losses may be the inevitable outcomes of the need to protect individuals not only from the state but also from the associations to which they belong.

Macedo's science of social groups enhances the likelihood that individuals, especially nonconformist ones, would be oppressed by both private associations and the state. Consequently, the radical and innovative potential of the civic sphere is likely to be curtailed for the sake of political stability. Indeed, following Kornhauser, Macedo chooses to stress the fact that the multiplicity of social groups and associations can shield the state from excessive social pressures. Civic associations, he argues, mitigate possible public pressures on the government by allowing political appeals to flow toward the center indirectly, fragmented and moderated by associations. "Shielded from direct, mass appeals and the pressures of an unorganized but homogenous and volatile mass opinion, political authorities may negotiate with a variety of groups and pressures."[24] In Macedo's model, then, the civic sphere changes its traditional role: its major role is no longer to balance and restrict the powers of the government or of the majority, to amplify the voices of individuals and encourage the emergence of alternative ways of thinking, but to promote political stability and civic education.

Macedo is not alone in calling upon the state to harness the power of associations to promote its interests. Cohen and Rogers, motivated by democratic egalitarian considerations, also argue that one way of counteracting many of the ills of modern societies and especially the adverse effects of splintering is to use public powers to "act directly on the associative environment of public action in ways that make associations less fractionalizing and more supportive of the range of egalitarian-democratic norms . . . [as] the 'right' sorts of associations do not arise naturally. It [the theory of associative democracy] then proposes to supplement nature with artifice: through politics, to secure an associative environment more conducive to democratic aims."[25] Cohen and Rogers attempt to create congruence between the values and goals of the state and its major associations; they offer to achieve this congruence through the use of state power.

This policy might seem quite innocent—why would anyone object to the desire to secure an environment conducive to democratic aims? The problem, however, is with the means rather than with the ends, with the attempt to recruit the civic sphere to support the social-political order. The debate, then, concerns neither the need to educate for democratic virtues nor to strengthen democracy, but the best ways of achieving these goals. Macedo and Cohen and Rogers argue that the price of preserving the autonomy of the civic sphere—mainly, exposing individuals to the harmful effects of non-democratic associations, lessening of civic commitments, and disruption of social union—are severe enough to force a redefinition of the role of this sphere. According to this instrumentalist-democratic approach to the civic sphere, state intervention in the civic sphere is both effective and justified. In what follows I challenge these conclusions.

One of the major problems of this approach is that it exaggerates not only the risks embodied in an autonomous civic sphere but, mainly, the benefits of state intervention in this sphere. To begin with, there is little evidence that the development of democratic virtues corresponds directly to one's experience in civic associations, be they schools, the workplace, unions, churches, or the family. There is no evidence, for example, that individuals educated in the authoritarian system of the British elite schools turn out to be less committed to liberal democratic values or less involved in public affairs than individuals who were educated in the democratic school system of the Israeli kibbutz movement. As Rosenblum rightly argues, qualities acquired in different associational environments may serve to complement those qualities that direct one's behavior in the political sphere, but "they could just as reasonably be seen as substitutes for one another, or as entirely independent of one another so that men and women interpret work situation [or any other associational situations] as requiring different qualities from them than citizenship."[26] The ability of civic associations, then, to contribute to civic education has yet to be proven.

Moreover, while a policy of nonintervention in the civic sphere may expose individuals to illiberal, nondemocratic influences, it has itself an educational value. A policy that grants all members of all associations regardless of their social effects—including authoritarian religious groups, traditionalist communities, even racist ones—an equal chance to express themselves and be heard sends a message to the society that all individuals, even those with unpopular views, have an equal right to associate and have a public voice (assuming they do so peacefully and do not incite violence).

There are, however, further reasons why the state should refrain from intervening in the civic sphere. State intervention might undermine the ability of civic associations to play four social roles that are essential for the functioning of a stable and healthy democratic system.

First, civic associations are assumed to reinforce the ability of isolated individuals to acquire influence in the political sphere, thus balancing the power of the government. In democracies, the citizens are independent and weak, Tocqueville argued: "they can do hardly anything for themselves, and none of them is in a position to force his fellows to help him. They would all therefore find themselves helpless if they did not learn to help each other voluntarily."[27] In order to serve this purpose, civic associations must emerge out of a system of mutual help that is grounded in the interest of private individuals rather than in the needs of the government.

Second, as Madison claimed, freedom of association is "a necessary guarantee against the tyranny of the majority,"[28] as the interplay of a multiplicity of groups defending their diverse interests prevents the consolidation of a permanent center of power. Freedom of association thus strengthens the legitimacy and fairness of majority rule and helps assure that it is not "the rule of a fixed group"—the Majority—on all issues; instead, it is the rule of shifting majorities, as the losers at one time or on one issue join with others and become part of the governing coalition at another time or on another issue. The result will be a fair system of mutually beneficial cooperation.[29] The distribution of powers among associations that makes communication and cooperation among associations necessary thus has a balancing and stabilizing effect. And yet, all these benefits are dependent on the fact that the state neither controls nor biases the division of powers among associations. Otherwise, the state might help to create a solid majority that reflects the interest of the government and would thwart the need and the ability to create shifting alliances among different associations.

Third, one of the main reasons why civic associations can contribute to the stability of a democratic political system is that they are peaceful in their objectives and the legal means they use, "and when they say that they only wish to prevail legally, in general they are telling the truth."[30] In the United States, Tocqueville argued, due to universal suffrage, members of each association know whether their association has, or could aspire to have, the support of the majority. If they can win such support, they will hope to do so by peaceful means; if they cannot, they will accept the public's verdict. But this is likely to be true only if civic associations are structured from the grass roots, "out of immediate affinities that people find they have in their everyday lives, in their neighborhoods, religious congregations, occupations, consumer interests, cultural expressions and orientations and their values and political commitment,"[31] rather than constructed from above, governed by the ends and needs of the state. Individuals would have less reason to accept the public's verdict if it reflects not merely the power of conviction of private individuals but the views and interests of the state.

Fourth, if the state—or, more exactly, the government—is given the right to decide which associations are of the "right" sort, it is likely to endorse those associations that support its own interpretations, values, and policies. Consequently, changes of governments will lead to changes in the distribution of power in the civic society. Consider, for instance, what would have happened were Macedo and Cohen representing the two leading parties in a liberal democracy. The debate between these parties regarding the kinds of associations that would be the most appropriate ones for fostering liberal democratic values—churches, organizations that promote family values, unions, single mothers' associations—would be hard to settle. Each party would naturally tend to offer support to "its own associations." Associations on their part would find it profitable to ally themselves with the leading parties in order to gain such support. Consequently, the border between the state and the civic society would be transgressed frequently. The civic sphere might then end up, as it did in Israel, as a reflection of the political map, where most associations—from charity organizations to soccer clubs—are divided along partisan lines. Every time the government would change hands between the Macedonians and the Cohenians, the structure of the public sphere would also change in a way that would support the government and stabilize its regime rather than balance its powers. When describing the attraction of the idea of a civil society to Eastern European intellectuals, Ignatieff emphasizes its independence of the regime. Instinctively, he writes, Eastern Europeans knew what the main characteristic of that sphere was; it was "the kind of place where you do not change the street signs every time you change the regime."[32] State intervention endangers this independence and hinders the ability of the civic sphere to fulfill its democratic functions.

It is interesting to recall in the context of our discussion the fascination of liberal democrats with the revolutionary energies embodied in the civic sphere within the Eastern European context. "The teachers, writers, and journalists of the Czech underground, the shipyard workers and intellectuals of Poland's Solidarity, and the pastors and layman who met in East German church crypts did more than dream of civic society," Ignatieff writes:

> they sought implementation in the very womb of communist society. The philosophical study groups in the basements and boiler rooms, the prayer meetings in church crypts, and the unofficial trade union meetings in bars and boxrooms were seen as a civil society in embryo. Within those covert institutions came the education in liberty and the liberating energies that led to 1989. In the revolutions of the year in Hungary, Poland, Romania, East Germany, Czechoslovakia, and the Baltic—civil society triumphed over the state.[33]

Is it then the case that the civil society should play different roles in democratic and nondemocratic societies, that in the former it ought to destabilize the government and in the latter support it? Such an approach seems to embody an undeserving democratic hubris and an unfounded assumption that democratic regimes can stand the temptation to abuse state power. Democratic regimes need the balancing powers and political and ideological stimulus that can emerge from an autonomous civic sphere. By giving up these social forces they can sink into ideological stagnation.

So far I have argued that the instrumentalist-democratic approach fails by its own standards as it ignores the considerable social and political losses that follow from the policies it offers. We have then good reason to adopt a rights-based approach to the civic sphere, which endorses an amalgam of libertarian and communitarian rights. And yet both approaches have their own limitations, to which I shall now turn.

LEAVING ASSOCIATIONS UNGUARDED

While restricting the role of the state and emphasizing the importance of freedom of association, Nozick—the most eloquent and convincing exponent of the libertarian view—is not at all concerned with the nature of the associations that individuals create and support, as long as the right to exit is preserved. The (minimal) Nozickian state is thus described as the heavenly kingdom of personal freedom in which individuals can pursue their interests free of threats or disturbances from both the state and fellow citizens.[34]

This utopian description ignores the fact that in reality individuals face insurmountable obstacles that limit their ability to exercise personal choices and liberties. One of these hindrances is the limited ability to join and exit civic associations. The degree of voluntarism associated with the civic sphere is then considerably more restricted than Nozick assumes. Many individuals are locked within the associations in which they were born, or locked out of all the associations they wish to join.

In Utopia, individuals may leave a group if they feel oppressed and discriminated against, but in reality the price of leaving might be so high that individuals might choose to remain even within associations that treat them unjustly, silence them, marginalize them, or oppress them.[35] Associations may then have an interest in raising the price of leaving or in preventing exit in other ways, such as keeping their members "ignorant of the nature of other alternative communities they might join, to try to prevent them from freely leaving their own community to join another."[36] The end result is that individuals are often unable to pursue their interests by joining the associations of their choice or to protect their rights by practicing their right of exit. For many individuals exit is almost impossible, especially in the context of a minimal state in which all services, including protection, are provided through associational affiliations. It thus seems as if the combination of a minimal libertarian state and unrestricted freedom of association could lead to the substitution of one form of oppression (that which is administered by the state) with another (that which is administered by a particular community).

The same objections could be raised against Kukathas's approach to cultural rights. Kukathas concentrates on the importance of cultural communities rather than of voluntary associations, and yet, like Nozick, he bases his model on freedom of association and argues that the main safeguard against communal oppression is the freedom to dissociate. If an individual, although free to leave, continues to live in a community that treats him or her unjustly, our concerns about the injustice, he argues, diminish: "What is crucially important here, however, is the extent to which the individual does enjoy a substantial freedom to leave. . . . The most important condition which makes possible a substantial freedom to exit from a community is the existence of a wider society that is open to individuals wishing to leave their local groups."[37] But in a libertarian state many of those who choose to exit an association may find that there is no public sphere they can join, no shelter offering them protection and support. The market society may indeed be a refuge for the educated, the talented, and the healthy, but it leaves the poor, the feeble, and the needy unprotected.

Concerns regarding the possibility of exercising exit rights are not merely theoretical; sociological evidences show that such cases are quite common. For example, Bell's examination of the case of Residential Community Associations suggests that quite often individuals subscribe to such associations with one purpose in mind and then find that the contract they have signed violates some of their rights.[38] In such circumstances individuals may still choose to remain within the associative framework in order to protect their property and their investments. This is especially true if individuals cannot find in the state an ally in their attempt to secure basic rights, goods, and services.

The libertarian model thus secures only the right of the powerful to choose with whom to associate, but it cannot defend the equal right of all members to join the associations of their choice. In fact, it cannot protect individual rights at all. Nozick himself recognizes that even within the framework of voluntary associations, "everyone has various rights that may not be violated, various boundaries that may not be crossed without another's consent."[39] Nevertheless, he offers no measures for protecting these rights.

By placing all the burdens on the right to exit while disregarding the actual difficulties of both leaving associations and protecting the rights of those who choose to remain in them, Nozick's theory misses its own professed goal: ensuring the rights and liberties of individuals. I will argue below that freedom of association can serve to protect these rights and freedoms, but only if it is exercised within the framework of a much thicker state than Nozick is willing to permit—a state ready to actively protect individual rights (including welfare rights) and balance when necessary the distributional inequalities that associational activities may bring about.

HOPING FOR THE BEST

The Nozickian model leaves not only the question of individual rights and opportunities unattended but also the question of social unity and social solidarity. This may not be surprising, for Nozickians are not concerned with these issues; they believe that social units should be held together by self-interested considerations. Once these expire, the framework will disintegrate. Yet democratic states do not take their integrity so lightheartedly. They attempt to ground it not merely in the convergence of self-interest, but also in a much larger set of ideological, historical, cultural, and political elements. They seek to establish civic friendship, social solidarity, and political cohesion, and may therefore be tempted to interfere in the civic sphere if they suspect that freedom of association will lead to social disintegration.

One cannot deny that the segregative powers of civic associations are a permanent feature of group life. Membership in any group—regardless of its particular nature—draws a line between insiders and outsiders and fosters favoritism of the former at the expense of the latter. Consequently, associational activities—even if beneficial to members of the in-group—endanger the cohesion of the larger society. This is evident on a small scale in the case of Residential Community Associations, and on a large one in the case of regional organizations. Both kinds of associations tend to adopt policies that are best characterized as NIMBY—not in my backyard.[40] Hence Residential Associations oppose "local zoning decisions to allow higher-density housing, commercial or industrial uses, and proposals to locate unwanted public facilities near their neighborhoods such as the hazardous waste dump sites, solid waste landfills, prisons, airports, drugs and school rehabilitation, and group homes for the mentally retarded."[41]

This kind of NIMBYism is but the first stage of social disintegration. The larger the range of social services that associations provide by themselves to their members, the more they aspire to free themselves from the regulatory and distributive powers of the central government. They question the justification of taxation as they become less and less dependent on public goods—or so they seem to think—and have less and less solidarity with fellow citizens who are nonmembers of their association. The logic of social disintegration is simple: If you cannot remove the harmful object from your backyard, you can, at least, dissociate yourself from your backyard, thus dissociating yourself from the aggravating object and freeing yourself from bearing responsibility for it.

This line of argument is used by spokespersons of the Lombardian League to convince the inhabitants of the affluent Italian north to dissociate themselves from the less developed and the more violent and corrupt south. The Italian example is worth considering, as it sheds new light on one of the scholarly works that initiated the renewed enthusiasm for the civic sphere—Putnam's examination of Italian civic society in *Making Democracy Work*. It is interesting to observe that the two communities that Putnam describes as the most civically oriented—Lombardia and Emilia Romagna—are those in which support for the Lombardian League and its claims for secession are the strongest, a fact calling into question Putnam's use of the term *civic*. In the most civic regions, Putnam tell us, "citizens are actively involved in all sorts of *local* associations—literary guilds, local bands, hunting clubs, cooperatives, and so on. They follow civic affairs avidly in the local press, and they engage in politics out of programmatic conviction."[42] Putnam might be justified in arguing that Lombardia's vibrant civic life turn Lombardians into more confident, savvy, and effective political agents. As a result of their participation in associative life, they may have become more aware of the needs of other members and of their responsibilities to them. But all these benefits do not turn them into better citizens if they restrict their concern to their specific reference group rather than broaden it to encompass all fellow citizens.

The question, then, is how social responsibility acquired though membership in secondary associations can be extended to include all citizens? Rawls seems to be offering the means for such an extension when he considers the development of the sense of justice, and yet his strategy is based on an unexplained leap. Note how smoothly his argument moves from attachment to particular associations and their members to a sense of commitment to the state and its citizens:

> The morality of association takes many forms depending upon the association and the role in question, and these forms represent many levels of complexity. But if we consider the more demanding offices that are defined by major institutions of society, the principles of justice will be recognized as regulating the basic structure and as belonging to the content of a number of important ideals. Indeed, these principles apply to the role of citizen held by all, since everyone, and not only those in public life, is meant to have political views concerning the common good. Thus we may suppose that there is

a morality of association in which the members of society view one another as equals, as friends and associates, joined together in a system of cooperation known to be for the advantage of all and governed by a common conception of justice.[43]

According to Rawls, the shift of citizens' loyalty from a plurality of particular associations to the overarching association of the state is based on the acquisition of a motivation to act in accordance with the principles of justice. Consequently, the citizen body, as a whole, "is not generally bound together by ties of fellow feelings between individuals, but by the acceptance of public principles of justice."[44] This end result presupposes that all associations will foster in their members adherence to the principles of justice, and will provide them with a justification to extend these principles to the whole of the citizen body, rather than to some smaller or larger entity. But there is no reason, theoretical or practical, to assume that this process of controlled extension of loyalty will take place. The scope of the net laid down by associations need not overlap that of the state, and if it does not, associational activities may become divisive rather than integrative.

The inherent tension between the ideal of freedom of association and social unity should be especially troublesome to those theorists who wish to see the political sphere as embodying a rainbow coalition based on fellowship among different social groups. It is thus worrying to find that advocates of such approaches tend to avoid the need to confront such tensions by presenting a dualistic picture of social relations: condemning the social effects of some associations (mainly interest groups) while fostering an unrealistic picture of social relations among other types of associations (mostly those who give expression to a particular social identity, be it gender, race, religion, or ethnic affiliation).

Young's theory exemplifies this problem well. Interest-group politics, Young argues, forestalls public discussion and decision making, as no group needs to consider the interests of others "except strategically, as potential allies or adversaries in the pursuit of one's own. The rules of interest group pluralism do not require justifying one's interest as right or as compatible with social justice."[45] The opposite, she argues, is true for a heterogeneous public, "where participants discuss together the issue before them, and are supposed to come to a decision that they determine as just or most just."[46] This dualism is unfounded; Young's criticism of interest-group politics seems just as powerful when used against the gender, race, ethnic, and culture-based associations she aspires to support. There is no reason to assume that the politics of difference inherently correlates with a desire for either social justice or altruistic tendencies.

It is therefore puzzling to find that when it comes to the question of social unity, Young, who gives such a brilliant account of the importance of power relations, tends to revive the old liberal belief in a social harmony guided by an invisible hand. This is the unavoidable, and unrealistic, outcome of the rejection of liberal principles as the basis for political discussion and decision making. If there are no general principles on which members of the different groups can agree, then idealized, invisible-hand solutions seem the only available fallback position. Ideally, Young claims,

> a rainbow coalition affirms the presence and supports the claims of each of the oppressed groups or political movements constituting it, and arrives at a political program not by voicing some "principle of unity" that hides differences but rather by allowing each constituent to analyze economic and social issues from the perspective of its experience.[47]

But here again the ideal and the real are worlds apart. In reality there is no basis for promoting an illusion of harmony within diversity. Doing so is as dangerous and oppressive as reviving the old liberal illusion of harmony grounded in state neutrality against which Young so wisely warns.

It seems, then, that active associational life cannot, by itself, promote civic responsibility and friendship. In a world in which ethnic groups are constantly competing with each other, or even killing each other, and where the rich and powerful appear to ignore their responsibility to the poor and needy, we should be more skeptical about the contribution of associations and social groups to the development of civic virtues and social responsibilities. The centrifugal and divisive power of associations must therefore be balanced by the state.

The strange consequence of the discussion so far is that in ignoring the importance of the state, the approaches examined in the last two sections miss their own target: the Nozickian approach neglects its initial commitment to individual rights, while Young's position leads her to ignore the need for fostering social unity and solidarity and leaves the task of developing civic friendship to be guided by an invisible hand. What we need then is an approach that will defend the freedom of the civic sphere, and see it as a sphere in which individuals exercise their right to associate in order to pursue their life plans, express their views and identities, and balance the powers of the state, but will be attentive to the dangers embodied in this sphere and will try to counter them.

CONTAINMENT WITHOUT COMPLIANCE

The major fault of the approaches to civic society examined so far is their one-sidedness; they tend to emphasize one set of values, goods, and liberties at the expense of all others. Democrats give priority to the need to foster civic virtue and democratic attitudes; they welcome social policies aiming to construct or support civic associations and ignore the damages embedded in hampering the independence of the civic sphere. Libertarians view the civic sphere through the prism of freedom of association and argue that the government should refrain from intervening in it, even at the cost of curtailing individual rights and welfare. Finally, communitarians support the formation or preservation of whatever associations individuals see as providing them with a public voice, but overlook the divisive properties of such associations and therefore fail to offer ways to confront the danger of social fragmentation.

In what follows I would sketch an approach to the civic sphere that balances democratic, libertarian, and communitarian considerations. Contrary to those approaches that view the civic sphere and civic associations as a means for advancing the purposes of the state, it sees this sphere as means of realizing the liberal ideal of freedom of association and the communitarian aspiration to a more vibrant communal life. The state, it argues, should indeed play an important role in fostering liberal democratic virtues, in encouraging political participation, public debate, and social cohesion, but it should not use the civic sphere for these purposes. This does not imply that the state should surrender democratic aspirations; on the contrary, it should increase its spending on public education and reinforce its democratic institutions.[48]

The main purpose of this approach, then, is to protect the independence of the civic sphere but to place it within the framework of a strong democratic welfare state that will refrain from intervening in the civic sphere but would act, through its institutions, to balance the activities of civic associations. Such a state would encourage and enable individuals to create their social environment and actively participate in associational life. And yet it would take into account the need to balance such activities and provide citizens with a network of state-sponsored services that would lessen their dependency on the associations to which they belong.

In order to make this position plausible I should clarify the difference between "intervening in" and "balancing" certain kinds of social activities. The state's relation to *the family* exemplifies this distinction. A liberal democratic welfare state ought not to intervene in the family life of its citizens; act as a matchmaker, criticize the kinds of families individuals form, supervise agreements between spouses, or decide how many children they should have. And yet the state ought to balance the social outcomes of family life: through state schooling it should attempt to provide children with equal opportunities and cultivate in them civic virtue; through its social agencies it should offer mental and financial help to individuals whose families are dysfunctional; and by progressively taxing households it should redistribute resources between families. Only in extreme cases in which basic rights are infringed upon and violence occurs is the state called upon to intervene directly in family life: to take children out of their homes, provide them with new custodians, give them medical treatment that can save their lives, order violent parents to stay out of the family home, and the like. We can extend this example and argue that the only way to allow social units—be they families, voluntary associations, or cultural communities—to function autonomously, protected from state intervention, without giving way to social chaos, profound inequalities, or oppression, is to develop a strong welfare state that places the welfare of *individuals* at the center of its concerns.

In a state of full equality—when resources, education, and social power are fairly distributed—the state will have no justification to actively support individuals in their attempt to exercise their rights and freedoms. It should, under such circumstances, intervene only in order to protect individuals from violence and the violations of their basic rights. But as long as social inequalities persist, one of the major goals a democratic welfare state must take upon itself is to equalize the worth of liberty for all its citizens. For that matter, a constitutional shelter that protects freedom of association and associational relationships from unwarranted state intervention might not be enough. The inability to enjoy the benefit of such a protection as a result of poverty or ignorance forms a constraint on liberty that must be removed, or at least alleviated, through public education and financial support. Moreover, as Young rightly argues, it justifies the establishment of mechanisms for allocating differential resources that would cultivate organizing capacities "in order to promote the self-organization of members of oppressed or disadvantaged groups, and to create compensatory political forms to ensure that such groups have an equal voice in agenda setting and policy formation."[49] Some of the associations that would be constructed as a result of such an encouragement might be neither liberal nor democratic. Nevertheless, state support should not be withheld on ideological grounds, as it is meant to allow individuals to make use of their associative rights irrespective of their beliefs (assuming they will act within the framework of the law). As a consequence individuals might form a wide range of associations including: authoritarian and exclusive ones that would restrict membership on the basis of gender, race, ethnic identity, or a particular moral approach, or ones that would violate certain social norms or strive against certain socially accepted ends. The state might thus find itself indirectly supporting associations whose actions lead to undesirable social effects. And yet, supporting individuals' attempts to associate only in those kinds of associations the state sees as constructive ones—that is, those that foster liberal democratic virtues—will invite the state to exert control over the associational life of members of disadvantaged groups who need the state's support in order to organize, while leaving the associational life of the wealthy unconstrained.

Some may still think it unwise, inconsistent, and inefficient to offer support to associations whose activities the state will eventually have to balance or contest. But I have previously argued that the damages caused by state intervention in the civic sphere might be just as profound. Moreover, a liberal democratic state ought to be ready to pay some social price for allowing individuals to enjoy their rights in the fullest and most satisfactory way. If we acknowledge that even oppressive cultures and associations can give individuals quite a lot, that they may "provide many of their members with all that they can get,"[50] we will find the support given to individuals to form such associations far less troubling.

How should the state support the ability of individuals to associate? One way of doing so is to permit collective money to seep through the state/association barrier: "This is especially important when taxes constitute a significant portion of the national wealth and when the state has undertaken, on behalf of all its citizens, to organize education and welfare. It can be done in a variety of ways, through tax exemptions and rebates, subsidies, matching grants, certificate plans, and so on."[51] This support must be progressive—namely, the least well off should get more substantial support.

Another way is to offer actual counseling: nurturing organizational skills, offering legal advice, and instructing individuals how to deal with the relevant authorities and how to apply for public funds and space. Some states and municipalities already endorse these kinds of policies. For example, the *New York Times* reported on a project uniting two nonprofit groups, East New York Urban Youth Corps and Cypress Hill Local Development Corporation, with the New York municipality to support the work of Lyndrew Nesmith in establishing tenants' associations aiming to reclaim buildings from drug dealers and users.[52] The freedom of association of the individuals organized by Nesmith was not hampered by any formal violation of their rights but by their unfamiliarity with the workings of political institutions and their organizational helplessness. They were unaware of their collective power, and lacked the motivation and the skills to organize.[53]

Claiming that the state should foster the organizational skill of its citizens but refrain from intervening in civic sphere does not imply that associational activities should go unguarded. Liberal democratic states have an interest in protecting the basic rights of their citizens, and especially their right to exist. They can do so in three different ways.

First, the state must develop a powerful system of public education that will teach individuals their rights, nurture civic virtues and beliefs, and encourage cross-associational respect. Second, the state has not only a right but also a duty to intervene in the activities of associations that threaten public safety or violate the rights of their own members. Third, the state must supervise the norms and practices of associations in those spheres that are irrelevant to the professed ends of the association. Namely, the state should assume that an association has only those ends it openly endorses, and if necessary, intervene and limit those activities that are not directly related to these ends. This was the view of the court in *Roberts v. United States Jaycees*. When evaluating the *Jaycees'* policy of excluding women from membership, the court examined the proffered aims of the association and concluded that according to these aims, it was unjustified in excluding women. The Jaycees did not view their associations as fostering a certain kind of male intimacy or promoting the kind of activities women might interrupt. Given their ends, then, the Court ruled that the act forcing them to open their chapters to women did not impose "any serious burdens on the male members' freedom of expressive association."[54]

The pivotal role my approach ascribes to the state may be a source of concern to some liberals. These concerns are legitimate, as we should always be attuned to the need to balance the power of the state, but we must also be attuned to the need to balance the effects of voluntary activities performed in the civic sphere. This is especially true in modern, multiethnic, multireligious societies in which class differences often overlap ethnic, race, or religious cleavages. Without a strong state as arbiter and guarantor of human rights, social equality, and democratic values, freedom of association may lead to more, rather than less, injustice and oppression. We must acknowledge then that "invisible hands are no substitute for the magistrate's sword,"[55] or for its caring and supportive hand.

NOTES

This paper was written while I was a Rockefeller fellow at the University Center for Human Values at Princeton. I am grateful for the many good comments, ideas, references, and support given to me by George Kateb and Elizabeth Kiss, and my fellow fellows: Daniel A. Bell, Christopher Bobonich, Hilary Bok, Samuel Fleischacker, Kent Greenawalt, and Steve Macedo. I would also like to thank Peter Berkowitz, Thomas Pogge, Sigal Rady, Amelie Rorty, Nancy Rosenblum, Cass Sunstein, and Dennis Thompson for their helpful comments. But most of all I am grateful to Amy Gutmann, whose perceptive comments were extremely helpful.

1. The terms *civic* and *civil* are used in the literature interchangeably. According to the Webster dictionary, both have the same meaning, namely, "of, or relating to, citizens." For purposes of consistency I have chosen to use *civic* rather then *civil*. (When citing other authors I use their terminology, although this might result in some unavoidable confusion.) The choice is rather random, as both terms are somewhat misleading. Not all associations are civil, in the sense that they do not always encourage the politeness, tranquility, and self-restraint implied by the term *civil*. Nor are they necessarily civic-minded, i.e., fostering public-spiritedness and citizenship. My preference for the term *civic* is mostly historical and emerges from my disapproval of the condescending undertones injected into the term *civil society* by the Scottish philosophers who coined it in order to distinguish modern capitalist societies from the savage and barbarous tribal societies they "observed" in the New World.

2. F. Zakaria, "Bigger Than the Family, Smaller Than the State," *New York Times Book Review*, August 14, 1995, p. 1.

3. R. Putnam, *Making Democracy Work* (Princeton: Princeton University Press, 1993), p. 113.

4. There is some overlap between the different clusters and some notions, such as *trust*, are likely to play a role in all of them.

5. Zakaria, "Bigger Than the Family," p. 1.

6. The state itself is also a particular type of association. Hence, a comprehensive categorization of the different types of associations must take it into account and analyze the special rights and duties associated with it. Such a discussion, however, exceeds the scope of this paper.

7. M. Walzer, "Multiculturalism and Individualism," *Dissent* (spring 1994): 188.

8. M. Walzer, "Pluralism: A Political Perspective," in *What It Means to Be American* (Marsilio, 1994), p. 66. Walzer's argument refers only to ethnic groups, but it can be applied to other social groups.

9. I. Young, "Social Groups in Associative Democracy," in E. O. White, ed., *Associations and Democracy* (London: Verso Press, 1995), p. 209.

10. Tocqueville, *Democracy in America* (New York: Harper and Row, 1969), p. 514.

11. N. Rosenblum, "Civil Societies: Liberalism and the Moral Uses of Pluralism," *Social Research*, 16, no. 3 (1994): p 542. Note that Rosenblum offers this description in order to reject it later on in the paper.

12. J. Rawls, *Theory of Justice* (Cambridge: Harvard University Press, 1972), pp. 471–72.

13. Ibid., p. 471.

14. The key difference between religious associations that are supportive of democratic regimes and those that play a subversive role, as Tocqueville observed, is the scope of the religious doctrine and precepts. If these extend to matters of state and to the character of the public sphere, adherents of this religion are likely to find themselves in conflict with the political authorities.

15. Tocqueville, *Democracy in America*, p. 445.

16. Rosenblum, "Civil Societies."

17. Putnam, *Making Democracy Work*, p. 221.

18. H. Eckstein, *Division and Cohesion in Democracy* (Princeton: Princeton University Press, 1966), pp. 282, 283.

19. S. Macedo, "Community, Diversity, and Civic Education: Toward a Liberal Political Science of Group Life," *Social Philosophy and Policy Foundation*, 13, no. 1 (winter 1996): 268.

20. Ibid., pp. 241–42 (my emphasis).

21. Ibid., p. 264.

22. The Tony and Susan Alamo Foundation is recognized as a nonprofit religious association, the Secretary of Labor filed action under the Fair Labor Standards Act (FLSA), charging the foundation with violating minimum wage and overtime provisions. The Supreme Court held in 1985 that the foundation's business was a commercial enterprise whose substandard wages gave it an unfair economic advantage over competitors.

23. N. Rosenblum, "The Moral Uses of Pluralism: Freedom of Association and Liberal Virtue, Illustrated with Cases on Religious Exemption and Accommodation" (paper presented at the Political Philosophy Colloquium, Princeton University, 1993), p. 27.

24. Macedo, "Community, Diversity, and Civic Education," p. 254.

25. J. Cohen and J. Rogers, "Secondary Associations and Democratic Governance," *Politics and Society* (1992): 427.

26. N. Rosenblum, "Democratic Character and Community: The Logic of Congruence?" *Journal of Political Philosophy* 2. (1994): 80–84. I do not explore this issue here, but one should be careful not to assume that there is significant transference between the social experiences and the values acquired within secondary associations and the development of liberal democratic virtues, at least not until sufficient evidence is available.

27. Tocqueville, *Democracy in America*, p. 192.

28. L. Guinier, *The Tyranny of the Majority* (New York: Free Press, 1994), p. 4.

29. Ibid, p. 4.

30. Tocqueville, *Democracy in America*, p. 194.

31. I. Young, "Social Groups in Associative Democracy," *Politics and Society* 20, no. 4 (1992): 531.

32. M. Ignatieff, "On Civil Society: Why Eastern Europe's Revolutions Could Succeed," *Foreign Affairs* 74, no. 2 (1995): 128.

33. Ibid., p. 128.

34. R. Nozick, *Anarchy, State and Utopia* (New York: Basic Books, 1974).

35. See Nozick's discussion of such costs in *The Nature of Rationality* (Princeton: Princeton University Press, 1993).

36. Ibid., p. 307.

37. C. Kukathas, "Are There Any Cultural Rights?" *Political Theory* (1991): 133, 134.

38. See chap. 9 of this volume.

39. Nozick, *Anarchy, State, and Utopia*, p. 325.

40. In "Taking Communities Seriously: Should Community Associations Have Standing in Maryland?" (forthcoming in *University of Maryland Law Review*) Michael Sarbanes suggests that despite the bad reputation of NIMBYism, such policies are justified in those cases in which an unfair social burden has been imposed on a community. Citing the claim of the Comm'n for Racial Justice, United Church of Christ, Toxic Wastes and Race in the United States that "race was the most significant variable in the location of commercial hazardous waste facilities," he suggests that attempts to reverse this trend are justified. Such actions may seem to fall under the definition of NIMBY but are of a different kind, as they could also be motivated by general considerations of social justice, rather than merely by community centered ones.

41. From an earlier version of chapter 9, this volume.

42. Putnam, *Making Democracy Work*, p. 97 (my emphasis).

43. Rawls, *Theory of Justice*, p. 472.

44. Ibid., p. 474.

45. I. M. Young, "Polity and Group Difference: A Critique of the Ideal of Universal Citizenship," *Ethics*, 99 (1989): 267.

46. Ibid., p. 267.

47. Ibid., p. 265.

48. This approach also demands far greater commitment on the part of individuals who cherish liberal democratic values to promote these values within their own liberal democratic associations. Would not it be desirable if liberal democrats would have accepted the accusation that comprehensive liberalism, unlike thin political liberalism, is a particularistic point of view and would follow the model of religious groups, and demand for their children comprehensive liberal education in special frameworks or Sunday schools?

49. Young, "Social Groups in Associative Democracy," p. 533.

50. Walzer, "Multiculturalism and Individualism," p. 76.

51. M. Walzer, "Pluralism: A Political Perspective," p. 75.

52. *New York Times*, August 2, 1995, pp. B1, B2.

53. A cynic might ask whether the state should also protect, or support, the right of drug dealers to associate and then restrict their activities. The answer is *no!* The state has a right, or even an obligation, to outlaw certain activities. There is, however, a wide range of legal associational activities that do not foster, or might even be in conflict with, liberal democratic virtues and should nevertheless be encouraged and supported.

54. See chap. 5 of this volume.

55. Ignatieff, "On Civil Society," p. 135.

Chapter Nine

CIVIL SOCIETY VERSUS CIVIC VIRTUE

DANIEL A. BELL

A GROWING NUMBER of social critics in the contemporary United States seek to reinvigorate a venerable yet neglected republican tradition of civic virtue. As against those who would condemn this tradition to historical obsolescence, such "republican" critics of modern American social and political life argue that increasing commitment to a common political project may be necessary to combat some of the more serious ills plaguing contemporary America. Those concerned with the swelling of corruption in government point out that institutional protections against the abuse of power by public and private authorities will not suffice in the absence of widespread civic virtue, for only citizens with the character that disposes them to support the common good above their own interests will be sufficiently motivated to resist corruption when it occurs.[1] Those concerned with increasing economic inequality and the marginalization of the "underclass" argue that any effective scheme of distributive justice presupposes a bounded political community of virtuous citizens willing to enshrine generous actions into laws that benefit the least well off members of the community.[2] Those worried about the fragmentation of national political life into competing ethnic, linguistic, and religious groups see a need to reaffirm and increase commitment to a common political project.[3] Such critics are not so out of touch with reality as to advocate the total elimination of self-interest à la Jean-Jacques Rousseau, but there does seem to be a widespread sentiment from across the political spectrum that the exclusive pursuit of self-interest in the public realm must be tempered somewhat by citizens acting from public or semipublic motives if America is to effectively resolve some of its most pressing political concerns.

In this essay, however, I simply assume rather than defend the claim that increasing civic virtue will likely have socially desirable consequences in the contemporary American context. My task here is to ask the question, how best to maintain and promote civic virtue in modern political life. Which groups and institutions, that is, are most likely to encourage the disposition on the part of American citizens to feel part of a common political project, to participate in politics animated by a certain amount of public-spiritedness, and to face harm for the sake of the political community if need be?[4]

According to the dominant theory of our day, one must look for such groups in civil society, the realm between the family and the state. Drawing on the insights of Alexis de Tocqueville, social and political thinkers such as Robert Bellah, Larry Diamond, Amitai Etzioni, Francis Fukuyama, Ernest Gellner, Robert Putnam, and Michael Sandel contend that intermediary associations are essential "springboards" for civic virtue.[5] Associations such as churches, community centers, labor unions, and parent-teacher associations are said to break down social isolation and allow people to cooperate and to discover common interests that might otherwise have gone unnoticed. They are, as Tocqueville put it, "large free schools" where citizens "take a look at something other than themselves."[6] In them, political interests are stimulated and organizational skills enhanced, thus countering the disposition to give precedence to personal ends over the public interest and leading to a broader notion of public-spiritedness.

This essay will rely on two politically significant yet seldom discussed case studies to question the premise that groups in civil society in fact serve to "school" individuals in the art of civic virtue. In the first section I argue that Residential Community Associations (RCAs), a rapidly growing intermediary association in the contemporary United States, tend to undermine rather than increase commitment to the common national good. In the second section I evaluate the civic effects of the National Park Service (NPS). While Tocquevillian theorists of civil society may be led to think that such a large-scale political institution ought to overwhelm isolated individuals and reinforce a tendency toward political alienation in the modern world, I argue instead that the NPS plays a crucial role in fostering an attachment to the common political good in the American context. I conclude this essay with the observation that the tendency to promote civic virtue will vary according to the aims and internal decision-making processes of groups and institutions.

CIVIC VIRTUE AND CIVIL SOCIETY

Civil society theorists, to be fair, generally do not claim that intermediary associations *always* produce beneficial consequences for the polity at large. Tocqueville himself made a distinction between "American" associations that allow for and encourage independent behavior and "French" associations that are tyrannical within themselves, thus producing passive and servile behavior instead of training members in the use of their energies for the sake of common enterprises.[7] Along these lines, some civil society theorists argue that in an overall authoritarian context, associations will reproduce hierarchical relationships within themselves and reinforce political apathy, whereas in a democracy citizens tend to freely and equally associate within groups, developing participants' taste for collective benefits and eventually forging a sense of common purpose in the wider political community.[8]

Senator Bill Bradley expresses a similar viewpoint in a recent issue of the *Responsive Community:* "Civil society . . . is the sphere of our most basic humanity—the personal, everyday realm that is governed by values such as responsibility, trust, fraternity, solidarity, and love. In a *democratic* civil society such as ours we also put a special premium on social equality—the conviction that men and women should be measured by the quality of their character and not the color of their skin, the shape of their eyes, the size of their bank account, the religion of their family, or the happenstance of their gender."[9]

The problem with this view is that a *liberal* democratic society also gives people a right to freely associate into communities not governed by such virtues as fraternity and social equality. If people want to form hierarchical and exclusivist communities like, say, the Mormon church, they have a right to do so.[10] And even if certain civic associations do allow members to freely and equally participate in the internal life of the community, there is no reason to expect that outsiders will be the beneficiaries of what can be termed "internal democracy": as Yael Tamir puts it, "the reality is that one necessary feature of group life is drawing a distinction between insiders and outsiders, and development of loyalty to the former at the expense of the latter. . . . Associations may foster among their members feelings of respect and reciprocity but they often promote self-interested behavior towards outsiders."[11] Such is the price of living in a liberal society—only a tyrannical regime would try to force people to join communities governed by a particular set of virtues meant to forge an attachment to the overall political community.

But what if associations in civil society begin to seriously undermine attachment to the polity at large, maybe even to erode the bare minimum of social cohesion and trust needed to promote social justice and sustain the democratic process? Unfortunately, this is more than a theoretical possibility in view of the worrisome social and political implications arising from a relatively new type of civic association known as Residential Community

Associations. Almost unnoticed by academics and government officials, more than *32 million* Americans—one in eight—live in homes and condominiums as members of over 150,000 RCAs, a number that may exceed 50 million by the year 2000.[12] Let us begin with some background material on RCAs, turning later to their civic consequences.

What Are Residential Community Associations?

A Residential Community Association is a form of communal home ownership that developers adopted in the early 1960s as land suitable for traditional suburban homes became scarcer and more expensive to buy and develop. Instead of building single-family homes surrounded by large private yards, developers turned to a more economical way of building a new kind of surburban home at a price most middle-class families could afford. Smaller individual lots were built and supplemented by common areas for recreation and other activities, areas owned and managed by the residents themselves as members of RCAs. New housing in all regions is increasingly RCA housing, but it is most common in the suburban areas of California, Florida, New York, Texas, and Washington, D.C. In 1990, 61 percent were classified as condominium associations (typically located in multifamily, multistory buildings) and 35 percent as home owner associations (detached single-family homes or townhouses with common areas).[13]

RCA developments have three distinct legal characteristics: common ownership of facilities used by all residents (e.g., swimming pools, parking lots, parks), who are assessed fees to pay for these facilities and for private services such as police protection, snow removal, and garbage collection; mandatory membership in a nonprofit home owner association; and the requirement of living under a set of private laws drawn up by the developer (known as "covenants, conditions, and restrictions," or CC & Rs) and enforced by fellow residents elected to a board of directors. Some CC & Rs are said to impinge upon quite intimate areas of the residents' private lives, such as how many people can spend the night in a home, and it is this characteristic of RCA development that has drawn the most controversy thus far.[14] This essay, however, will discuss the impact of RCAs on nonmembers and the overall effect of RCAs on civic commitment in American political life.

RCAs and Civic Virtue

RCAs seem to exemplify many of the characteristics of civic associations celebrated by Tocqueville and his intellectual heirs. They are generally small in number (the average association has approximately 150 units), are well-organized, and provide the opportunity for participation in local public affairs. One might thus be led to expect that RCAs foster norms of generalized reciprocity and social trust that contribute to the benefits of associational life as described by Robert Putnam in his now-famous article "Bowling Alone": "better schools, lower crime, faster economic development, longer lives, and more effective government."[15]

Not surprisingly, RCAs are in fact promoted on the grounds that they provide all the benefits of village democracy. As the Urban Land Institute put it in one of their studies, "the homes association is an ideal tool for building better communities. . . . The explosive growth of our cities, their trend to gigantism, and the high mobility of their residents are rapidly destroying a sense of community among individuals in America. . . . The best possible way to bring about—or to revive—a grass roots sense of community is for home owners to control nearby facilities of importance to them and through this to participate actively in the life of their neighborhoods."[16] On this view, participation in RCA governance encourages people to become more knowledgeable about local political affairs, to view the world from the perspective of the neighborhood as a whole, thus broadening the participants' sense of self and developing habits of public-spiritedness that spill over into the larger political world.

The reality, however, may be almost the inverse of the myth. In the eyes of critics such as Evan McKenzie,[17] RCAs do not function as facilitators of civic virtue. Instead, RCAs allow and encourage "citizens" to act as privatized individuals who participate in public affairs only for the most narrow of self-interested reasons, with profoundly detrimental consequences for the public at large.

Some of the consequences are indirect, not necessarily the effects of conscious political decision making. RCAs give middle- and upper-income city residents the opportunity to leave the urban setting, either literally as in a move to a new suburban community or in the functional sense of moving to a fortified condominium in a gentrified downtown neighborhood. This amounts, McKenzie argues, to a gradual secession of the well off that would leave the city stripped of much of its population and resources, exarcerbating the social and economic problems of the city and the cleavage between rich and poor.[18] As a warning on the likely effects of RCA housing, McKenzie invokes the voice of Charles Murray: "I am trying to envision what happens when 10 or 20 per cent of the population has enough income to bypass the social institutions it doesn't like in ways that only the top fraction of 1 per cent used to be able to do. . . . The Left has been complaining for years that the rich have too much power. They ain't seen nothing yet."[19]

Murray predicts that cities will come to be viewed in much the same way mainstream America views Indian reservations today, as places of squalor for which the successful will acknowledge no responsibility.

Perhaps this grim diagnosis of the future could be avoided if RCAs served as forums for lively political exchanges and debates, with members learning to think about common purposes and eventually entering the political realm with a certain amount of civic virtue and concern for the less well off. Few members, however, actually participate in RCA meetings or vote in RCA elections (though Robert Jay Dilger notes that RCA member turnout at general membership meetings is higher than the turnout rate for all adults at local government elections).[20] According to a California survey, most RCA members collectively participate in their association's business only when they feel threatened by its decisions or the actions of outsiders.[21] More worrisome, polical activity seems to take the phenomenon of NIMBY (not in my backyard) to new heights. For example, RCA members in Indiana sought to prevent the creation of a group home for developmentally disabled individuals within their subdivision. Covenants that governed the subdivision restricted the use of lots within the subdivision to "single-family or two-family dwellings," and while the state had enacted a statute invalidating restrictive covenants that prohibited the use of "property as a residential facility for developmentally disabled or mentally ill persons," association members went to court and won. The statute was struck down because it was said to violate the contract clause of the state constitution, insofar as it applied to preexisting restrictive covenants. (The court considered such covenants to be issues of private concern, rather than of public policy.)[22]

In California, RCA members mobilized with the aim of opposing a proposal to build a second high school for the city of Redlands near their homes. Dilger notes that twenty-nine out of thirty speakers at a local government public hearing identified themselves as members of RCAs, and they were unanimous in their view that building the high school at the proposed site would increase traffic, litter, criminality, loitering, drug use, and noise in and around their neighborhoods, thus adversely affecting their property values and their neighborhood's aesthetic appearance. The local school board was apparently impressed by these arguments and subsequently announced that the new high school would be built in a location where there were few existing homes or RCAs to contend with.[23]

It is unlikely that participation in this kind of local politics teaches the "lessons" that Tocqueville had in mind. Instead of being "schooled" in civic virtue and increasing their commitment to the good of the overall society, participants learn to act *in opposition* to the interests of the wider community and to evade their responsibility for a fair share of the burdens (e.g., housing the mentally ill) that political communities normally undertake.

Critics point to another manifestation of RCA politics, with the same negative effects on nonmembers in the polity at large. Local government officials and even state legislatures are facing increasing demands from RCA members for tax reimbursements for the provision of local services such as snow and ice removal, street lighting, and the collection of garbage. RCAs argue that since they pay for their own services through their home owner associations, why should they pay property taxes for duplicating public services that they do not need? The problem, as McKenzie explains, is that for RCA members, "tax equity" means that they would provide for their own private parks and private streets, from which the public could be excluded, while members would still make use of outside services such as public parks and streets, for which they would not have to pay.[24] And one may add that RCA members in all likelihood would expect federal disaster relief aid if, say, severe floods or earthquakes hit their suburban "fortresses" in California and Florida.

Nonetheless, the issue of double taxation is gathering steam among those who live in RCAs. In Naugatuck, Connecticut, according to McKenzie, an organized RCA contingent made double taxation an issue in a local election and claimed to have "turned the town around from being completely Democratic controlled to Republican controlled. . . . We were a force to be reckoned with. We turned this town on its ears."[25] In New Jersey a law was recently approved requiring all cities to reimburse RCAs for the cost of providing for their own snow removal, street lighting, leaf recycling, and trash collections.[26] On an even larger level, a nationwide RCA voting bloc is a possibility. As Dilger explains, "Another tax equity issue involves the national government. It allows taxpayers to deduct their property taxes from their taxable income when determining national tax liability. RCA members are not allowed to deduct their association fees from their taxable income even though a portion of their fees is used to provide services similar to those provided by property tax dollars. To promote tax equity, RCA members want the national government to allow them to deduct from their taxable income the portion of their assessment fees used to pay for services that are provided by their local government to other residents in their community."[27]

The consequences of greater political participation by RCA members are predictable: for members, a decreasing sense of loyalty and commitment to the national community and the local communities in which their RCAs are located; for nonmembers, a decreasing tax base to provide for public services; and for the nation as a whole, greater alienation from the political system and an increasing gap between rich and poor.[28] A recent front-page article in the *New York Times* aptly summarizes the dilemma facing the nation: "One of the biggest consequences of this trend [the rise of RCAs], urban experts and even many residents of the new tracts say, is that the nation will surely become more balkanized. Critics worry that as homeowners withdraw into private domains, the larger sense of community spirit will disappear."[29]

A Political Response?

If the above diagnosis is at least partly correct, the United States needs to pay more attention to the baleful effects of RCAs on the public sphere. Whereas extremist forces among certain ethnic groups may be a more visible cause for worry—for example, Diane Ravitch worries about the possibility that "if all we have is a motley collection of racial and ethnic cultures, there will be no sense of the common good. Each group will fight for its own particular interests, and we could easily disintegrate as a nation"[30]—in actual fact RCA mobilization constitutes a far more serious long-term threat to the public good. RCAs are more numerous, more powerful, wealthier, and potentially better organized than any marginalized ethnic group can ever hope to be now or in the foreseeable future.

So what can be done to make RCA growth a matter of public debate and concern? First and foremost, it is important to emphasize against libertarians reluctant to endorse political intervention in the affairs of civil society that the development of RCAs is not "natural." They scarcely exist in the rest of the industrialized world.[31] But in the United States, the national and local governments facilitate the formation and expansion of RCAs. Developers make contributions to local politicians, who then provide municipal assistance of various kinds (e.g., infrastructure, public regulation of the land surrounding RCAs) that help to keep development costs as low as possible. Sales are promoted by providing transportation (especially freeways) near RCAs. And most explicitly, the Federal Housing Administration helps by advocating RCA construction in its own publications and by providing developers with federal mortgage insurance and, hence, assuming much of the risk should RCA projects prove to be unprofitable.[32]

In short, various levels of government in the United States play an active yet seldom acknowledged role in promoting the growth of RCAs. Thus, one can question to what extent public authorities should continue to encourage the construction of RCAs as opposed to, say, insuring loans for modernizing older homes or building more cooperative housing. Moreover, local governments could use their local zoning powers to make entry-level housing more affordable by encouraging developers to build smaller lot sizes and placing public parks and other recreational amenities within walking distance of these homes. Richard Sennett notes that zoning could also be used to help promote home construction in relatively heterogenous settings with a mixture of social classes, cultural groups, and residential and commercial uses: "For instance, 'active edge' planners have sought to direct new building away from local centres and towards the boundaries separating communities; as in some experiments in East London, the aim is to make the edge a zone of interaction and exchange between different groups. Another strategy is to diversify central spaces; planners in Germany are similarly exploring how pedestrian zones in the centres of cities can regain light manufacturing."[33]

Given that RCAs are here to stay, however, public authorities can also contribute to a process of reorganizing RCAs around principles more beneficial to the polity at large—for example, granting favorable zoning decisions and mortgage subsidies to RCAs with covenants that privilege mixed-income home owners and mixed-use neighborhoods. And the government can intervene in more direct ways to ensure that RCAs bear a fair share of social responsibilities; Nancy Rosenblum notes that "New York enacted a policy of 'community residences' to meet the needs of the mentally disabled, and in an effort to avoid 'mental hygiene ghettos' provided a mechanism for overriding local exclusionary zoning rules that limited use to single-family homes. . . . Under authority of this law, the New York court refused to enforce an RCA by-law against an owner who had violated the restrictive covenant by leasing his house for the care of eight severely retarded adults."[34]

The statement (by historian Kenneth Jackson) that "no agency of the United States government has had a more pervasive and powerful impact on the American people over the past half-century than the Federal Housing Administration"[35] may be a slight exaggeration. But there is no doubt that more public scrutiny must be brought to bear on the social and political implications arising from the FHA's administrative preferences and the zoning authority delegated to local governments.

Civic Virtue and the State

The previous section argued that associational life in civil society may sometimes undermine civic virtue. Whereas the Tocquevillian view on civil society predicts that small, well-organized intermediary associations affording ample opportunity for participation in local public affairs transform individuals into public-spirited citizens with the capacity to exercise an effective influence on broader public issues, it turns out that some associations in fact encourage self-seeking activity at the expense of the interests of the community as a whole, diminishing rather than strengthening social cohesion in the overall political community.

This section will evaluate a corollary of the Tocquevillian theory on civil society, namely, the view that large-scale political institutions tend to be inimical to civic virtue. Few deny that in wartime the state can imbue citizens with national spirit and effectively mobilize patriotic sentiments to counter real or imagined foreign enemies, but in peacetime, Tocquevillians argue, modern political institutions impede republican sentiment.[36] Instead of cultivating civic virtue and allowing individuals to acquire the capacity to exert an effective influence on public issues, complex and bureaucratically centralized power structures overwhelm isolated individuals and reinforce a tendency toward atomization and political alienation in the modern world.[37] Thus arises the need for a more vibrant civil society composed of intermediary associations small and intimate enough for free individuals to meaningfully participate in public affairs.

But if Tocquevillians tend to idealize civil society, it may also be that they underestimate the crucial role of some large-scale political institutions in fostering identification with and attachment to the overall political community. More specifically, I try to show below that one political institution seldom discussed by political theorists—the National Park Service (NPS)—makes a positive contribution in terms of maintaining and promoting a desirable form of civic virtue in an American context. Next, I suggest that NPS government officials may be justified in imposing certain limits on associational life for the purpose of allowing the NPS to fulfill its function of educating the public in national affairs and fostering a sense of identification with a common political project.

The National Park Service and Civic Virtue

Contrary to popular belief, the NPS is not merely entrusted with the management of the nation's most precious natural resources. The NPS is also charged with the task of protecting and interpreting the nation's most significant *cultural* resources, such as the White House, Ford's Theatre in Washington, D.C. (where President Lincoln was shot in 1865), the Jefferson Memorial, and Walnut Canyon in Arizona (cliff dwellings inhabited by

Pueblo Indians about eight hundred years ago). In fact, more than half of the 368 NPS units are national historic sites, national monuments, national memorials, and other "man-made" cultural sites.

Why does the nation need a state policy to designate, preserve, and manage valuable natural and cultural resources? The answer is provided in a work published for the seventy-fifth anniversary of the National Park Service entitled *National Parks for the 21st Century: The Vail Agenda:*

> The resources protected by the national park system harbor lessons that the nation wishes and needs to teach itself and replenish in itself, again and again, visitor after visitor. Thus, just as it is the responsibility of the system to protect and nurture resources of significance to the nation, so must it also convey the meanings of those resources and their contributions to the nation and to the public in a continuing process of building the national community. . . . The ability of our national historic sites, cultural symbols, and natural environments to contribute to the public's sense of a shared national identity is at the core of the purpose of the National Park Service. . . . Hence, park use has meaning and purpose higher and apart from purely recreational, entertainment, or economic values. It is partly an act of nation building.[38]

In short, the mission of the NPS is to protect and interpret those resources most likely to imbue Americans with a sense of shared national identity and commitment to the common national good.[39] It is a political institution with the explicit aim of promoting civic virtue in the United States.

Does the NPS, a large and bureaucratic organization, succeed at its mission? Contrary to the expectation by Tocquevillian civil society theorists that large-scale political institutions contribute to political alienation, available evidence suggests that the NPS is one of the most respected and admired public organizations in the United States. According to a nationwide Roper poll, the NPS is "America's favorite federal agency."[40] Numerous public opinion polls show that the citizenry strongly support use of additional tax dollars for operating the national park system.[41] Visits to Park units have increased 25 percent over the last ten years to 270 million per year, and government officials expect the volume to double within the next fifteen to twenty years.[42]

Interestingly, the National Parks attract more than 75,000 volunteers, as against 15,000 permanent employees,[43] a good sign of genuine commitment to the institution. Few groups in civil society can claim to match the five-to-one ratio of volunteers to paid employees.

If the above data can serve to refute the thesis that large-scale, centralized power structures tend to impede interest and participation in the op-

eration of political institutions, it can still be argued that in the eyes of most
NPS patrons, park use is "mere" recreation (no different than, say, a visit to
Walt Disney World) and hence that the NPS may not fulfill its "republican" function of instilling national pride and increasing commitment to the
good of the national political community. But the available evidence suggests otherwise. Cultural and historical sites account for more than three-
quarters of the total visits to the NPS.[44] According to a 1991 national survey of adults conducted for Citibank, 69 percent said that they visited the
parks "to see history."[45]

In any case, one need not invoke empirical evidence to imagine the "patriotic" effect of a visit to the Statue of Liberty or the Lincoln Memorial.
Even natural wonders are likely to inspire an attachment to the national
community, a sense of pride that one is a member of a country with unique
"crown jewels" safeguarded for future generations of Americans. As one el-
derly visitor put in the Citibank questionnaire, "I have travelled all of the
lower forty-eight states and. . . . Yellowstone is the American Garden of
Eden."[46]

Liberal Concerns

According to a dominant strand of the Anglo-American liberal tradition,
the state should not involve itself in the maintenance and the promotion of
an officially designated culture. Right-liberals (or libertarians) such as
Robert Nozick argue that the role of the state is to secure the personal freedom of individuals to seek the good in their own way,[47] and left-liberals
such as Ronald Dworkin favor considerable state intervention to ensure a
fair distribution of opportunities and material resources required for meaningful freedom,[48] but both groups generally agree that it is not the business
of the state to promote or safeguard particular cultural outlooks. The government, on this view, must be neutral between particular conceptions of
the good life, for only then can it respect the equal freedom that all persons
should have to pursue their freely chosen ways of life.[49]

Other liberal thinkers recognize the fact that most liberal democracies
do allow for substantial governmental promotion of particularistic cultural
values and practices. Michael Walzer, for example, points out that governments in Norway, France, and the Netherlands "take an interest in the cultural survival of the majority nation; they don't claim to be neutral with reference to the language, history, literature, calendar, or even the minor
mores of the majority. To all these they accord public recognition and support, with no visible anxiety. At the same time they vindicate their liberal-

ism by tolerating and respecting ethnic and religious differences and allowing all minorities an equal freedom to organize their members, express their cultural values, and reproduce their way of life in civil society and the family."[50]

In contrast, Walzer argues that a different kind of liberalism informs the official doctrine of immigrant societies like the United States. This liberalism "is committed in the strongest possible way to individual rights and, almost as a deduction from this, to a rigorously neutral state, that is, a state without cultural or religious projects or, indeed, any sort of collective goals beyond the personal freedom and the physical security, welfare, and safety of its citizens."[51]

As an account of the actual situation in the United States, however, Walzer's description of American-style liberalism is misleading. Recall that one federal agency—the National Park Service—is entrusted with the task of identifying, safeguarding, and interpreting natural and cultural resources of national significance. It is not just that as an (unfortunate?) consequence of selecting valued resources the NPS's "preservation policy goes beyond simply saving certain objects and becomes a symbolic shaping of the national agenda. It serves as a banner announcing what the nation represents, or at least what it aspires to represent."[52] Rather, as noted above, the core purpose of the NPS is precisely to preserve valued resources as a *nation-building strategy*—that is, what the NPS does is explicitly justified with reference to the aim of creating a shared national identity.[53]

Perhaps the liberal argument about state neutrality in matters of culture is offered as a account of how things ought to be rather than as a description of actual liberal societies. On this view, the liberal critic can concede that the NPS exists and seems to be flourishing, but nonetheless proceeds to argue that this kind of political institution is fundamentally illegitimate and should be abolished in liberal societies or at least in an American context (Walzer?). Needless to say, this would be a radical political stance to adopt in view of the widespread public support for the NPS, but even so, for the record it is worth noting that abolishing the NPS seems to be an unavoidable political implication of the liberal argument for state neutrality in matters of culture.

Rather than spending more time criticizing liberal theorists for their lack of political realism,[54] however, we might be better off pondering the likely fate of valued natural and cultural resources in the absence of the NPS. Consider the state of affairs prior to the establishment of the Yellowstone National Park (the first national park) in 1872. As Joseph Sax notes, vast public domains were being recklessly exploited by the profit-seeking pri-

vate sector. Thus, "the purpose of these initial efforts [at nature conserva-
tion] was to slow the pace of destructive resource exploitation—which had
already decimated the beaver and buffalo, levelled ancient forests, and
wreaked vast harm through erosion—by establishing national forests and
national parks."[55] The expansion and diversification of the park system to
include the protection of important historical monuments and artifacts was
partly justified by a similar fear that valuable (cultural) resources were being
lost due to greed, ignorance, or indifference.

This is not to say that America's "natural crown jewels" and historically
significant cultural resources will necessarily be destroyed without intervention by the federal government. Some may be bought by successful businessmen and kept for private benefit in the way that paintings are acquired
for private collections. Others may be owned by private entrepreneurs who
charge high fees for entrance in order to make a substantial profit. But the
point is that private funding can be unstable and insufficient to properly
manage and preserve valued natural and cultural resources. And if the aim
of the NPS is also to educate Americans about the special landscapes and
historical events that shaped a common heritage, to increase attachment to
a common national project, then only govermental funding and management can ensure easy and affordable access to valued resources by all seg-
ments of the population.

Let me turn to more specific liberal worries regarding a state policy that
designates public artifacts as having special value.[56] The first is a concern
about due recognition for *diversity* in American history. By promoting sites
of national significance for purposes of increasing commitment to the overall national community the NPS may play up the "Great Men" in American history and ignore the contributions of the diverse groups and individuals not part of the traditional history curriculum. The many NPS sites
honoring the contributions of the Founding Fathers, presidents, and military heroes in American history lend some credence to this fear.

In response, one may note with approval increased commitment to the
value of diversity on the part of the NPS. The contributors to the report
entitled *National Parks for the 21st Century: The Vail Agenda* make this explicit: "since cultural diversity is our national experience (*E Pluribus Unum:*
out of many, one), the national park system must be a collection of culturally diverse resources. The criterion for inclusion must be national significance, but of a special kind: the significance should relate to the building of
the nation out of so many different peoples and environments."[57] In practice, recognition of the contributions of diverse peoples has led the NPS to
add such sites as the Ellis Island Museum (opened in 1990), which contains

displays and films telling the story of the nearly fifteen million immigrants who were processed through this immigration station.[58]

If the United States is in part a "nation of immigrants" who voluntarily came to this country to start a new life, the descendants of two other groups—First Nations and African Americans—experienced a very different history, which is recounted in other NPS sites. For example, recent additions to the NPS system include the Martin Luther King, Jr., National Historic Site established in Georgia in 1980 to honor King's achievements, and Washington, D.C.'s Frederick Douglass National Site established in 1962 in honor of the nation's leading nineteenth-century African American spokesman. In order to celebrate the contributions of First Nations, the NPS added to its sites the Cape Krusenstern National Monument, established in 1978 in Alaska to preserve archaeological sites illustrating the history of Eskimo communities, and the Nez Perce National Historical Park, established in Idaho in 1965 to preserve and interpret the history of the Nez Perce people.[59]

To be sure, not all NPS choices will be met with unanimous approval. Like any other organization, the NPS seems to have its institutional biases—three conservationists, John Muir, Frederick Law Olmsted, and George Perkins Marsh, are each given an NPS site, but not a single Nobel prize–winning scientist or sporting hero is similarly honored. Some groups such as Asian Americans and Americans of West Indian descent seem to be largely absent from the NPS system for no better reason than the fact that they lack political clout. But overall, the NPS has been successful in terms of increasing its commitment to recognizing the diverse contributions of various groups to the common national heritage, and this can only help in terms of the nation-building mission of the NPS—the more members of groups are made to feel that they have made significant contributions to a common national project, the greater the likelihood that national bonds will be strengthened.

The second liberal worry concerns the issue of "whitewashing" history. By highlighting the positive contributions of groups and individuals to the common national heritage, the NPS risks downplaying the many injustices inflicted upon marginalized groups and oppressed individuals in American history. The critic can point to the fact that plantation agriculture is not a focus of interpretation on signs along the Colonial Parkway, an NPS-owned road in Colonial National Historical Park in Virginia that connects the historic towns of Yorktown, Jamestown, and Williamstown. As Ary Lamme explains, "plantations are a controversial theme for the Park Service. Because of the association of plantation life with slavery, questions of how to interpret this phase of our nation's history for the public is a hotly debated topic. . . . However it is done, there is a need for interpretation of colonial plantation life."[60] In the same vein, one may fault the NPS for authorizing two parks to commemorate the European American victims of massacres committed by native Americans (Little Bighorn Battlefield National Monument in Montana and the Whitman Mission National Historic Site in Washington State) while glossing over the unpleasant reality that, as the *Economist* puts it, "the country rests on a wholesale [ethnic] cleansing of its native people."[61] In another case the NPS manages the Perry's Victory and International Peace Memorial on the site in Ohio where, as an official NPS publication puts it, "Commodore Oliver H. Perry won the greatest naval battle of the War of 1812"[62] instead of establishing a site at Sackets Harbor, New York, where on May 28, 1813, "confusion among American officers had led to the self-destruction of most American supplies and several U.S. ships."[63]

As with the issue of recognizing the contributions of diverse peoples to the common national heritage, however, the NPS has become more sensitive of late to the need to educate the public about shameful and embarrassing episodes in America's past. One recent NPS publication explains that "we tell the stories of civil rights and Civil War, of invention, and of national *shame* and honor."[64] In practice this means, for example, that the Ellis Island museum displays vicious cartoons from the 1920s of Uncle Sam cowering against waves of "riffraff immigration"[65] as well as several other anti-immigrant exhibits from this era. One educational function of these displays is quite obvious—to teach about past "mistakes" so they will not be repeated in the future. But for our purposes it is important to note that bringing to light shameful chapters from America's past can also serve a patriotic end—the knowledge that one's political community is willing to confront the past in an honest and truthful way can be a source of national pride in the present. Put differently, a political community that consciously lies about its past or neglects to make amends for immoral deeds risks alienating a large proportion of its victimized or conscience-stricken populace.[66]

Liberal thinkers may also be troubled by the fact that the NPS manages nine military parks and eleven national battlefields, among other military action sites, thus seeming to encourage an aggressive and martial form of nationalism. Is the United States any different in this respect from countries such as Iraq, where it may seem more obvious that a bellicose government manipulates military symbols for war-making purposes?

But battle sites and war monuments can be interpreted in different ways.

The same site can reinforce a tendency toward violence or be understood as a symbol for peace. As Ary Lamme puts it,

> Since American sites tend to highlight American military victories, a battlefield can represent an ultimate win. This is, of course, one of the reasons that Gettysburg was not as popular among southerners. To others a battle site calls for deeper insight. The fact that conflict is past and peace restored prompts some to ask whether it was worth it, whether the conflicting principles were important enough to justify loss of life.
>
> Historical perspective almost always suggests that the battle could have been avoided in the search for resolution of disagreements. Hence, although battle sites may be visited by those who revel in the imagined glories of military action, such places may also serve as inspiration for renewed dedication to peace.[67]

Consider as well the impact of a visit to the Saratoga National Historical Park in Saratoga Springs, New York, to honor the American victory over the British in 1777 that was the turning point of the Revolution. Does the visitor emerge with a sense of increased antagonism and hatred toward the British? Not very likely in view of the century-long amicable state of relations between the United States and the United Kingdom ("that's history," may be the impression of most visitors, with no implications for the present). Even if relations were to deteriorate, it is difficult to imagine that cynical government officials could effectively make use of Saratoga National Historical Park to stimulate warmongering sentiments.

In short, different military action sites can have a wide range of meanings, and the same site can be interpreted differently by different people. But this is not to say that the NPS must take a hands-off approach with the hope that visitors will emerge with "enlightened" feelings. The NPS itself recognizes that it can, in the words of the contributors to *The Vail Agenda*, "encourage managers and interpreters to better interpret controversial events and sites and incorporate multiple points of view into interpretive programs. . . . Participants should include both mainstream and radical historians, natural scientists, public educators, park superintendents, and field interpreters."[68]

The Vietnam Veterans Memorial established as an NPS unit in 1980 is a case in point of a monument consciously designed not to foster jingoistic tendencies but rather to accent tragic loss and challenge the principles of blind obedience and unquestioning service. With its list of the names of the dead and its black color, according to Richard Rhodes, "it implies that the individuals were victims rather than heroes, and that it is a monument to their deaths, not to their glory."[69] In her description of the violent imagery that inspired the Vietnam Memorial, designer Maya Lin seems to point an accusing finger at the institutions of a government that called for an unnecessary sacrifice in a faraway land:[70] "I guess I just imagined taking a knife, cutting open the earth, opening it up, pointing one end to Lincoln, one to the Washington and having names be chronological."[71]

None of the above is meant to deny that the NPS has a legitimate role to play in managing and interpreting battle sites of national significance. There is no doubt that many such sites are associated with major turning points in American history and contribute to the aim of fostering knowledge of and commitment to a common national heritage. To quote Lamm once again: "It is at places like Gettysburg that people come to commune with and appreciate fellow citizens of 125 years ago; one nation of the people, across the ages, coming together."[72] But the point is that battle sites need not foster martial outlooks or aggressive feelings toward outsiders.

The fourth and last liberal worry concerns the growth of "Big Government." Looking at the NPS in historical perspective, it is clear that its mandate has grown from protecting and managing America's natural "crown jewels" to that of managing and interpreting cultural and historical sites of national significance. Moreover, conceptions of "significant" contributions to the common national heritage have multiplied to include not only the contributions of Founding Fathers, presidents, and great military heroes but also those of the many diverse cultural groupings that have played a role in American national life. Moreover, the NPS has felt a greater need to commemorate episodes of national shame as well as episodes of national honor. Is there a limit to this ever-expanding mandate?

It is possible to exaggerate this concern. If the task of the NPS is to manage and interpret cultural resources of *national* significance for the purpose of fostering a common *national* identity, it follows that the NPS should not be managing sites that are primarily of local or regional significance. Take for example the Keweenaw National Historical Park established in the Upper Peninsula of Michigan in 1992. The park includes the world's largest steam hoist and a once-active copper mine, but it is really no different from numerous other mining regions of the country, some of which are already included in parks. According to the *Wall Street Journal*, "Keweenaw supplies a small trickle of curiosity seekers with a closeup look at crumbling commercial buildings, slag piles and a Superfund hazardous-waste site, as well as a distinctly modern shopping center currently under construction within Park boundaries."[73] So why was this site established as a National

Park? It seems that "the true purpose of the park, championed by Democratic Sen. Carl Levin and former Republican Rep. Bob Davis, is to prop up the economy of a remote area on Michigan's Upper Peninsula by attracting visitors and creating jobs."[74] Even the park superintendant (who also happens to be the president of the Keweenaw Tourism Council) admits that the park was established to promote regional economic development, noting that "national parks are good places [for Congress] to spend money."[75]

Whatever one thinks of governmental support for economic development, it goes well beyond the mission of the NPS. Critics of the Keweenaw National Historical Park argue that with the NPS budget near the breaking point, valuable resources are being diverted from other park units in desperate need of additional funds.[76] One may add that if the NPS extends its mandate to manage resources that are primarily of local and regional interest, this can serve only to devalue the significance of NPS-managed resources elsewhere.[77] Thus, the NPS may benefit by withdrawing its participation from the Keweenaw site and other such projects, either selling off its facilities to the private sector or passing them on to a different government agency responsible for promoting economic development and the promotion of regional cultural artifacts.[78]

Nor is the prime mission of the NPS to provide recreational facilities for fun-seeking tourists. Some visitors to NPS sites may well view their visits as satisfying recreational needs, but if the NPS site cannot be also be justified in terms of its function of educating the visitor about the national significance of a natural or cultural resource, then the NPS has no business managing the site. Take for example the Amistad National Recreation Area, established as a national park in Texas in 1990. According to an official NPS brochure, "Boating, watersports, and camping highlight activities in the U.S. section of Amistad Reservoir on the Rio Grande."[79] If the sole task of this recreational area is to provide facilities for water sports and camping, there is no reason why this site cannot be managed by the private sector.[80]

In short, strict application of the criterion of "national significance" may in some cases justify *curbing* rather than *expanding* the activities of the NPS. But at this point I want to return more directly to the topic of associational life and civic virtue. If the NPS is indeed quite successful at fostering civic commitment in American political life, and if the NPS promotes a kind of national commitment that on balance meets liberal concerns about dangerous or undesirable forms of civic virtue, then the state may sometimes be justified in limiting associational life for the purpose of allowing the NPS to properly fulfill its mission.

On the Need to Limit Associational Life

In some cases, this may mean curbing commercial activity on park grounds that is incompatible with the required atmosphere of tranquility and respect at NPS grounds. A tawdry and commercialized park site is not likely to build civic commitment and inspire attachment to a common political project. Consider the recent example of T-shirt sales on national park grounds in Washington, D.C. Soon after the Park Service in 1994 disclosed that it would allow the sale of merchandise on federal parkland so long as it was a cause protected by the First Amendment, the grounds of the Washington Monument, the Lincoln and Jefferson Memorials, the Vietnam War Memorial, and the Smithsonian Institution were crowded with hundreds of all-night souvenir stands. T-shirt vendors took advantage of the NPS rule by "politicizing" their items with small, unobtrusive messages such as "D.C. 51st State," messages that were often printed in removable dye. A *Washington Post* editorial commented that "because of [a] loophole in park-use regulations, T-shirt merchants turned America's monuments into a gross national flea market."[81] In response, the NPS prohibited T-shirt sales on national park grounds in Washington, D.C. A coalition of seven nonprofit groups then filed suit, alleging that the new regulations violated their right to free speech, and a decision by the U.S. District Court judge was imminent at the time of this writing.

Whatever the outcome of this case, one can argue that the obtrusive commercial activity may disturb the tranquility necessary for conveying the history in the various NPS-managed Washington, D.C. memorials and monuments.[82] As the American Alliance for Rights and Responsibilities (AARR) put in a friend-of-the-court brief defending the NPS, the prohibition of T-shirt sales is a "reasonable, narrowly-tailored and content-neutral" effort to preserve the accessibility and reverential atmosphere of the monuments to the nation's history.[83] As a matter of constitutional interpretation, the AARR added that "the First Amendment does not guarantee a right to rent-free retail space."[84]

This need to maintain an atmosphere of reverence and contemplation at cultural resource sites of national significance can sometimes also have implications that go beyond park grounds.[85] Consider the case of the NPS-managed Gettysburg National Military Park in Pennsylvania, "an important memorial to national reconciliation and individual dignity."[86] The NPS recognized that if developments outside the park can affect the atmosphere inside, land-use control can be employed to minimize the deleterious effects of surrounding landscapes. In the words of a general management plan that sets guidelines for operation of Gettysburg National Military Park, "Zoning provides for all the needed land uses in a community, while guiding their location and where appropriate in minimizing impacts on neighboring properties. The types of controls that will complement the park's historical lands include the establishment of agricultural and historic districts, clustered development, screening, height restrictions and other actions to minimize visibility of development in sensitive areas."[87]

The problem, however, is that surrounding communities may not always be persuaded to adopt land-use controls that suit NPS purposes, particularly if an important economic interest is at stake. In 1970 a private businessman, Thomas R. Ottenstein, informed the NPS that he was forming a corporation to build a three-hundred-foot observation tower just outside Gettysburg National Park. The Park Service in Washington opposed the plan, but concluded that legal opposition was unlikely to succeed. The Commonwealth of Pennsylvania then used its own legal staff to try the case, submitting expert testimony opposed to the construction of the tower. For example: "It is my opinion that the construction of a 300-foot tower near or in Gettysburg National Military Park is a long step in the process of cheapening and commercializing the battlefield. The battlefield is an historic site which means a great deal to the people of Pennsylvania and the United States. A tower of this size and of such proximity to the Park will detract from the historic meaning of this area." A local Adams County Court judge, however, ruled in favor of Ottenstein, explaining that arguments about the tower being out of scale were too subjective and that Gettysburg was already commercialized. The tower opened in 1974, and the result is what Ary Lamme describes as "an obscenity on the landscape." According to an NPS survey that did not specifically ask about the tower, 25 percent of respondents indicated that they had been distracted by modern structures, and a majority of these referred to the tower when they used the write-in section ("an eyesore" was the most popular description).[88]

Lamme concludes from this episode that "the federal government may need to intervene under its mandate to conserve historic resources for all people."[89] Sometimes, however, close work with citizens' groups in surrounding communities can lead to the voluntary adoption of land-use controls.[90] If that fails, financial incentives may do the trick. Consider the case of Waterford, Virginia, a pristine colonial town that has been labeled a National Historic Landmark, one of only three locations in the United States to have that designation applied to an entire village. Because of the area's proximity to Dulles International Airport, the village and the surrounding landscape was threatened by encroaching development. The Waterford Foundation believed that if Waterford's surroundings were marred by excessive development, the village would be spoiled as a historic landmark.

The foundation's response, aided by a grant from the World Wildlife Fund, was to prepare

> an agreement that the foundation hopes to enter into with each of the five farming families owning property surrounding the village within the landmark's boundaries. Under the compact, landowners will be encouraged to agree to perpetual restrictions on the amount and type of development on their property in exchange for money representing the shortfall between the development permitted under the agreement and the permissible level of development. Restrictions on the siting of development are also a vital part of the agreement. New buildings and roads are to be placed out of view from the village. Should the owner decide to sell, the foundation also has right of first refusal to purchase the land at fair market value.[91]

One of the farmers has agreed to the compact's terms, and the foundation is working to have the four owners of surrounding farms agree to similar terms.

In sum, NPS goverment officials may be justified in limiting some associational activities both inside and outside park sites that disrupt an atmosphere of tranquility, reverence, and historical continuity at NPS sites and thus have the effect of undermining the NPS mission to maintain and promote a sense of shared national identity and commitment to the overall political community in the United States. Legal prohibitions and zoning controls may be necessary to curb disruptive associational life, but the NPS also has a wide variety of educational and financial measures at its disposal.

Conclusion

This paper began with the claim that there may be a need for more civic virtue in the contemporary United States. I then asked the question of how one can identify the groups and institutions most likely to promote civic virtue. According to the dominant theory of our day, one must look for such groups in civil society, the realm between the family and the state. But this Tocquevillian view, first formulated over 150 years ago, may no longer be as persuasive in the modern age. In the first part of this paper I argued that Residential Community Associations, an increasingly widespread intermediary association in the United States, has largely detrimental effects on civic virtue. And in the second part I tried to show that the National Park Service, a large state agency entrusted with the task of increasing commitment to the common national good in the United States, is generally successful at promoting a desirable form of civic virtue and may in some cases be justified in limiting associational activities in civil society that interfere with its mission.

What can one conclude on the basis of these two politically significant counterexamples to the Tocquevillian view on associational life? As against social scientists inclined to merely count the number of small-scale voluntary associations in society at large—the more, the better—it may be more important to analyze what in fact particular associations are trying to do. No one expects that groups formed for the direct purpose of challenging the very idea of a large-scale political community, such as armed militias and separatist ethnic associations, will help to forge broader communal bonds. But the effects of class-based groups such as Residential Community Associations formed primarily to secure the economic interests of members—interests that are seen to conflict with the interests of nonmembers in the larger political community—may not be all that different. Even groups formed for the explicit purpose of promoting a patriotic attachment to the nation, such as the Daughters of the American Revolution, can be counterproductive if they are widely seen as endorsing an outmoded and exclusivist concept of nationhood. There is simply no reason to expect that "virtuous" outcomes will emerge as a happy by-product of such intermediary associations.

Nor can one neglect the actual internal decision-making processes of intermediary associations. Tocqueville pointed out that associations that are tyrannical within themselves will produce passive and servile behavior instead of training members in the use of their energies for the sake of common enterprises, but even groups that provide ample opportunities for political participation need not have "virtuous" effects if members tend to participate only when they think their interests are threatened by outsiders. Moreover, groups that favor some members over others based upon economic criteria—such as RCAs, which give extra votes to the wealthier property owners—cannot be expected to foster widespread commitment to a political community of free and equal citizens.

What this means in terms of politics should be made explicit. If the concern is the promotion of civic virtue, economic support (e.g., by means of charitable contributions) and political support (e.g., by means as tax breaks) for intermediary associations should be given only—assuming such support is effective—to groups whose purposes and internal decision-making processes are conducive to the promotion of ties to the broader political community. These groups, however, may not be as plentiful in the United States as Tocqueville led us to believe. The good news is that neo-Tocquevillians such as Robert Putnam need not always mourn the supposed decline of local groups and associations.

The further good news is that some large-scale political institutions can also help to foster widespread ties to the political community, and that this need not take the form of mobilizing "the people" against imaginary enemies at home and abroad. Organizations designed with the explicit aim of promoting attachment to a particular national community such as the National Park Service can be surprisingly effective. This organization works in part because it does not foreclose the question of which national values and symbols should be promoted by the state, but tries instead to account for the contributions of various groups in a rapidly changing immigrant society. This inclusive, multicultural approach can only help to foster national cohesion.

It may be equally important to examine the internal operations and decision-making processes of large-scale political institutions. Here we can invoke Tocquevillian insights about the benefits of volunteerism and decentralization. The National Park Service is effective in part because it relies to a great extent upon volunteer help. Such institutions can also be effective if local communities are given extra say in the management of particular sites, so long as this does not conflict with overall nation-building goals.

In short, the size of an organization is only one among many factors that may contribute to civic virtue. Relatively small organizations are more likely to provide settings for teaching organizational skills and stimulating an interest in public affairs. Smaller is better, other things being equal. But other things are rarely equal, and factors such as the purpose of the group and its decision-making processes can easily override the benefits of size. Inclusive and decentralized large organizations that depend in part on volunteer support will do a better job at promoting civic virtue than small, class-based, and undemocratic voluntary associations.

Notes

I am most grateful for comments by Amy Gutmann and Amitai Etzioni, and for Mary Abdella's outstanding research assistance. I would also like to thank the Center for Communitarian Policy Studies at George Washington University for providing the setting and the resources that allowed me to research and write this article. An earlier version of the first section of this piece was presented at the 1995 annual meeting of the American Political Science Association and published as an article entitled "Residential Community Associations: Community or Disunity?" *Responsive Community*, 5, no. 4, (fall 1995): 25–36. I would also like to thank Kent Greenawalt, Stephen Macedo, and Nancy Rosenblum for their useful comments on the first section and Karl Hess, Jr., for helpful discussions on the second section.

1. The general argument about the connection between civic virtue and corruption is that if people feel atomized and alienated from a common political project, they are likely to tolerate corruption so long as it does not impinge significantly upon their own interests (Shelley Burtt, "Children and the Claims of Community," [paper delivered at the annual meeting of the American Political Science Association, N.Y., September 1994]). In the American context the argument is that politics is hobbled by "special interests, drawing on deep-pocketed PACs, [which] have gained ever more power since the mid-seventies" (Amitai Etzioni, *The Spirit of Community* [(New York: Crown, 1993], p.225). This "built-in corruption" has the consequence that elected representatives often enact policies favorable to the special interests on whom they depend for campaign contributions rather than to the public interest. And since reform is unlikely to come from the same politicians who have grown more dependent on PAC money, "our salvation will have to come from some other quarter. The public at large, those who care about the whole and not merely the parts, must get into the act" (ibid.).

2. See, e.g., David Miller, *On Nationality* (Oxford: Clarendon Press, 1995), chap. 3; his article "The Ethical Significance of Nationality," *Ethics* (July 1988); and Yael Tamir, *Liberal Nationalism* (Princeton: Princeton University Press, 1988), pp.117–21. The general argument here is that the politically relevant choice for those concerned with helping the worst off is not between a national solidarity that underpins measures to help materially deprived citizens and a universal solidarity with all poor and oppressed human beings; rather, the choice is between national solidarity and a selfish indifference to the plight of the less fortunate. In an American context the argument is that only a renewed commitment to the American nation-state can counter what Michael Lind terms the "Brazilianization of America . . . Brazilianization is symbolized by the increasing withdrawal of the white American overclass into its own barricaded nation-within-a-nation, a world of private neighborhoods, private schools, private police, private health care, and even private roads, walled off from the spreading squalor beyond. Like a Latin American oligarchy, the rich and well-connected members of the overclass can flourish in a decadent America with Third World levels of inequality and crime" (Michael Lind, "An American Nation?" *Dissent* [Summer 1995]: 362).

3. See, e.g., Amitai Etzioni, *The New Golden Rule* (New York: Basic Books, 1996), chap. 7. The general argument here is that the fragmentation of national political life into competing ethnic, linguistic, and religious factions can pose a serious threat to social peace. In the contemporary United States the claim is that increasing polarization along racial lines means that "we could easily disintegrate as a nation, becoming instead embroiled in the kinds of ethnic conflicts that often dominate the

foreign news each night" (Diane Ravitch, "Pluralism vs. Particularism in American Education," *Responsive Community* 1, no. 2 [1991]: 36).

4. Alasdair MacIntyre notes that "How much each of us cares for or is concerned about any person, group, institution, practice, or good is measured—cannot but be measured—by the degree to which we would be prepared to take risks and face harm and danger on their behalf" (*Whose Justice? Which Rationality?* [London: Duckworth, 1988], p. 40). In the context of this paper civic virtue in the United States can be measured by the extent to which Americans are prepared to take risks and face harm for the sake of the national community.

5. See Robert Bellah, Richard Madsen, William Sullivan, Ann Swidler, and Steven Tipton, *Habits of the Heart* (Berkeley: University of California Press, 1984); Larry Diamond, "Economic Development and Democracy Reconsidered," *American Behavioral Scientist* 35 (May/June 1992) 4,5; Etzioni, *New Golden Rule*, p. 27; Francis Fukuyama, *Trust: Social Virtues and the Creation of Prosperity* (New York: Free Press, 1995); Ernest Gellner, *Conditions of Liberty: Civil Society and Its Rivals* (London: Hamish Hamilton, 1994); Robert Putnam, "Bowling Alone Revisited," *Responsive Community* 5, no. 2 (spring 1995); and Michael Sandel, *Democracy's Discontent: America in Search of a Public Philosophy* (Cambridge: Harvard University Press, 1996), p. 314.

6. Alexis de Tocqueville, *Democracy in America* (New York: Doubleday, 1992), p. 510.

7. Ibid., p.198.

8. See, e.g., Larry Diamond, "Civil Society: Toward Democratic Consolidation," *Journal of Democracy*, 5, no. 3 (July 1994): 7–8, 14–5.

9. "Civil Society and the Rebirth of Our National Community," *Responsive Community* 5, no. 2 (spring 1995): 4.

10. This is not to imply that all liberals agree on the extent to which the state should defer to the internal workings of associations in liberal societies. But part of what makes liberalism a distinctive doctrine is the thesis that the "morality" of associational life need not correspond exactly to the "morality" of liberal political institutions designed for free and equal citizens.

11. Yael Tamir, "The Freedom of Association," (paper presented at the 1995 annual meeting of the American Political Science Association), p. 3.

12. Evan McKenzie, *Privatopia: Homeowner Associations and the Rise of Residential Private Government* (New Haven: Yale University Press, 1994), p.11 (relying on statistics provided by the Community Associations Institute, a group created by the Urban Land Institute and the National Association of Home Builders to provide institutional support to RCA boards).

13. Robert Jay Dilger, *Neighborhood Politics: Residential Community Associations in Neighborhood Governance* (New York: New York University Press, 1992), p. 17 (according to McKenzie, *Privatopia*, p. 11, however, in 1990, 51 percent of RCA units were planned-unit developments of single-family homes and 42 percent were condominiums). Since home owner associations tend to be surrounded by walls and defended by armed gatekeepers, they seem to embody the more worrisome aspects of RCA developments and it may seem important to distinguish between home owner associations and condominiums for purposes of analysis. In practice, however, entrance to condominiums can be just as restricted as entrance to "walled towns," and

as far as I know there is no evidence that condominium residents are any less inclined to participate in NIMBY and "double-taxation" movements qua RCA members. McKenzie (in *Privatopia*) and Dilger (in *Neighborhood Politics*) also seem to be working on the assumption that home owner associations and condominiums have similar political effects and they therefore do not distinguish between the two types of RCAs for purposes of analysis. And Nancy Rosenblum points out that "it is well to recall that an enclave-like atmosphere does not require gates or affluence and is not unique to RCAs" ("Corporate Culture and Community at Home," [manuscript] p. 87). What may be distinctive about "walled communities," however, is that they tend to emerge when fear of violent crime becomes quite widespread (see n. 31).

14. I discuss this argument in my article "Residential Community Associations: Community or Disunity?" *Responsive Community* 5, no. 4 (fall 1995): 27–31.

15. Putnam, "Bowling Alone Revisited," p. 20.

16. Quoted in McKenzie, *Privatopia*, p. 24.

17. Ibid., chap. 8. See also Dilger, *Neighborhood Politics*, chap. 7.

18. McKenzie, *Privatopia*, pp. 186–92.

19. Quoted ibid, p. 187.

20. Dilger, *Neighborhood Politics*, p. 147.

21. Ibid., pp. 140–41.

22. See the discussion in Clayton P. Gillette, "Courts, Covenants, and Communities," *University of Chicago Law Review* 61, no. 4 (fall 1994): 1433–34.

23. Dilger, *Neighborhood Politics*, pp. 5–7.

24. McKenzie, *Privatopia*, p.196. In the same vein, Nancy Rosenblum argues that "'double taxation' is a misnomer because the analogy between association assessments and local taxes fails. RCAs provide services exclusively to their members, and statutes require them to match association benefits to assessments (and owners expect to recapture their assessments directly or in the increased value of their unit). . . . By contrast, local taxes are levied on the basis of property value, unrelated to the provision of goods. There is only a loose fit between a given taxpayer's burden and what he or she can expect to receive in services. Montgomery County, Maryland, allows cash payments to RCAs for street maintenance, provided they allow general access to the street. That, of course, is the key reason why 'double taxation' is misleading and does not merit support. RCA residents have use of public facilities; local residents do not have access to exclusive RCA services and facilities; they are luxuries owners purchase for themselves" ("Corporate Culture and Community at Home," pp. 96–97).

25. Quoted in McKenzie, *Privatopia*, p. 193.

26. Ibid., p. 195.

27. Dilger, *Neighborhood Politics*, pp. 29–30.

28. It is worth noting that the sudden growth of RCAs—from 55,000 associations in 1980 to 150,000 in 1992 (McKenzie, *Privatopia*, p.11)—parallels the worsening income inequalities in the Reagan/Bush years. Of course it is difficult to establish a causal link between the growth of RCAs and income inequality, but it is not implausible to suggest that worsening income inequalities can be explained partly by the fact that RCAs have a built-in structure that makes it easier to participate in NIMBY movements and to organize for the purpose of opposing "double taxation" (in contrast to local governments, which may not have been as responsive

to the NIMBY preferences of a group of residents, nor would they have the same capacity to unite on state and national policies likely to worsen income inequalities).

29. Timothy Egan, "Many Seek Security in Private Communities," *New York Times*, September 3, 1995, pp. A1, A22.

30. See Ravitch, "Pluralism vs. Particularism in American Education," p. 36.

31. The possible exception is South Africa. According to the *Economist*, whites in South Africa are increasingly moving "into entire walled towns, encircled by fortifications and defended by armed gatekeepers" (December 2, 1995, p. 45). Although a house in a walled town costs a third more than an equivalent one elsewhere, a surge in violent crime is driving many wealthy whites into such developments. Just as important may be "the urge to retreat, to escape. The end of apartheid has put a stop to racial discrimination, but not to racial fear. Black South Africans, if they can afford it, are as entitled to buy a property in a walled town as anybody else. But few can; these places are almost entirely white. In their artificial re-creation of a lost era, they neatly shut out the poor black realities of post-apartheid South Africa life" (p.46). In the same vein, Evan McKenzie argues that restrictive covenants in the United States developed partly in response to the end of legally enforceable racial exclusion in the form of racial zoning laws: "Homeowner associations and restrictive covenants shifted their emphasis to class discrimination, which is legal, from race discrimination, which is not. . . . The result is still increased homogeneity, and, given economic disparities between white and nonwhite Americans, this approach inevitably contributes to continuing racial segregation" (*Privatopia*, p. 78).

In contrast to the United States, however, it is interesting to note that residents of walled towns in South Africa have yet to mount a successful protest over "double taxation": residents still pay rates, collected by the walled town's administrators, to the local council.

32. See McKenzie, *Privatopia*, pp. 88–93.

33. Richard Sennett, "Something in the City," *Times Literary Supplement*, September 22, 1995, p. 15. For another suggestion to encourage variety in kinds of housing, see Witold Rybczynski, "Downsizing Cities," *Atlantic Monthly*, October 1995, p. 46.

34. Nancy Rosenblum, "Corporate Culture and Community at Home," p. 17. It should be noted, however, that Rosenblum favors state regulation of RCAs in the interests of social justice only as a last resort: "if local community is to be infused not just with the fact but also with ideals of heterogeneity and social justice, and with interests besides residence and family—work, say, or unconventional individual lifestyles, if zoning (and the fiscal resources that go with it) is to be exercised on behalf of a wider polity, then the place to begin is with challenges to local government authority and recast federal arrangements, not RCAs" (p. 83).

35. Quoted in McKenzie, *Privatopia*, p. 64.

36. See, e.g., Bellah et al., *Habits of the Heart*, esp. pt. 2.

37. Andrew Buchwalter argues persuasively that Hegel anticipated Tocqueville on this point (see Buchwalter, "Hegel's Concept of Virtue," *Political Theory*, [November 1992]: 572).

38. This report emerged from a symposium on the future of the NPS held in Vail, Colorado, in October 1991 that brought together nearly seven hundred persons from inside and outside the Service to consider the future of the NPS. It was

published with the assistance of the National Park Foundation. I quote from pp. 14, 15, and 74.

39. It is interesting to compare the national park systems in Canada and the United States, both large countries with diverse ecosystems and a history of European colonization followed by mass migration from different parts of the world. The two countries' national park systems have similar origins—the establishment of Yosemite and Yellowstone set the precedent for Canada's first national park (Banff) in 1885, and the first Canadian Parks commissioner, James B. Harkin, was deeply influenced by the writings of American preservationist John Muir (Canadian Environmental Advisory Council, *A Protected Area's Vision for Canada* [Ottawa: Ministry of Supply and Services Canada, 1991], pp.19–21)—but differences in philosophical orientation soon become significant. As Michael Kammen notes, conservationist goals in the United States become subordinated to nation-building efforts "during the 1930s when the Park Service, like so many New Deal cultural projects, connected patriotism with populism as its guiding spirit. Verne Chatelain, the chief historian working for the Park Service, explained its interpretive mission in 1935 in these words: 'to recreate for the average citizen something of the color, the pageantry, and the dignity of our national past.'" (Michael Kammen, *Mystic Chords of Memory: The Transformation of Tradition in American Culture* [New York: Vintage, 1991], p. 465). In 1958, a National Park Service historian asserted "that national parks should inculcate "true patriotism" in order to overcome "provincialism" and localism" (p. 646).

By contrast, national parks and historic sites in Canada have been managed primarily for ecological and aesthetic (rather than patriotic) reasons. More generally, Kammen points out that federal public authorities in Canada have done comparatively little to promote the transmission of a shared national identity: "National holidays have never enjoyed the prominence in Canada that they have in its southern neighbor. . . . There are virtually no national holidays that honor heroic individuals (like Washington, Lincoln, and Martin Luther King, Jr.), and only three of any kind that are observed in all provinces. . . . Some celebrations, moreover, such as St. Jean Baptiste Day (June 24) and Orange Day (July 12) are more likely to aggravate sectionalism than to foster Canadian cohesion. . . . [P]ublic monuments have not been common in Canada and they attract little notice. Nor are there counterparts to such mythic or sentimental sites as Plymouth Rock, Independence Hall and Liberty Bell, or Gettysburg Battlefield. . . . Canadian schools have not been used to promote national consciousness and assimilation to anything like the same degree as in the United States. As one observer remarked: 'The teaching of a national history creates national myths which facilitate nationalism—but there are ten versions of Canadian history taught in the schools'" (pp. 523–24).

Perhaps in response to worries over national fragmentation, in June 1993 Parks Canada separated from the Department of the Environment and moved to the newly created Department of Canadian Heritage, and the goal of employing National Parks for the purpose of "strengthening a shared sense of Canadian identity" was made more explicit (*National Historic Sites Systems Plan Review* [Ottawa: Parks Canada, 1994], p. 12). It may already be too late, however.

40. Quoted in a recently published NPS pamphlet entitled "The NPS: A Fresh Look" (1993), p. 3.

41. *The Vail Agenda*, p. 97.

42. See Tony Snow, "National Parks: Too Big a Bargain," *USA Today*. August 21, 1995, p. 11A; and *The Vail Agenda*, p. 11.

43. "The NPS: A Fresh Look," p. 5.

44. *The Vail Agenda*, p. 67.

45. Ibid., p. 69.

46. Ibid. In the early part of this century the rationale for public protection of natural resources of great beauty in the United States explicitly included a patriotic justification known as "scenic nationalism." The idea that, for example, "our mountains are better than Europe's" (p. 75) was employed as a means to increase national pride.

47. Robert Nozick, *Anarchy, State, and Utopia* (Oxford: Basil Blackwell, 1974).

48. See, e.g., Ronald Dworkin, "Why We Are All Liberals" (paper presented at New York University seminar in political philosophy, fall 1995).

49. It should be noted that some contemporary Western liberal thinkers offer persuasive critiques of the ideal of state neutrality from within the liberal tradition—see esp. Stephen Macedo's *Liberal Virtues* (Oxford: Clarendon Press, 1991). Others such as Amy Gutmann argue that the liberal state can legitimately promote policies justified by particularistic outlooks so long as they emerge from an open and fair process of democratic deliberation and do not conflict with basic human rights (see Amy Gutmann and Dennis Thompson, *Democracy and Disagreement* [Cambridge: Harvard University Press, 1996]). But while it may be possible to formulate a defensible "non-neutralist" version of liberalism at the level of high philosophical theory, the fact remains that the value of neutrality informs many of the actual political practices and legal judgments in the United States as well as much popular thinking about life and ethics (this argument is developed in Michael Sandel's book *Democracy's Discontent: America in Search of a Public Philosophy*).

50. See Walzer's comment in Amy Gutmann, ed., *Multiculturalism*, 2d ed. (Princeton: Princeton University Press, 1994), p. 100.

51. Ibid., p. 99.

52. Joseph Sax, "Is Anyone Minding Stonehenge? The Origins of Cultural Property Protection in England," *California Law Review* 78 (1990): 1543, 1544.

53. I make the distinction between the consequences of NPS policies and the justification for NPS policies in order to counter liberal theorists such as Charles Larmore who may be inclined to argue (if they were to apply their theory to the NPS) that since the liberal view on state neutrality in matters of culture has to do with how political decisions are *justified* as opposed to the idea that government action should have neutral consequences, therefore the NPS is a legitimate political institution from a liberal point of view (see Larmore, *Patterns of Moral Complexity* [Cambridge: Cambridge University Press, 1987]), p. 44. For an argument that John Rawls has to be interpreted as endorsing this sort of neutrality, see Will Kymlicka, "Liberal Individualism and Liberal Neutrality," *Ethics*, [July 1989]: 883–86).

54. Joseph Sax points to the tension between widespread adherence to the value of state neutrality in matters of culture and an equally widespread attachment to NPS-type institutions designed and maintained for the purpose of promoting a common national heritage: "as uncontroversial as heritage preservation may appear when one thinks of historic monuments and artistic masterworks, the idea of an of-

ficially designated culture seems greatly at odds with modern sensibilities. The very idea of government involving itself in cultural life raises the unwelcome specter of censorship on one side and official propaganda on the other. In addition, there is the more general question of cultural policy as a tool of a paternalistic state that aspires to make its citizens good, a notion that has lost all cachet in our time. In short, state cultural policies appear to be out of harmony with modern ideas about the role of government. Nonetheless, they flourish. Obviously there is some very strong attraction to the idea of a common heritage: a people and a community bound together in some shared enterprise with shared values" ("Heritage Preservation as a Public Duty: The Abbé Gregoire and the Origins of an Idea," *Michigan Law Review* 88 (April 1990): 1142). Sax seems to be suggesting that if people are made consciously aware of the conflict between the value of state neutrality in matters of culture and attachment to national institutions designed to promote an official culture, most would opt for the latter.

55. Joseph Sax, "Nature and Habitat Conservation and Protection in the United States," *Ecology Law Quarterly* 20 (1993): 47. See also Joseph Sax, "Helpful Giants: The National Parks and the Regulation of Private Lands," *Michigan Law Review* 75 (December 1976): 237. In another article Joseph Sax argues that the origins of cultural property protection in the United Kingdom can be traced to a similar fear that many ancient ruins were being threatened by a mid- to late-eighteenth-century development boom ("Is Anyone Minding Stonehenge? p. 1543).

56. I have to rely on my imagination on this point, as I do not know of any liberal political theorist who has written at length on this topic.

57. *The Vail Agenda*, p. 75.

58. One personal note. In communication with the eminent American sociologist Daniel Bell it was established that his grandfather Avram Bolotsky and my great-grandfather Daniel Beletsky both immigrated to the United States from Minsk via Ellis Island in 1905. Upon visiting the Ellis Island Museum I realized that this may not have been as remarkable a coincidence as I once had thought—roughly three million Jewish immigrants from Eastern Europe arrived to the United States via Ellis Island, and more generally over 120 million Americans can trace their ancestry via immigrants processed at Ellis Island!

59. Some NPS sites designated to celebrate the contributions of First Nations, such as the Canyon de Chelly National Monument established in 1931 to protect the ruins of Indian villages built between A.D. 350 and 1300, have a longer history. But the purpose of establishing First Nation sites in the early part of this century seems to have been that of reinforcing the policy of forcing aboriginal peoples into reservations rather than for celebrating the contributions of First Nations.

60. Ary Lamme III, *America's Historic Landscapes: Community Power and the Preservation of Four National Historic Sites* (Knoxville: University of Tennessee Press, 1989), p. 84.

61. *Economist*, September 23, 1995, p. 18.

62. *The National Parks: Index 1993*, p. 72.

63. Lamme, *America's Historic Landscapes*, p. 114.

64. *The NPS: A Fresh Look*, p. 3, my emphasis.

65. Clyde Haberman, "Ellis Island: A Visit Cures U.S. Amnesia," *New York Times*, September 24, 1995, p. 43.

66. Of course, it is certainly possible that some conservatives may be disinclined to favor the use of a national political institution to remind Americans of shameful episodes from the past (one thinks of the protests by the American Legion and the Air Force Association that forced the Smithsonian to withdraw an exhibition on the nuclear bombing of Hiroshima). But others recognize that there is nothing incompatible between patriotism and a willingness to confront the fact that one's nation has committed injustices in the past—for example, General Colin Powell, a man with a fairly conservative outlook, spent many years raising money to create a memorial at Fort Leavenworth, Kansas for "Buffalo Soldiers," the U.S. Army's black regiments that were victims of the army's racism and "were treated as cannon fodder" in late-nineteenth-century wars against native Americans (*New Yorker,* October 9, 1995, p. 31).

67. Lamme, *America's Historic Landscapes,* p. 188.

68. *The Vail Agenda,* p. 90.

69. Quoted in Karen Anderson, "It's Not a Monumental Time in America, Is It?" *New York Times,* September 10, 1995, p. E4.

70. More visitors to the Vietnam War Memorial are likely to have this impression now that even Robert McNamara, one of the architects of the Vietnam War, has sought to make amends for the war (see Robert McNamara, *In Retrospect: The Tragedy and Lessons of Vietnam* [New York: Times Books, 1995]).

71. Quoted in Janet Maislin, "Paying Tribute to History in a Personal Way," *New York Times,* November 3, 1995, p. C12.

72. Lamme, *America's Historic Landscapes,* p. 176. To be sure, not all visitors from the South will experience this sort of sentiment at Gettysburg. Lamme suggests that it may have been a mistake to remove Confederate bodies from Gettysburg, as "the healing of our nation would have been quickened by Northern and Southern burials in the Cemetery at Gettysburg. Historic landscapes have that kind of power" (176).

73. Timothy Noah, "Tired of Mountains and Trees? New Park Features Superfind Site, Shopping Mall," *Wall Street Journal,* July 28, 1995, p. B1.

74. Ibid. Steamtown National Historical Site in Pennsylvania, a park that interprets the story of early-twentieth-century steam railroading in the United States, is another notorious example of a "Park Barrel." This park "stands as a memorial to Rep. Joe McDade, R-Pa." according to *USA Today,* August 21, 1995, p. 11A.

75. Quoted in Karl Hess, Jr., et al., "Tarnished Jewels: The Case for Reforming the Park Service," *Different Drummers,* 2, n. 1, (winter 1995): p. 25.

76. See Terry Anderson's op-ed piece "The Forests and the Fees," *New York Times,* June 28, 1993.

77. Similarly, "rights inflation" in the United States may have the unintended consequence of weakening all appeals to rights by devaluing the really important ones (see Mary Ann Glendon, *Rights Talk* [New York: Free Press, 1991]).

78. This is easier said than done. The problem is that Park Service policies are responsive to congressional funding, which to a growing extent emphasizes activities that provide the greatest political return in the forms of parks that function more as local development projects than as sites of national significance designed to promote attachment to a common national heritage. The NPS itself is aware of the worrisome trend toward the creation of parks of primarily regional significance, and

some of these parks are created over NPS objections (see *The Vail Agenda*, pp. 118–19).

But (contrary to the view expressed in Hess et al., "Tarnished Jewels") the problem may not be Congressional funding per se. Park funds have always come from congressional appropriation of tax dollars, yet it is only recently that "park barrel" construction projects have become commonplace (as Michael Frome puts it, "Years ago the NPS built a reputation as a bureau powered by professional ethics, free of political pressures. This is no longer the case. Democratic and Republican administrations alike and congressional power brokers have politicized the agency, influencing personnel selection and treating the parks like political pork," *Chicago Tribune*, March 8, 1992). This change can be explained in large part by the fact that the NPS has recently undergone a rapid expansion of functions in the absence of a clear national plan that can guide the establishment of new park units. Thus in the midst of uncoordinated and unplanned expansion for a myriad of purposes, it may be more difficult to resist congressional proposals for adding new parks designed to promote regional economic development and increase the likelihood that representatives will be reelected. But a congressional representative would not be able to readily justify the establishment of a park that clearly conflicts with a national plan defining the NPS's role in preserving America's heritage relative to other federal, state, and private efforts.

79. *The National Parks: Index 1993*, p. 80.

80. The NPS could potentially justify its role managing recreational facilities if money earned from such sites were used to help fund the management of nationally significant natural and cultural resources. As it turns out, however, not a single one of the 368 NPS managed sites (including recreational facilities) has turned a profit of late.

81. Quoted in *The American Alliance for Rights and Responsibilities* (monthly newsletter), July 1995, p. 2.

82. See *The Vail Agenda*, p. 21.

83. *The American Alliance for Rights and Responsibilities*, July 1995, p. 2.

84. Ibid.

85. Note that I am referring to cultural resource sites, and not to natural resource sites. In an unpublished report prepared for the Center for Communitarian Policy Studies (entitled "The National Park System: For the Nation or the Environment?"), I argue that the NPS should distinguish between two "missions": the protection and interpretation of significant *natural* resources, which should be justified primarily on ecological grounds, and the protection and interpretation of significant *cultural* ("manmade") resources, which should be justified first and foremost as a nation-building exercise. Thus I do not mean to imply that the state can restrict associational freedoms at natural resource sites on the grounds that it is important to maintain an atmosphere of tranquility at these sites (as a precondition to fostering civic commitment). But it may be that the state can legitimately restrict commercial and recreational activities at natural resource sites if these interfere with the aim of ecological management.

86. Lamme, *America's Historic Landscapes*, p. 137.

87. Quoted in ibid., p. 149.

88. Ibid., pp. 150, 175, 162–63.

89. Ibid., p. 150.

90. The Sonoran Institute, based in Tucson, Arizona, is a nonprofit group that seeks to anticipate conflict between "gateway communities" and national parks. The Sonoran Institute sponsored community workshops in Greenwater (a "gateway community" surrounding Mt. Rainier National Park) in May and June 1994, resulting in a decision to maintain current zoning to restrict residential development and to establish a business zone with traditional "Cascadian" architecture ("Sonoran Institute Communiqué on Mt. Rainier Gateway Communities Project," 1994).

91. *World Wildlife Fund*, "Creating Success in Conservation: Final Report of the Innovation Grants Program" (Washington, D.C.: World Wildlife Fund, 1992), p. 16.

Chapter Ten

INSIGNIFICANT COMMUNITIES

Sam Fleischacker

TWO CONCEPTIONS of society:

> Each man must forget himself and see himself only as part of the whole of which he is a member, detach himself from his individual existence, . . . belong only to the great society and be a child of the fatherland.[1]

> [O]ur regard for the individual [does not] arise from our regard for the multitude: but . . . our regard for the multitude is compounded and made up of the particular regards which we feel for the different individuals of which it is composed.[2]

Consider, first, a crowd singing "We Shall Overcome"; second, several people making dinner, perhaps chatting now and then, or all listening to the radio but mostly doing different things. To the first, one might assimilate dances, rallies and demonstrations, or group therapy sessions; to the second, the experiences "shared" by people in a bar, a small social lounge, a cocktail party or a public square. I shall call the first kind of community "significant" or "solid," with a polemical eye on the word *solidarity* and the strong bonds across people with which it is usually associated. I shall call the second community "insignificant" or "particle," with an equally polemical eye on its apparent inability to transcend the atomization of individuals, its tendency not to "signify" any moral or other evaluative commitments, and its consequent dismissal by many theorists. The polemics are perverse, for it is my hope to reverse the value signs. Solid community I consider dangerous and to be regarded with suspicion by anyone who values freedom, while the insignificant, particle communities are precisely the ones we can all love, and those of us who embrace "liberalism" should pursue as much as communitarians do. Unfortunately, community is far too often identified with the first rather than the second.

. . . . .

Insofar as there is a liberal case for communitarianism, the best version of it, I believe, is one based on the claim that participation in some sort of community greatly enriches our rational deliberations, especially over our higher ends.[3] We correct the ends we already happen to have in conversation with our friends; otherwise, we can barely see what might be wrong with them. This is partly because we are historical creatures, unclear about our own identity because it is enmeshed with the identity of others and in a past we do not fully know, and partly because our emotions, and emotional investments in certain relationships and courses of action, can blind us to the longer-term interests those investments are supposed to serve.[4] If we see ourselves this way, we see our freedom as enhanced by the help of our friends. Micheal Sandel writes: "Uncertain which path to take, I consult a friend who knows me well, and together we deliberate, offering and assessing by turns competing descriptions of the person I am, and of the alternatives I face as they bear on my identity. To take seriously such deliberation is to allow that my friend may grasp something I have missed, may offer a more adequate account of the way my identity is engaged in the alternatives before me."[5] I shall not elaborate this point further: in essence it was put already by Aristotle, and it has been recently enlarged superbly by Sandel, Will Kymlicka, and Yael Tamir, among others. If community is a precondition for *freedom*, it clearly deserves liberalism's protection.

But not just any community will do, and for some individuals isolation will reasonably appear more freeing than all communities. *If* I see myself as essentially a historically and socially enmeshed being, I must accept Sandel's conclusions, but if I refuse to "take seriously" the notion of friendly deliberation he describes, it is hard to show that I *must* be unfree.[6] Even if I do accept his argument, moreover, I may find no wise friends. Maimonides, who urges life in community from an even more Aristotelian perspective than Sandel's, at the same time advises someone surrounded by corrupt communities to live alone:

> If all the states known to [a man], or of which intelligence has reached him, be followers of a path which is not good, . . . or, if he be unable to migrate to a state whose rules of conduct are good, . . . he should isolate himself and live in seclusion, even as it is said, "Let him sit alone and keep silence." (Lamentations 3:28). And, if the inhabitants of his state be evildoers . . . who deny him the right of residence in the state unless he become assimilated with them, . . . he should go forth and dwell in caves, or cliffs, or deserts.[7]

A hermit's existence is better than being led astray by foul communities. Only good communities enhance our ability to make wise choices, and thus only the *possibility* of community is something a politics concerned with liberty must preserve. After childhood, a "free spirit" might want to leave the possibility unused. There are free hermits, after all, and very unfree members of communities. Liberal nationalists and communitarians have thus made a case only for *some* kinds of community, and for participation in those kinds of community to be an option for everyone. What kinds, and how to ensure that participation remains optional, is the burden of this paper.

. . . . .

That the distinction between solid and particle communities is often missed comes out nicely in the following, highly influential passage from Charles Cooley:

> By primary groups I mean those characterized by intimate face-to-face association and cooperation. They are primary in several senses, but chiefly in that they are fundamental in forming the social nature and ideals of the individual. The result of intimate association, psychologically, is a certain fusion of individualities in a common whole, so that one's self, for many purposes at least, is the common life and purpose of the group. Perhaps the simplest way of describing this wholeness is by saying that it is a "we"; it involves the sort of sympathy and mutual identification for which "we" is the natural expression. One lives in the feeling of the whole and finds the chief aims of his will in that feeling. . . . [The unity of this "we"] is always a differentiated and usually a competitive unity, admitting of self-assertion and various appropriative passions; but these passions are socialized by sympathy, and come, or tend to come, under the discipline of a common spirit.[8]

The small groups Cooley describes seem to be simultaneously the "face-to-face" particle associations, "always differentiated and . . . competitive," in which we grow up—families, neighborhoods, and the like—and the sort of unhealthy cults and mobs in which one "lives in the feeling of the whole," "fuses" oneself with others, and submerges one's ends to the "common life and purpose of the group."[9] I want to keep such groups firmly apart.

To do so, let me spend a moment on the phenomenology of group life. If we say, as I want to do, that the second quotation at the beginning of this paper (from Adam Smith's *Theory of Moral Sentiments*) represents a society where the company of other people serves primarily as a source of moral examples, and morally helpful approval and disapproval, to each individual, while the first quotation represents a society where individuality itself is superseded, we can construct a continuum between the two poles that Cooley has collapsed. Using "society" as a general term for significant numbers of people living together for a significant period of time, and "community" to designate the subset of such arrangements in which the presence of others *matters* to each of the people, let us begin with the endpoints of no community, on the one hand, and the completely oppressive crowd on the other. At the bottom end of the continuum is the person who lives among others but is entirely isolated—for instance, someone locked up in a bare and windowless cell. A bare notch up, still well shy even of Robert Putnam's "bowling alone," is one who has only books or newspapers for company, or who, like Chauncey Gardiner in *Being There*, sits in front of the television all day. This person has human images to emulate, human actions to admire or condemn, but unreal ones, and presumably will soon lose the ability, if she ever possessed it, to distinguish between the more and the less realistic among the images passing before her. In addition, of course, the emulation is all one way—the figures in the books or on the screen cannot take direction from her example, much less give her approval or disapproval.

In fact, compared with these extremes, Putnam's lonely bowlers are positively social butterflies,[10] but to preserve the point he wants to make, we have to imagine them bowling in complete indifference to other people in the room. There are staff and other bowlers all around them, but they do not take any of these people as examples, as people to watch in admiration or contempt, much less to talk to or share a drink with. They live in the presence of real other people, but do not interact with them in any way.

One step above this, the first I think into a society worth cultivating, is a room where people silently but consciously share the same project. We are all preparing dinners for the same charity, or doing our individual bests to pull survivors out of a collapsed building, but we work in our own corners on our own chosen parts of the effort. Here there really is a community, although nothing is explicitly shared or coordinated. We are "alone together": both halves of that paradoxical phrase are entirely apt. I look over, brazenly or out of the corner of my eye, at a particularly hardworking person over there or a lazy shirker in the corner and try to emulate the former or distinguish myself from the latter; the shirker, perhaps, puts in a bit more of an effort if he notices my contemptuous glare. Or perhaps I pick up a practical tip by watching someone do something particularly clever. We learn from one another and we influence one another, although we remain each entirely free in our actions.

Three grades of richer community can be constructed from this one by adding, successively, conversation among the participants, some participatory structure for organizing the activities, and some activity or activities that people actually perform together. Mutual exemplification becomes a clearer business once the first is added—that apparently accusatory glance can be explained away as a mere twitch—and a subtler one: a smile can be accompanied by criticism. And once activities are jointly organized or carried out, the stakes of participating in community are raised. One may gain from the material results of joint efforts or simply from the increased emotional warmth that talking and acting together can bring, but one also loses a certain amount of independence. The initial, silent community provides human interaction with the lowest possible amount of pressure by one on the other to conform. Conversation increases the opportunities for emotional coercion, and as one moves on to shared ways of distributing labor and to shared labors, pressure to conform necessarily increases. So there is a trade-off between the gains communal efforts can offer in satisfying human needs—for material goods and for the alleviation of loneliness—and a loss in immediate control over one's own actions. Some would call this a straight trade-off between pleasure and freedom. Others, to some extent surely correctly, would mitigate the trade-off by distinguishing "immediate control" over one's actions from freedom, noting that one sometimes gains more of the latter by mediating one's decisions through the process of rational conversation about one's motives and intended effects with other human beings. But the compromises that governing structures, however participatory, usually require, and that shared human activities must require, quickly outstrip even a generous conception of those actions I would choose to do differently after conversation with others. I might still prefer, on the whole, to be part of a social group that requires such compromises than to do the things I individually want to do while living entirely alone, but this preference is not primarily, if at all, a *moral* one. Most of us want to be part of some social group or groups, and for that we relinquish some amount of our individual autonomy. And this is not strictly forbidden by morality, even of a Kantian variety, as long as the compromises do not require choices that themselves are strictly forbidden (or disallow choices that are required of us).

At the top end of our continuum, we have societies in which the individual is supposed to "merge" into a larger group. Individual boundaries supposedly melt away, and each finds his or her "true essence" in a higher group identity to which he or she belongs. Ultimately, I guess, since it is incoherent to seek "my" self in a realm where the distinction between "me" and "you" has disappeared, one kicks away the ladder of individual identity altogether and enters the mysteries of *Geist*, or some other collectivist conception of human nature. I shy away from the metaphysics here, since they are probably incoherent on any reading, but examples of social groups that claim some such thing as their aim are plentiful. Ancient orgiastic rites and modern mass rallies are the most obvious examples, although they are perhaps too short-lived to count properly as a society. Longer lasting examples might be political and religious cults like the Red Brigades or the Nation of Islam, where membership is contingent on an effort to avoid disagreeing with the rest of the group in speech and thought.

Finally, beyond even these groups in the search for "solidarity" are the societies Hannah Arendt labeled "totalitarian": every moment and aspect of every individual life is monitored, and as much as possible controlled, by some group standing for the social whole, usually by means of terror. The familiar paradigms are Nazi Germany, Stalinist Russia, and Communist Cambodia, Romania, and Albania. This must serve as the extreme other end of our continuum because it is in essence a point at which community again ceases to exist, where each individual is bound to others and the whole by means of force alone, and has lost any sense that interaction with others might be an extension of his or her own autonomy.

We thus have nine stages, which we might summarize as follows: (1) complete isolation, (2) illusory community, (3) societies of indifferent atoms (bowling alone), (4) societies of pure example, (5) exemplary and conversational anarchies (4 plus conversation), (6) exemplary and conversational polities (5 plus some structure of governance), (7) communitarian polities (6 plus some group activities), (8) anti-individualist society, and (9) totalitarian society. The point of laying out this continuum is to make clear that friends and foes of promoting community are usually arguing over the optimal point *between* two very ugly extremes. When a libertarian suggests that 1, 2, or 3 is actually a healthy way for human beings to live, then it is perhaps understandable that a communitarian might veer to the equally ludicrous extreme of praising 8 or 9, but in the range between 4 and 7 freedom and community do not have so much as a serious conflict with one another. A healthy debate can be conducted over the morally best mix to be found between 4 and 7, and over the proper governmental role in promoting one or more of these kinds of community. That debate is skewed when just one condition is presented (individual freedom without any social bonds) versus just one other (the *Aufhebung* of individuality into its social essence).

Particle Communities: Historical Considerations

Rather than argue directly about how best to steer between atomism and *Aufhebung*, I want here simply to lay out a model of community that fits roughly my level 5 (exemplary and conversational anarchy). I hope thereby to show that many of the moral gains of community can be achieved without the high level of participation emphasized by those who view voluntary associations as a training ground for citizenship. Anarchic associations strike most political theorists as too amorphous to deserve much attention, and incapable of developing any politically interesting virtues. I shall try to show that this is not so, at least if the main point of communal involvement is to allow us to achieve a more thoughtful, and less egoistic, understanding of ourselves and our ends. And I shall argue that promoting the anarchies I have called "particle communities" is the best way for liberals to grant the central criticism communitarians have urged on them without violating the constraints of neutrality.

The notion of community I want to advocate has a precedent in the writings of Adam Smith, and it will be helpful to look at this precedent to explain how it might work. Eighteenth-century liberal thinkers are often caricatured as atomistic individualists who neither recognized the social nature of human beings nor cared much whether or not people entered into communities. This is especially ridiculous in the case of Smith, whose *Theory of Moral Sentiments*[11] is one of the most astute sociological treatises before the twentieth century. Smith took the human need for community extremely seriously, but also saw it as raising moral problems, and for that very reason was concerned to develop thoughtful ways of reconciling social bonds with individual autonomy. Any attempt to foster a properly liberal kind of community, one with bonds weak enough to preserve freedom but strong enough to allow for morally fruitful interaction, faces serious philosophical difficulties. The reward Smith generally receives for appreciating these difficulties is that the notion of community in his writings gets overlooked. But he in fact seems clearly to want to forge, out of the church, an institution in which the kind of civic friendship Aristotle recommended can be developed. Smith hopes that a separation of church and state will transform churches into groups that primarily encourage moral action rather than supernatural belief. In fact, he entitles the chapter in the *Wealth of Nations* in which he discusses churches, "Of . . . Institutions for the Instruction of People of All Ages," and intimates in the first sentence that churches just *happen* to be the main forum in which people are educated after adolescence. The tone of the chapter as a whole suggests that he would have preferred secular institutions to provide "instruction for all ages," had he known any that might be effective. Let us see what we can glean by considering this chapter in depth.

. . . . .

Book V, chapter 1 of the *Wealth of Nations* is officially devoted to "the Expences of the Sovereign or Commonwealth,"[12] and Smith, who follows his own announced programs with a scrupulousness that borders on the obsessive, shapes everything he ever managed to publish about the legitimate functions of a state to fit this awkwardly budget-sized wrapper. A wealth of interesting insights into education and military policy become mere colorful illustrations to an overall argument about the difference between the amounts ancient and modern states need to spend on schools and armies; an entire theory of how the interests of a government official should be linked to those he or she attempts to rule gets buried in a subsection of an argument about expenditures on "publick Works." Similarly, what Stephen Macedo has rightly identified as Smith's intriguing, quite unusual contribution to our understanding of associative life is buried, and somewhat distorted, by appearing as a mere digression to a chapter on churches.[13] To make out exactly what Smith wants to say about associations, we therefore need to work backward, from the overall purpose of the chapter to the argument, in the light of that purpose, about the associative value of churches to, finally, the way that argument belongs with Smith's general conception of how society contributes to its members' moral development.

So, first of all, what is Smith doing discussing churches at all? The simple answer to that is that an established church traditionally formed one of the most significant of government expenses, and an even more significant part of the spending of the population as a whole—above all, in the form of lands ceded to church officials that could otherwise be used for housing or agriculture. Smith takes this expense up, therefore, as something any reader would expect a "sovereign or commonwealth" to spend money on. I put the point in this roundabout way because it turns out that Smith actually recommends, in the opening pages of the chapter, spending *no* money on religion: the "plan of . . . no ecclesiastical government" that had been advocated by the Independents in England and that the Quakers had established in Pennsylvania strikes him as the best (*WN* V.i.g.8). Against this recommendation stand two things: the opinion of Smith's close and brilliant friend David Hume, who wanted the state to pay clerics precisely so as "to bribe their indolence" (as he put it in a delightfully perverse passage that Smith quotes at length), and virtually the entirety of political experience up until Smith's time. So after extolling the merits of complete disestablishment, Smith resigns himself to the political improbability of such a plan and proceeds to show how the advantages of disestablishment might be approximated even where a state church is maintained. Warning that an established religion puts the sovereign's own security in doubt unless he can significantly "influenc[e]" the teachers of that religion, he devotes the rest of the chapter to a history and set of policy recommendations designed to show how such influence can best be achieved. His conclusion: pay your clerics poorly. Money that goes into church coffers can better be directed to other expenses of the state (*WN* V.i.g.41). Universities, in particular, gain greatly if they can draw intelligent young scholars away from a clerical career, and it is better that scholarship take place in a university environment (*WN* V.i.g.39–40). "Mediocrity of benefice," finally, has agreeable effects on the demeanor and moral behavior of clerics (*WN* V.i.g.38, 42).

The whole chapter thus exudes suspicion, cynicism, and distaste both for churches and for the people who run them. Smith wants governments as much as possible to avoid endorsing religious doctrines (*WN* V.i.g.18), and at two points he suggests using the universities actively to *counter* such doctrines: once, as noted above, at the end of the chapter and once, earlier, when he tells us that encouraging "the study of science and philosophy" is the best "antidote to the poison of enthusiasm and superstition" (*WN* V.i.g.14). To set Smith's favorable notes about churches as social institutions in this context is therefore to show, in the first place, that any moral advantages churches have to offer have to be weighed against some extremely serious *dis*advantages. I will use that point, in the next section, to take Smith's suggestions in a more secular direction. In the second place, we will see that Smith picks out sociological facts to the virtual exclusion of doctrinal ones as what matters to politics about religion. No Burkean talk here about the value of religious traditions for instilling a respect for the past, nor any utilitarian suggestions that a belief in divine reward and punishment will keep the citizenry well behaved. What makes a church morally useful has almost nothing to do with what it officially teaches, for Smith; the distinction between a good and a bad church depends on the size of the church and the way its teachers get paid. From this perspective, Smith can afford to offer more tolerance to the many different doctrines people believe than did most of his predecessors, while urging the government to take a remarkably activist line against certain *modes* of belief ("enthusiasm") and to the encouraging of some and discouraging of other institutions for sharing beliefs.

We can now turn to what Smith does find to praise about churches. Recall that Hume recommended funding clerics "to bribe their indolence." He worried that the little religious sects that spring up where there is no established religion tend to be rather crazier, and more effective, than an established religion ever is. Smith opens by quoting Hume's view, then defends disestablishment with the argument not only that it contributes to a general climate of "philosophical good temper and moderation with regard to . . . religious principle," but that even zealous little religious sects can provide some real social benefits. Specifically, they offer communities that keep the common people away from the disorderliness and self-destruction of vice. "The vices of levity are always ruinous to the common people, and a single week's thoughtlessness and dissipation is often sufficient to undo a poor workman for ever, and to drive him through despair upon committing the most enormous crimes" (V.i.g.10). But unless a person feels watched by some social group whose approval he craves, he may slip, nevertheless, into the "thoughtlessness" that will undo him. Small sects provide the surveillance necessary to keep poor people from thoughtlessness.

Smith's spectator theory of moral development flashes by us for a moment here. According to his *Theory of Moral Sentiments*, we are initially awakened to reflect on our own conduct by the approval and criticism of others:

> Were it possible that a human creature could grow up to manhood in some solitary place, without any communication with his own species, he could no more think of his own character, of the propriety or demerit of his own sentiments and conduct, of the beauty or deformity of his own mind, than of the beauty or deformity of his own face. All these are objects which he cannot easily see, which naturally he does not look at, and with regard to which he is provided with no mirror which can present them to his view. Bring him into society, and he is immediately provided with the mirror which he wanted before. It is placed in the countenance and behaviour of those he lives with, which always mark when they enter into, and when they disapprove of his sentiments. (*TMS* III.1.4)

We then internalize these external responses:

> [O]ur first moral criticisms are exercised upon the manner and conduct of other people; . . . But we soon learn, that other people are equally frank with regard to our own. We become anxious to know how far we deserve their censure or applause, and whether to them we must necessarily appear those agreeable or disagreeable creatures which they represent us. We begin, upon this account, to examine our own passions and conduct, and to consider how these must appear to them, by considering how they would appear to us if in their situation. We suppose ourselves the spectators of our own behavior, and endeavour to imagine what effect it would, in this light, produce upon us. . . . If in this view it pleases us, we are tolerably satisfied. We can be more indifferent about the applause, and in some measure, despise the censure of the world; secure that, however misunderstood or misrepresented, we are the natural and proper objects of approbation. (*TMS* III.1.5)

And, finally, at least in the ideal case, this "impartial spectator" within ourselves replaces external response as our primary criterion for whether we are behaving well or badly:

> The man of real constancy and firmness, the wise and just man who has been thoroughly bred in the great school of self-command, . . . never dare[s] to suffer the man within the breast to be absent one moment from his attention. With the eyes of this great inmate he has always been accustomed to regard whatever relates to himself. . . . He does not merely affect the sentiments of the impartial spectator. He really adopts them. He almost identifies himself with, he becomes himself that impartial spectator, and scarce even feels but as that great arbiter of his conduct directs him to feel. (*TMS* III.3.25)

On a psychological level, however, even this ideal internalization, this move toward freedom, usually requires that real other people reinforce our self-judgments: "Their approbation necessarily confirms our own self-approbation" (*TMS* III.2.3). And on an epistemic level, real other people keep our self-judgments honest: "The man within the breast, the abstract and ideal spectator of our sentiments and conduct, requires often to be awakened and put in mind of his duty, by the presence of the real spectator. . . . The propriety of our moral sentiments is never so apt to be corrupted, as when the indulgent and partial spectator [in our selves] is at hand, while the indifferent and impartial one is at a great distance" (*TMS* III.3.38, 41).

This account makes moral behavior dependent on social sanctions, not in the deterministic sense that we are incapable of acting well except as a sort of performance to win approval, but in the sense that we *learn* to turn inward only from society. For Smith, social approval is an implicitly rational teaching method and an appropriate response to virtuous conduct, not a means of Pavlovian conditioning. Ultimately we seek not praise but praiseworthiness—"to be that thing, which, though it should be praised by nobody, is, however, the natural and proper object of praise[:] . . . so far is the love of praise-worthiness from being derived altogether from that of praise, that the love of praise seems, . . . in a great measure, to be derived from that of praise-worthiness" (*TMS* III.2.1, 3). But to understand this, first we have to live out our desire for praise: to experience its satisfactions and disappointments. Becoming virtuous, pace Mandeville, is thus not incompatible with understanding the process of socialization by which one has so developed,[14] and if one succeeds in internalizing the ideal, merely *potentially* external spectator against which to judge one's own actions, one can act more or less freely, and contribute more or less freely to the standards of judgment in one's society, regardless of having been directed toward such judgment *by* one's society.

So individually free action and the social construction of the self are compatible, for Smith, even dependent on one another, which means that he is not proposing religious sects as a means of controlling poor people in particular, but as a special case of the societal influence that he regards as necessary to encourage virtue in anyone. "A man of rank and fortune is by his station the distinguished member of a great society, who attend to every part of his conduct, and who thereby oblige him to attend to every part of it himself."[15] What distinguishes the poor, in a large urban environment at least, is that they lack a group with which they can interact in a morally reinforcing way:

> A man of low condition, on the contrary, is far from being a distinguished member of any great society. While he remains in a country village his conduct may be attended to, and he may be obliged to attend to it himself. In this situation, and in this situation only, he may have what is called a character to lose. But as soon as he comes into a great city, he is sunk in obscurity and darkness. His conduct is observed and attended to by nobody, and he is therefore very likely to neglect it himself, and to abandon himself to every sort of profligacy and vice. (*WN* V.i.g.12)

And it is to *this* problem that religious sects provide a solution:

> He never emerges so effectually from this obscurity, his conduct never excites so much the attention of any respectable society, as by his becoming the member of a small religious sect. He from that moment acquires a degree of consideration which he never had before. All his brother sectaries are, for the credit of the sect, interested to observe his conduct, and if he gives occasion to any scandal, if he deviates very much from those austere morals which they almost always require of one another, to punish him by what is always a very severe punishment, even where no civil effects attend it, expulsion or excommunication from the sect. (*WN* V.i.g.12)[16]

"Regular and orderly" morals are strongly urged by members of little sects on one another, indeed excessively so: "The morals of [these] little sects . . . have frequently been rather disagreeably rigorous and unsocial." Smith recommends that the state counter this disagreeable rigor and exclusiveness to some extent, by spreading science and philosophy and by providing frequent and gay "public diversions"—the latter to include comedies that ridicule religious fanatics.[17]

So secular efforts at community should fit neatly into Smith's highly sociological account of moral behavior—but it is the power of example alone, the power that comes of the human desire to meet with other people's approval, that ought to govern such communities. In the small sect, each serves as an example for the others. The poorly paid clergy that Smith recommends as the best to be gotten out of establishment achieve whatever they do achieve by setting a good example (*WN* V.i.g.37–38, 42), and by attending closely enough to their parishioners to provide the latter with someone for whose approval *they* might behave well. The power of example is very different from the powers churches have historically tended to wield: powers based on material wealth at their disposal or on the promise of divine reward and punishment. The power of example requires neither physical force nor dishonesty—indeed, it is normally incompatible with dishonesty—hence, it cannot readily be used to manipulate someone. And it cannot readily be exercised in front of very large groups, in fact in hardly any setting outside of direct, face-to-face interaction.

I draw from this two political morals for the broader purposes of this paper. First, Smith's analysis makes smallness extremely important to keeping religious sects healthy rather than dangerous. In Smith's *ideal* picture, where groups like the Quakers rather than austere fanatics predominate, the

> teachers of each little sect, finding themselves almost alone, would be obliged to respect those of almost every other sect, and the concessions which they would mutually find it both convenient and agreeable to make to one another, might in time probably reduce the doctrine of the greater part of them to that pure and rational religion, free from every mixture of absurdity, imposture, or fanaticism, such as wise men have in all ages of the world wished to see established. (*WN* V.i.g.8)

Only where the teachers of each sect *find themselves almost alone* is this moderate and rational religion likely to come about. And when Smith, moving one step closer to reality from his ideal, considers the larger, more fanatical sects that are actually likely to predominate after disestablishment, he retains the notion that they must be "sufficiently numerous, and each of them consequently too *small* to disturb the publick tranquillity" (my emphasis) for their good effects to outweigh their evil ones. Finally, when Smith takes a second step away from his ideal and concedes the political inevitability of establishment, at least for the foreseeable future, he calls for a *presbyterian* clergy: only clerics responsible strictly to a local presbytery, it seems, can provide the nice examples of modesty and kindness that he regards as a cleric's true moral purpose. For various reasons—to keep each

sect constrained by the need to get along with others, to keep all sects politically and militarily powerless, and to keep leaders locally responsible, responsible to people they have to see—the voluntary associations Smith advocates must be *small*.

Second, we see here how the supposed "atomism" of classical liberal doctrine can go with a very rich and deep understanding of how individuals belong in and need community, an understanding that may get overlooked because the conception of community at work is so finely spun as to be
invisible. The connecting thread between any two members is thin enough
to be broken with a shrug; the texture of the threads is so light that it shows
up more as background to a spider here or a fly there than as anything one
might easily see in itself; but the web is still very much there, pervasively
structuring every participant's actions. I belabor the web metaphor because
it illustrates nicely how something thin can be wrongly dismissed as nonex-
istent, and how thinness might, for some purposes—like the spider's—be a
strength. Smith's thin web of communal bonds enables a resolution of the
tension between our individual freedom or independence and our need to
interact with and learn from others. It is not unreasonable to suppose that
resolution at a thicker level is impossible.

PARTICLE COMMUNITIES: PHILOSOPHICAL PROBLEMS

Smith is thus generally suspicious of churches, reluctant to accept them in
their traditional, specifically "Christian" form. I take his discussion as a
model for my own, more secular proposal for fostering community. In the
late-eighteenth century, the church served as a paradigm for a community
bound together explicitly by the pursuit of moral ideals, and that is all Smith
wants from the institution. What is politically acceptable and what is
morally necessary are things he keeps firmly apart, but for that very reason
a notion of moral community supplements, and importantly limits, his notion of political society. He thereby manages to resemble libertarians in his
theory of *justice* but communitarians in his account of the human *good*. I propose to follow him in this. Anything I say about religious communities
should thus be taken as a stand-in for whatever kind of communities might
properly be called "moral": communities that help individuals develop their
sentiments or articulate their highest ends. Religious communities are simply a convenient example of such communities, since for a long time they
have been the only groups even purporting to have such aims—however in-
effectively and corruptly they may have pursued them.

I begin, therefore, with a small observation from my own religious experience. As a nominally "Conservative" Jew, I have attended both traditional and untraditional Jewish services.[18] The various reform movements Judaism has undergone in the past two centuries have been strongly influenced by Enlightenment notions, like Smith's, of religion as a means for fostering moral community. Some reformers explicitly say that the essence of Judaism is the fulfillment of moral duties, and the ritual trappings of the tradition should be understood as something that merely preserves a community within which people can encourage each other to moral action. Religious services, on this view, have a purely communitarian purpose, and it is felt that they ought to reflect, in their structure and content, the freedom, equality, and fraternity of an ideal human community. So Reform, Conservative, and Reconstructionist services often try to loosen the hierarchical bonds with which traditional Judaism supposedly represses individualism and equality by (1) arranging the seats in a circle rather than behind the prayer leader, (2) encouraging the community to say as many sections of the service together, rather than in response to what the leader calls out, and (3) adopting modern texts—poems, political statements, theological reflections—in place of the standard liturgy. Whenever a service has all three of these features, and often when it has any one or two of them, I tend to feel *more* repressed, *less* able to "be myself," than in traditional services.

Why? First of all, in the untraditional service, everyone watches everyone else: the seating arrangement ensures that. In traditional communities, perhaps members of the congregation are *supposed* to monitor each other, but everyone faces in the same direction, which makes such surveillance difficult—and everyone is too busy carrying out his or her own direct obligation to pray[19] to pay much attention to what others are doing. Second, the mode of prayer reinforces this difference in social surveillance. In the untraditional service, one chants together with everyone else—in "solidarity," as it were; in traditional services, varying degrees of cacophony are tolerated or even encouraged. Chanting together leaves little room for individual expression, and to keep up at all, one must be concerned first and foremost with what everyone else is doing. Finally, the adoption of modern texts means that each community has to agree on standards of theological and political "correctness" for the excerpts it will read aloud. Generally, the modern bits praise the state of Israel, reinterpret, deny, or submerge traditional doctrines like the importance of sacrifice or the resurrection of the dead, and exhort people to work for left-of-center political causes. Idiosyncratic interpretations of these goals, let alone utter disagreement with them, have no room for expression: the texts chosen are literal and clear, so that no one will miss the "message." The traditional texts, by contrast, precisely because they are so very out of date—and are, besides, mostly vague, allusive, and metaphorical—demand constant interpretation and reinterpretation. So the imposition of a set text goes with a freedom for wildly different interpretations of that text, and in *fact* each individual winds up with a unique prayer. In each of three ways, then, the attempt to tailor services to the needs of free, egalitarian individuals has wound up stifling individual expression instead.

We can learn from this in structuring secular associations. Community is possible where people are doing quite different things, even where they do not directly pay attention to one another and where they do not share texts, or specific aims, or sentiments—although they probably need some overlap in each of these areas. This runs against the rhetoric of both patriotism and "multiculturalist" consciousness raising and against the practices advocated by both communism and communitarianism. Rich and warm communities can be built out of individuals who are mostly wrapped up in their own particular activities, while communes of love and work, tighter divorce laws, artificial protection of languages, and celebrations of communal achievements often fail to so much as bind people together, let alone bind them in a way allowing individuals freely to express their differences. In short: communitarianism does not have to be achieved directly.

I want in fact to urge a stronger thesis: that communitarianism *cannot* be achieved directly. Communities fall apart where individuals share only those goals, projects, or attitudes, with each other that they share with every human being, but communities also flourish only where the possibility of such falling apart is allowed for; *free* bonding across individuals requires such a possibility. This becomes clearer if we stress the last element of the contrast I drew between traditional and untraditional Jewish religious services, although it is an element where the analogy between religious and political community begins to break down. Traditional Jewish communities take a set text as given, imposed from on high, but differ widely, from individual to individual, in how to interpret that text, while less traditional communities allow their members a say in choosing the text of their prayers, but look for one in which the meaning is reasonably obvious, and expect all to conform in expressing that meaning once the text has been selected. In this way, the traditional communities tend to preserve individual freedom of thought while the untraditional ones tend insidiously to submerge it— because the former *have a goal beyond community itself.* Because traditional Jews feel that their prayer together is supposed to serve "the will of God," however they interpret that phrase, they can individually differ and correct one another in the name of that higher goal. This diversified, individualistic community is not, of course, always achieved, but at least a rich language for it exists. One is perfectly in line with the purpose of a traditional community to insist on differing from what everyone else is doing, or even to say that everyone else is doing something wrong. In an untraditional community, where the experience of community itself is the purpose of coming together at all, this type of dissent literally makes no sense. If most of the people want to do something a certain way, let alone if everyone wants that, then that simply *is* the way to achieve the group's purpose. But not only does the possibility of individual dissent keep the goods of community compatible with liberalism; by an important and often overlooked irony, only such room for the individual to make his or her own place allows true *community itself* to occur. Only communities where the individual can dissent from communal practices in the name of a higher good can be truly willed by their members, kept in existence by active individual commitments. A community kept in existence by the need for community itself, by contrast, must require a conformity that eventually erodes its members' sense that they have individually chosen to be part of it. As Daniel A. Bell has argued with regard to Singapore, "communitarianism" imposed by authoritarian leaders destroys community itself.[20] I think the imposition of community even by individuals on themselves will destroy community. Willed community exists where the community aims at something outside of itself, where community is a by-product of the joint pursuit of other ends, not where joint pursuit is itself the end individuals are trying, jointly, to pursue. A shared end *other* than community holds together the insignificant communities in which individuals remain free.

This is not simply a brute irony: in a community that exists for the sake of community only constant monitoring and pressure on those who fail to "stay in line" constitute the group as a united entity at all. Where a community exists by dint of discrete individuals sharing some specific aim, on the other hand, the shared interest in that aim can define the community, and this need not be (although it often is) supplemented by direct pressure to conform. Such a community can therefore open itself to dissent and idiosyncrasy.

We might here want to recall Jon Elster's famous notion of "states that are essentially by-products."[21] In Elster's own examples, I cannot will myself to behave un-self-consciously or to fall asleep by becoming indifferent to my own insomnia, nor can a group of people achieve self-respect or class consciousness by political action aimed precisely at those ends. Similarly, I would say, we cannot achieve the goods of community by aiming directly at them.[22] No state-imposed policies can make people like one another or learn from one another, nor will even private, voluntary efforts to promote family life or neighborliness succeed if the goal of these efforts is simply the good of human contact itself. People get together in emotionally and morally enriching ways when they have some other end for which they need help, whether it be as lofty as moral reinforcement or as lowly as tournaments to bowl in. The state can thus encourage insignificant communities only by encouraging these other ends.

But this raises an enormous philosophical problem for liberalism. Practically all the loftier ends for which people associate are precisely the sorts of things that a liberal state must avoid promoting. Political as opposed to comprehensive liberalism especially teaches this neutrality with regard to citizens' chosen ends, but comprehensive liberals too, although they may in principle believe in promoting some ends over others, are uncomfortable in practice with such promotion when it threatens to give a small elite the power to draw possibly invidious distinctions.[23] But how can one support the activities that promote community without supporting religious believers over the nonreligious, or some religions over others? One might, with Yael Tamir and Will Kymlicka, support cultural as opposed to religious groups, but this too requires taking far too much of a stand on what is truly important to human life. Kymlicka proposes that cultural structures and their languages are the social institutions par excellence in which each of us finds the psychological "security" and role models that allow us agency.[24] However intuitively plausible this may seem, there is plenty of evidence against it, and Kymlicka brings almost no evidence for it. Even if he had done so, surely the decision *about* whether we need cultural ties to make our own decisions is politically too important, too fundamental to people's comprehensive conceptions of the good life, to be left up to social scientific experts and the data they may adduce. Tamir, although she takes care to call for policies that treat all communities alike, writes that "the American Communist party, . . . stamp collectors, [and] many other groups . . . are not entitled to the same rights as national minorities."[25] What proves that stamp collecting is less important to people's true identity than ethnic origin or religious affiliation?[26] Again, Tamir says that "[a]boriginal people should have priority when competing for land with others wishing to build a golf club, but their case would be much weaker if they were competing with members of a persecuted religious group" (41); the rationale for this is supposed to be that cultural and religious affiliations "belong in the category of constitutive choices," while playing golf does not. But it is far from clear what theory of human nature is so well justified philosophically as to guarantee that national origin or religious belief necessarily "constitutes" an individual, while hobbies and political beliefs do not. If liberalism is above all a political doctrine that tries to finesse philosophical questions about the ultimate ends of human life, then the liberal promotion of community, if justifiable at all, requires building institutions and funding activities without favoring the preservation of religious or cultural identity over stamp collecting and golfing.[27]

Indeed, I would like to suggest that liberalism and the promotion of community can be most easily reconciled by directing resources precisely to the more trivial, the less lofty of the reasons why people get together. Funding neighborhood barbecues—or "midnight basketball"—raises fewer troublesome issues than giving tax exemptions to churches does. From a political perspective, the point of a church, says Adam Smith, is to provide, for each person in a large urban environment, that "his conduct may be attended to, and he may [therefore] be obliged to attend to it himself."[28] But then the specifically religious function of churches falls away as irrelevant or worse. If a liberal state's interest in associations is only to ensure that everyone has some society "attend[ing] to his conduct" and therefore obliging him to attend to it himself, then insignificant communities, communities arising as a by-product of barbecues or basketball, are rather more appropriate places to put money than the portentous, often oppressive organizations claiming to be agents of God's will.

. . . . .

Suppose we distinguish now between low- and high-level ends. Low-level ends are ends that enable us to pursue other ends—ends incorporated into the higher-level ends we set as our explicit, and important, purposes. This distinction can be taken either in a relative or in an absolute way, and I intend to exploit both meanings. Relative to any given higher end, there are lower ends that must be met: one might be politically active for the romantic opportunities campaigns afford or might date in order to make political connections, and what makes the difference is precisely which end one regards as lower and which as higher. Ends are always interlocked with one another, and always hierarchical, but the hierarchies differ significantly from one person to another. If the English eat to live while the French live to eat, we can quite readily say that a comprehensive conception of the good life (high-level end) for the latter is a mere "primary good" (low-level end) for the former.

In the absolute sense, however, there are ends that all of us have to have in order to survive, to keep going from day to day. Because they are needed to pursue any other end, these absolutely low-level ends tend to be widely shared and thus uncontroversial. Yet because goods of many different kinds can meet our lower-level ends, and because ends are networked and hierarchical—because higher-level ends can be used to interpret lower-level ends, and therefore to select among the variety of specific goods that satisfy them—even our absolutely low-level needs are not "universal" in any simple sense. What kind of architectural structure people require will vary with climate as well as with cultural, historical, and socio-economic setting, as will the kind of food they eat, mating rituals they pursue, intellectual skills they use, entertainment they enjoy. But these things are, to some extent anyway, ends that all people need to partake of whatever other ends they set themselves. High-level purposes, by contrast, are those we normally take as making a significant contribution to whatever we take our lives to be about *beyond* mere survival, and here difference can, and usually does, widely erupt.

Now, where a group defines itself by some high-level purpose, a great deal of flexibility can and usually does open up among its members' low-level purposes. Here, precisely which purposes count as low level is largely a relative matter. A group for whom the propagation of Christian faith is primary can afford to pay little attention to what, precisely, its members choose to eat; a group committed to gourmet dining as its main purpose cannot allow itself that kind of toleration. The traditional Jewish services I mentioned earlier can afford cacophony; a choral society, obviously, cannot.

But another way flexibility in low-level purposes can be introduced is if the group has *no* central purpose, or if attendance at it is a low-level purpose for practically all its members. A public square, even one regularly filled by people talking or demonstrating or performing song-and-dance routines, can reasonably be said to have no high-level purpose. When it was designed, its purpose may have been to serve as a place of political gathering, say, or to provide "breathing space" in some urban planner's conception of how the neighborhood should work. Now that it has been built, even that thin layer of purposiveness may well have been overridden. Instead of political, perhaps artistic events primarily take place here, or drug dealing, or a farmer's market, or simple chatting. Or the "breathing space" has drawn in people from all over the city, even from out of town, and hotels now vie for the buildings around it, making it no longer *that* neighborhood's breathing space.[29] At any rate, low-level purposes of all sorts can be pursued, along with high-level purposes of all sorts, since the square itself prescribes nothing.

As far as its owner is concerned, by contrast, an English pub has a clear high-level purpose: alcohol consumption. But the owner's purpose usually fails to dominate what people actually do there. *If* the people coming to a pub pursue alcoholic consumption with the single-mindedness of the National Rifle Association's opposition to gun control or the Audubon Society's concern for bird habitats, eventually only very hard drinkers show up. Where this is not the case, the owner's high-level purpose is furthered but not necessarily shared by her customers, who often indeed have no high-level interest in coming to the pub at all. They may regard their investments in their family or job, their church or association for the promotion of atheism, their literary pursuits or numismatic interests as of much greater importance. *Precisely for this reason*, they may find a kind of relief in coming to the pub. Stripped of what they regard as their really important concerns, they can talk to people, play a game of pool or backgammon, or have a quiet drink while listening vaguely to the ambient music and chatter, without the pressure of wondering whether or how all this fits into their higher-level ends. Sociability under such circumstances is often the most pleasant kind of sociability, and also a sociability where people are willing to open up, temporarily at least, to hearing about other ways of living, to receiving criticism of their political, or moral, or religious positions, to playing with other ends they might take on, ends they might adopt but have so far resisted adopting, ways of life they might regard as reasonable alternatives to their own. Political and religious arguments often do take place in pubs, probably because people allow themselves there a greater openness to positions than they show in other public settings. It is this kind of community, united by no thick activity and no great end, catering instead to low-level purposes like casual drinking, that I think a liberal state can and should encourage. How does one encourage community as a place for moral exemplification and conversation without encouraging any of the specific ends around which communities form? By encouraging communities of low-level ends, insignificant and particle communities.

I want therefore to recommend, perhaps as a constitutional matter and certainly as a matter of liberal political philosophy, that states foster communal structures that have either no high-level purpose, like the square, or a purpose that fails to dominate the participants' activities, like the pub. Furthermore, both where it funds these "insignificant communities" and when it helps more traditional groups like church-based schools or charities, it should aim low in its funding; it should seek to promote low-level but not high-level ends. This means, first, that it can invest in group activities built around general biological human needs—eating, exercise, and the like—and second, that if it allows its support to extend to groups perform-ing religious, political, or "moral" activities, it should target its support at the lowest level of the ends those activities achieve. Ideally, one wants to support ends that, because biological, all human beings fairly uncontrover-sially share, but to support them in a context in which higher ends are also being pursued: where the biological needs, rather than being pursued for their own sake and thus possibly constituting a general conception of the good life by themselves, fit low into a hierarchy of other purposes. The state would thereby have some assurance *both* that it is funding communities with ends other than community itself *and* that its funding does not go directly into the communities' highest purposes. It would have imposed on itself a discipline of funding comprehensive conceptions of the good life only as a "double effect," a by-product of its direct actions. Thus it could fund churches and church schools, along with similar secular institutions, while directing its moneys to the food and drinks they serve, the buildings they construct, their community-wide social or athletic services, rather than to their educational programming, much less their proselytizing. This way the direct purpose of the funding will always cut across secular/religious lines, as recent Supreme Court decisions have urged such funding to do.

Particle Communities: An Idealized Example

I would like in this light to describe an imaginary political institution. Sup-pose that in every village or rural community and in every urban neigh-borhood large enough to support a school and a church, the government provided funds for a building, open twenty-four hours and protected where necessary with guards or police, for amusement, learning, and political dis-cussion. For want of a better name, I will call these buildings "Social Houses." A Social House would have rooms, let us say, for bridge and chess games, lounges or a café for talking or sitting quietly, perhaps a pool room, perhaps a library and classrooms, and always a large auditorium that could be used for movies or concerts and would in any case be used for political speeches, assemblies and debates. Anyone acting violently or offensively would be thrown out. What specific activities would be available—what kinds of classes would be taught, what games arranged, what music fea-tured—would be determined, through some sort of democratic procedure, by each neighborhood for its own local Social House. In addition, there would be some ground rules of affiliation that every community would have to follow, above all ensuring that everyone living in the relevant neighbor-hood of a Social House could go to the building at any time and attend any of its events. Individuals would also be allowed to join Social Houses in neighborhoods other than their own if they were willing to pay some nominal fee or to do volunteer work in the relevant neighborhood. And if the neighborhood for a particular Social House so decided, it might open some or all of its events to the general public. The net result of all this is that I could walk out at night on the antisocial streets of New York or drive along the anonymous strip of Route 202 and find a place where there would be things to do and people to talk to, and I could do this regardless of whether my income level, professional activity, type of housing, or religion provided me with any other source of community.

What advantages would such an institution have? Well, first of all, it could offer a source of comfort to lonely people and an outlet for the ordinary unhappiness people experience in families—not so much physical or sexual abuse, which requires more serious measures, but the frustration of husbands and wives who have had a fight or of adolescents who feel neglected or oppressed. Secondly, it would provide an opportunity, outside of formal educational curricula or state or municipal arts programming, for people to study their cultural traditions. Neighborhoods that so chose could have classes or reading groups on African or African American history, on Urdu literature or Sunni law, on native American art or Finnish cuisine. This might defuse some of the animus currently fueling multiculturalism: the availability of opportunities for adults to study and celebrate their culture could drain away some of the need to insist that every non-Western culture be brought into school curricula. Third, Social Houses might create or even discover community where none as yet exists. The area where my wife comes from is a particularly drab and commercialized section of New Jersey where the people who drive in and out of their single family homes have nothing evidently in common with one another. But if there were a local Social House, then perhaps the very planning of its activities would bring out the fact that a large number of them were Poles or Italians, or jazz enthusiasts, or Marxists, or followers of New Age religions. Finally, it seems likely to me that people who often get together simply for low-level pleasures are more likely to become interested in learning together, and that people who already are friends and intellectual companions are more likely to become able to have productive political discussions with one another, to enlighten one another on issues and greet visiting candidates for elective office with thoughtful questions. (Hence the placement of political assembly rooms in each of these Houses.) Aristotle's three types of friendship might be understood as a progressive hierarchy, where the educative friendship builds on the friendships of use and pleasure. And Aristotle is in good part right to say that friendship is more important to a state than justice is, that broad networks of friends are precisely the right locus for moral and political education among adults.

We can round out this picture of what a Social House is by saying a little about what it is not. It is not, first, a library, because it is not a place where one is expected to be quiet, and it is not open just during working hours. It is not a community center either, if only because I am imagining a lot *more* Social Houses than there are community centers, which means that Social Houses would be more accessible to everyone and vary a lot more in what they have to offer. The institution in contemporary American life it probably most resembles is a bar, but in America a significant amount of drinking is expected among those who regularly patronize a bar, so it is hard to imagine them as places that encourage deep and educative friendships. The English pub is closer to what I have in mind, as are the Italian cafés from which one watches the local *passagiata*, the public parks to which families regularly take walks in some parts of Europe and Israel, and the town squares in small Indian villages. This may well mean that Social Houses are not necessary in every country, even every country with liberal political institutions, and indeed the problems that have given force to the communitarian critique of liberalism seem more pronounced in the United States, and perhaps in Canada and Australia, than they are in many other places. At the same time, the increasing ubiquity of multinational corporations, of the television, of cars and cities planned around cars, and of the science and philosophy of science that make local traditions look silly to their adherents mean that the loneliness and monotony of American life is likely to be everyone's problem soon.

Finally, the Social House is neither a school nor a church, although it resembles both to some degree. It is not a school, a YMCA, or a youth center, because those are institutions aimed at the young, and precisely what I am worried about is education and community for adults. We are happy, as liberals, to spend money on institutions for the education of children, but reluctant to build anything similar for adults. Perhaps this is because of a vague combination of the notions that education is always somehow coercive, and that coercion is unproblematic with children but forbidden with adults—both misleading notions, at best, in my opinion[30]—or perhaps we are simply making the empirical mistake of thinking that education is unnecessary after one has the tools to get a job and read the *New York Times*.[31] Adam Smith showed better judgment than we do, including "Institutions for the Instruction of All Ages" as well as "Institutions for the Instruction of Youth" among the public goods that liberal states should take pains to foster.

It is important, in my proposal, that nobody is coerced, in any way, either to go to a specific Social House or to go to any Social House at all. If I do not like the religious or ethnic or political inclinations of the community in which I live, I can always affiliate with a Social House in a different neighborhood or simply stay home. Nor, when going to a Social House, do I have to participate in any particular kind of activity: I can go just to talk, or even to be alone in the company of others. And if I do not like the more structured communal events currently taking place, I have a say in coming up with new ones. This combination of voice and easy exit[32] means that the community fostered by a Social House will be truly a liberal community, a community created out of the choices of individuals. At the same time, the point that communitarians love to stress, that individual choices are always already based in part on identification with certain communities, is given indirect expression in the fact that one's choices about which Social House to join and how to participate in it will normally reflect one's larger ethnic, religious, professional, or other group identity. This is expression enough— a more direct acknowledgment of the social structuring of individual choice would conflict with liberal principles.

Finally, in line with Rawlsian political liberalism, Social Houses respect the priority of the right over the good. They may resemble churches more than anything else, in the array of educational and communal activities they carry out, but unlike churches, they are explicitly designed not to pursue any single conception of the good. A liberal government may provide the space in which communities can form, reflect on themselves, and develop, but it must take care at the same time to leave every individual ample room to exit communities that claim her, to shape the communities she chooses to join, and, if she so desires, to avoid community altogether. I have imagined Social Houses to be open, fluid, and multilayered, both in the kinds of activities they offer and in the structure by which individuals affiliate with them. They offer opportunities for friendship and education by which a person may change her preferences, but they begin *from* people's given preferences rather than from any theoretical position about what human aims and practices ought to be.

Real Examples

What sort of institutions already in existence approximate the ideal of the Social House? Pubs, public libraries, and community centers capture some of its features, while others are reserved to the exclusive religious communities of the mosque, the synagogue, and the church. Much town planning, especially if influenced by the English "garden city" movement, has aimed at the placement of homes in close enough proximity to parks, playgrounds, and schools to bring families into frequent public contact with one another. Clinton's "midnight basketball" was a wonderful indirect attempt to build community; blindness to the importance of community in the United States helped kill off the proposal. I conclude with three tips we might pick up from Britain, the country with the longest and richest tradition of informal sociability—Tocqueville's claims to the contrary notwithstanding.[33]

Institutions for the Athletic Training of People of All Ages. Around the corner from where my wife and I lived in Edinburgh stands the Warrender Swim Centre, an old, elegantly tiled public bath that has been converted into a sort of community fitness center. The building comprises a small exercise room, a nursery where children can be placed for a half hour or so while their parents use the facilities, and a beautiful central pool, along with well-maintained showers and changing rooms.[34] Exercise and swim classes are offered for both children and adults, and for a couple of hours every week the pool is reserved for "fifty-plus" activities. The cost is low in general (around $1.80 per visit), and substantially reduced for students and the unemployed. One tends thus to meet a wide cross-section of one's neighbors in and around the pool, and if one has a fairly low income, one feels that the city respects one's interests as well as those of its better situated citizens, and that one has a real place in a community even if one cannot afford the social venues of the rich. In a total of about three years in New York City, my wife and I looked all over for something like this and found nothing equivalent. Only students or those who can afford several hundred dollars for club membership can swim in New York. Of course the well-grounded suspiciousness New Yorkers have of one another helps explain this difference. But then again, it is due in good measure to the absence of institutions like the Warrender Swim Centre that New Yorkers are so suspicious of one another.

The Garden City Movement. Just at the time when Americans were being carried away by the grandiose visions of Chicago's "City Beautiful" movement—summed up by Daniel Burnham's admonition to "make no small plans"[35]—Ebenezer Howard in England proposed a scheme in which groups of no more than around thirty thousand people, drawn from a variety of social classes, would jointly own tracts of land and develop them into a mix of town and country, with their own schools, cultural facilities, and places of work (rented out to external private industries and divided off from the residential sector) all within a short daily walk. Should the town need to grow, it would establish another town "beyond its own zone of 'country,' so that the new town may have a zone of country of its own."[36] Thus a cluster of town-country combinations, each virtually self-sufficient as a civic entity—"towns of moderate size, complete communities in which people both live and work, on a background of green country"[37]—might eventually come to replace the congestion and anonymity of the large modern commercial center. Dismissed as too utopian even by members of the Fabian society,[38] the scheme bore fruit in the creation of two English towns in Howard's lifetime (Letchworth and Welwyn), and at least twenty-five more after his death; in Radburn, New Jersey, and in the three greenbelt cities created by the New Deal across the ocean; and to some extent in urban planning models used all over the world. Radburn added to Howard's original ideas

> a consideration of the automobile and a more conscious use of design as a sociological tool to enhance social contact. For their purposes, they invented the "superblock." Bounded by traffic streets, a superblock contained thirty to fifty acres. Small clusters of housing lined its perimeter, while much of the interior was utilized for landscaped park. A person could walk through Radburn by way of interior parks and a system of underpasses without crossing a single street.[39]

Today Radburn has a waiting list for homes and is still beautiful; one can still walk through it by way of interior parks alone; and it still fosters an active civic life. Letchworth and Welwyn maintain their green belts, their mix of classes, most of their original housing (plus new, ugly, but still small-scale 1960s constructions), and their distinction between an industrial and a residential sector. This is a far better success rate than other modes of urban planning, both public and private, have had. The Cities Beautiful are now blighted and dangerous; the massive public housing projects inspired by Corbusier have become slums, and the speculative developments underwritten in recent years by private investors are depressing, unlovely, sometimes oppressive settings for suburban malaise.[40] What we should note about the garden cities, I think, is (*a*) their smallness, and the corresponding low scale of their housing, (*b*) the way they provide space for "work, life, and play" together, and (*c*) the way their aesthetic and safety features give people reasons to join them independently of any direct desire for sociability.[41] When Howard's concerns for scale are ignored or his greentowns reduced to bedroom communities for a larger urban workplace, what results is nothing more interesting than America's typical sprawling suburbs—as anonymous an environment as any congested urban one. When communes have tried to draw people in by social ideals alone, on the other hand, without the aesthetic and safety features, let alone the tolerance for capitalist enterprise, that allow people to come to a garden city for selfish reasons, they have tended to disband angrily in less than a generation. So Howard's utopianism, when taken as the rich whole it is, provides a better model than anyone ever expected for the "Peaceful Path to Real Reform" that the subtitle of his 1898 book promised. It is hard to imagine what would offend against liberal political principles about a government's widely disseminating information about such communities, or offering tax breaks and even direct subsidies to those who start them.[42] Putnam stresses "the power of zoning regulations to influence where and how [social] networks are formed."[43] I am proposing only a slightly more activist urban policy than that.

Friendly Societies. The early days of the Industrial Revolution in Britain saw the widespread growth of so-called Friendly Societies. By 1801 there are said to have been 7,000 such clubs, with over 600,000 members; by the mid-nineteenth century, it is estimated, almost half the male population of England and Wales belonged to a friendly society.[44] The main, "official" purpose of these societies was to provide, out of a pool of funds, some sort of health and life insurance,[45] along with provisions to cover funeral expenses "in an age where the poor dreaded a pauper funeral, whether for themselves or their children."[46] But they also met, minimally once a month and usually at a public house, to discuss business and collect funds over a convivial meal. In addition, they had a regular annual or biannual feast, sponsored meals after every funeral, and held occasional processions, fairs, and sports meetings.

Both historians of the working classes and politicians at the time when friendly societies reached their heyday have tried to play down the convivial side of these groups. Historians of the working classes tend to have socialist sympathies, and see Friendly Societies as but inadequate expressions of the needs that later expressed themselves in the formation of trade unions.[47] And if the struggle against masters of all sorts is the main point of working-class solidarity, Friendly Societies did lack the large-scale impact, or interest in striking, that has made unions a force to be reckoned with.[48] That they were far better than unions in instilling "civic virtue" has not, to my knowledge, received any attention.

Government officials had an almost opposite reason for stressing the "self-help" over the associational benefits of the Friendly Societies. Indeed,

England's Combination Laws of 1799–1800, which forbade trade union activity, specifically exempted Friendly Societies from their strictures.[49] The reasons for such favorable treatment are obvious: both Tories and Liberals saw much to gain from workers taking care of their own insurance rather than requiring public aid. At the same time, they saw nothing of value in the state's contributing, even indirectly, to workers' amusements. Thus Friendly Societies received legal protection, of various kinds, for their work as insurance agencies,[50] while being constantly discouraged from pursuing their social activities. Such practices as the use of club funds to purchase liquor were "strongly condemned by the actuaries, the clergy, the government and all those who gave advice, as it were, from above," and government figures did their best to root out all hidden ways by which such expenditures might be concealed.[51] In addition, after the societies were enabled and encouraged to register with the government in 1851, those who did so were required by law to distinguish between "necessary" and "unnecessary" expenses, to include all "[p]ayments for anniversaries, processions, bands [and] regalia" in the "unnecessary" category, and to cease using club funds for such payments.[52]

So legal doctrine, informed by the paradigm of liberal political philosophy, mandated that the associational benefits of the Friendly Societies be treated as unimportant, detracting from their "true aim." Yet it was precisely for these benefits, apparently, that most of the members joined:

> The idea of paying a regular premium for insurance against sickness and funeral expenses simply did not appeal strongly enough to working men of the late eighteenth or nineteenth centuries for it to be possible to run the societies as purely insurance businesses. . . . [Monthly meetings and an annual feast] appear to have been the least that a member demanded of his friendly society.[53]

For the legal privileges gained by registration, wrote one club secretary to Sir George Young in 1874, the members would not give up their feast and monthly beer: "They don't see no good in a club without it, they say."[54] There in fact existed large organizations offering the economic benefits of the Friendly Societies without their social activities, but these attracted far fewer members than their convivial rivals—60,000 people, in 1874, as opposed to 2.25 million in the Friendly Societies.[55] Clearly, those actually joining the societies sought companionship in the face of an increasingly isolated world first and foremost, insurance for themselves and their families only secondarily. Were these expressed preferences so irrational?

Moreover, the strictly social benefits of these societies went beyond friendly talk and conviviality. An initiation ritual and set of secret symbols guaranteed that a member of the Oddfellows, the largest of the Friendly Societies, "travelling far from his home district might gain admission to a strange lodge."[56] Trust, therefore, and the correlative possibilities for protection were generated by a sort of artificial equivalent of the customs that enable members of small ethnic and religious groups to identify one another. Other functions of religious communities were taken over: the societies provided some programs of adult education, in the form of scientific and literary lectures, as well as a newsletter sent out to all members. The societies also made strenuous efforts to encourage each other in certain virtues. From the beginning they had codes imposing fines for "being drunk on the Sabbath, striking another, 'calling one another bye-names,' coming into the clubroom in liquor, taking God's name in vain," or more generally for offenses against "Intemperance, Animosity, and Profaneness."[57] Finally, they were generally structured such as to provide practically an ideal example of a small, local group governed by the equal participation of all.[58] Cutting across religious lines and professional occupations, these societies are perhaps the closest the West has come to a widespread secular church. But that "church" was as successful as it was because it centered around the humblest of companionable activities, while it received government aid because it served social purposes quite apart from companionship. As we have seen, far from recognizing community building as itself a worthy end, successive governments did what they could to squelch that aspect of the societies' activities. A modern liberalism, informed by the core of truth in communitarianism, should want to do everything it can to revive friendly societies with their convivial meetings intact.

· · · · ·

One possible way of doing this would be to encourage what Putnam calls "tertiary associations" to transform themselves into secondary ones by removing tax exemptions from movements that rely primarily on direct mailing and giving them instead to groups, whether or not they are politically, religiously, or charitably inclined, holding small local gatherings with food, speakers, and the like. Thus a neighborhood association that holds regular barbecues would receive tax breaks while Planned Parenthood and the Sierra Club would not. Planned Parenthood and the Sierra Club would then have an incentive to raise money by means of local gatherings rather than mass mailings. And the interest liberals have in voluntary associations, I have been arguing, is directed much more to ensuring that these associations have a local, small-scale structure than to the ends they happen to pursue.

It follows that the debates over how a liberal government can promote the goods of association without establishing religion are as misguided as they are endless. Churches should be understood as but one example of a moral community. Then we will see that liberal governments can support moral communities without paying any attention to their ultimate purposes. There is no intrinsic conflict between supporting community and refraining from telling people how, overall, they ought to live. A liberalism that aids insignificant communities, that supports community via the low-level activities that bring people casually together, can achieve the associational bonds it needs without so much as appearing to promote one set of ultimate human ends over another.[59]

NOTES

1. Guy-Jean Target, in Simon Schama, *Citizens* (New York: Knopf, 1989), p. 291.
2. Adam Smith, *The Theory of Moral Sentiments* (1759; reprint, Indianapolis: Liberty Classics, 1982) II.ii.3.10. "The moral primacy of individuals for which Smith argues here is a basic feature of his moral philosophy, which is often reflected in his language." Knud Haakonssen, *The Science of a Legislator* (Cambridge: Cambridge University Press, 1981), pp. 88–89.
3. Two other, roughly liberal arguments do rather more poorly:

1. Community, social bonding of some sort, is a "higher end" of all human beings. Like Millian higher pleasures, however, one does not necessarily know one desires community until one tries it first. So governments should provide us with ample opportunities to sample community, even perhaps impose it on us in our early years, until we realize that we like it for ourselves. Sanctions making divorce difficult are one way of going about this; making group activities, jointly graded, a large part of the public school curriculum might be another. Thoroughly paternalist in approach, not only are the assumptions of this position questionable but its mode of argument can easily be, and has often been, used to defend a multitude of other oppressions in the name of "our own good." Unfortunately, traces of it can be found in the utterances of many recent communitarians.
2. Social bonds, a warm sense of community, civic virtue, etc., are "public goods." Each person benefits if other people have them, but either does not benefit from them herself at all, or benefits so little that competing interests she has will always override this one. If, as seems likely, strong social bonds diminish crime, increase voter participation, and allow businesses to rely more on trust than on the enforcement of contracts, then each of us has an interest in there being a lot of strong social bonds around. But if these goods are all that the bonding achieves, we cannot individually do enough to bring about that bonding to

make it worthwhile for us to put our own money into our local church, community center, etc. So the government can here do what it does elsewhere to encourage environmental conservation and the like: spend our money for us on such institutions, or establish a series of incentives making it more worthwhile for each of us to do so ourselves.

Aside from the oddity of an argument designed to show the value of institutions that take us "out of ourselves" being based on the crudest of appeals to already established individual preferences, this approach has an even more offensive paternalism about it than the last one. Social bonds, of the kind provided by churches and cultures at least, remain strong only as long as those who participate in them think they are serving some higher purpose. People do not commit themselves to a religion to bond with one another; they bond with one another because they are committed to the same religion. If the value of the religion is actually only that it creates social bonds, the bonding is bought at the price of delusion. So this argument, unlike other public good arguments, justifies encouraging an activity that truly benefits *only* those who do not participate in it. We intellectuals can be individualists while the hoi polloi keeps itself out of trouble by bonding communally to pursue illusory goods. A liberal whose concern goes out to every person in his or her society should find this disturbing. The public goods offered by communal institutions can be justified in liberal terms only if those institutions can be shown to benefit, without delusion, the individuals who actually participate in them.

4. On the first issue, see Michael Sandel, "Justice and the Good" in his collection *Liberalism and Its Critics* pp. 171–75 (New York, 1984). On the second, see Amélie Rorty's account of how emotions outlast their fit with the situations that originally evoke them (*Explaining Emotions* [Berkeley: University of California Press, 1980], p. 180); and my *Integrity and Moral Relativism* (Leiden: E.J. Brill, 1992) chap. 3, and *The Ethics of Culture* (Ithaca: Cornell University Press, 1994) chap. 4.

5. Sandel, "Justice and the Good," p. 174.

6. Am I then living in false consciousness? Perhaps not: perhaps I have just chosen to *reject* my particular history or social enmeshment—given some histories, an eminently reasonable choice! Or perhaps I *am* living in "false consciousness," but so what? I may not care if I am, or see it, with Sartre, as inevitable whatever I do.

7. Maimonides, *Mishneh Torah* (vol. 1 [Book of Knowledge], "Hilchot De'ot," 6.1), trans. Simon Glazer (New York: Maimonides Publishing Company, 1927), pp. 217–18.

8. Charles Cooley, quoted in Michael Olmsted, *The Small Group* (New York: Random House, 1959), pp. 17–18.

9. Other evidence of the confusion that concerns me can be found among some of the contemporary neo-Tocquevillians, who too often assimilate large political or religious movements to the small-scale, face-to-face societies that promote companionship, trust, and moral education (see also below, note 33, on Tocqueville himself). Fukuyama at one point lumps together fundamentalist churches with the Marine Corps (*Trust* [New York: Free Press, 1995], p. 289; Robert Solow notes the foolishness of this comparison in his review, in the *New Republic*, September 11, 1995, p. 39); a columnist criticizing Bill Bradley's concern for civil society cites the high church attendance in the United States as proof that our civil society is in fine shape (Matthew Cooper in the same issue of the *New Republic*, p. 14). Since

Fukuyama's concern is what makes people *loyal* to groups, regardless of whether the loyalty is instilled by manipulative means or not, it is perhaps not surprising that he thinks it is praise for a church to be compared with a Marine troop, or that he manages to call the Mormons "highly individualistic" merely because the doctrines of the group differ significantly from those of other Christian sects (pp. 292–93). In any case, he entirely misses the distinction between forced and willed human bonds. The columnist, similarly, obliterates any distinctions there might be among church groups. Attending one's neighborhood storefront church is one thing; showing up at the Riverbend Baptist Church in Austin is quite another:

> "The No. 1 rule of church growth is that a church will never get bigger than its parking lot," says the Rev. Gerald Mann, pastor of the 3,000 member Riverbend Baptist Church in Austin, Texas. On Sundays, therefore, Mann employs a squad of off-duty police officers to direct traffic around the church's 51-acre complex. (*Newsweek* December 17, 1990 p. 52. I am indebted to Stanley Hauerwas for this reference)

Here "church attendance" has precious few social advantages over walking through Times Square. Even worse, of course, are the memberships that I and so many others have in Amnesty International, the Democratic Party, and the like. We pay our dues and get on with our isolated lives. Voluntary associations, in the morally and socially positive sense, these most certainly are not. Robert Putnam has introduced a useful distinction between secondary and "tertiary" associations, claiming rightly that "From the point of view of social connectedness, the Environmental Defense Fund and a bowling league are just not in the same category" ("Bowling Alone: America's Declining Social Capital," *Journal of Democracy* 6 no. 1 (1995): 70 [on-line edition, p. 4])

10. Even without a league, there are other bowlers to impress and be impressed by, let alone the unremarkable other players, ticket sellers, managers, etc., whom one can so easily annoy or amuse by bumping into them, fumbling for cash, dressing badly, smelling badly, making strange noises, etc., etc. So even those who bowl alone are likely to have incentive and example enough to keep themselves minimally socialized. What they lack is anyone with whom they might self-consciously share goals, who could try to set them an example, or for whom they might try to set an example of any higher pursuit than keeping physically out of other people's way.

11. Hereafter, citations will be given in text as *TMS*.

12. All quotations from the *Wealth of Nations* come from Adam Smith, *An Inquiry into the Nature and Causes of the Wealth of Nations*, R. H. Campbell, Andrew Skinner, and W. B. Todd (New York: Oxford University Press, 1976). (hereafter *WN*)

13. Stephen Macedo, "Community, Diversity, and Civic Education: Toward a Liberal Political Science of Group Life," *Social Philosophy and Policy*, 13, no. 1 (1996): 242–52. Macedo's paper brings out Smith's relevance to discussions of voluntary associations in wonderfully rich detail. I shall be stressing, however, the severely qualified nature of Smith's praise for churches somewhat more than he does.

14. Smith here distinguishes himself both from Mandeville's identification of virtue with hypocrisy (as Nicholas Phillipson has wonderfully explained in "Politeness, Sociability, and the Science of Man: Adam Smith in Context," manuscript) and from the blind emotional determinism of Hume. The pleasure in praiseworthiness

and displeasure in blameworthiness arise from the presence or absence of a rationally appropriate object—from whether, in truth, we *deserve* praise or not—rather than from a behaviorally programmed response to external stimuli.

15. *WN* V.i.g.12; Compare, with this and the following quotation, *TMS* I.iii.2.1: "The poor man goes out and comes in unheeded, and when in the midst of a crowd is in the same obscurity as if shut up in his own hovel. . . . The man of rank and distinction, on the contrary, is observed by all the world. . . . His actions are the object of public care."

16. Vicious behavior rather than heretical doctrine is the sole reason Smith gives here for excommunication: that this is wildly out of synch with historical fact underlines how much Smith wants to see the sects in a purely ethical, nonreligious light.

17. "The state, . . . by all sorts of dramatic representations and exhibitions, would easily dissipate, in the greater part of [the people], that melancholy and gloomy humour which is almost always the nurse of popular superstition and enthusiasm. Publick diversions have always been the objects of dread and hatred, to all the fanatical promoters of . . . popular frenzies. . . . Dramatick representations besides, frequently exposing their artifices to publick ridicule, and sometimes even to publick execration, [are] upon that account, more than all other diversions, the objects of their peculiar abhorrence" (V.i.g.15). Jerry Mueller makes a great deal of a casual stipulation in this passage that the diversions be "without scandal or indecency": this is perhaps his main prooftext that Smith would have supported restrictions on pornography and the like, as against the contemporary libertarians who claim him as their mentor (*Adam Smith in His Time and Ours* [Princeton: Princeton University Press, 1993], 161, 202–3). Well, Smith indeed was not a libertarian, but the overall tone of this paragraph, as the excerpt I have quoted should make clear, is precisely to *encourage* offending against stuffy moral sensibilities. Nothing in Smith suggests that the flouting of conventional sexual mores would have particularly disturbed him (see V.i.g.10 for a suggestion of the opposite), and the equivalent of pornography in flouting religious mores—"heresy" or "blasphemy"—appeared to him, from the evidence of this paragraph, as something positively good, something to be encouraged. The attempt to enlist Smith in the service of contemporary neoconservativism seems to me hopeless. Smith was a proud exponent of the Enlightenment, admiring no one more than Voltaire: artistic offenses against people's sensibilities like those of Salman Rushdie, Martin Scorsese, and Andres Serrano would surely have delighted rather than outraged him. We should take the stipulation that public diversions be decent and without scandal to be more a reassurance that he does not envisage a full-fledged campaign against conventional morality, a sort of "outer limit" of offense to what the state should underwrite, rather than a constitutive guideline for what some future National Endowment for the Arts ought generally to fund.

18. I use "traditional" instead of "Orthodox" throughout, here, because there are both traditional and untraditional brands of, at least, Conservative Judaism. The main liturgical difference between the former and Orthodox Judaism is that the Orthodox maintain a strict separation of men and women, and allow only men to run the services. I do not think any part of my point here turns on gender issues. I thank Amy Gutmann for showing me the need to comment on this—and I hope that the

possible confusion, brought to my attention by both Jeff Spinner Halev and Arthur Applebaum, between "Orthodoxy" and "ultra-Orthodoxy," will also be allayed by this substitution. ("Orthodoxy" embraces a broad span of communities, including many liberal and worldly wise ones, while "ultra-Orthodoxy" normally characterizes only the tightly knit, atavistic world represented by Hasidic sects.)

19. As opposed to the reformers' *indirect* obligation to pray, in order to carry out the direct obligation to support morally reinforcing communities.

20. Relying in part on Chee Soon Juan, the opposition leader and author of *Dare to Change: An Alternative Vision for Singapore:* see "A Communitarian Critique of Authoritarianism," *Political Theory* 25, no. 1 (February 1997): esp. 11–14, 17–18 and nn. 20, 27, 80.

21. Jon Elster, *Sour Grapes: Studies in the Subversion of Rationality* (Paris: Maison de Science de l'Hommes; and Cambridge: Cambridge University Press, 1983), chap. 2. Elster quotes the psychologist Leslie Farber:

> I can will knowledge, but not wisdom; going to bed, but not sleeping; eating, but not hunger; meekness, but not humility; scrupulosity, but not virtue; self-assertion or bravado, but not courage; . . . commiseration, but not sympathy; congratulations, but not admiration; religion, but not faith; reading, but not understanding. (50)

Roughly, although not exactly: I can will certain *activities*, but not their ends, external trappings but not what is supposed to be thereby entrapped. Similarly, I want to say, I can will the activities or appearances of community but not the bonds of affection and learning that are supposed to come about thereby. What matters then is what kinds of activities make the ends more *likely* to come about, and it may happen that quite indirect ones are better for this purpose than the ones we would think of first.

22. Elster himself criticizes Tocqueville's assessment of America for overlooking this point: *Sour Grapes*, 95–97.

23. The latter, just as much as the former, will run into no end of trouble should they try to distinguish which moral and religious organizations deserve public support on the basis of the specific ends they pursue. Even among self-declared "liberal" organizations, one might be hard put to decide whether it is the social democrats or the libertarians, the First Wave or the Second Wave feminists, who best serve liberal ends. It should therefore not matter to this paper whether we favor a political or a comprehensive construal of liberalism. I am grateful to Alan Ryan for making me think more about this matter—although I am far from confident that what I now say on it is yet adequate.

24. Will Kymlicka, *Liberalism, Community, and Culture* (Oxford: Oxford University Press, 1989), pp. 165–68, 175–78.

25. Yael Tamir, *Liberal Nationalism* (Princeton: Princeton University Press, 1993), pp. 46–47, 54–55, 76.

26. Alan Ryan has suggested to me that the fact that people go to war over the latter, but not the former, will suffice as a proof. I think that fact can be used in precisely the opposite direction—what we kill for may well be the ideals we are *least* certain of—and in any case, the bloodiness of ethnic and religious conflicts gives liberals reason to urge people toward more peaceful forms of self-identification.

27. And Robert Putnam's evidence for the social value of groups devoted to these latter activities lends empirical support to the notion that the secular, political need for community is met by bowling leagues as well as churches.

28. *WN* V.i.g.12. See the section on particle communities, above.

29. Rittenhouse Square in Philadelphia strikes me as a bit like this.

30. On the first, see the distinction between authority and power in my *Ethics of Culture*, chap. 4; on the second, see Samuel Bowles and Herbert Gintis, *Democracy and Capitalism*, (Ithaca: Cornell University Press, 1994), esp. pp. 121–27.

31. The young, I suspect, are actually likely to participate *more* in institutions that are primarily used by adults: as long as thirty and forty year olds prefer bars to programs at the Y, teenagers will also see the bar as a sexier means of entertainment than basketball at the local community center.

32. Kymlicka, *Liberalism, Community, and Culture*, p. 59: "As Rosenblum notes, there are two aspects to the liberal conception of freedom of association. Liberalism 'encourages both access to groups in which one has a "voice" and the possibility of "exit" from them as equally important parts of freedom of association.'" The exit/voice distinction comes originally from Albert Hirschman, *Exit, Voice, and Loyalty* (Cambridge, Cambridge University Press, 1970).

33. Was Tocqueville really such a good observer? The British show the "spirit of individuality," he says, while the Americans display the "spirit of association" (Tocqueville, *Journey to England and Ireland*, trans. G. Lawrence and K. P. Mayer, ed. J. P. Mayer [London: Faber and Faber, 1958], p. 88]. Today such a statement looks extraordinary: if anything, we would expect the reverse. Tocqueville enthusiasts probably assume that things were just different in the mid-nineteenth century. But I am not convinced that they were. It is remarkable that, in Tocqueville's notes on his journeys to England, he could report that "the principle of association [is] not used nearly [as] constantly or adroitly there" as in the United States, while never so much as mentioning the Friendly Societies as a possible counterexample—this at the time, as we shall see below, when Friendly Societies alone embraced *50 percent* of all working British males!

Let us look closely at his famous chapter on associations. In throwing suspicion on his observational powers, I am not talking about his understanding of human psychology or the imaginativeness with which he probes the effects of institutions on individual minds. The advantages of voluntary associations he indeed grasped more sharply than had anyone before or after him: "Feelings and ideas are renewed, the heart enlarged, and the understanding developed only by the reciprocal action of men one upon another" (*Democracy in America*, ed. J. P. Mayer, trans. George Lawrence [Garden City, N.Y.: Doubleday, 1969], p. 515) The question is whether he was right to see these virtues especially well realized in the *American* society he visited. He speaks of Americans forming associations "of a thousand different types" but then goes on to list almost only associations with a grand mission of human improvement: seminaries, churches, groups that distribute books or "send missionaries to the antipodes"; hospitals, prisons, and schools; undertakings to "proclaim a truth or propagate some feeling." (513) Robert Putnam, citing Tocqueville's discussion, gives choral societies and bird-watching clubs as examples of associations that teach "self-discipline and an appreciation for the joys of successful collaboration" (Putnam, *Making Democracy Work* [Princeton: Princeton University Press,

1993], p. 90), but Tocqueville mentions no groups with such low-level ends. And the contrast he goes on to develop between aristocratic and democratic nations shows how large social projects require association in democratic countries but can be run by a single wealthy or powerful person in an aristocracy (514–15); nothing in the argument shows why *small* social groupings might be necessary.

If anything, there is a current in his account that runs in the opposite direction. He says: "As soon as several Americans have conceived a sentiment or an idea that they want to produce before the world, they seek each other out [and] . . . unite. Thenceforth they are no longer isolated individuals, but a *power conspicuous from the distance* . . . ; when it speaks, men listen" (516, my emphasis), and gives the following example:

> The first time that I heard in America that one hundred thousand men had publicly promised never to drink alcoholic liquor, I thought it more of a joke than a serious matter and for the moment did not see why these very abstemious citizens could not content themselves with drinking water by their own firesides.
>
> In the end I came to understand that these hundred thousand Americans, frightened by the progress of drunkenness around them, wanted to support sobriety by their patronage. (516)

But a hundred thousand people is no longer a small group of friends giving each other advice and help. And in the following chapter, on the importance of newspapers to what associations do, Tocqueville says explicitly that "In a democracy an association cannot be powerful unless it is numerous" (518). Indeed, it is precisely for that reason that there is a "necessary connection between associations and newspapers":

> Those composing [a numerous association] must . . . be spread over a wide area, and each of them is anchored to the place in which he lives by the modesty of his fortune and a crowd of small necessary cares. They need some means of talking every day without seeing one another and of acting together without meeting. So hardly any democratic association can carry on without a newspaper. (518)

Here we are in the realm of what Putnam calls "tertiary associations," where "the only act of membership consists in writing a check for dues or *perhaps occasionally reading a newsletter*" ("Bowling Alone," p. 70 [on-line, p. 4], my emphasis), and where social connectedness is hardly the object. One hundred thousand men pledging publicly never to drink alcohol is very far from a network of face-to-face interactions. Earlier in *Democracy in America*, Tocqueville had stressed the advantages of small, local over large, centralized government, praising above all the New England township, but he does not give equal attention to the advantages of small, local over large, centralized organizations. Perhaps we need to understand this in the light of his overriding concerns with political liberty: both strong municipalities and voluntary associations large enough to be "conspicuous from the distance" provide a buffer against the threat of despotism. But the moral concerns of an Aristotle or a Sandel are not thereby addressed. The "reciprocal action of men one upon another" by which "[f]eelings and ideas are renewed, the heart enlarged, and the understanding developed," the networks of face-to-face interaction by which people set examples for one another and give each other advice, are not the large groups that get noticed from a distance. Tocqueville elides the difference between these kinds of groupings a bit too readily for those interested in the way community inspires individuals to moral growth.

What matters about this historical point is that Tocqueville's famous observations may actually be evidence for the opposite of the empirical conclusion usually drawn from them. Rather than simply having "a propensity for civic associations," as Putnam, for one, puts Tocqueville's thesis ("Bowling Alone," p. 65 [on-line, p. 1]), perhaps Americans have always had to struggle *harder* to achieve social connectedness than have other people; perhaps the many churches and especially political associations we consciously form are and always have been an inadequate substitute for the long entrenched structures of intimacy in the villages and small towns of Europe. The tension between individualism and communalism in America is something Tocqueville himself stresses, and he is not always optimistic about our ability to resolve it. Neither the tension, nor his worries about it, however, appear prominently in his contemporary followers. Fukuyama calls us "hyperactive joiners" of such things as "4-H Clubs, the NRA, the League of Women Voters, and so on," without seeming to notice that one can belong to many of these groups without ever having to meet another member (Fukuyama, *Trust*, p. 272; see Robert Solow's criticism of this passage in his *New Republic* review of Fukuyama, September 11, 1995, p. 39). And if Putnam's evidence of a recent decline in social capital really shows that a long-term tendency toward individualism has gotten worse, that the weak dams we erected in the past against the deluge of alienation have now been swept away, then he weakens his point by using Tocqueville to suggest that we once had an easy fondness for association. Complacency about the fundamental health of our social institutions is out of place: we cannot trust that we have *ever* had a "spirit of association" to which we might return.

By contrast, the local, primarily convivial Friendly Societies of Britain, founded above all "to cement more firmly the bonds of social feeling and sympathetic intercourse between man and man," represent the kinds of groups in which Aristotelian friendships may be achieved extremely well. (The quotation, brought by P. Gosden [see below, n. 45], p. 127, is from *Oddfellows' Magazine* 1, (1829): 146, citing Masonic principles as the philosophic basis of their order.) A tradition of "informal sociability and . . . voluntary social institutions providing settings for this sociability" goes back in Britain at least as far back as the mid-seventeenth century:

> Coffee and chocolate houses thrived, their clients (or groups among them) often forming clubs. The same sorts of development also often took place in inns and ale houses. Some of these new institutions were very nebulous, others came to have definite memberships and rules. . . . Some were general in membership, others confined to people with particular interests, literary, scientific or political. In the Scottish masonic lodges many evidently sought, and found, existing institutions which provided a framework for this craving for sociability and ritual. (David Stevenson, *The First Freemasons* [Aberdeen, 1988], p. 10)

34. The beauty of the pool is no distraction from the main issue. Community centers all over the United States founder for lack of attractiveness. A slipshod initial structure—badly lit, carelessly designed, made with cheap and ugly materials—

which then receives inadequate maintenance can draw only those young enough or poor enough to have no other option. If most of those who attend the center are children or are socially marginal, that fact itself keeps others from coming—and ensures that the center's constituency will have too little political pull to keep it publicly funded. So the maintenance level gets worse, the attendance gets worse, and a long day wears on . . . Only an initial investment sufficient to establish an attractive facility and to maintain it properly for at least its first few years can give these structures so much as a chance of achieving their purpose.

35. "[M]ake no small plans, for they do not have the power to stir men's blood": quoted in Stanley Buder, *Visionaries and Planners: The Garden City Movement and the Modern Community* (New York, 1990), p. 157. Sometimes writers wrongly assimilate the two: "Another important question asked about the modern pattern by the British was whether beauty and emotional satisfaction do still deserve a priority among the most basic considerations in urban and country life. There was something arresting in the fact that the thirst for environmental beauty should reach its peak in Britain in the 1890s, just when the garden city was being invented, as it did in America with the City Beautiful movement" (Walter L. Creese, *The Search for Environment: The Garden City, Before and After* [New Haven: Yale University Press, 1966], p. viii). A focus on the movements' shared aesthetic concerns here serves to obscure the City Beautiful movement's complete inattention to problems of scale. Architectural critics like Creese are sometimes blinded, I think, by aesthetic considerations: these are not unimportant (see previous note) but are hardly the only criteria for judging a building or town. Howard, but not Burnham, understood that.

36. Ebenezer Howard, *Garden Cities of Tomorrow*, ed. F. J. Osborn (London: Faber & Faber, 1965), p. 142.

37. Frederick J. Osborn, *Green-Belt Cities* (New York: Schocken, 1969), p. 133.

38. Osborn, preface to Howard, *Garden Cities*, n. 21 and p. 11 and note.

39. Buder, *Visionaries and Planners*, 169.

40. See Daniel A. Bell, "Residential Community Associations: Community or Disunity?" *Responsive Community* 5, no. 4 (fall 1995); and "Civil Society versus Civic Virtue," chap. 9 in this volume.

41. Clarence Stein reports that in the first twenty years of Radburn's existence and the first ten of the Greenbelt cities, the four had a total of three deaths and two injuries from traffic accidents (*Towards New Towns for America* [Cambridge: Cambridge University Press, 1966], pp. 51–52). From Stein's figures, which are a bit confusing, this seems to be about half the death rate and 2 to 3 percent of the injury rate in towns of similar size across the country.

42. For information about the Garden City movement, in addition to the sources already cited, see Dugald MacFadyen, *Sir Ebenezer Howard and the Town Planning Movement* (Manchester, 1970); and Carol A. Christensen, *The American Garden City and the New Towns Movement* (Ann Arbor: University of Michigan Press, 1986). Buder and Christensen present some of the problems the movement has faced.

43. Putnam, "Bowling Alone," p. 29.

44. Barry Supple, "Working-Class Self-Help and the State," in Neil McKendrick, ed., *Historical Perspectives: Studies in English Thought and Society* (London, 1974), p. 215.

45. They sometimes maintained their own doctors, rather like a health maintenance organization: P. H. J. H. Gosden, *The Friendly Societies in England, 1815–1875* (Manchester: English University Press, 1961), pp. 140–41.

46. Supple, "Working-Class Self-Help," p. 217.

47. See, for example, E. P. Thompson's *The Making of the English Working Class* (Harmondsworth: Penguin, 1968); or Robert Leeson's *Travelling Brothers: The Six Centuries from Craft Fellowship to Trade Unionism* (London: George Allen and Unwin, 1979). Peter Mathias explicitly calls them "incipient trade unions": Mathias, *The First Industrial Nation*, 2d ed. (London: Methuen, 1983), pp. 187 and 188.

48. Engels apparently complained to Marx in the 1850s that the "widespread adoption of bourgeois values" represented by the friendly societies threatened the development of any real proletarian solidarity: Mathias, *First Industrial Nation*, 191.

49. Of course this exemption simply made Friendly Societies in fact become, in many cases, a cover for trade union activity: see Thompson, *Making of the Working Class*, pp. 166, 181, 500, 505, 651; or Leeson, *Travelling Brothers*, p. 113

50. The right to incorporate, with all its attendant advantages; exemption from stamp duties and favorable interest rates on their funds; at one early point (1757), even a regulation mandating that employers help fund such societies (Gosden, *Friendly Societies*, pp. 5–6, 173–74).

51. Gosden, *Friendly Societies*, pp. 117–18. This, despite the fact that the societies disapproved of intemperance in general, took measures to discourage it in their members, and therefore could have been regarded as *channeling* the desire for relaxation by means of alcohol into limited, socially harmless circumstances.

52. The standard letter sent out by the registrar in response to inquiries about the proper use of club funds ran as follows (Gosden, *Friendly Societies*, p. 123): "Sir,— In answer to yours of . . . , I beg to acquaint you that no portion of the funds of a friendly society can lawfully be applied otherwise than in payment of the benefits granted by the rules and of the NECESSARY EXPENSES of management.

Each Society must determine for itself what, under its rules, are necessary expenses.

Payments for anniversaries, processions, bands, regalia are clearly unnecessary, and therefore unlawful.

The Registrar will decline to certify any rule purporting to authorise such payments."

53. Gosden, *Friendly Societies*, p. 115.

54. Ibid., p. 122.

55. Supple, "Working-Class Self-Help," pp. 216–17.

56. Gosden, *Friendly Societies*, p. 128.

57. Thompson, *Making of the Working Class*, pp. 418–19. See also the whole discussion from 418–424, placing the societies centrally in the "growth in self-respect and political consciousness" (424) that marks the difference between the nineteenth-century working class and the eighteenth-century mob: "[A]nyone familiar with procedure and etiquette in some working men's clubs today will recognise the origin or still extant practices in several of the [Friendly Societies'] rules. Taken together, they indicate an attainment of self-discipline and a diffusion of experience of a truly impressive order" (420).

58. "The more conventional 'local societies,' many of them very small, were characterized by complete independence and self-government" (Supple, "Working-Class Self-Help," pp. 216). See also Thompson, *Making of the Working Class*, p. 421.

59. I want to thank Alan Ryan, Gary Jacobsohn, Mark Reinhardt, and Jeff Weintraub for their extensive comments on drafts of this paper, and the participants in Princeton's Program in Ethics and Public Affairs for a conversation about it I enjoyed and learned from tremendously. I am entirely responsible, of course, for all remaining errors in judgment and fact.

Chapter Eleven

THE CITY AS A SITE FOR FREE ASSOCIATION

Alan Ryan

THIS IS AN ESSAY in a somewhat unorthodox form of political theory. It speculates about the relationship between political and moral allegiances and the built environment, a topic that has not been prominent among the philosophical and historical interests of American and British political theory over the past fifty years. It is, however, a topic with a respectable pedigree. I begin with the thought that political theory is what John Dewey claimed it was, an inquiry into the problems of "associated living." I begin, too, where Dewey did: with the thought that in the modern world there are opportunities for freedom that earlier ages lacked; that we have in principle a wider choice of associates and a wider choice of associations, a wider range of goals that we may pursue in association with others. One of the modern world's major problems, however, is that the freedom available in principle may be undermined by our practice; in particular, the exercise of one freedom may frustrate the exercise of another. So, liberating the individual from many forms of social control may subvert the institutions that allow individuals in association to achieve their goals, both individual and collective, and the unintended and unforeseen consequences of uncoordinated attempts by individuals to improve their conditions individually often destroy exactly what they are trying to achieve.

Instances abound: a college faculty not compelled to attend faculty meetings will find it impossible to control their teaching and working conditions as they would like; teenagers emancipated from the unofficial social sanctions wielded by their neighbors and relatives may not only destroy the peace of a neighborhood, but may make it virtually uninhabitable for themselves; motorists wanting to spend a quiet day at the beach are more likely to spend much of their day parked on the Long Island Expressway. In all these cases, there are real gains for freedom at one level and losses at another. Assessing the extent to which a particular society has achieved as great a degree of freedom for its members as possible, we must balance not only the "quantity" of different particular freedoms we can exercise, but make some obviously contestable overall judgment of their value to us.

The political theorist is likely to think that there exists a conflict between two different conceptions of freedom on which much else hangs; the first is what is sometimes called "freedom of self-government," the second, "freedom as laissez-faire." If a community is to have the first kind of freedom, that is collective control over its own existence, it may need to restrict the second, that is, the freedom of individuals to do as they choose; conversely, if people wish only to be allowed to pursue their private avocations without interference by the law or the informal pressures of their neighbors, they may have to forego the kind of collective control over their lives that the enthusiasts for republican liberty desire. Faculty who wish to be free from demands for attendance at innumerable committee meetings will find they are governed by hierarchical and bureaucratic arrangements that they very much dislike. Faculty who try to govern themselves in even a semidemocratic fashion will find that they have less free time than they would like. There is no room for evasion here; more freedom of one sort is more than likely to lead to less freedom of another. I do not mean that they are always in competition or that there are no occasions when more of one will bring with it more of the other—when a former police state removes travel restrictions on its citizens, they may go where they choose, and one of the things they may well choose to do is attend meetings that enable them to organize politically and achieve self-government; conversely, one thing that a self-governing group may well choose to do is to relax restrictions on its members' activities. I observe only that the two sorts of freedom come into conflict sufficiently often to lend some color to the claim that their opposition is *the* central dilemma of the modern search for freedom.[1]

Not only do I want to bring questions of town planning, zoning, public transportation, and the like into the purview of the liberal theory of self-government; I also want to stretch the concept of free association somewhat, and to leave the well-explored terrain of First Amendment constitutional debate for the terrain of urban culture. Here I discuss free association both instrumentally as a political phenomenon, properly treated by citizens as a device for securing responsive and intelligent government, and noninstrumentally as one of the cultural benefits of urban living. Arguments from authority possess no intellectual authority: so it is only by coincidence that Aristotle's treatment of political association has the same structure as my own.

．　．　．　．　．

Every political theorist who takes an interest in classical political thinking starts with the thought that the city is the first home of politics, and thus the place where citizens can conduct their common affairs as free men. In the festivals and drama of the Athenians of the democratic era, the city—their city above all, of course—was presented as a place where *politics* was practiced and the patriarchal, vengeful, violent actions and reactions of warring families and their dependents had been brought under the rule of law. In the last pages of *Eumenides*, Athena comes to live in the city and tells the subjects of Theseus, the future Athenians, not only that they will become the "school of Hellas" that Pericles boasted of in his funeral oration, but that they will henceforth live under the rule of law. Athena brought them justice and reason, and these were the preconditions of freedom.

John Dewey admired classical Athens because, he thought, the Athenians had been the first people to *think* about ethical issues, the first to see that what he termed "the problems of associated living" might be made amenable to intelligent action.[2] Dewey believed that a democratic politics and, more importantly, the habits of discussion and reflection that would characterize a thoroughly democratic society were the quintessential expression of social intelligence. Indeed, Dewey's account of the nature of "sociality" led him to the conclusion that democratic social relations amounted—to the extent that the concept of an essence was admissible within his political philosophy—to the revelation of the essence of social existence. The thought that democracy is society par excellence, if it is true at all, is something that needs a good deal of argument to sustain it, and I shall not try to provide that here. The thought it rests on is that individuals can come to a full appreciation of their own deepest desires and their own full powers only when they are in freely self-revelatory communicative relations with their equals. Since Dewey defined democracy as full communication on the basis of freedom and equality, it was not a great stretch to argue that democracy expressed the inner meaning of social existence as such. The price paid for this argument, however, is that the criteria for the existence of a democratic society are a good deal more complex, not to say vague, than the more narrowly political criteria of universal suffrage, competitive elections, and the like.

But we can begin without begging the question of the validity of that account. We may start from the thought that the city sustained social intelligence because it sustained freedom of association, even when the *politics* (narrowly speaking) that it sustained was not in the modern sense democratic. It can hardly be denied that many of the virtues of urban culture were to be had under oligarchical regimes, though it can obviously be complained that the advantages of those regimes were characteristically confined to very few members of the society. But this was true under the regimes that the classical world regarded as democratic. Hegel's observation that under the Greek, highly politicized conception of freedom only "some were free" catches nicely the thought that classical democracy was far from meeting our conception of a democratic society: a society in which membership of the political community was decisive would exclude women, children, foreigners, slaves, and manual workers from the class of truly free persons. Indeed, taken in the way in which Hegel intended his remark to be taken, it points to two distinct failures. The first is what we have just pointed to, namely, the exclusion of whole classes of person from citizenship and, thus, from the most valuable of Athenian freedoms; the second is a narrowness in the idea of freedom itself rather than in the class of people who have access to it, and that is the restriction of freedom to political freedom.

Hegel's observation fails, in fact, to do complete justice to what Pericles himself said about the Athenians. He said that they were free inasmuch as they did not think it necessary to dragoon one another into behaving in a public-spirited fashion. The idea that the city was a high-spirited place that could rely on its members' loyalty to it and to each other to sustain a common life came closer to boasting that Athens had achieved what we should nowadays want from a free society than Hegel suggested. That is, Pericles does not appear to suggest that political participation is the only aspect of freedom that a rational man would be concerned with. Certainly he says that a person who takes no interest in the public business of Athens is a man with "no business" here, and he excludes women from the benefits of Athenian freedom without suggesting that there is even a question of their having a stake in that freedom, but there is at least some suggestion that what made Athens so free was precisely that people could have many interests besides their interest in the politics of their society, and nobody would make long faces about it.

What made it possible for Pericles to advance this claim was a variety of complicated factors. One was that Athens was unusually prosperous among the city-states of the ancient world. Many of the sources of her prosperity were not admirable; they included the more or less open exploitation of the other states that belonged to the Delian League. How much difference this made to Athenian life is controversial; it must have made some difference to the ability of the Athenians to involve their poorest citizens in public office, since the Athenians uniquely paid those who would have been economically unable to attend the assembly to do so, and paid them to serve on special juries and the various functional equivalents of the modern committee by which Athens governed itself.

The silver mines at Laurium, worked by slaves whose lives were abbreviated by overwork, accident, and lead poisoning, are another source of Athenian wealth that one flinches from. But the good luck of the natural fertility of Attica, the natural energy and quickness of the Athenians, and their readiness to trade all over the Mediterranean must have made more difference than anything. Prosperity made for social confidence, permitted the citizen to raise his head from the toil of securing a living, and allowed the city to create spaces where the citizens might meet. To be sure, prosperity might have made the Athenians lazy, greedy, and fearful of losing what they had acquired. The inhabitants of Corinth were accused of having become so. The recipe for success is not, then, mere "wealth," but "wealth rightly used." Some paradoxical qualities come into the equation. The Athenians did not trust their leaders, even when they admired them and followed them into rash adventures. They took it for granted that men with sufficient time, energy, and money would wish to become political and military leaders, and they understood quite well that such men might betray them, might run away in battle, might waste the city's resources, and might sacrifice the general good to the interests of their family and friends. They did not deny the need for leadership, but they insisted on the need to keep it under control. The ability to harness talent for public purposes is what any political system that proposes to govern itself by appealing to public opinion has to acquire; and the lesson the Athenians taught their successors is that at least in city-states of a certain size, and at least with citizens of sufficiently high morale and political intelligence, it was possible to get the citizenry together to choose generals, cashier financial officers for misconduct, and govern themselves as free persons.

I do not want to dwell on the virtues of the Athenians. Nostalgia is dangerous, and nowhere more so than in politics. I do wish to borrow two ideas from their practice, however. The first is that if people are to be self-governing, they must associate with each other in natural and unforced ways from which their political association can spring. It is clear enough that a country the size of a continent, with a population of almost three hundred million, cannot replicate the immediacy of contact that characterized classical Athens. Aristotle, after all, thought ten thousand citizens was the upper limit of properly political association because he wished everyone to be known to everyone else. When John Dewey expressed the wish that the entire American society should somehow embody the sensibilities of the small-town "face-to-face" community, he was notably silent about how this feat was to be accomplished.[3] It is evident enough that the politics of a large, modern democratic state must be pluralistic and multilayered in a way that no Greek of the Periclean age would have comprehended. It is one of the arguments of what follows that some of the tendencies of modern urban culture are exactly what is needed for the purpose, and others exactly not.

There is a second thought that animates what follows. If questions of city and regional organization have instrumental implications for the politics of free association, this politics, and the social and cultural life associated with it, has expressive implications for the shape of our habitat. The Spartans were proud of the fact that they had no city walls: their "walls" were their army with its motto Every Man a Brick. The absent walls were a visible symbol of the Spartan conviction that every citizen would die before he or she abandoned the post assigned to them. The Acropolis was more than an expression of Athenian power and a site for assorted ritual observances. Or rather, the way in which it was both of those things called attention to Athens's leadership of and membership in the Delian League, and reminded everyone who walked up the sacred way of Athens's relationship to its allies. Conversely, the democratic quality of Athenian politics shone a vivid light on the fact that the agora was the physical hub of decision making; the fact that it sheltered a mixture of everyday commercial activity and political activity was a vivid reminder of the fact that democracy brought decision making into the street and gave a role in it to the man in the street. Similarly, the readiness of Americans to abandon large areas of their cities to dereliction and decay, and to litter much of the landscape between the cities of the northeast with abandoned factories and warehouses testifies to an antiurban sentiment that I think bodes ill for American politics and for American cultural life more generally.

· · · · ·

Leaping two thousand years ahead, I want to begin with a writer who proves my point by negation. This is Edward Bellamy, the author of *Looking Backward*, whose immensely successful utopian fantasy was published in 1888. *Looking Backward* described Boston in the year 2000 as it had become after the triumph of a form of corporate socialism that Bellamy called "nationalism." (Bellamy knew that what he was describing was socialism, but thought that the term "socialism" conjured up images of beards and free love. His readers would be happier with "nationalism"; since the book was second only to *Uncle Tom's Cabin* among American best-sellers in the nineteenth century and sold 200,000 copies in its first two years in print, he cannot be said to have been wrong.) Bellamy's nationalism was not bellicose; it was the view that an ethos of public service and the disciplined corporate organization of late-nineteenth-century capitalism pressed to its limit were the only possible basis for a successful industrial society. Bellamy's vision of a revitalized Boston was of a city that expressed these values. Industrialists and their workers must share the spirit that animates soldiers fighting for a just cause; in a rationally ordered society, managers and generals were one. Bellamy's successors were heard to say that presidents of the republic and presidents of General Motors were the bearers of the same organizational ethos. Bellamy's utopia was to be governed by bureaucratic, scientific, meritocratic rationalism, and the architectural and countrywide planning system lightly sketched in *Looking Backward* reflected those virtues.

The prevailing atmosphere, both in Bellamy's social theory and in his sketch of the new Boston, is an obsession with uniformity, regularity, and hygiene; this is emphasized by the burial of utilities and a kind of "factory in a garden" form of planned landscape that spreads as far as the eye can see. It is the visible embodiment of one sort of justice—the justice expressed in strict economic equality. It is not, however, an expression of either freedom as laissez-faire or freedom as self-government. This is a proposition that Bellamy would have resisted. Bellamy set out to explain how it was that the freedom of the individual to which Americans were so attached had not been at all impaired in his rational utopia. The paradox is that what makes Bellamy's utopia so depressing and so chilling stems from a kind of concern with the freedom of the individual as worker and consumer that entirely overlooks our need to be free in association with others.

Bellamy tried to square the circle by appealing both to American individualism and to the new corporatist enthusiasm: each worker could choose just what occupation to take up so long as it lay within his abilities, but the "income" the worker got was exactly the same as everyone else's. It was essential to his account that although work was compulsory—idlers were to be jailed in utopia—individuals could choose their occupations according to talent and taste. Society's managers would ration training according to talent, but each worker could choose which of the tasks for which she or he was qualified would be his or her occupation. The hours of work that were demanded would be adjusted to bring supply and demand into balance. The plausibility of this in economic terms is not great, of course; Bellamy made the heroic assumption that public demand for goods and services was predictable enough to enable the planners to know in advance how much labor was needed, and that technological change was slow enough to allow them to adjust the supply of labor to the demand for it in a rational way. The point lay elsewhere. What the inhabitants of Bellamy's utopia get is the knowledge that each of them is contributing exactly what he or she should contribute to the functioning of society; that is, each person gets a certain sort of moral tranquillity. But each gets it as a private gift. The relationship between individuals and the smoothly functioning society is in essence one of complete individual subservience to the needs of the whole society, those needs being determined by expert managers, not by the community itself.

Everything in *Looking Backward* was organized in such a way as to emphasize the individual's dependence on public provision. Paradoxically—as witness Bellamy's account of shopping and dining in utopia, and his chilling account of the way piped music is to replace the concert hall—everyday consumption is more privatized than it is under capitalism. One does not need to have adopted Born to Shop as a motto to find Bellamy's description of the new model department store pretty bleak: all the goods stocked by different stores are identical; the clerks may not encourage shoppers to buy anything in particular, and are there only in order to supply additional information about the goods on display and to take orders for them. The idea that the commercial interactions of everyday life have their valuable human aspects as expression of individual tastes and enthusiasms was utterly foreign to Bellamy. It then becomes clear what a passion for free association is: it is the thought that going to a concert is better than listening to excellent music piped into the home because people's common experience of hearing music together, the interaction of audience and performers, the interaction of listener and listener as each takes a cue from the responses of the others are all valuable both in themselves and as aids to a full understanding of the music itself. It is the thought that even buying relatively mundane goods can provide a basis for forms of interaction that allow us to develop and display our own individuality—the salespersons may fake much of their enthusiasm for their products, but probably not all of it; they may lie about how we look in the clothes we wonder whether to buy, but probably not always; and we can turn what philosophers are all too prone to dismiss as mere "consumption" into a distinctively human enjoyment of what the world offers us. Not to see any of this is to overlook the poetry of everyday life.

· · · · ·

So, armed with a clearer conception of what it is like not to succeed in visualizing what we are after, we may move on to connect urban culture, free association, and the rise and fall of the modern city. Much of what is worth saying is obvious, though perhaps underremembered. If human beings are to form intelligent, self-governing communities, they need places in which such communities can form. Although my own taste is for the great cities of the world, such as London, Paris, and New York, they are not obviously well designed for this purpose. In that sense, Dewey was quite right that the small-town face-to-face community is a more plausible basis for a quick and easy perception of a common good requiring common action. When Tocqueville looked at America in the early 1830s and commented on the American talent for "association," it was the America of little country towns that he had in mind. He was decidedly anxious about what the newly ar-rived immigrants in the rapidly growing early industrial cities might mean for the future of democracy. In fact, the immigrants eventually brought a new vitality to American democracy; it socialized them into new allegiances far more often than not. It was able to do so for a reason that is worth bear-ing in mind, however; the cities became places of innumerable neighbor-hoods, and political parties adapted themselves to that urban phenomenon by adopting the system of ward captains and precinct bosses that enabled them to trade favors for votes in a frequently corrupt but always impressive fashion. If we are to combine democracy and megalopolis, it will have to be by ensuring that megalopolis is a city of many villages as well as a place where a distinctively urban high culture can flourish; the aspiration is not absurd, for we have done it once already.

This is a thought that has been made much of by the late Christopher Lasch. Reflecting on the declining power of the American working class in national politics, Lasch blamed many features of modern social and eco-nomic life, including the cosmopolitanism of the American upper classes and the shallow hedonism fostered by television and the movies. But one crucial cause, he thought, was the decline of the traditional neighborhood. Unlike most American writers, Lasch refused to associate American democ-racy with an ideology of social mobility. Not merely did he notice the ob-vious incoherence of the idea that we can *all* rise in a social scale that is or-dered precisely by the fact that some people are at a higher level than others; he repudiated the ambition itself. What ordinary people need is not to rise, but to receive self-respect. The politics of self-respect are essentially popu-list politics, but not necessarily liberal politics; they are the politics of work-ing-class self-reliance, and for these the two great necessities are steady, useful work, on the one hand, and a territory that working-class political organizations control, on the other. To sustain the latter, the unofficial in-stitutions of city life are needed—the pub, the café, the corner shop.

The reminder of the importance of locality and what one might call lo-calness can be divorced from Lasch's strictures on the cultural attachments of financial and academic elites. What it cannot be divorced from is the importance of what others have described as "ends that are essentially by-products."[4] That is to say, it would be impossible to make a café or a pub attractive to its patrons *in virtue of* its political consequences, however much we wanted those political consequences. Telling people to go to such and such a café in order to promote political cohesion and political activity is like telling people to be happy; there are many things they can do that will make them happy, but aiming directly at being happy is not one of them. Having a pub or café in the middle of shops that people have to use in order to get the food for dinner is an infinitely more plausible route. People who meet in the café are then likely to be drawn into conversation, and to discover that they do (or do not) have shared interests, shared political opinions, or whatever else. Similarly, we may think that the rise of the out-of-town shopping mall is something of a political as well as a planning disaster; in destroying the downtown shopping areas of American cities, they have destroyed the capacity of those cities to control their own affairs—not only by removing the tax base on which the cities depended, but by removing the managerial talent that they needed, and by making the cities and their inhabitants increasingly unimportant to the careers of the politically ambitious. But however forseeable such consequences might be, it is implausible to think that we can somehow prop up commercial and other institutions. There are things we can do, and more rational zoning is certainly one of them, but the piecemeal subsidizing of commercial enterprises is not likely to be one of them. People go to cafés because they want to see one another in that setting; they go to the shops they do because they enjoy the shopping experience. Unless cities serve genuine functions, they will surely continue to crumble. Filling storefronts with local government advice bureaus and welfare agencies—as in what was once the center of Poughkeepsie, say—only draws attention to the fact that the city center has lost its raison d'être.

This raises a familiar question. If people continue to move out to the suburbs, is it anything better than nostalgia on the one hand or snobbery on the other to reproach them for so doing? We have to steer a careful line. On the one hand, it surely is simple snobbery to reproach people with seeking in the suburbs what anyone in their right minds is likely to want for themselves and their children—fresh air, clean surroundings, enough space to live in comfortably, quiet nights to get some sleep in, and so obviously on. To say only that a person would be a boor if he sacrificed proximity to the Metropolitan Opera or the Guggenheim Museum in order to breathe clean air, have undeafened ears, and enjoy sufficient space for everyday life without sacrificing his entire salary for the purpose is to cut oneself off from the possibility of rational argument about the political use of space. But to say that whatever choices people turn out to have made must be accepted just because they have made them is to elevate the accidents of the market-place to a position of moral unchallengeability that they surely do not deserve.

The case I wish to offer is that suburbanization as it has taken place under the impulse of the motorcar and a general hostility to planned land use—a hostility that often has its roots in the fact that planning invariably means that some landowners are deprived of gains they might otherwise have made from selling their land—is not only an aesthetic disaster but a social and therefore a political one. The case is not original with me; indeed, it was well understood a hundred years ago, when the English town planner and urban theorist Ebenezer Howard originated the idea of the "garden city," a new town of modest size that would be built at a distance from major metropolitan centers, but that would be a genuine town, surrounded by open country, and itself sufficiently endowed with green space to be an attractive place in which to live and bring up children. The point of creating new towns was to secure the cohesion that city life can create, without creating too much traffic, pollution, noise, and general inconvenience. The thought was that almost everything would be accessible on foot, that people could walk to work, that there would be dispersed but adequate shopping and social facilities, and that the town would thus be comprehensible, manageable, and within the citizenry's grasp.

It is obviously possible to create such places on a suburban basis. The original Main Line suburbs on the train route west from Philadelphia might be taken as illustrations. When the exigencies of train travel and the absence of private motorcars meant that settlement had to cluster quite tightly around the train station, one got quite naturally a focus to the settlement in terms of the location of shops, entertainment, and eating places. In essence, the old-fashioned suburbs were strung like beads along the railway tracks. Such places lacked one element of the new town scheme, which was putting housing and the workplace in close proximity to one another; this naturally had one political consequence, which was the separation of political organization via work from political organization at the place of residence. This is more important than it might seem, since electoral politics are mostly based on residence rather than on work. A man who lives in a safely Republican suburb may well be a loyal union member and a devout Democrat, but his vote will do no great good where it is cast, and it will be harder to get him to return to the city at weekends and evenings than it would have been had he never left there in the first place.

Thus far, then, nothing has been said to suggest that "small town" virtues are not virtues, and that it is the vast urban agglomerations of the twentieth century that we ought to look to for a home for free association. Indeed, observers of the United States in the nineteenth century were quite sure that it was the free associations of small towns that were the backbone of American democracy. What Tocqueville saw, or thought that he saw, were vigorous little country towns. He may well have exaggerated the impact of the New England township meeting, a form of political organization that was really on its last legs by the 1830s. But the little towns whose local newspapers got up campaigns for civic improvements of one sort and another and whose inhabitants always numbered *somebody* capable of taking the lead in matters of self-government were rarely places with more than a thousand or so inhabitants. The contrast Tocqueville was struck by was between the thriving small towns of the Anglo-Americans and the unambitious, introverted little villages of the French Canadians. Large cities worried him just as Paris worried him. A society divided between the respectable middle and upper classes and an urban mob was no basis for democracy.

The modern suburb, however, is not the small town of the nineteenth century. That is, the phenomenon of ribbon development and suburban sprawl, where low-density, single-family housing is spread out over multi-acre tracts, built without any particular orientation to shopping, schools, medical care, or, indeed anything other than access to a highway, has produced something quite other than the older suburb, let alone the nineteenth-century small town. Such dormitory accommodation has no "natural" center or focus; it forces its inhabitants to rely on the car for every activity other than gardening in their own backyards. It renders anyone who is either too old to drive or not yet of an age to obtain a driver's license just about wholly immobile—particularly since dedicated cycling tracks are a luxury most speculative builders are loath to provide—and it makes parents slaves to their children's weekend and evening transport needs.

The impact of these arrangements on quality of life, the possibilities of civic association, and thence on the vitality of politics is something on which one ought not to pronounce too dogmatically. Before attempting to provide some nondogmatic comments, however, I should answer the obvious question: if these arrangements are bad news politically, socially, and culturally, why do people create them? The answer is that when people pursue rational ends in an uncoordinated fashion, they very often create results that none of them had in mind, and that they would have rejected before the event if other alternatives had been available. Another answer lies in the nature of the motorcar. The cost of a reliable car is for most people a considerable expense; add in the cost of registration and insurance, and much of the car's cost to its owner is incurred before the car rolls an inch. Conversely, the cost per mile of gasoline is very low, so the owner has every reason to drive the vehicle as far as possible, and none to prefer public transport. Yet another lies in an overestimation of the virtues of the profit motive and an underestimation of the usefulness of government as a mechanism of coordination.

This latter usually means that regional planning is slighted, and that planning is left in the hands of local boards whose powers are limited, whose vulnerability to lawsuits by disappointed speculative builders is great, and whose incentives to think about the spillover effects of their behavior on neighboring communities are few. If they allow the erection of a shopping mall on low-grade farmland, their municipality will receive the taxes paid by the mall, but the traffic problems will very likely fall on some other municipality entirely. Similarly with housing, they will have more incentive to resist new development since families will mean children, and children will mean schools, and schools mean taxes; but the first farmer to be allowed to grow single-family homes on his potato fields will reap a windfall, and the argument that once Farmer Jones has harvested a million, it is unfair not to allow his neighbor to reap a million of his own is one to which local governments are very vulnerable.

This would make no difference if there were not a demand for suburban life. Nobody deliberately builds houses that no customer wishes to buy, and nobody erects a shopping center that no customer wants to set foot in. The explanation for the demand is not very complicated. People looking for enough space to bring up their children in tolerable comfort without bankrupting themselves are not looking for anything wicked or peculiar; people wanting to get to work on quieter rather than busier roads are not foolish; people wanting to be able to spend more time at home and less time commuting are entirely rational. But put them all together, and we get a sprawling mess. The quiet roads become clogged; either they are rebuilt on a massive scale or the wretched commuter has lost everything he or she had just gained. One housing development on a green-field site has lots of elbow room; so attractive is that elbow room that other developments crowd in, and the elbow room is lost. Firms see the logic of following their employees to where they live—intrinsically a very rational move—but the logic is so compelling that they all situate themselves next door to one another and the commute again stretches out.

Nobody has done anything wicked or corrupt, but the end result is a peculiarly unattractive form of human habitat, what one might call the thinned-out suburb, where the density of population is just enough to wreck the countryside and just too little to support most of the amenities of civilized life. But is it politically debilitating, too? It is harder to know than one might wish. The observation that suburbanization had coincided with the decline in party loyalty and a decline in voter turnout might be met with the retort that party loyalty was the product of the years when trade unions were at their peak and class-based politics made more sense than they do now. And low turnout might be blamed on the demands that American government places on the voters rather than on a lack of civic virtue on the part of the voters: a rational woman will have few views or none on the merits of one candidate rather than another for the post of deputy assistant courthouse clerk, and if asked to fill in a ballot for many such posts will rationally decline to do so.

On the other hand, there is almost certainly something in the view made famous by Robert Putnam's essay "Bowling Alone." If fewer and fewer people join such entities as bowling *leagues*, as distinct from just going bowling in a family or a group of friends, then there are fewer people getting any practice at acting as secretary or treasurer of a club or a league, fewer people learning the arts of government on the small scale—learning the compromises needed to get a program to work, the diligence needed to construct a program of any length, and the several arts of personal diplomacy. If that is right, then what one might call the small night schools of democracy will not be serving their proper function. It is as well not to pass over the drawbacks of the lifestyle that Putnam laments. All too often, the situation was that while the men went out for bowling, beers, and pizza, their wives and children stayed home and entertained themselves as best they could. If people who "bowl alone" bowl as families, there have been gains as well as losses. Moreover, the acquisition of "political competence" is not quite the same thing as the acquisition of democratic or liberal allegiances. The Orangemen of Northern Ireland are strong in the collective qualities whose absence Putnam laments among late-twentieth-century Americans. They form Orange Lodges, organize pipe-and-drum bands, look after the families of their members who have fallen on hard times; their capacity to act as a unit is impressive. But the ends to which this is all directed are extremely unattractive—involving as they do the continued intimidation of the Catholic population of the province.

One might wonder, in the same vein, how many of those who once bowled together were also adept at fixing the politics of urban Chicago so that no black could find decent accommodation or the sort of city-paid employment that had got the Irish, Polish, German, and other immigrants into the city, out of poverty, and onto the ladder that led to middle-class prosperity. It is not clear, for the matter of that, that we should lament this as a failing of democracy. It may be that the right thing to say is rather that it shows that an effective democracy can be exceedingly unjust unless it is animated by a liberal and inclusive spirit that encourages those who are effective participants to share the benefits of government activity and public employment with those who have not so far been able to benefit. At all events, I would not wish to be read as suggesting that suburbanized America is uniformly a bad thing, and that we should look back to the days of more organized urban politics with unmitigated nostalgia. Rather, we ought to ask a more complicated question: what we can do to restore a sense of common purpose and an appreciation of the need for effective government to implement common purposes among people whose (highly constrained) choices of where to live and work have done much to unravel them.

The obvious suggestion is that we need forms of regional government and regional planning that cut quite awkwardly across the existing pattern of state and local government. We also need what we are extremely unlikely to get, which is some kind of national pact to prevent states from poaching employment from other states near and far. The two things are connected. The "beggar my neighbor" policies practiced by New York, New Jersey, and Connecticut for too many years have left the whole conurbation that stretches from Stamford to Trenton underresourced and excessively at the mercy of corporations that can blackmail their temporary hosts with threats of imminent departure for Alabama or Arkansas in order to enjoy cheap utilities, lower local taxes, and anti-union legislation. There are certainly many industries that ought to be encouraged to depart, but not in that kind of fashion. If there was better control of regional land use, together with effective constraints on the way communities adapted to new transportation demands, the citizenry might live in more manageable communities, and just because they were more manageable might take more interest in their management and find themselves with more time for the purpose. It would not be any sort of panacea, but it might be an improvement on the present situation.

Lastly, I return very briefly to the thought that "free association" is not only a subject of *political* interest. It is not entirely true that the great cities of the world are indispensable as the homes of a culture that can draw people to enjoy it collectively and *as* a knowledgeable public. It may be that opera in the United States needs New York City, but it cannot be said that opera in Italy needs Rome in quite the same way; even in the United States, there is opera in smallish towns such as Santa Fe and summer resorts such as Cooperstown, New York. But it is hard to believe that they would survive in the absence of the Metropolitan Opera. Similarly, it is no doubt true and important that Albert Barnes's wonderful collection of impressionist and postimpressionist paintings is housed in Merion on the Philadelphia Main Line, and that the Clarke Institute is attached to Williams College in a small town in western Massachusetts. Still, it is hard to believe that anywhere other than New York City or Chicago or Los Angeles could have housed something on the scale and with the impact of the Museum of Modern Art. It is for the matter of that hard to believe that without the great cities we would have had collectors who wanted the paintings that eventually form the collections of such places.

What galleries and concert halls, city parks, monuments, and other such places provide is on this view a site for a different form of free association—for communities to come together, group by group and interest by interest, from the baseball fan to the devotee of serial composition, or from the rock addict to the fan of the aleatoric "drip" style of painting. To the degree that this is irreplaceable by seeing and hearing it all on television or on the stereo system, it encourages people to understand themselves as members of one society, engaged in a multitude of competing but also cooperative projects. A society that does not understand this about the basis of its cultural resources is a society in danger of losing them. At present, we seem to be such a society.

NOTES

1. The two forms of freedom are distinguished in Michael Sandel, *Democracy's Discontent* (Cambridge: Harvard University Press, Belknap Press, 1996).

2. See John Dewey, *The Public and Its Problems* (1927), in *The Later Works of John Dewey* (Carbondale: Southern Illinois University Press, 1981–), 2: 235ff; *Liberalism and Social Action* (1935), in *Later Works* 11; 31ff.

3. Dewey, *The Public and Its Problems* pp. 304ff.

4. The idea is developed in Jon Elster, *Sour Grapes* (Cambridge: Cambridge University Press, 1983).

Chapter Twelve

TRADE UNIONISM IN A LIBERAL STATE

STUART WHITE

TRADE UNIONS represent the interests of millions of workers in countries like Britain and the United States and thus remain an important element in the associational life of these countries.[1] In both countries, however, trade unions have unambiguously declined in membership and influence in recent years.[2] Many, casting an eye back to the stagflationary 1970s, might regard this as a welcome development, as signaling the much needed emasculation of a once disruptive, destabilizing social force. Over this same period, however, earnings and income inequality, along with absolute poverty, have increased significantly, and the decline in union power has been one important factor behind these alarming trends.[3] It is against the background of these developments that I would like in this paper to reopen the question of how a liberal state—a state committed to the realization of liberal justice—should structure its relationship with trade unions.

The question of how a liberal state should structure its relationship with a given type of secondary association, whether it be trade union, church, or sports club, can be usefully broken down into (at least) three more specific questions. Firstly, to what extent should a liberal state adopt a stance of neutrality toward specific associations or types of association, seeking neither to encourage nor discourage their emergence and continuation? Secondly, to what extent must a liberal state uphold the individual's freedom not to join and freedom to exit a given association or type of association, as well as his/her freedom to join them? Thirdly, to what extent may, and should, a liberal state regulate the internal organizational arrangements of specific secondary associations or types of association?

Having set out a working conception of liberal justice in the first section of the chapter, in subsequent sections I explore each of these questions as they typically arise in policy debates about the state's relationship with unions. The second section considers whether a liberal state must adopt a position of neutrality in relation to unionism or should seek actively to encourage (or discourage) it. Next follows an examination of the legitimacy of the so-called union shop, in which union membership is made a condition of employment, an arrangement that many regard as fundamentally compromising the individual's associational liberty. The final section considers whether a liberal state may, and should, regulate the internal organizational arrangements of trade unions—specifically, whether it may and should legislate for internal union democracy and equal opportunity membership policies.

As we set about the task of exploring these questions, we shall also be assessing the relevance in this context of an influential model of how a liberal state ought to structure its relations with secondary associations. For reasons that will become evident below, we may refer to this as the religion model of state-association relationships. This model equates liberalism with a stance of strict neutrality toward secondary associations and strict adherence to principles of voluntary membership and organizational autonomy (which respectively require the state to uphold the individual's freedom to refuse membership of associations and to refrain from dictating associations' internal organizational arrangements). I believe that this religion model exerts considerable influence over public discussions of state-association relationships. Certainly, participants in debates over state policy toward trade unions frequently appeal, albeit selectively, to its constitutive principles. I shall argue, however, that the religion model is not appropriate as a model of state-association relations in the trade union context. In the case of state-union relations, liberal justice may in fact require a nonneutral, promotive stance on the part of the state and, relatedly, may require, or at least permit, selective and limited departures from the putative principles of voluntary membership and organizational autonomy— departures sufficient to allow for the operation of union shops (albeit subject to an important qualification) and to allow the state to legislate for union democracy and equal opportunity membership policies.

I should say at the outset that I do not claim nor do I think that all of the questions concerning how a liberal state should structure its relationship with trade unions can be entirely resolved at the philosophical level. Too many of the key steps in the various arguments are of a contestable, empirical nature. Nevertheless, I do think that a discussion of the key philosophical issues at stake can facilitate ongoing debate at the political level over state-union relations; in particular, if such a debate is to be properly framed, then it is important for us at least to see what the key philosophical questions are, and just how our answers to them depend on specific factual assumptions. I hope that in this chapter I can at least help to clarify the appropriate terms of this necessary ongoing democratic debate.

LIBERAL JUSTICE AND THE RELIGION MODEL OF STATE-ASSOCIATION RELATIONS

In order to discuss the appropriate relationship between a liberal state and secondary associations in general, and trade unions in particular, we must first have at hand a working conception of liberal justice. The first task of this section is to outline such a conception. Having done so, I shall then try to clarify the connection between liberal justice and the putative principles of state neutrality, voluntary membership, and organizational autonomy alluded to in the introduction. I shall argue that these principles do indeed have strong presumptive force in the design of state-association relations in the case of what we may call expressive associations: associations whose primary purposes necessarily concern the exploration or propagation of a specific view of the good life or controversial ideology of the good society. Trade unions are not necessarily associations of this expressive kind, however, and, for this reason, it is not clear that these three principles should regulate the way a liberal state structures its relationship with trade unions.

The core elements of our working conception of liberal justice follow from the underlying liberal conception of society as, ideally, a cooperative community of free and equal persons.[4] The norm of freedom inherent in the liberal social ideal refers, centrally, to the freedom to form and pursue a conception of the good life—that is, to formulate one's own, personal response to fundamental questions of value and meaning and then to live authentically in accordance with this personal response. This entails a commitment to establish and maintain a system of basic liberties and securities adequate to the task of ensuring that the individual has sufficient space, immune from external interference, to formulate and live authentically in accordance with his/her response to these questions. Rights of bodily integrity and freedoms of movement, conscience, expression, and association all fall within the category of securities and liberties that are basic in this sense. It would be somewhat irrational, moreover, to be concerned to uphold these liberties without also being concerned to maintain their worth to the individual who holds them—with ensuring, in particular, that the ability to exercise them is not fundamentally compromised by material desperation.[5]

The norm of equality inherent in the liberal social ideal requires, firstly, that the state treat citizens on equal, nondiscriminatory terms and, in connection with some social goods, that it also protect citizens from discriminatory treatment by other citizens: at least ordinarily, one citizen should not have preferential access to strategic goods like income and wealth over another citizen simply in virtue of "morally arbitrary" characteristics such as gender or race, or in virtue of his/her specific conception of the good life. If this basic intuition is pursued, the norm of equality can be seen to have some more general implications for justice in the distribution of income and wealth. It is a matter of some controversy as to exactly what these implications are, a controversy that I shall not attempt to summarize, let alone resolve, here.[6] At the very least, however, the norm may be taken to imply that each citizen should have equal opportunity for leading a "decent" life (a life above some minimum threshold level of well-being and capability for agency), and that the ground rules governing the distribution of income and wealth should consequently be structured so as to ensure that each citizen has access to the resources standardly necessary for such a life—that is, to ensure that no citizen falls below the relevant threshold as a result of bad "brute luck" in the natural or social lotteries or as a result of exploitation.[7] Our working conception of liberal justice is thus centrally defined by two complementary core commitments: to basic liberty and basic opportunity.

Let us now consider what connections there are between this conception of liberal justice, and the liberal social ideal that underlies it, and the putative principles of state neutrality, voluntary membership, and organizational autonomy to which I alluded in the introduction. The nature and extent of these connections is most easily seen, I think, by focusing on the case of religious associationism (obviously a case of profound historical significance for liberals).

Consider first the putative principle of state neutrality. To conform to this principle, a state must not bring forward policies with the aim of encouraging or discouraging the emergence or continuation of a given secondary association or type of association. Now, in the case of religious associationism there is a clear and strong connection between state neutrality, so defined, and the norm of equality inherent in the liberal social ideal. The norm of equality requires that the state treat citizens with different conceptions of the good life with equal respect, and ordinarily this will require that the state refrain from deliberately encouraging some religious groupings over others or encouraging religious associationism in general.[8]

Departures from the putative principles of voluntary membership and organizational autonomy in relation to religious associations are, on the other hand, clearly in violation of the norm of freedom inherent in the liberal social ideal, and of the core commitment to basic liberty derived from this norm. (Such departures will also violate the norm of equality insofar as they also entail a departure from the stance of neutrality.) If, for example, the state departs from the principle of voluntary membership by denying its citizens the effective freedom not to join or the freedom to exit a particular religious association, then the state is obviously curtailing the freedom of its citizens to live authentically in accordance with their own personal responses to fundamental questions of value and meaning. The state would similarly restrict the freedom of its citizens to live authentically in accordance with their conceptions of the good life if it were to depart from the principle of organizational autonomy and legally require all religious associations to arrange their internal affairs in, say, a democratic and egalitarian manner. Many quite reasonable views of the good life may require some degree of inequality or hierarchy within the associations dedicated to the pursuit of these views, and these views of the good life would thus become more or less impossible to pursue authentically if the state were to require that the associations in question be internally democratic or egalitarian.

In the context of religious associationism, then, adherence to the putative principles of state neutrality, voluntary membership, and organizational autonomy does seem to follow directly from a commitment to uphold the norms of freedom and equality inherent in the liberal social ideal. Adherence to these three principles in this context is therefore to be regarded, at least presumptively, as a requirement of liberal justice. Such a position is, in this context, constitutive of the liberal ideal of toleration.

We should be careful, however, not to exaggerate the range of applicability of this *religion model,* as we might call it, of how a liberal state ought to structure its relations with secondary associations. Religious associations are prime examples of what we may term "expressive" associations. An association is expressive, as I am here using the term, when its primary associational purpose is necessarily tied to the exploration or propagation of a specific conception of the good life or a specific, controversial ideology of the good society (so that by joining and participating in the association one thereby necessarily gives expression to one's own views about the nature of the good life or expresses support for a controversial ideology of the good society). An expressive association, in this sense, is a community whose members are united by sharing a distinctive set of religious or ideological beliefs. The religion model of state-association relations has an immediate and strong claim to applicability in relation to associations that are distinctive communities of shared belief in this sense.

By no means all associations are of this expressive type, however. It is possible to imagine, in contrast, a wholly "instrumental" association: an association whose primary purpose is to secure for its members improved access to strategic goods, such as income and wealth, the possession of which is important from the standpoint of more or less any conception of the good life. The goals of such an association are independent of any particular conception of the good life or controversial ideology, and participation in such an association cannot be said, therefore, necessarily to express commitment to any particular conception of the good life or controversial ideology. Moreover, because participation in such an instrumental association is not necessarily tied up with the pursuit of any particular conception of the good life or controversial ideology, it will not be as immediately clear that the state is violating the norms of equality and freedom inherent in the liberal social ideal if and when, in relation to such an association, it acts in ways that contradict the principles constitutive of the religion model of state-association relations.

Of course, in practice an association may have a complex nexus of purposes so that it is not possible to characterize it reductively as *either* expressive *or* instrumental. The expressive quality of an association can be a matter of degree, depending on the relative importance of expressive commitments (to specific views of the good life or ideologies of the good society) to its overall purposes. In general we can say that the more important these commitments are, the more expressive an association is, and, therefore, the stronger the presumption in favor of the religion model in thinking about the proper relationship between the association and the state.

Where do trade unions fit into this expressive-instrumental model? It is certainly possible for them to take a strongly expressive form. It is not hard to find historical examples of trade unions organized around controversial ideologies of the good society (Marxist, syndicalist, and so on), or of unions with strong organic connections to other strongly expressive associations, such as particular churches or political parties. Nevertheless, the primary purposes of a trade union, qua trade union, are essentially instrumental in kind: to increase members' access to certain all-purpose goods such as employment and income. To be sure, a trade union may often articulate its instrumental ambitions by reference to an overarching set of ideas about distributive justice and democratic citizenship. Indeed, from a liberal standpoint, it is highly desirable that it should. But this does not necessarily make the union an expressive association, in the above sense, if the values to which it is appealing are, as they may well be, part of the shared public moral vocabulary of a liberal society. The union becomes an expressive association, in the sense here relevant, only when it identifies its objectives with a specific, controversial ideology of the good society or grounds its claims in an appeal to a specific religion or distinctive conception of the good life (e.g., Catholicism). Unions can, and often do, have this "sectarian" character. But they can also readily take a "secular" form, pursuing instrumental goods like employment, education and training, income, workplace safety, and so forth, in a manner that is informed by broad notions of justice and democratic citizenship that are part of the shared political culture of a liberal society, but without committing to any specific view of the good life or controversial ideology of the good society.

In policy debates about "trade union reform"—for example, in debates about the desirability of the union shop or about legislation regulating strike ballots and the election of union officials—appeal is often made, if implicitly, to the religion model of state-association relations. Something like the principle of voluntary membership is appealed to—by those on the Right—to discredit the union shop, for example; and something like the principle of organizational autonomy is appealed to—by those on the Left—to discredit legislation regulating union decision making procedures. However, precisely because participation in a union cannot be said necessarily to express commitment to any particular view of the good life (or controversial ideology of the good society), it is not immediately clear that the state violates the norms of equality and freedom inherent in the liberal social ideal if and when, in relation to unions, it acts in ways that contradict the putative principles of state neutrality, voluntary membership, and organizational autonomy. The religion model may thus have limited relevance when we come to think about how a liberal state ought to structure its relationship with trade unions. Various departures from its constitutive principles in this context may be consistent with, or even required by, liberal justice.

In the next three sections I shall make the case that a liberal state may, and in order to promote basic opportunity and maintain the value of basic liberty probably should, depart from these three principles in certain specified ways in structuring its relationship with trade unions.

AGAINST NEUTRALITY: THE CASE FOR A PROMOTIVE STANCE

In this section I look at the question of whether a liberal state may, and should, eschew a stance of neutrality toward trade unionism in favor of what we may call a promotive stance. I first clarify in concrete terms what it would mean for a liberal state to adopt a neutral or, by contrast, promotive stance toward trade unionism. I then present the basic argument in favor of the promotive stance. Next I show how this basic argument can be most plausibly elaborated in the contemporary circumstances of the advanced capitalist countries.

Defining Neutrality and the Promotive Stance

What, concretely, would state neutrality toward trade unionism entail? As a first stab at an operational definition, we might say that the absence of any legal prohibition on the formation and membership of trade unions is sufficient for neutrality to obtain. Let us call this the formal conception of neutrality. The state permits unions to form but does absolutely nothing to promote union formation or even to protect union formation in the face of employer resistance (aside from enforcing basic background rights of bodily integrity and so forth in the face of, say, hired thugs sent out to intimidate pro-union activists).

Under the formal conception of neutrality, employers remain at liberty to dismiss workers who attempt to form or join unions or who attempt to engage in various forms of collective action. Given the typical imbalance of bargaining power between employers and individual sellers of labor power, however, the retention of this power of dismissal under the formal conception can be expected to have a severe chilling effect upon union formation and collective action. The probable severity of this effect, combined with its utter predictability, must then raise serious doubts as to the genuine neutrality of intent of the state toward union formation and activity. So long as there are significant background inequalities of bargaining power between employers and individual sellers of labor power, the mere absence of any legal prohibition on union formation looks less like a strategy of neutrality than a strategy for indirectly discouraging unionism.

If we reformulate our operational definition of neutrality to take account of this background inequality of bargaining power—that is, if we formulate a suitably power-adjusted conception of neutrality—then the following basic categories of rights (in addition to the mere absence of a legal prohibition on forming or joining trade unions) would seem necessary for neutrality to obtain: (*a*) a right to form and join unions without threat of dismissal; (*b*) clear and fair procedural rights to achieve recognition of unions from employers as proper bargaining representatives;[9] and (*c*) a right to take strike action in pursuit of union objectives without threat of dismissal.[10] Taken together, these rights amount to what we may call a *minimally substantive right to organize and strike*. They establish a more level playing field between labor and capital in the struggle over unionization by depriving employers of the opportunity to use the threat of dismissal as a way of chilling union formation and activity.[11]

To adopt a promotive stance toward unionism, a state must respect the minimally substantive right to organize and strike defined by (*a*) through (*c*) above, and then do something further that can reasonably be expected to foster union formation and influence. One possibility, for example, would be for the state to incorporate trade unions, along with parallel employer organizations, into publicly sponsored bodies with consultative and supervisory public policy functions. Such bodies might focus on wage policy, for example, attempting to thrash out guidelines for pay settlements for local pay bargainers to follow; or on education and training policies, having a responsibility to identify skill needs and to coordinate and oversee action to meet them. In such cases, the state endows unions (and parallel employer organizations) with a share in public governance, institutionalizing the input of such organizations into policy making and into the execution of broad policy mandates.[12] By incorporating unions into the tasks of public governance in this way, the state directly promotes union influence, enhances the public utility of unions, and may also thereby enhance the legitimacy of unions in the eyes of the wider citizenry, so encouraging union growth.

Hopefully, we now have a more concrete sense of what a promotive stance toward unions on the part of the state would involve. But may a liberal state adopt a promotive stance toward trade unionism? And, even if it may do so, should it do so?

The General Form of the Argument for the Promotive Stance

The principle of state neutrality has strong presumptive force in relation to associations that have a strongly expressive character. This follows directly from the norm of equality inherent in the liberal social ideal. However, as I pointed out above, the primary associative purpose of a trade union, qua trade union, is not necessarily related to the advancement of any specific conception of the good life or good society. Thus, if the state acts to promote unionism in general, it will not necessarily be giving proponents of one religious or ideological viewpoint special advantages over citizens with other religious or ideological viewpoints (as would be the case, for example, if the state took it upon itself to promote religious associationism in general). This is most obviously the case where unionism is what I referred to above as secular in kind. However, even if unions are sectarian, the state would not display unequal respect for citizens if, in order to encourage unionism in general, it offered certain benefits to all such unions on equal terms (for example, subsidies specifically to help meet the costs of collective bargaining).[13] Given, then, that the usual equality-based objection to departing from the stance of neutrality does not necessarily apply in this context, what is the positive argument for the state adopting the alternative promotive stance toward unionism?

The argument stands or falls on the claim that in the context of a capitalist economy, a strong trade union movement is a necessary part of the institutional framework for securing basic opportunity for the individual and, relatedly, for maintaining the value of his/her basic liberty.[14] At least five potential functions or effects of trade unionism are relevant here:

1. The substitution of collective bargaining for individualized bargaining directly reduces the market vulnerability of those selling their labor power (particularly unskilled or low-skilled workers), and thereby helps to prevent exploitative exchanges that would otherwise threaten basic opportunity and/ or the value of basic liberty.[15]

2. In almost any capitalist society strong unions will be necessary to achieve a balance of interest representation in the political process and, thereby, to help secure the enactment of legislation that may be vital to basic opportunity (e.g., minimum wage laws or wage councils, state-sponsored training programs, welfare programs, health and safety legislation).

3. Policies to promote basic opportunity and protect the value of basic liberty must not only be adopted and well designed, but must also be properly enforced. In certain areas, like health and safety, where it is almost impossible for the state itself effectively to supervise employer compliance with relevant legislation, unions can perform an essential supervisory function so as to improve compliance.[16]

4. Unions can perform educational functions that serve the basic opportunity and basic liberty commitments. They can, for example, educate their members against racial or gender discrimination. Or they can help their members come to appreciate the value of training, and so help to maintain their employability.[17]

5. Unions can be (and historically often have been) vehicles for resource-pooling among poorer individuals. They can, for example, organize insurance against costly contingencies such as poor health or unemployment, or pool members' resources to help finance education and training.[18]

For future reference we may refer to these as the *collective bargaining, legislative, regulatory, education,* and *resource-pooling* effects or functions of trade unionism. This list is only illustrative of the ways in which unionism can serve liberal ends, of course, and not exhaustive.

The general form of the argument for the promotive stance may then be set out as follows. A liberal state is obliged to promote those institutions that are necessary for the realization of liberal justice. Through the exercise of the various functions enumerated above (and perhaps others not presented here) trade unions can make a significant, indeed indispensable, contribution to the realization of liberal justice. Therefore, a liberal state should promote unionism—at least to the extent that, in so doing, it can promote unionism in that form (or those forms) which, by making optimal use of the above functions in the prevailing circumstances, can be reliably expected to make a significant contribution to the realization of liberal justice.

The qualification contained in the last sentence is important. If a liberal state is unable to promote unionism in a form that can be reliably expected to promote liberal ends, then the liberal argument for the promotive stance obviously fails. Two structural features are of general importance in helping to ensure that a union movement does indeed serve liberal ends: firstly, the union movement must achieve an encompassing representation of worker interests; secondly, its constituent associations must have a well-developed capacity for coordinated decision making.[19] Where unions are not encompassing they lack an *incentive* to pursue policies that are of benefit to all workers, and may consequently adopt policies that promote the well-being of their members at the expense of other workers. As I shall stress in my discussion below of union membership policies, it is important in this respect that unions encompass not only those currently in employment, but also extend a form of membership to the unemployed. Moreover, even if a union movement is appropriately encompassing, it will lack the *capacity* to act effectively in the interests of all workers if its constituent associations are unable to coordinate policy making. Coordination and assurance problems will then plague decentralized collective bargaining and reduce the efficiency of its outcomes in ways that may also damage significantly the basic material interests of some workers. Centralization of decision making is one way of establishing the necessary capacity for coordinated decision making, but may not be the only way.[20]

In general, then, in seeking to promote unionism, a liberal state should seek to promote a unionism that is both encompassing and that possesses strong capacities for coordinated decision making.[21] If this is beyond the power of a liberal state at a particular time and place, then the case for the promotive stance is correspondingly weakened.

A Contemporary Argument for the Promotive Stance

Any application of the argument for the promotive stance involves showing exactly how the various union effects or functions listed above can make a significant, indeed indispensable, contribution to realizing liberal justice in the specific economic circumstances of the day. By way of elaboration, let us therefore see how unionism, through the exercise of these functions, can make such a contribution in the contemporary economic context of advanced capitalist countries like Britain and the United States.

One of the distinguishing features of the present economic context in these countries is the growing need for skilled labor and, related to this, the deteriorating position in the labor market of the relatively unskilled worker. During the so-called Golden Age of the 1950s and 1960s, there were plentiful employment opportunities for relatively unskilled workers in the advanced capitalist countries, especially in the manufacturing sector where firms needed large pools of such workers for their "Fordist" product market strategies centered on the price-competitive mass production of standardized goods for large, stable domestic (and expanding foreign) markets. In the future there is likely to be much lower demand for unskilled labor in successful capitalist economies. In part this is a reflection of technological changes (especially computerization) that have already helped produce a significant shift in relative labor demand away from unskilled to skilled workers, exerting downward pressure on their employment prospects and wages.[22] But it is also a reflection of economic "globalization" and, in particular, of increased competition from newly industrialized countries where firms, taking advantage of lower wage rates, can often pursue Fordist product market strategies much more cheaply than in the advanced capitalist countries. Some firms in some countries have responded (or have been simultaneously constrained and enabled to respond) to this competitive pressure by adopting alternative "flexible system" product market strategies, based on the batch or unit production of more differentiated goods for a range of smaller, changing markets and on a selling point that resides less in price than in qualitative features such as precise orientation to specific customer needs.[23] In the long run, it will become increasingly difficult for firms in the advanced capitalist countries to retain a competitive edge while continuing to pursue older, mass-production strategies, and it is therefore imperative that the governments of these countries orient their economies toward the adoption of the newer, flexible systems strategies.[24] Such strategies entail a much lower demand for unskilled labor, however. Successful adoption of such strategies depends, rather, on a plentiful supply of broadly and highly skilled workers, capable of taking initiative and flexibility across tasks.

In this economic context, trade unions have a critically important—indeed, indispensable—role to play in facilitating skills acquisition. By performing this function, unions will increase labor market security and reduce market vulnerability at the individual level and, as I shall explain below, may help to prevent firms from responding to the increased pressures of international competition in ways that generally threaten satisfaction of the basic opportunity commitment for those currently most disadvantaged in the labor market. The state committed to realizing liberal justice should therefore promote unionism and, in the process, encourage and enable unions to concentrate their energies in this area, helping unions to recast themselves as *human capital agencies*, centrally focused on maintaining the skills and employability of their members.

To support these claims, let us now clarify, firstly, just how unions can contribute, through the effects and functions enumerated above, to the promotion of skills formation; secondly, why their role in this area is an indispensable one; and thirdly, how the state can encourage them to make the most of their potential in this area.

Firstly, unions can exert legislative influence to secure the enactment of public policies that promote education and training. They can contribute, through the political process, to the fixing of public goals in the area of education and training; to the establishment of managerial structures at national and local levels, incorporating an ongoing union input, to oversee the pursuit of such goals; and to the establishment of programs of financial assistance for education and training. Within such a framework of public intervention, secondly, unions can exercise their regulatory function to ensure that employers respect such goals and adopt appropriate industry and firm-level policies to raise or maintain investment in workforce skills.[25] Thirdly, even in the absence of such a framework, they can exercise their collective bargaining function, at firm or industry level, to the same end. Fourthly, they can perform an educative function within their own memberships to increase awareness of the importance of skills formation and of training and job opportunities. The importance of this educative function should not be underestimated as research shows that those most lacking skills are also often those least appreciative of their importance.[26] Finally, unions can also pool member resources to help finance education and training.[27]

It is not, moreover, just that unions *can* promote skills formation. We *must* look to unions to do so because employers, left to themselves, will not do so to an adequate extent (adequate, that is, to ensure satisfaction of the basic opportunity commitment). Firms in a free market will underinvest in skills because they run the risk of having the workers they train "poached" by other firms who have not contributed to the cost of the training.[28] There is in addition the problem that while flexible-systems product market strategies may be more profitable in the long run, as competition from newly industrialized countries intensifies, they may be less profitable in the short run, precisely because of the higher training costs they entail. Where firms are encouraged by the character of capital markets or internal processes of financial review to maximize short-term profits, they may consequently refrain from adopting flexible-systems production strategies and assessing their skill needs accordingly.[29] To the extent that the state then delegates the lead in education and training policy to employers' organizations, such "short-termism" can affect not only the training policies of individual firms, but the orientation of the whole education and training system. As in the British case, the economy may consequently become trapped in a "low-skills equilibrium": a self-reinforcing cycle of selecting product market strategies that demand low-skill requirements and producing a workforce with a level and distribution of skills that is unsuited to the widespread selection of anything other than these strategies.[30] Adjustment to flexible-systems production becomes patchy and sluggish in this situation, and employer and governmental energies consequently become focused solely on cutting labor costs in the face of international competition, with attendant downward pressure on the living standards of the country's low-skilled workforce (or else upward pressure on unemployment if wages are not cut). Active union involvement in the formulation and implementation of education and training policy, from the national level down to the firm, is therefore essential to pull employers in the direction of high-skilled flexible-systems production, and, in the process, to block these alternative responses to international competition that currently threaten satisfaction of the basic opportunity commitment in the advanced capitalist countries.

However, it does not follow that just because unions can do something desirable, and that they alone can be expected to do it, that unions *will* do it. Admittedly, unions presently have an incentive to recast themselves as human capital agencies. This provides a very tangible way of displaying their continuing relevance to workers, and so of increasing the demand for unionism.[31] But there may be a useful role for the state here too. In the very process of promoting unionism, the state can directly engage unions with this policy area (see the example I gave above of how a state might promote unionism); and, without unduly infringing their organizational autonomy, the state can add significantly to the pressure on unions to engage with it. One possibility, for example, would be for the state directly to sponsor the establishment of *employee mutuals:* organizations owned by their members that would "organise, manage and sell" their members' labor power, developing this labor-power through ongoing education and training, and then deploying it on a flexible basis according to employers' changing needs.[32] Institutional competition from state-supported employee mutuals would increase the incentive of existing trade unions to move in the direction of becoming human capital agencies, organized on similar mutualist lines.

To sum up: satisfaction of the liberal's basic opportunity commitment in the present economic context centrally requires a high level of skills acquisition at the individual and aggregate level; unions, through the exercise of the various functions described above, have an indispensable role to play in securing the necessary level of skills acquisition; a liberal state should therefore adopt a broadly promotive stance toward unionism, while structuring union incentives to help ensure that unions thoroughly recast themselves to meet the demands of this role.

The Principle of Voluntary Membership and the Legitimacy of the Union Shop

Assume that the case for the promotive stance set out in the previous section is valid. One practice that could serve to consolidate the position of unions, and so perhaps contribute indirectly to the realization of liberal justice, is the union shop, the practice of making employment within a given plant or firm conditional upon union membership.[33] It may be objected, however, that union shop arrangements contradict the principle of voluntary membership that requires the liberal state to uphold the individual's freedom not to join a given association or type of association. Is the union shop compatible with the liberal state's commitment to protect basic liberty?

One might argue that the union shop involves no violation of basic liberty because the individual can readily escape the putative obligation to join a union simply by choosing not to take a job with an employer operating a union shop. However, this seems a somewhat disingenuous response. Very often, the costs of not accepting the relevant job offer will simply be too high for the individual to have any meaningful choice about whether or not to accept the job in question. We cannot then say that he/she is free, in a sufficiently substantive sense, to escape the putative obligation to join a union by refusing the relevant job. Rather than denying that the union shop introduces an element of coercion into union membership, I think we would do better to consider whether the coercion involved does or does not violate the individual's basic liberty.

When membership of an association requires the individual to give support to a particular conception of the good life or controversial ideology of the good society, the freedom to refuse association is clearly fundamental to the individual's freedom to live authentically in accordance with his/her own ethical and political beliefs. Thus, insofar as unions do have strong expressive commitments, as when they are religiously oriented or oriented through their constitution to a controversial ideology of the good society, the freedom not to join a union must indeed be regarded as a basic liberty. Union shop arrangements that make employment conditional upon membership of unions with strong expressive commitments of these kinds would appear, therefore, to be straightforwardly incompatible with liberal justice.

However, even a secular union may get involved in wider political campaigns whose character some union members will see as incompatible with their ethical and political beliefs. In the course of a campaign to get health and safety legislation enacted, a union might, for example, donate money to an avowedly "socialist" party that promises to introduce such legislation. Even a union member who values health and safety and who supports such legislation may nevertheless not want to give support to this particular political party. She could plausibly object that being forced, through her union dues, to contribute to this party's coffers is relevantly analogous to being forced to contribute funds to support a particular church, and that as such it constitutes a violation of her freedom to live authentically in accordance with her own ethical and political beliefs.

This is an important point, but one we can apparently accommodate without surrendering the principle of the union shop. Developing the approach set out by Justice William Brennan in his *Machinists* opinion,[34] one might argue that the obvious solution is simply for unions to separate out the financing of those political activities that have a clear partisan character and to give union members the freedom to opt out of contributing to this specific campaign fund while remaining under an obligation to contribute to the cost of the union's other activities (at a minimum, to its core collective bargaining activities).[35]

A critic, however, can now raise a further objection to the union shop that is grounded in this same concern to protect the individual's integrity as an ethical agent. Union membership carries with it an obligation not only to provide the union with certain funds but, on occasion, to withdraw one's labor in support of a strike, at least where strike action has been decided upon through a fair, democratic procedure. However, some people may think strike action immoral in the same way that some people believe war-making is immoral; they may be "industrial pacifists" with principled reasons against taking strike action. Even if the union in question is a secular union, the freedom of these individuals to live authentically in accordance with their sincere and deeply held ethical beliefs *is* jeopardized by compelled union membership, at least given the assumption that union membership carries with it an obligation to act in support of (democratically determined) strike action.

A supporter of the union shop might try to handle this problem by developing further the Brennan approach for handling the problem of unions' partisan campaign work. To put the response concretely, imagine that on joining a union an individual is presented with a form requesting specific financial contributions to cover: (*a*) general union operations and campaigning costs; (*b*) the provision of mutual insurance benefits; (*c*) the establishment of a strike fund; and (*d*) partisan campaign work. The supporter of the union shop has already conceded that all union members must be free to opt out of the contributions covered under *d*. We might now add that the industrial pacifist must be given the right both to opt out of strike action and to opt out of the financial contribution covered under *c*. He need not strike, and need not subsidize others who do so.

At this point, however, one might reasonably begin to wonder whether the union shop is not about to suffer a death by a thousand cuts. How many more cases can we think of in which individuals find themselves in conscientious disagreement with what their union is doing to an extent that they can reasonably wish, in all integrity, to disassociate themselves from the union's actions? Are we going to go on multiplying the number of things we allow union members to exempt themselves from in an effort to respect the claims of freedom of conscience? Would it not be a lot easier if we just retreated from the principle of the union shop and accepted that union membership should be wholly voluntary?

We do not have to go quite that far. Instead of trying to anticipate all of the ways in which individuals might find themselves in conscientious disagreement with union policies or practices, and offering multiple exemptions from specific union duties targeted at each of these specific sources of conscientious disagreement, we could instead just admit one blanket exemption from union membership on grounds of genuine conscientious disagreement with some aspect of union policy or practices. There is obviously a risk that individuals could abuse this right of conscientious exemption, taking advantage of it merely to avoid contributing to the costs of unionism while they continue to share, gratefully, in the benefits that unionism provides. However, this is a risk that we can readily minimize by requiring all those exercising the right of conscientious exemption to bear an equivalent monetary burden to that borne by union members, for example, to make a financial contribution to a recognized charity equal to the dues they would have to pay if they were union members.[36] This reduces the incentive to abuse the right of conscientious exemption for material gain without weakening the right itself in any significant way. Providing this general right of conscientious exemption is acknowledged, the union shop cannot be said to threaten the integrity of the individual as an ethical agent and, thus, to violate his/her basic liberty.[37]

A liberal state may therefore permit this qualified form of the union shop. From this, however, it does not follow that a liberal state should permit the union shop, let alone that it should encourage it. To take those further steps in the argument and justify the infringement of nonbasic liberty that even the qualified union shop necessarily involves, one must be able to point to some significant social benefit that the union shop achieves (a benefit, moreover, that could not be achieved by any lesser infringement of non basic liberty). Supporters of the union shop argue that the institution produces a range of significant social benefits: that it consolidates the bargaining position of otherwise vulnerable wage workers and thereby promotes basic opportunity; that it ensures a fair distribution of the burdens of unionism among all those who receive its benefits, thereby preventing opportunistic individuals from free riding on the contributions of, and so exploiting, union members; and that it helps to reduce transactions costs in the workplace, an efficiency gain that is to the advantage of all parties. In response, critics argue that the union shop reduces the incentive of union leaderships to make unions attractive to workers, and may thus lead to a unionism that is more attuned to the aspirations of union leaders than to the needs of ordinary members. I shall not try to adjudicate between these competing claims here. The crucial point is simply that if the union shop, qualified by the general right of conscientious exemption, does produce a significant net social benefit, then the liberal state may legitimately proceed to permit or encourage it, for, in so doing, it will not thereby be supporting an institution that violates basic liberty.

Legislating for Union Democracy: Against the Principle of Organizational Autonomy

During the 1980s, the Conservative government in Britain introduced a series of reforms of the way in which trade unions consult their members

about strike action and elect union officers.[38] The declared aim of these reforms was to "democratize" the unions, and so "give the unions back to their
members." According to one commentator, however, the reforms "involved
the most intrusive involvement by the state in the internal affairs of trade
unions in the western world,"[39] and many within the British labor movement opposed the reforms on the grounds that it is simply illegitimate for
the state to dictate to secondary associations their internal organizational
arrangements. Opponents of the reforms thus appealed to the putative
principle of organizational autonomy, introduced above, which holds that
the state should leave secondary associations free to determine such
arrangements by themselves. Is a liberal state in fact required to abide by
such a principle in its dealings with trade unions? Or may, and should, it set
this principle aside and legislate directly for union democracy?

There ought to be a strong general presumption in favor of legislating
for union democracy simply because union democracy is likely to be a necessary feature of a unionism that reliably acts to promote basic opportunity
and to protect the value of basic liberty. Most obviously, genuinely democratic procedures of policy making and selecting union officials will serve
to protect union members from the possible predations of union leaderships and, more generally, to help orient union leaders toward serving union
members' genuine needs. It is hard to imagine how unions can reliably promote basic opportunity if they are not structured to be attentive to their
members' needs in this elementary way.

Extending this point, one can argue that as part of the process of full democratization, a liberal state must also be prepared to legislate to require
unions to respect equal opportunity principles in relation to rights of membership and officeholding. Such equal opportunity rules will serve to prevent union policy from becoming insensitive to the interests of otherwise
vulnerable minorities. One vulnerable minority, often neglected in these
discussions, is the unemployed, and the state may need to insist on a very
particular measure of democratization in order to help prevent the emergence of an "insider-outsider" dynamic in the labor market that is detrimental to the interests of the unemployed. Specifically, if the state requires
unions to allow members who become unemployed to retain membership
rights for a period after losing their jobs, and to submit all wage policy proposals to a discussion and vote by all union members, then this may help to
ensure that union wage policy is formulated with the interests of the unemployed "outsiders," and not just the employed "insiders," in mind.[40] Recent economic research does suggest that centralized and encompassing
union confederations can play a constructive role in effecting wage adjust-

ment to macroeconomic shocks so as to prevent unemployment.[41] But, once again, if unions are not genuinely democratic organizations, it is hard to see how such agreements made in the course of centralized pay bargaining can hope to maintain their legitimacy, and thus their stability, over time in the eyes of rank and file union members.

The general presumption in favor of legislating for union democracy is especially strong in the context of the union shop. Since union shop arrangements obviously have the effect of reducing the individual union member's power to exit the union if he/she so desires, they may also reduce the individual's power of "voice" within the union. In these circumstances, unions may be less democratic than their members wish, and it can be argued that the liberal state then has a special responsibility to step in and regulate union decision making procedures in order to ensure that these are indeed genuinely democratic. The liberal state must substitute its own direct regulatory power for the indirect regulatory power of exit that the individual union member is no longer readily able to exercise.[42]

There is, then, a strong case for legislating for union democracy and equal opportunity policies. Nevertheless, we have yet to consider whether this case is sufficiently strong to justify departing from the principle of organizational autonomy, the principle that the state should refrain from determining the internal organizational arrangements of secondary associations.

The principle of organizational autonomy has presumptive force, I have argued, in relation to secondary associations that are expressive in kind, such as religious associations. The presumption in favor of the principle is significantly weaker in relation to associations that lack this expressive character. To the extent that trade unions are not expressive associations in the relevant sense, there is thus no presumption in favor of full-blown organizational autonomy to start with. Therefore, given the way union democracy serves the basic opportunity commitment, legislating for union democracy seems clearly justified.

It might be objected, however, that some unions do have strong expressive commitments. May a liberal state override the principle of organizational autonomy and insist on public standards of internal democracy (and equal opportunity) in relation to these unions? Given the probable importance of union democracy to basic opportunity, I think that in this instance the presumption must still be in favor of overriding the principle. To defeat this presumption, the union in question must show two things: firstly, that specific expressive commitments are indeed central to its associational mission;[43] secondly, that the ability of its members to live authentically in accordance with these commitments would be significantly damaged by the union's conformity to the relevant standards of internal democracy and equal opportunity. These requirements will be hard to meet unless the union itself is the primary associational vehicle for these commitments, which frequently will not be the case.[44]

Of course, none of this should be taken to imply that any and all public regulation of internal union organization is legitimate. There is a clear distinction, firstly, between regulations to ensure that unions operate in a genuinely democratic manner and regulations that limit the scope of union democracy, for example, rules prohibiting Communist Party members from holding union offices.[45] By depriving the individual of the opportunity to hear a full range of viewpoints or to campaign or vote in accordance with sincerely held political beliefs, rules of this latter kind violate the individual's basic liberty.[46] In addition, it is also necessary to attend to a more subtle distinction between regulations that are strictly necessary to ensure genuine union democracy and regulations that are not strictly necessary in this way but that do increase decision making costs within unions and thereby inhibit collective action. For example, an insistence that all union votes on strike action be conducted by secret ballots seems eminently reasonable, but an insistence specifically on *postal* ballots, as reflected in recent British legislation,[47] seems unnecessary to ensure genuine democracy and merely calculated to make strike action more burdensome to the union. In view of the way this may discourage collective action, one might wonder whether such legislation is compatible with a stance of neutrality toward unionism, let alone with the more exacting promotive stance for which I have argued here.

CONCLUSIONS

My conclusions may now be briefly summarized as follows:

The appropriate relationship between a liberal state and secondary associations is sometimes conceived of in terms of a religion model according to which a liberal state must not seek to discourage or encourage the emergence of any particular association or type of association (the principle of state neutrality); must uphold the individual's freedom not to join an association as zealously as it guards his/her freedom to join an association (the principle of voluntary membership); and must not legislate to determine associations' internal organizational arrangements (the principle of organizational autonomy). Debates concerning state policy toward unions often make tacit appeal to the principles constitutive of this model of state-association relationships.

A liberal state is not required, however, to adopt a stance of neutrality in relation to trade unionism. Indeed, a strong case can be made that a liberal state ought to adopt a promotive stance toward trade unionism. The ground for the promotive stance lies in the contribution that a strong trade union movement can be expected to make, through collective bargaining, legislative, mutual insurance, and other functions, to securing satisfaction of the liberal's core commitments to basic opportunity and the value of basic liberty. A contemporary argument for such a promotive stance would focus, in particular, on the potential role of unions in facilitating the acquisition of skills by individuals, thereby helping to prevent advanced capitalist countries from becoming locked in a low-skills equilibrium that, in the present global economy, threatens satisfaction of the basic opportunity commitment. As part of its broadly promotive stance, a liberal state may and should take action to encourage unions to adapt to the role that, in the circumstances, is most conducive to liberal ends (e.g., in the present context, by sponsoring a degree of constructive institutional competition in the form of state-supported employee mutuals).

A liberal state may permit the operation of union shops, under which union membership is made a condition of employment, but only providing it guarantees a general right of conscientious exemption from union membership. Whether, subject to this qualification, a liberal state should permit or even encourage adoption of the union shop then depends on a highly contextual judgment about the wider social benefits or costs of the institution.

A liberal state is not obliged to adhere strictly to a principle of organizational autonomy in its dealings with trade unions. In general, it may and probably should legislate for union democracy and, relatedly, for equal opportunity practices within unions. No interest of ethical integrity is at stake (certainly in the case of secular unions, and often also in the case of sectarian unions), and genuinely democratic and equal opportunity practices will usually be necessary structural features of a unionism that can be reliably expected to contribute to the realization of liberal justice.

The general conclusion of this paper, which follows from the specific conclusions summarized in the preceding three paragraphs, is that the religion model of state-association relations does not readily apply in the case of relations between the state and trade unions. This model actually has a very specific and limited range of application, and we should therefore be wary of arguments in the public debate over state policy toward trade unions that uncritically invoke presuppositions peculiar to it.

NOTES

1. Earlier versions of this paper were presented to the Nuffield College Political Theory Workshop, Oxford, and the Program in Ethics and Public Affairs at Princeton University. I would especially like to thank Robin Archer, Oliver Avens, Selina Chen, Cecille Fabre, Diana Gardner, Robert Goodin, Amy Gutmann, Gil Harman, George Kateb, Christine Korsgaard, Meira Levinson, Richard Locke, David Miller, Alan Ryan, Marc Stears, Nadia Urbinati, Ramon Vela Cordova, and Stewart Wood for their verbal or written comments.

2. In Britain, union density (the proportion of civilian employees belonging to unions) fell from 53 percent in 1980 to 39 percent in 1990. In the United States union density has fallen from 25 percent in 1970 to 16 percent in 1990. In the private sector, density was down to a mere 11 percent by 1992.

3. See Richard Freeman and Lawrence Katz, "Rising Wage Inequality: The United States vs. Other Advanced Countries," in Richard Freeman, ed., *Working under Different Rules* (New York: Russell Sage Foundation, 1994), pp. 29–62.

4. See especially John Rawls, *A Theory of Justice* (Oxford: Oxford University Press, 1972); and *Political Liberalism* (New York: Columbia University Press, 1993).

5. See Norman Daniels, "Equal Liberty and Unequal Worth of Liberty," in Daniels, ed., *Reading Rawls* (Oxford: Basil Blackwell, 1975), pp. 253–281.

6. Central to this controversy are arguments about Rawls's difference principle and Dworkin's conception of "equality of resources." See Rawls, *A Theory of Justice*, pp. 75–83, and Ronald Dworkin, "What Is Equality? Part 2: Equality of Resources," *Philosophy and Public Affairs* 10 (1981): 283–345.

7. On the significance of brute luck inequality, see G. A. Cohen, "On the Currency of Egalitarian Justice," *Ethics* 99 (1989): 906–44.

8. Departures from the baseline of strict neutrality may on occasion be justifiable, but only by reference to the advancement of basic interests that individuals have in common regardless of their specific conception of the good life, and never by appeal to the supposed superiority of one conception over another.

9. Thus, we might stipulate that a union automatically acquires a right of recognition so that employers are obliged to bargain in good faith with it if it can demonstrate that it has the support of 50 percent or more of the workforce in a given workplace. As in the Canadian case, demonstration of this support could require nothing more than that a sufficient number of workers sign a card indicating a desire for union representation.

10. Since the value of the right to associate in this case is clearly and significantly diminished if it is not accompanied by a right to strike, I think it legitimate to treat the right to strike here as if it is an integral part of the right to associate.

11. The United States provides a good example of an industrial relations system that falls well short of the demands of power-adjusted neutrality. The right to strike without being dismissed is effectively undermined by employers' right to hire "permanent replacement workers" in place of strikers, rehiring strikers only as new jobs subsequently become available. The system also fails to provide adequate protection against employee dismissal for pro-union activity in struggles for union recognition—by the late 1980s unlawful employee terminations occurred in one in three

workplace elections on union representation, with no fewer than one in six pro-union voters in such elections being illegally discharged. For a succinct review, see Charles B. Craver, *Can Unions Survive? The Rejuvenation of the American Labor Movement* (New York: New York University Press, 1995), esp. pp. 28–31, 47–51, 126–55.

12. See Joshua Cohen and Joel Rogers, "Secondary Associations and Democratic Governance," in Erik Olin Wright, ed., *Associations and Democracy* (London: Verso, 1996), pp. 7–98, esp. pp. 55–58. My development of the argument for the promotive stance here is heavily indebted to their discussion.

13. Nor would the state violate the norm of equality if it were to give particular encouragement to secular unions over sectarian unions. Indeed, there may be a case for doing this if it helps to bring about a less divided union movement over the long run, more capable of co-ordinated policy making.

14. I do not think anything important in the general argument for the promotive stance depends on assuming a capitalist rather than a socialist economy, though the argument would have to be elaborated differently in the context of a socialist economy (as indeed it has to be for different types of capitalist economy).

15. For a pertinent discussion of vulnerability and exploitation, see Robert E. Goodin, *Protecting the Vulnerable* (Chicago: University of Chicago Press, 1985), pp. 195–96.

16. The importance of effects/functions 2 and 3 is explored in connection with a wider range of secondary associations in Cohen and Rogers, "Secondary Associations and Democratic Governance." See esp. pp. 42–44.

17. For an illustrative account of this educative function of unionism among a large group of women workers in the United States, see Dorothy Sue Cobble, *Dishing It Out: Waitresses and Their Unions in the Twentieth Century* (Chicago: University of Illinois Press, 1991), esp. pp. 120–27, 140–44.

18. In the British context, trade unionism emerged as part of a broader associational movement that included the Friendly Societies, associations through which working-class households pooled resources so as to protect themselves against various kinds of costly contingencies, and trade unions themselves gradually adopted many of these mutual insurance functions. See Henry Pelling, *A History of British Trade Unionism*, 4th ed. (London: Macmillan, 1987), esp. pp. 7–81. In the United States context, see also Cobble, *Dishing It Out*, pp. 131–36.

19. On the general importance of the encompassingness of interest groups, see Mancur Olson, *The Rise and Decline of Nations* (New Haven: Yale University Press, 1982), esp. pp. 47–53. The importance of encompassingness and centralization (as a means for coordination) are also stressed in Cohen and Rogers, "Secondary Associations and Democratic Governance," pp. 48–49.

20. Within the overall framework of coordinated policy making, it may also be important to ensure that particular groups of workers with specific vulnerabilities have special rights in the determination of policy, e.g., that workers in the highly competitive exports sector of the economy are empowered to take the lead and wield veto power in the determination of wages policy. I thank Richard Locke for discussion of this point.

21. The features of encompassingness and centralization seem to have been particularly important, for example, in determining the effect of unionism on unemployment in the advanced capitalist countries in recent years. Where union move-

ments have been encompassing and centralized they have had both the incentive and the capacity to adopt wage policies that promote full employment. See Matti Pohjola, "Corporatism and Wage Bargaining," in Jukka Pekkarinen, Matti Pohjola, and Robert Rowthorn, eds., *Social Corporatism: A Superior Economic System?* (Oxford: Oxford University Press, 1991), pp.44–81.

22. See Freeman and Katz, "Rising Wage Inequality," and in the British context, Stephen Machin, "Changes in the Relative Demand for Skills," in Alison Booth and Dennis Snower, eds., *Acquiring Skills* (Cambridge: Cambridge University Press, 1996), pp. 127–46.

23. See Charles Sabel and Michael Piore, *The Second Industrial Divide: New Possibilities for Prosperity* (New York: Basic Books, 1984); Wolfgang Streeck, "Diversified Quality Production," in his *Social Institutions and Economic Performance* (London: Sage, 1992), pp. 1–40.

24. Not that adoption of the "high road" strategy, based on high-quality, high-skill production, will necessarily enable the advanced capitalist countries to escape all pressure for downward adjustment in real wages. Other countries also have significant numbers of highly skilled workers, and these workers have relatively modest real wage expectations. For illustration of this point in the context of trade between the United States and Mexico, see Harley Shaiken, "Going South: Mexican Wages and U.S. Jobs after NAFTA," *American Prospect* (Fall 1993): pp. 58–65.

25. For further discussion of this point see Cohen and Rogers, "Secondary Associations and Democratic Governance," esp. pp. 82–87.

26. This point is made in the British context by Euan Keep and Ken Mayhew, "Evaluating the Assumptions that Underlie Training Policy," in Booth and Snower, *Acquiring Skills*, pp. 305–34, specifically p. 316.

27. This model of the contemporary trade union as human capital agency is clearly set out in Wolfgang Streeck, "Skills and the Limits of Neo-Liberalism: On the Enterprise of the Future as a Place of Learning," *Work, Employment, and Society* 3 (1989): pp. 89–104. For a discussion of how, in the German context, unions may have begun to adapt their strategies accordingly, see also Howard Kern and Charles Sabel, "Trade Unions and Decentralized Production: A Sketch of Strategic Problems in the West German Labor Movement," *Politics and Society* 19 (1991): pp. 373–402.

28. See especially Streeck, "Skills and the Limits of Neo-Liberalism," pp. 93–95.

29. On the problem of short-termism, see Keep and Mayhew, "Evaluating the Assumptions that Underlie Training Policy," esp. pp. 318–20, 323–25.

30. On the concept of the "low-skills equilibrium," see Daniel Finegold and David Soskice, "The Failure of Training in Britain: Analysis and Prescription," *Oxford Review of Economic Policy* 4 (1988): 21–53.

31. There are certainly clear signs that at least some British trade unions are currently moving in this direction. See Robert Taylor, *The Future of the Trade Unions* (London: Andre Deutsch, 1994), esp. pp. 153–59.

32. See Geoff Mulgan and Tim Bentley, *Employee Mutuals: The 21st Century Trade Union?* (London: Demos, 1996). There are notable historical precedents in the United States for the form of unionism I am advocating here. See, for example, Cobble's discussion of "occupational unionism" among waitresses in *Dishing It Out*, pp. 137–50.

33. Under the union shop, one is required to become a member of the union once one has obtained employment in the relevant plant or firm. This is distinct from what is called, in the United States, the closed shop, under which one must first be a member of the union even to be eligible for employment. I think the argument I make here concerning the union shop also carries over to the closed shop.

34. *International Association of Machinists v. Street*, 367 U.S. 740 (1961).

35. For a similar view, see Sheldon Leader, *Freedom of Association* (New Haven: Yale University Press, 1992), pp. 91–119.

36. We might also stipulate that the conscientious objector provide a short written statement explaining the basis of his/her objection to union membership. I am grateful to Diana Gardner for helpful discussion of this issue.

37. This general right of conscientious exemption might readily be combined with the more specific right of exemption from contributions to union partisan campaign work. On entering a place of employment, the individual would thus be faced with three options: (*a*) joining the union and paying full dues, including contributions to partisan campaign work; (*b*) joining the union, but with an exemption from contributions to support partisan campaign work; and (*c*) full conscientious exemption from union membership.

38. The 1984 Trade Union Act required unions to hold secret ballots for the direct election of union executives at least once every five years and to provide secret balloting of union members before strike action, the ballot taking place at least four weeks before commencement of any strike action. The 1988 Employment Act went a step further, giving union members the right to a postal ballot in all union elections and prestrike ballots; and the 1993 Trade Union Reform and Employment Rights Act made postal balloting for prestrike ballots compulsory.

39. Taylor, *The Future of the Trade Unions*, p. 45.

40. For a more general discussion of the need to "enfranchise" outsiders, see Assar Lindbeck and Dennis Snower, *The Insider-Outsider Theory of Employment and Unemployment* (Cambridge: MIT Press, 1988).

41. See Pohjola, "Corporatism and Wage Bargaining."

42. This point was prominent in early congressional arguments for the regulation of union government. According to one account of the passage of the Taft-Hartley Act of 1947: "Senator Robert A. Taft held that union security provisions made it incumbent upon Congress to guarantee the rights of workers in relation to their unions. The choice before Congress, according to Taft, was between legislating an open shop or an open union. Taft favored the latter alternative, and Congress accepted his approach." See Sar A. Levitan and J. Joseph Loewenberg, "The Politics and Provisions of the Landrum-Griffin Act," in Marten S. Estey, Philip Taft, and Martin Wagner, eds., *Regulating Union Government* (New York: Harper and Row, 1964), pp. 28–64, specifically p. 29.

43. This will require showing that the relevant expressive commitments are an important part of the typical member's understanding of what it means to be a member of this specific union and of his/her motivation for joining the union.

44. For example, while the ability of, say, a Catholic to live authentically in accordance with his/her conception of the good life would be significantly damaged by requiring the Catholic Church itself to be internally democratic and egalitarian, it is by no means clear that requiring a Catholic trade union to conform to public

standards of democracy and equal opportunity would seriously burden the individual's ability to live authentically as a Catholic.

45. Under the Taft-Hartley Act of 1947, each officer of a union had to file annually an affidavit to the effect that he/she was not a member of the Communist Party or else the union would lose its legal protections against unfair labor practices.

46. Most liberal theories accept that there can be circumstances of supreme emergency in which it is excusable to violate basic liberties, and supporters of such rules, e.g., in the cold war United States, would doubtless try to excuse them in these terms. I cannot explore this important issue properly here. Suffice it to say that the criteria of "supreme emergency" must be drawn with great care if this doctrine is not to pose an intolerable ongoing threat to the basic liberties of various dissident groups whom the wider society merely happens to suspect and dislike; and that, on any plausible account of these criteria, a situation of supreme emergency did not obtain in the United States in the late 1940s or 1950s.

47. As noted above, the 1993 Trade Union Reform and Employment Rights Act made postal balloting for prestrike ballots compulsory in Britain.

CONTRIBUTORS

DANIEL A. BELL teaches political philosophy at the University of Hong Kong. He is the author of *Communitarianism and Its Critics* and of the forthcoming book, *East Meets West: Human Rights and Democracy in Asia.*

PETER DE MARNEFFE, Associate Professor of Philosophy at Arizona State University, is author most recently of "Liberalism, Liberty, and Neutrality" and "Contractualism, Liberty, and Democracy."

SAMUEL FLEISCHACKER, Assistant Professor of Philosophy at Williams College, is the author most recently of *The Ethics of Culture.*

KENT GREENAWALT, University Professor at Columbia University School of Law, is author most recently of *Fighting Words* and *Private Consciences and Public Reason.*

AMY GUTMANN, Laurance S. Rockefeller University Professor at Princeton University, is the author most recently of *Democracy and Disagreement* (with Dennis Thompson) and *Color Conscious* (with Anthony Appiah).

GEORGE KATEB, Professor of Politics at Princeton University, is author most recently of *The Inner Ocean* and *Emerson and Self-Reliance.*

WILL KYMLICKA is Visiting Professor of Philosophy at the University of Ottawa and at Carleton University. His most recent book is *Multicultural Citizenship.*

NANCY L. ROSENBLUM, Henry Merritt Wriston Professor and Professor of Political Science at Brown University, is author most recently of *Membership and Morals: The Personal Uses of Pluralism in America.*

ALAN RYAN, Warden of New College, Oxford, and until recently, Professor of Politics at Princeton University, is the author most recently of *John Dewey and the High Tide of American Liberalism.*

YAEL TAMIR, Senior Lecturer in Philosophy at Tel Aviv University, is author most recently of *Liberal Nationalism.*

MICHAEL WALZER, UPS Foundation Professor of Social Science at the Institute for Advanced Study at Princeton, is author most recently of *Spheres of Justice* and *On Toleration.*

STUART WHITE, Assistant Professor of Political Science at the Massachusetts Institute of Technology, is currently completing a forthcoming book, *The Civic Minimum: An Essay on the Rights and Obligations of Economic Citizenship*.

also affirmative action; occupations; public employees; trade unions; unemployment
Employment Act (1988), 355n.38
Employment Division v. Smith (1990), 125–26, 127, 128, 142nn.48, 50
employment opportunity. *See* equal opportunity
Engels, Friedrich, 312n.48
English colonists, 198
English dining, 291
English garden city movement, 298–300, 311n.35, 324
English Independent churches, 280
English language: Canadian immigrants and, 194; civic nationalism model and, 208; Hispanic immigrants and, 209, 210; marginalized sects and, 183; mother-tongue literacy and, 203, 204; naturalization and, 198, 199; pluralist multiculturalism and, 184, 200, 201; preeminence of, 180; societal integration and, 181, 204–5
English pubs, 293, 296, 297, 310n.33
English soccer hooliganism, 219
Enlightenment, The, 287, 306n.17
Environmental Defense Fund, 305n.9
environmental groups, 117, 121
envy, 97
Equal Credit Opportunity Act, 85
equal opportunity: associational freedom and, 156; for disadvantaged groups, 13, 58, 87, 233; fundamental rights and, 58–59; Jaycees and, 13, 14, 15, 16, 84–86; juvenile church membership and, 143n.67; liberal ideal of, 333; nondiscrimination and, 80, 189; private sector and, 188; racial nondiscrimination and, 7, 8; religious discrimination and, 114, 116–17; school leaving and, 124, 125; sex discrimination and, 153; skills acquisition and, 343, 344; state interest in, 22, 82; subsidized housing and, 24; unionism and, 331, 339, 347, 348, 349, 351. *See also* affirmative action
equal protection before the law, 142n.44; Brennan on, 57, 58; child custody and, 143n.63; congruence demands and, 78–79; nondiscrimination and, 140n.32; Rehnquist on, 42
equal status. *See* social equality
Eskimos, 253
established churches, 280, 285
establishment clause, 142n.57

ethnic associations, 177–213; Friendly Societies and, 302; illiberal, 219; political instability and, 218; RCAs and, 246; restrictive, 216–17; separatist, 261
ethnic conflict, 231, 263–64n.3, 307n.2
Etzioni, Amitai, 240, 263n.1
Europe: colonization by, 267n.39; cultural policies of, 250–51; immigration from, 269n.58, 327–28; mountains of, 268n.46; national minorities of, 182, 185; public parks of, 296; revolutions in, 225; small municipalities of, 310n.33; totalitarianism in, 278
European Americans. *See* white citizens
Evacuation Day Parade, 139n.13
evangelical Christians, 65, 70
Exclusive Brethren, 133–34, 135, 143n.67
excommunication, 142n.50, 284, 306n.16
exiles, 186, 209. *See also* refugees
exit rights, 23, 226, 227, 331
export workers, 353n.20
expressive associations: civil wrongs and, 127; commercial associations and, 81; constitutional protections of, 10, 136–37; custody issues and, 135; discrimination by, 116, 119, 139–40n.20; donations to, 139n.12; fundamental rights and, 54; ideological discrimination by, 120; illiberal, 22; internal discipline by, 132; legal exemption of, 31; membership policies of, 11–12; noninstrumentality of, 53; O'Connor on, 12, 55–56, 104n.18, 115, 116, 122, 139n.13; religion model and, 334, 335; state neutrality and, 338; unionism and, 332, 335, 349–50
expressive freedom. *See* speech freedom

Fabian Society, 299
Fair Labor Standards Act (1938), 221, 237n.22
families: allowances for, 73; Brennan on, 45–46, 48, 113; contention in, 70; in Edinburgh, 298; educational decisions of, 126; entertainment of, 327; gay imitation of, 67; immigrant, 201, 204; involuntary membership in, 65; judgments on, 121; promotion of, 290; self-denial for, 94; shunning in, 131; small businesses of, 89; state relations with, 232–33; in suburbs, 242, 325; unhappiness in, 295; walks by, 296. *See also* children; parents
Farber, Leslie, 307n.21

identity (psychology) (*cont.*)
  tivism and, 277; competing sources of,
  290–91; friendship and, 274; fundamental
  rights and, 52, 53, 54; intimacy and, 49,
  113; intrinsically valuable relationships
  and, 47–48, 52; self-fashioning of, 70–71
identity groups, 230, 297
ideology, 115–16, 120. *See also* philosophy;
  religious doctrines
Ignatieff, M., 225
illegal immigrants, 186, 209
illiberal associations: civic virtue and, 261,
  262; indirect support of, 234; liberal
  democracy and, 22–23, 110; proliferation
  of, 219; reciprocity and, 25. *See also* hate
  groups; oppressive associations
illiberal convictions, 60–61, 78, 102, 223
immigrants: to Canada, 193, 194, 196,
  267n.39; cartoons of, 254; in Chicago,
  327–28; cultural neutrality and, 251;
  democracy and, 322; at Ellis Island, 253,
  269n.58; English language and, 180, 198;
  illegal, 186, 209; to Israel, 192; marginalized sects and, 183; multiculturalism of,
  20, 184, 196–208, 211; naturalization of,
  179, 182, 194, 198, 199; Rousseau on, 69;
  self-government issue and, 21. *See also*
  Hispanic immigrants; integration (assimilation); resident aliens
imperialism, 185, 196, 198, 267n.39
impressionism, 329
incarceration, 38
incest, 163
income, 335; distribution of, 333; inequality
  of, 97, 246, 263n.2, 265–66n.28, 266n.31,
  330; redistribution of, 72–73. *See also*
  wages
incorporation, 312n.50
Independence Hall (Philadelphia), 267n.39
Independent churches, 280
India, 296
Indiana, 244
Indians. *See* native Americans
individualism, 100–101, 310n.33, 320
individuality. *See* personhood
industrial enterprises. *See* business firms
industrial pacifists, 346
industrial relations. *See* labor relations
Industrial Revolution, 300
industrialists, 320. *See also* businessmen
inequality. *See* social equality
inns, 310n.33

insignificant communities, 27, 273–313
instrumental associations, 334–35
instrumental value, 47; Brennan on, 44–45,
  50, 113; fundamental rights and, 52–53;
  trade unions and, 336
insurance, 339; Friendly Society, 300, 301;
  mortgage, 246; mutual, 346; unemployment, 142n.53
insurrections, 19, 147, 225
integration (assimilation), 178; choice of,
  184; criticism of, 20; language and, 192;
  mother-tongue use and, 204; multiculturalism and, 200, 203; nation-building and,
  181, 185; native resistance to, 207; official
  resistance to, 186; promotion of, 202,
  205, 208, 209; psychological aspects of,
  206, 212n.20; rejection of, 191, 196–97
integration (desegregation), 59, 92
intellectual freedom. *See* speech freedom
intemperance, 309n.33, 312n.51
interest groups, 230–31, 263n.1, 353n.19
intermediary associations. *See* secondary associations
Internal Revenue Service, 6, 24
International Association of Machinists v. Street
  (1961), 345, 346
international competition, 341, 342, 343
Internet, 145
interracial marriage. *See* miscegenation
intimate associations: actions unjustified by,
  131; associational freedom and, 3–4, 35;
  Brennan on, 44, 45, 46–47, 112; constitutional protections of, 9–10; discrimination in, 93; "essential to democracy"
  argument and, 148; interethnic, 206; judicial attention to, 37, 38; legal exemption
  of, 31; moral rights to, 164, 169, 172n.24;
  paternalism and, 162–63; *Roberts* justices
  on, 9, 113, 121; selfhood and, 49. *See also*
  families; marriage
intrinsic value: Brennan on, 44–45, 46, 47,
  112–13; of expression, 51–52, 53; unintimate relationships and, 49
invisible hand theory, 231, 235
involuntary association. *See* compulsory association
involuntary servitude, 146, 253, 318
Iraq, 254
Irish Catholics, 99, 327
Isaac (patriarch), 66
Islam: apostasy from, 143n.58; family law
  of, 201; fear of, 207; holidays of, 200,